CHILDREN'S JUSTICE

CHILDREN'S JUSTICE

BY BRENDON MAROTTA

HEGEMON MEDIA

Published by Hegemon Media.
HegemonMedia.com

Copyright © 2022 by Brendon Marotta.
All rights reserved.
BrendonMarotta.com

Children's Justice
Edition 1.0

Hardcover   ISBN 978-1-7351134-2-5
Paperback   ISBN 978-1-7351134-4-9
Ebook   ISBN 978-1-7351134-3-2
Audiobook   ISBN 978-1-7351134-5-6

For Marco

TABLE OF CONTENTS

1	Social Justice	1
2	Critical Theory	17
3	Systemic Issue	27
4	Epistemic Injustice	40
5	Subaltern Status	52
6	Oppression's Origins	62
7	Intersectional Identity	71
8	New Discourse	78
9	Power/Knowledge	87
10	False Consciousness	94
11	Patriarchal Pedagogy	104
12	Gender Theory	113
13	Medical Gaze	123
14	Biopower Brutality	132
15	Created Problems	141
16	Medical Socialization	149
17	Human Capital	159
18	Fragile Pushback	174
19	Racial Trauma	185
20	Deconstructing Race	198
21	Cultural Stress	208
22	Restorative Justice	224
23	Diverse Allies	235
24	Liberating Tolerance	245
25	Liberal Critique	253
26	Further Issues	263
27	Future Vision	272
EPILOGUE	Mutant Meme	280
	Acknowledgments	289
	Bibliography	290
	Notes	294
	Index	339

CHILDREN'S JUSTICE

CHAPTER 1
SOCIAL JUSTICE

Children's Justice is the idea that the treatment of children is a social justice issue. If social justice is about protecting the vulnerable, the minority, and the oppressed, then there is no minority more vulnerable or oppressed than children. Children are the weakest members of society in every society, and any movement based in social justice must eventually face the reality that children are oppressed and have been since the beginning of history. If we want a just world and children are our future, we must begin with Children's Justice.

THE ORIGINS OF CHILDREN'S JUSTICE

Two events lead to the creation of this book: the rise of critical social justice and my own interest in children's rights issues. The collision of these two interests would lead to an experiment that would go far beyond either individual interest and have implications for the whole of society.

I have always had an interest in Children's Justice. I just didn't have that name for it. The closest name I had was "children's rights," a topic I have been reading about since high school. Even as a child,

I could feel something about how I was treated was wrong. Adults told me I would "get over it" and understand when I was older. Looking at their behavior as an adult, it seems like they had never gotten over their own childhood trauma and simply repressed it to inflict on others. As a child, I knew every adult around me must have also been a child at one point, yet they seemed to have forgotten what it was like to experience the pain of childhood. I remember making a silent promise to myself that I would remember, and when I was older and in a position of power, I would do something about it. In some ways, this book is the fulfillment of that promise I made to my younger self. The child was not forgotten, but lives inside me still, watching me write these words in his defense to protect future children the way he could not protect himself.

After college, I became interested in how early childhood trauma impacts people later in life. I began looking at my own childhood and practicing various healing methods to clear out the ways that trauma had negatively impacted my own life. That self-development process eventually led me to direct a film to bring awareness to one of those forms of trauma. Over the course of six years, I directed a feature-length documentary titled *American Circumcision*, which explored the modern debate around infant male circumcision, and the growing Intactivist movement, which believes that all human beings have the right to their own bodies and to cut off a part of someone's body without their consent is a violation of human rights. The film was on Netflix, and I toured across the country speaking about the issue. The film and subsequent media I've created have led me to connect with people in other movements dedicated to protecting children, including natural birth, peaceful parenting, and unschooling. It was actually at a conference I was speaking at for the Association for Pre and Perinatal Psychology (APPPAH), an organization dedicated to exploring birth psychology and the lifelong impact of early life experiences, that I proposed to my wife. During the writing of this book, we married and had a child of our own.

Despite the personal success I was having, the issues I cared about were not receiving the same attention. Most of the activists I knew were struggling to create change, grow their organizations, and raise funds. I once saw the leader of a major organization literally pass a hat around an event and ask for donations to cover their travel expenses. Though these activists cared deeply about their cause, they weren't getting the support they needed. At the same time, social justice movements were having a cultural moment. Over the summer of 2020, *#BlackLivesMatter* became an international social justice phenomenon. The Black Lives Matter Global Network Foundation raised over 90 million dollars.[1] The founder of Twitter gave 10 million dollars to Ibram Kendi's Center for Antiracist Research.[2] Numerous celebrities, politicians, and corporations endorsed the antiracist movement.[3] While I'm sure these activists would say there is still a lot of work to be done, they are in a much better position to do that work with international name recognition, celebrity endorsements, and millions of dollars than they would be if they had to pass a hat around events to cover their expenses.

I became curious. What were these movements doing that we weren't? Whatever you think of modern social justice movements, they have had a massive cultural impact. Rather than be jealous of their success, I had the humility to acknowledge that their greater results were likely because they were doing something better, and sought to learn from them. I did what anyone who wants to improve their performance should do: I looked at others who were already more successful in my field and sought to model their process. In this case, my field was social change, and the more successful model was critical social justice activists.

The children's movements I was familiar with were based in human rights. When I looked at social justice movements, I discovered they were not using the language of human rights. They were using something called critical theory.[4] One could approach racial justice issues with the discourse of human rights. For example, police brutality is clearly a human rights violation. Yet, these movements were choosing not to use human rights and instead speaking about systemic power. They had an entirely different intellectual foundation. This distinction is true not just of racial justice movements, but of most modern social justice movements, including those around gender, disability, decolonization, etc. Modeling children's movements after modern social justice movements would mean more than just borrowing a few tips and tactics, but changing the entire intellectual roots of children's movements and reimagining them using critical theory. So I did.

This book began as a thought experiment to answer the question: What would children's issues look like if based in critical social justice theory, rather than human rights? To conduct this experiment, I focused on the issue that I knew best from working on my documentary, but this analysis has implications for all issues related to children or social justice. The results of this experiment were so successful, that it moved beyond being a mere experiment into a new conclusion, and an entirely new way of viewing children's issues known as Children's Justice. Prior to this experiment, I was skeptical of all things "woke," and more familiar with the "cancel culture" headlines about social justice movements than the underlying theory behind them. Applying critical theory and social justice ideas meant I had to immerse myself in theory, and read all that I could. Reading theory led to me doing the rarest act anyone can do in American politics: I changed my mind. Now I love theory and read it for fun. You might notice as you continue to read this book, that it moves from skeptical of the ideas I'm exploring to enthusiastic because that was the intellectual journey I went on writing this book. I've tried as much as possible to make the book a cohesive whole through editing, but no amount of revision has been able to remove all signs of my own personal growth.

Whatever your perspective on social justice and critical theory, this book has something to offer you. I've designed this book to be both understandable to those who have never read any critical social justice theory before and to offer new ideas to longtime social justice activists. Even those who consider themselves "anti-woke" or opposed to modern critical social justice politics might find this book fascinating or discover that it changes their mind, as writing it changed mine. If you continue reading, it might change yours as well. Continue reading only if you're willing to explore new ideas.

CRITICAL SOCIAL JUSTICE

What is social justice? The best-known American social justice movement was the Civil Rights Movement, specifically the African-American Civil Rights Movement of the 1960s. The Civil Rights movement is best known by Martin Luther King's famous quote that people should "not be judged by the color of their skin, but by the content of their character."⁵ The movement sought to end racism and discrimination by removing laws that categorized people on the basis of race. After this movement, a dominant understanding emerged that Americans should be "color-blind," and see each other as individuals, rather than by their racial group.

Modern social justice movements are different. They are based in what is known as critical theory or critical race theory.⁶ Whereas the Civil Rights Movement sought to see people as individuals, critical theory says that people are not merely individuals, but participate in systems. Those systems can be oppressive, racist, or discriminatory even if the individuals participating in them do not consciously wish to harm others.⁷ Critical theory does not focus just on individuals, but systems and systemic oppression. For clarity, I will refer to this version of social justice as critical social justice.⁸

Critical social justice attempts to end systemic oppression by getting people to see how they participate in social systems. It asks people to commit to not just ending their individual racism or discrimination but to examine and change the ways they participate in systems that perpetuate oppression. Two of the most popular texts of critical social justice are the bestselling books *White Fragility: Why It's So Hard for White People to Talk About Racism* by Robin DiAngelo and *How To Be An Antiracist* by Ibram X. Kendi. *White Fragility* contains a strong critique of the popular understanding of Martin Luther King's "content of their character" quote, calling it "color-blind racism."⁹ She writes that "we are taught to think about racism only as discrete acts committed by individual people, rather than as a complex, interconnected system"¹⁰ and that "I understand racism as a system."¹¹ *How To Be Antiracist* argues that racism is not just about individual prejudices, but any policy or idea that results in "racial inequity."¹² Kendi suggests that the solution to racism is antiracism, which "locates the roots of problems in power and policies."¹³

Critical social justice prioritizes ending systemic oppression above previous Civil Rights era legislation intended to protect individual rights. For example, in June 2020 the California State legislature voted to remove the legal prohibition against discrimination, striking the following words from their state constitution: "The state shall not discriminate against, or grant preferential treatment to, any individual or group on the basis of race, sex, color, ethnicity, or national origin."[14] This change would have allowed the state to hire based on the basis of race. From the perspective that emerged after the Civil Rights movement, hiring someone based on their race rather than the content of their character is racism. From the critical social justice perspective, making sure you hire more people from races or backgrounds that are underrepresented in a particular field is antiracism. Civil Rights thinking focused on equality of opportunity or making sure everyone has access to the same opportunities, whereas critical social justice theory focuses on equality of outcomes or what is known as equity, or making sure each group of people receives equal outcomes.[15]

Since both critical theory and the Civil Rights Movement are known as social justice movements, many are not aware of the difference between these two perspectives. The Civil Rights Movement has been lionized with a mythic status in Americans' minds. When institutions adopt critical social justice, some may think they are carrying on the legacy of the Civil Rights movement, when they are actually affirming texts that directly critique the popular understanding of that movement.[16] Yet, critical theory has been adopted by universities, schools, corporations, politicians, banks, churches, media, entertainment, social media, and government agencies. Given the number and power of institutions that have adopted critical theory, critical theory could be described as having a hegemony, meaning that it is the dominant cultural power in America.

MEDICAL ORGANIZATIONS AND SOCIAL JUSTICE

There is a second reason for writing this book. Because critical social justice has power in American institutions, any movement which wishes to change those institutions must either oppose or work within the confines of that power. That includes the medical institutions which children's movements have sought to change since every major medical organization has released a statement in support of social justice.

The American Academy of Pediatrics (AAP) released a policy statement in 2019 titled *The Impact of Racism on Child and*

Adolescent Health which defines racism as a "system of structuring opportunity and assigning value based on the social interpretation of how one looks (which is what we call 'race') that unfairly disadvantages some individuals and communities, unfairly advantages other individuals and communities, and 'saps the strength of the whole society through the waste of human resources,' as described by Camara Phyllis Jones, M.D., Ph.D., M.P.H."[17] This definition of racism as a system rather than individual prejudice is from critical social justice, not the previous definition of individual prejudice, and the rest of the statement is written in the language of critical social justice. The AAP also had *How To Be An Antiracist* author Ibram X. Kendi as a featured speaker at their 2020 convention.[18]

The American Medical Association released a statement against police violence in 2020,[19] that defines racism as "a system that assigns value and structures opportunity while unfairly advantaging some and disadvantaging others based on their skin color and 'saps the strength of the whole society through the waste of human resources,' as described by leading health equity expert Camara Jones, MD, MPH, Ph.D."[20] (Yes, both statements quote the same academic literature by the same author.)

The American Academy of Family Physicians released a 2019 statement condemning racism that reads: "The American Academy of Family Physicians (AAFP) recognizes that racism is a system," and then goes on to define that system in the language of critical social justice.[21] (Camara Jones is not cited in this paper, but she has spoken at one of their events.[22])

The list goes on. We could fill the pages of this book with boilerplate statements from medical organizations condemning racism, but the important aspect of these statements is that across the board these statements cite the definitions and language of critical social justice theory that racism is not merely an individual action but systemic one and that to end racism or reduce its influence in our world we have to not just look at our individual actions, but how the systems we participate in perpetuate unequal or unjust outcomes.

These statements often use the same language and share similar ideas because they come from the same academic literature. When major organizations want to release a statement on a subject, they go to whomever they consider an expert on the subject. The experts on racism come from critical theory. Notice for example that the author cited in multiple statements brands herself as being an expert in health equity. Equity has a very specific meaning in critical social justice. Whereas equality is often used to mean everyone getting the same thing, equity recognizes that not everyone has been afforded the same advantages and that remedying this might mean giving some unequal treatment. Like we mentioned earlier, equality is often used to mean equality of opportunity, whereas equity is used to mean equality of outcomes.[23] Health equity is this concept applied to medicine. Whereas equality might mean everyone receiving the same standard of care, health equity would mean recognizing that in order to achieve equal outcomes, some might need to receive different or unequal treatment.[24]

Whether or not you agree with the ideas of critical social justice, it is important to understand them, since their influence is felt in nearly every institution of American life, including medical institutions. This new value system is so important that when it conflicts with other statements from the medical system, medical institutions will choose the values of critical social justice over their own previous health advice.

For example, during the COVID-19 epidemic, when Americans took to the streets in support of Black Lives Matter, many medical organizations also declared racism a health epidemic[25] and voiced their support for mass protests.[26] This contradicted previous advice saying that Americans should stay home and avoid mass gatherings to stop the spread of COVID-19.[27] Medical professionals that had previously shamed people who refused to stay home used their medical credentials to say "racism is the real virus."[28] As one letter signed by over a thousand epidemiologists and health workers reads "White supremacy is a lethal public health issue that predates and contributes to COVID-19… As public health advocates, we do not condemn these gatherings as risky for COVID-19 transmission. We support them as vital to the national public health."[29] Later, health experts cited in the New York Times in connection with the Center for Disease Control (CDC) proposed prioritizing vaccine distribution to historically marginalized racial groups over elderly people and essential workers, because those at greatest risk were "very white."[30]

This statement and others like it indicate that many medical organizations now see the harm of injustice, as framed by critical social justice theory, as even greater than the most significant epidemic in recent history.[31] This is important because it means when previous medical advice conflicts with critical social justice, social justice can win as the more dominant value.

Given that critical social justice can be of a higher value than previous medical advice, including even prevention measures during an epidemic, it seems that every medical practice must be reevaluated in light of this new way of thinking. If critical social justice can be more important than a worldwide epidemic, surely it is more important than common non-emergency medical practices. No practice is more common in American medicine and in need of re-evaluation from a social justice perspective than infant circumcision.

CIRCUMCISION AND SOCIAL JUSTICE

Why focus on circumcision? The dominant American narrative about circumcision is that it is not an important issue. Yet, circumcision affects every person in America, either directly because it was done to them, or indirectly because it was done to their children, partner(s), relatives, and people they know, or because they live in a culture that practices genital cutting. It affects people in the most intimate ways possible, creating a permanent change to their body, sexuality, and psyche. The issue of circumcision intersects with some of the most important aspects of social justice, such as sexuality, gender, consent, capitalism, etc., and can be understood using social justice tools that examine power dynamics, language, and social constructions. If any other social justice issue affected every American this personally, it would dominate political discussions. The fact it does not, and large hegemonic cultural narratives prevent public discussion of the issue only indicates its importance.

Doing justice to each issue where children are oppressed would require an entire book per issue. There is greater understanding to be gained from deeply exploring one issue to derive the underlying principles we can use to understand other Children's Justice issues than skimming the surface of each. Examining the issue of circumcision will reveal larger truths about how we treat children, the same way a deep examination of slavery would reveal larger truths about race and racism in America. No one would question why a book about racism might focus on slavery. If the dominant culture saw slavery as trivial or hid the issue entirely, it would be essential for a book about racism to address this before moving forward on other commentaries. In the same way, it makes sense for a book about the treatment of children to address the fact that American culture normalizes cutting parts of children's genitals off. It is essential to address circumcision in a culture that sees genital cutting as trivial and often hides the issue entirely. In the same way that there is much more to the issue of race than just slavery, there is much more to Children's Justice than just the issue of circumcision, and we will name some of those issues by the end of this book. However, it is important to address this issue first, because understanding this issue of genital cutting will unlock the principles by which we can apply Children's Justice to all other forms of injustice perpetrated against children.

Circumcision is the removal of part of the penis. I mention this because many Americans do not even know what circumcision is. In the opening of my documentary, *American Circumcision*, an older man approaches an activist and asks if circumcision involves removing tissue or is "just an incision." This man had made it into his elder years without ever learning what circumcision involves. Despite the majority of American men undergoing genital cutting, most Americans are deeply unaware of this issue. Many believe it to be a simple one-time decision made by comparing the "benefits and risks," which does not have a long-term impact and will not be considered ever again. The reality is that even after interviewing every major expert on both sides of the issue for my documentary, speaking with people across the world after the release of the film, and connecting even more through podcasting, writing, and activism, there are still new aspects of the issue I continue to discover.

If you are previously unfamiliar with this issue, it is important to ask if you are willing to receive new information. Ronald Goldman, author of *Circumcision, The Hidden Trauma: How an American Cultural Practice Affects Infants and Ultimately Us All* and Executive Director of the Circumcision Resource Center, told me he often begins conversations about the issue of circumcision with the question, "are you open to new information?" This question is important because the book you are reading now will present you with a lot of new information. Do not continue reading this book unless you are willing to receive new information, perspectives, and ideas, because this book will give you many. This question is also important because before we can explore this issue, some basic information is required, including information that the majority of Americans are systemically denied. Despite the majority of American men having been circumcised, the majority of the world does not circumcise.[32] Most parents around the world would not even consider circumcision, because circumcision is not medically necessary. Children do not need to be circumcised. Much of the world considers circumcision harmful.[33] How then do American medical organizations justify continuing to cut children's genitals?

MEDICAL ORGANIZATIONS AND CIRCUMCISION

All of the major American medical organizations previously mentioned in the context of medical organizations adopting the values of critical social justice, including the AAP, AMA, AAFP, and CDC, also support or allow their membership to practice infant male circumcision.[34] Medical organizations frame circumcision as an individual choice parents have to make. In their last policy statement, the American Academy of Pediatrics (AAP) suggests that parents and doctors make decisions on circumcision by weighing what they call its "benefits and risks".[35] How do they determine benefits? How do they determine risks? How do they weigh them against each other?

Right now, medical organizations like the AAP define both benefits and risks using only certain data from peer-reviewed research in Western academic journals. This definition excludes other forms of knowing such as the testimony of people's lived experience. It also excludes research, including even peer-reviewed research, around the emotional, cultural, or ethical impact of circumcision. In other words, medical organizations define "benefits and risks" by a very narrow set of publications that they control. While this is framed as an open process, it actually creates a power structure where only the medical system can determine what information is relevant or valid.

This method of gathering information in peer-reviewed Western medical journals provides no inherent ethical framework to evaluate that information. For example, if research shows that there is a ten percent rate of surgical complications from circumcision,[36] how do we evaluate that information? Is that acceptable or unacceptable? At what percentage of complications would circumcision become unethical? This data is only information, and there is no way to evaluate it until we apply an ethical framework to it. What ethical framework we apply will change what conclusions we derive from that information. One ethical framework might suggest that any harm to a child is unacceptable. Another might suggest that it is okay if some children are harmed if the majority are okay. A third might suggest that this information is irrelevant and that there is some other factor that matters more. What ethical framework is the medical establishment using?

The ethical framework the medical establishment has used to evaluate other important ethical dilemmas is critical social justice or social justice based in critical theory. For example, during the COVID-19 epidemic, many in the medical establishment weighed the benefits of mass gatherings in support of Black Lives Matter as greater than the risks of staying home to slow the spread of COVID-19. This "benefits and risks" analysis was not based merely on COVID-19 transmission data but occurred within an ethical framework grounded in critical social justice. The medical system saw the benefits of standing against racial injustice as greater than the risks of spreading the COVID-19 virus. A different ethical framework might prioritize slowing the spread of the virus over mass protests, and might not even recognize the cause of the protestors as important at all.

Different ethical systems do not just evaluate information differently but have a different way of determining which information is important or worth evaluating. The idea that the most reliable or important information comes from peer-reviewed research in academic journals is based in Western enlightenment ideas about science and reason. Western enlightenment thinking views the scientific method as the best way at arriving at truth, and as a universal tool anyone can use. No matter your race, gender, or background, if you correctly conduct an experiment, you will get the same result as anyone else who does the same.

Critical social justice has a different view of knowledge. In the view of critical theory, the Western scientific method is just one way of knowing.[37] Other ways of knowing, such as the testimony of lived experience, are equally valid.[38] There might be relevant information, such as people's feelings, subjective experiences, or the cultural influence of an action, which cannot always be arrived at through scientific experiments. Western science is only one way of knowing. In critical social justice, claiming that the way knowing invented by white European culture is superior to all others is white supremacy because it prioritizes Western culture's way of knowing above all others.[39]

A view of the "benefits and risks" of circumcision based in critical social justice would not just include peer-reviewed research from Western academic journals, but other ways of knowing, such as the lived experience of those affected by circumcision. The entire method of evaluating information and determining truth that the medical establishment has used on this issue is not just obsolete, but in the view of critical social justice is actually a form of oppression. The medical establishment's frame of circumcision as an individual parental choice goes against the heart of critical social justice, which views us not just as individuals, but participants in larger systems.[40] Critical social justice would not suggest that this is a decision that individual parents can make in isolation, but that understanding circumcision requires seeing the larger systems it intersects with. Circumcision clearly intersects with larger systems around gender, sexuality, and other cultural systems.

The old justifications for circumcision directly contradict the dominant values of both medical institutions and the dominant culture. Given that circumcision involves systemic issues, affects the majority of Americans, and is done based on values that are no longer dominant, we must re-evaluate this practice in light of the new values of American culture. An organization whose view of circumcision fails to include a larger systemic perspective and does not include the lived experience of those affected by the practice has no actual interest in social justice and is merely appropriating the name for public relations. If medical organizations are serious about social justice, then they must reconsider circumcision in light of new values.

INTACTIVISM AND SOCIAL JUSTICE

Medical institutions are not the only group involved in the circumcision debate. Much of the circumcision debate is now centered on the rising human rights movement against circumcision known as Intactivism.[41] The current Intactivist argument is simple: Every human being has the right to their own body. To cut off a part of someone's body without their consent is a violation of their human rights. Intactivists oppose all forms of non-consensual genital cutting, including intersex genital cutting, female genital cutting, and male genital cutting, because every human being deserves the right to an intact body.[42] This argument is clear and obviously correct to anyone who accepts the ethical framework of human rights.

What if the intended audience for Intactivist arguments does not support human rights? Intactivism was rooted in human rights because the human rights framework was the dominant ideology of the Western world, and has been since the movement began.[43] Plus, many activists are genuine believers in the idea of human rights and see themselves as part of a larger historical cause to ensure equality and rights for all. Activists in the Intactivist movement have compared their work to the Civil Rights movement, the gay rights movement, and even the abolitionist movement to end slavery. Many have been mystified as to why institutions that claim to support human rights have not adopted their cause when it makes so much moral sense to do so.

Human rights based in liberalism is no longer the lone dominant ideology of Western institutions and is rapidly being replaced by critical social justice theory. Critical theory is explicitly "suspicious of another liberal mainstay, namely rights" according to the most definitive textbook on critical race theory.[44] Critical social justice does not believe in prioritizing human rights above equitable outcomes and sees the liberal emphasis on individual rights as blind to systemic oppression.[45] Arguments based on individual rights will fall on deaf ears if made to institutions that prioritize critical social justice theory over individual rights.

A movement against circumcision could be rooted in any ideology that opposes harming children. It is the rarity that any movement or ideology believes you should hold down children and cut off parts of their genitals. Although Intactivism has been based in human rights, it does not have to be. It is just that human rights have been the dominant ideology of Western countries during the modern Intactivist movement, so an appeal to human rights was an appeal to the dominant principles of Western powers.

What would Intactivism look like if appealing to a different dominant power? Pretend for a minute you were living under the rule of the Catholic church in the Middle Ages of Europe. Would you make an argument to the church based on human rights? Of course not. The Catholic church of the Middle Ages would never acknowledge human rights-based arguments. You would make an argument based on the values of Christianity. If arguing against circumcision, one might quote the Apostle Paul's statement that "if you let yourselves be circumcised, Christ will be of no value to you at all"[46] and the verses where he calls those who want to perform circumcision "mutilators of the flesh."[47] You could also reference Jesus's quote that "it would be better for them to have a large millstone hung around their neck and to be drowned in the depths of the sea" than to harm a child.[48] Plus there are many church fathers decrying circumcision you could cite, and a history that indicates the ending of circumcision was one of the primary differences between Judaism and Christianity. An Intactivism based in Christianity would look different, but it could reach the same conclusions without referencing human rights.

The dominant power activists appeal to in modern times is not the church, but a different belief system. Until recently, human rights based in liberalism was the uncontested dominant ideology of the Western world. Many Intactivists are so convinced of the truth of human rights values that they never had to question the assumptions their arguments are based on. Now, a new hegemonic power is emerging in the form of social justice based in critical theory. What does it mean for Intactivist human rights organizations if major Western institutions no longer hold individual human rights based in liberalism as their dominant ideology and begin focusing on systemic social justice issues based in critical theory?

CHAPTER 2
CRITICAL THEORY

This book is an attempt to see what the issue of circumcision and treatment of children would look like if it was rooted in critical social justice theory. To be clear: I am not saying this is the only way to understand this issue or even the best way. The idea that circumcision is harmful could be rooted in *any* ideology or system. It's just that critical social justice theory is the dominant ideology of establishment organizations. This is what those in power say they believe.

Circumcision has never been deeply examined through the lens of critical theory. Using this lens may require you to drop previously held beliefs and assumptions about this issue and to be willing to question and critically examine those assumptions. We will be using an entirely different set of tools, values, and questions to examine the issue of circumcision than either the medical "benefits and risks" model or the individual human rights model. The medical model asks "do the benefits outweigh the risks?" The Intactivist model asks "do we have the right to our own bodies?" Critical theory asks "what systems of power does this perpetuate?" It is a very different question that deconstructs the assumptions and power structures of the medical system. The tools of critical theory suggest a more radical approach than any organization currently involved in the circumcision debate has previously explored.

PRINCIPLES OF CRITICAL THEORY

Since the analysis of this book is based on critical theory and its modern application in social justice, it is worth defining what that means. Critical social justice is complex, and one could write entire books defining what social justice or critical theory means. The term critical theory originally refers to the Marxist theories developed at the Institute for Social Research in Frankfurt, Germany, better known as the Frankfurt School (1918–1933).[49] Unlike traditional theory, which is intended to merely explain the world, critical theories are meant to transform the world.[50] Based on Frankfurt School member Max Horkheimer's definition of critical theory, "a critical theory is adequate only if it meets three criteria: it must be explanatory, practical, and normative, all at the same time. That is, it must explain what is wrong with current social reality, identify the actors to change it, and provide both clear norms for criticism and achievable practical goals for social transformation."[51] By this definition, many left-wing movements which followed the Frankfurt school could be considered branches of critical theory. In modern politics, the term is often used as a short-hand for critical race theory, a movement examining race, power, and racism,[52] or as a catch-all term to describe social justice politics and the intellectual influences on those politics.[53] In this book, I will be using the broadest possible definition for critical theory and its application to social justice, since we are concerned with the current dominant worldview, not merely historical movements.

I recognize that no definition of critical theory or critical social justice will satisfy every activist. Each social justice activist and critical theorist has their own perspective, some of which contradict each other. If you were to ask ten critical social justice activists their definition of social justice, you might get eleven different answers. This does not mean that critical social justice cannot be defined or that activists do not share certain ideas. If you were to ask ten Christians to define what it means to be a Christian, you might also get eleven different answers. Those from different denominations like

Catholic or Orthodox might have significant disagreements. However, they would have more in common with each other than non-believers, and most answers would share certain ideas about Jesus, the Bible, and being saved from sin. Those with different focuses like queer theory or racial justice might also have disagreements, but they would have more in common with each other than those from opposing perspectives, and their answers would likely share certain ideas about social constructs, equity, and systemic oppression. Just as we could define the principles of Christianity even though Christian beliefs might vary, we can define the principles of critical social justice even though the ideas of theorists also vary.

Though the ideas of critical social justice go far beyond the summary below, for the purposes of this book I've condensed the method by which I will be applying critical theory to this issue to five principles shared by many critical social justice activists:

First, social problems are systemic.[54] Social problems do not arise merely because of bad individuals, but due to a confluence of systemic factors. For example, most people do not want pollution, yet our current system consistently produces pollution. This is not because any individual wants pollution, but because the economic incentives of our current system reward cheap goods over sustaining the environment. With pollution, we have a systemic issue, not an individual one.

Second, people are not merely individuals but participate in larger systems.[55] It is possible for everyone involved in a system to be well-intentioned, yet for a system to produce bad outcomes. To continue the above example, you might not want to create pollution, but you need to drive your car to get to work, you have to buy food that comes in plastic packaging, your home appliances need power, etc. You as an individual might not see yourself as a "polluter," yet you participate in systems that produce pollution. You know you have a systemic problem when, despite your best intentions, you sometimes still contribute to an outcome you don't want to create.

Critical social justice theory suggests that the same might be true of systems that produce racism, inequality, or other forms of oppression.[56] I use the example of pollution because most people do not have an emotional charge around the idea that if they contribute to systems that produce pollution they are a "polluter," but they do have an emotional charge around the idea that if they contribute to systems that produce racial inequality they are a "racist." Reducing your pollution might require critically examining the systems you participate in. For example, you might personally not create much pollution, but if you patronize a business that harms the environment, you are systemically participating in that harm. A critical examination of your environmental impact would suggest avoiding high-pollution businesses. Likewise, reducing racial inequality might also require a similar critical examination. For example, you might not personally discriminate against others, but if an institution you participate in consistently produces unequal outcomes there might be a way you are also participating in that inequality. Critical social justice activists call this active commitment to reducing your participation in systems that create racial inequality antiracism.[57]

Third, systems can be judged by their outcomes.[58] Since problems are systemic, and everyone involved claims to have good intentions, we can only address these systems by looking at what they produce. People say they do not want to contribute to pollution, racism, inequality, etc. yet they participate in systems that consistently produce these outcomes. Fixing these problems will require moving beyond people's individual intentions to focus on results. We do not track pollution by seeing how much companies claim they are "not polluters" and "support the environment." We track it based on their outcomes, or how much pollution they produce. Critical social justice suggests that we can track problems like racism the same way. It doesn't matter if institutions say they are "not racist" and support everyone. What matters is their outcomes, or how much inequality they produce.[59]

Fourth, to fix systems, create more equitable outcomes.[60] This should be obvious if we accept the three previous principles. If the problem is outcomes, change the outcomes. We fix pollution by mandating that companies produce less pollution. Critical social justice suggests we can fix other issues the same way, by mandating that institutions produce less inequality. While this might seem heavy-handed, it shifts the focus from mind-reading people's intentions, which may or may not be the source of the problem, to focusing on the measurable impact on those affected by the problem.

LANGUAGE AND POWER

The last principle is the most crucial. As we've already established, critical social justice holds that systemic problems are the result of large social systems people participate in. These problems are visible in the outcomes of social systems and will only be solved once those outcomes are altered. This means that enacting change will require achieving power over large social systems. By what method does critical social justice achieve this power?

Every system of power rests on a system of language.[61] For example, the systems that produce pollution would not be possible without a complex system of language around money. This system frames protecting the environment as costly, but polluting it as cheap. These systems both create and obscure power. Although an institution might not be able to see the cost of pollution through the economic system they are working in, the cost is still there. For example, an institution's pollution might harm the health of everyone who works near that institution, passing the cost of their pollution onto people's bodies. If people become tired, sick, or unhealthy due to pollution, that is a cost of pollution, even if the institution responsible does not directly pay for it. Showing the harm of this system might require deconstructing the economic language that frames environmental harm as "cheaper," while obscuring costs that are passed on to others.

Change might also require deconstructing some of the narratives and premises on which this system rests. For example, the system that produces pollution requires us to view nature as a separate resource we can exploit, rather than an environment we are a part of and depend on. If we are not separate, then the damage to nature is not damage to something else, but damage to ourselves and our home. Changing this system might require changing our language. For example, if we referred to "the environment" as "our home," would we have a different attitude about polluting it? It would be harder to frame this harm as separate from us if it was happening to "our home." Part of the reason social justice activists are so focused on language is because they believe that language creates power, and if language were changed, certain power systems could no longer function.

Critical theory holds that many systems are entirely socially constructed. For example, money has no real value. While money might attempt to represent something real, money itself is just ink on paper or pixels on a screen. Yet, this system runs the world. No one can deny the power of money. Even if you and many of the people who participate in this monetary system know that money is "not real," it does not reduce the systemic power of the social construction of money. You can't pay your bills by telling people "actually, money is just a social construct." If you actually wanted to take power away from money, you'd have to deconstruct this system. Critical social justice suggests that there are other systems around race, gender, and social class which are also "not real," yet have real power through their social constructions. While these categories might claim to represent something real, they are also identities created through language. Critical theory suggests that if you want to change these power systems, you might have to deconstruct the social constructions that create them.

This point that every system of power rests on a system of language might be less obvious than the previous four principles discussed because it requires us to think more abstractly. Yet, the idea that power flows from language is the heart of critical theory. Previous philosophical systems viewed language and theory as descriptive rather than prescriptive. Words were used to describe reality, and theory was used to explain it. These words and theories were seen as neutral attempts to understand reality. Critical theory suggests that language is not neutral, but contains certain assumptions and power structures within it.[62] For example, money is framed as a neutral store of value, yet it does not produce neutral outcomes. This system values certain things more than others. We all agree that raising a child is one of the most valuable things a person can do. Most people would not trade the impact of a parent's love in their life for a few dollars cash. Yet, parenthood has no direct economic value. People do not get paid for loving their children. Instead, raising a child most typically costs people money. If the monetary system reflected what we value as human beings, there would be nothing more profitable than loving your children. Spending time at home with children has little monetary value despite everyone agreeing that it has immense human value. In this way, the monetary system is not a neutral system, but one that creates a power structure that values certain labor over human connection.

Critical theory suggests that all systems of knowledge also produce systems of power.[63] One of the most famous theorists to explore this issue was French philosopher Michel Foucault, who said, "there is no power relation without the correlative constitution of a field of knowledge, nor any knowledge that does not presuppose and constitute at the same time power relations."[64] When applied to social justice issues, critical theory suggests that the language we use to describe race, gender, and other forms of identity actually create assumptions and beliefs about those identities and can even create entire forms of identity in and of themselves.[65] The reason critical social justice activists are so concerned with language is because they believe that the systems that oppress us are held up by a power structure based in language. This means that the fifth and final principle by which we will be applying critical social justice theory is: **To achieve power, change language.**

APPLYING CRITICAL THEORY

One of the biggest misconceptions about critical theory among both its critics and proponents is that critical theory implies a certain set of values and politics. Even opponents of critical theory take its claim that theory is critical, not neutral, at face value. However, the process of critical theory is a tool, not a conclusion. One can deconstruct the language, systems, and outcomes of anything. When applied in a certain way to topics such as race, critical theory has been used to create highly political conclusions. When most people think of critical theory, they think of these conclusions. Yet, the conclusions are not the theory. Just as the scientific method is different from the scientific establishment, critical theory is different from those who currently apply it on social justice issues. Just as the scientific establishment might apply the scientific method to building better bombs or extending human life depending on the values of their culture, critical theorists can also apply their method selectively to particular problems. In Western society, critical theory has been applied to adult identity issues such as race, gender, sexual orientation, and social class.[66] It has not previously been applied to children, childhood, or the institutions that impact children. Someone using the scientific method to extend life would be just as much a scientist as someone who uses the method to construct bombs. Likewise, if we apply critical theory and social justice principles outside previously explored identity issues, we are still critical theorists and social justice activists, because we are using the methods of critical theory and social justice. Even if we reach radically different conclusions, we are still using the method. The method is a process, not a conclusion.

If you do not like critical social justice or the way that certain social justice activists behave, you can still use this book and get value from critical theory. Often, those who dislike critical social justice debate the validity of critical theory because they are upset by the conclusions of certain theorists and activists. This is like doubting the scientific method because you don't like bombs. If you had only seen science used to produce weapons of war, you might think you did not like science, when what you really disliked is war. Throwing out the scientific method entirely would be a mistake because you would lose out on the other potentially useful applications of that method. You also would have no way of understanding what scientists were doing or way to prevent them from using their method for war. Likewise, merely because critical theory can be used to lead to conclusions you might not like doesn't mean that critical theory is not useful. Critical theory is just a way of understanding power, especially systemic power, and how power is created through language. Applying critical theory to new issues might lead to new conclusions entirely.

Critical theory is correct in asserting that problems are systemic, that language creates power, and that systems can be evaluated based on their outcomes. Would anyone argue the opposite? That the problems of the world are entirely down to the individual, that language has no power, and that the outcomes don't matter? Of course not. While some might debate the beliefs of certain critical social justice activists, the process of breaking down how language creates power or problems can be caused by systems rather than just individuals is valid. This process of understanding power can lead to power. If you know how a system works, you can change it. The evidence that theory works is visible in the success of critical theorists. You can see how much cultural change has been created by those who use critical theory. If you think the power of critical theory is being used for bad, you should seek to understand the source of their power so that you can wield it for good.

For those who support social justice and critical theory, it is worth exploring what this theory means when applied to new issues and understanding it deeper. The earliest critical theorists did not apply their work directly to identity issues. Critical theory was applied by later authors to identity issues like race and gender.[67] However, there are still areas where critical theory has not yet been applied. Since critical theory views problems as systemic and intersectional, these new applications might lead to new conclusions that recontextualize previously explored issues. If new discoveries intersect with previous conclusions and issues, those previously explored issues might have to be reevaluated in light of these new intersectional perspectives. Each new discovery has the potential to change all previous beliefs.

If we support critical theory, we must be willing to critically examine the systems we participate in, even if this leads to new conclusions or changes our conclusions on previously explored social justice issues. This willingness to reevaluate our beliefs based on a critical examination of the systems we participate in is at the heart of critical theory and its application to social justice issues. Reaching a new conclusion that contradicts previous social justice thinking shows a commitment to social justice, especially if it comes from applying the principles of critical theory and social justice to examine the potentially oppressive systems you might participate in. If this process leads somewhere new, it is because we are deepening our understanding of social justice issues.

Understanding and using critical theory is of interest to both those who support and oppose the current conclusions of critical social justice. If you oppose the current application of critical social justice, then understanding and applying it to a new issue might lead to a new conclusion. If you support it, then applying critical theory to new issues will lead to a deeper understanding of and commitment to critical social justice. Regardless of where you stand, it is worth undertaking the process of critical theory and exploring the systems of power we participate in. The fact you are reading this book is proof that you are willing to explore a new perspective on these ideas.

This book explores the application of critical theory and social justice principles to children and specifically focuses on the issue of infant circumcision in the United States of America. While this might not seem like a deeply significant issue at first, remember that issues are systemic, and this issue has the potential to change every other issue it intersects with. In the analysis of this book, we will use much of the work of previous critical social justice authors, even as we reach new conclusions beyond their work. Each application of critical theory has the potential to recontextualize everything. Continue reading this book only if you are ready to change your mind.

CHAPTER 3
SYSTEMIC ISSUE

What makes a problem systemic? Systemic issues are those that cannot be solved by one person but involve multiple aspects of society. They often involve language, culture, identity, socialization, and other underlying social aspects. They involve institutions and social structures. Systemic issues create a web of causation, where the initial issue impacts other systems, moving like a domino through the world. In other words, systemic issues are not limited to one sphere but bleed into the whole of society.

Although framed by the American medical discourse as an isolated issue, circumcision is clearly a systemic issue. Infant circumcision occurs as an inciting event in a child's life, shortly after birth. The institution perpetuating circumcision has the word 'system' right in the name: the medical system. Every system impacted by the medical system or birth is in some way touched by circumcision. Like a stone cast into a pond, the initial impact of infant circumcision ripples through a man's life and everyone he interacts with, impacting our family systems, our bodies, identities, relationships, religion, language, sexuality, families, the way we socialize children, and many other systems which we will discuss over the course of this book. Circumcision is encoded so deeply into our understanding of nearly every system it interacts with that many are not even aware of its presence until our attention is called to it.

If we are understanding circumcision systemically, we can't just look at one system, but all the other systems circumcision intersects with. This is a core concept of critical social justice theory known as intersectionality. Intersectionality is the idea that each aspect of a person's identity or experience interacts and intersects to create their experience.[68] For example, a black person might have one experience of the world, and a woman might have another experience of the world, but a black woman will have a third experience of the world that is uniquely different from just being black or a woman. To understand her experience of the world, you have to not just understand the experience of being black or a woman, but understand how each of those identities intersects. Each additional identity increases the intersectional experience. For example, if that black woman is straight or queer, this adds a new intersectional experience to her identity that we must understand if we want to understand her full experience.

Likewise, if we want to fully understand circumcision, we cannot just explore one issue it intersects with. We certainly cannot understand it just through a Western medical lens. We cannot even understand it fully through the lens of only gender or consent. Intersectionality suggests that we have to understand circumcision by investigating how all of the issues it involves intersect. We actually cannot even understand all of those issues individually. We have to understand how they affect each other and create a new experience involving all of them.

INTERSECTIONAL CIRCUMCISION ISSUES

What issues does circumcision intersect with? Circumcision clearly intersects with gender, since in Western countries it is only done to children deemed biologically male. Genital cutting is also enforced on intersex children to alter their genitals to make them look like what the dominant culture deems "normal." Many of the justifications given for circumcision also have to do with appearance, such as "it looks better" or claims that the foreskin is somehow "gross" or "dirty." In this way, circumcision also insects with issues such as body shaming and body acceptance.

Western societies have a strong taboo against female genital cutting but often treat male genital cutting as normal. In this way, circumcision intersects with sexism, because Western societies treat male bodies as more harm-able and disposable, while female bodies are to be nurtured and protected. Biologically, male and female genitals are made out of the same tissue and nerve endings.[69] While those nerve endings might be formed into different structures, to suggest that cutting into a bundle of nerve endings on someone deemed "male" is somehow different from cutting into a bundle of nerve endings on someone deemed "female" is a form of institutional sexism.

The vastly different Western attitudes towards male and female genital cutting are also a form of imperialism. Female genital cutting is typically carried out by African, or Muslim societies, whereas male genital cutting is carried out in Western societies. The idea that the genital cutting African and Muslim societies practice is "barbaric," while the genital cutting Western societies carry out is "cleaner," is a form of imperialism and white supremacy, because it suggests Western cultures are somehow superior when carrying out an equivalent act. This double standard is even extended to labiaplasty or cosmetic genital surgeries on women in Western societies, which often remove the same tissue that is removed in some forms of female genital cutting.[70] Western societies treat this form of female genital cutting as beneficial, while the same genital cutting carried out in non-Western societies is treated as harmful.

Circumcision also intersects with consent, because circumcision is done to infants who cannot consent. No infant ever willingly agrees to be circumcised. The Western medical system justifies touching the genitals of non-consenting minors by saying that the parents consent. However, consent cannot be given by anyone but the person consenting, infants cannot consent to sex, and parents cannot consent to sex on behalf of their children.

When circumcision is performed the doctor palpates the infant's penis in order to make it larger.[71] "Palpates" is the medical term doctors use to avoid saying what they are really doing: sexually stimulating the infant's penis until the child has an erection. When doctors rub the child's penis, even to apply antiseptic, they are sexually stimulating the child. Some doctors do this intentionally to make the penis larger and easier to operate on. As former nurse Marilyn Milos puts it, "this is the child's first shared sexual experience."[72] After the child is sexually stimulated to an erection, a blunt probe is inserted into the child's foreskin to separate the foreskin from the glans. The foreskin of newborn infants is fused to the glans, much like the fingernail is fused to the finger. This process of breaking away the foreskin involves forcibly penetrating the child, causing immense pain. Forcible penetration is the legal definition of rape in America,[73] and so circumcision is rape and sexual assault. Even if the forcible penetration was not enough, holding someone down and cutting off parts of their genitals amounts to sexual assault and violence.

The term rape culture describes the beliefs and values that normalize sexual assault or rape.[74] Many of the justifications given for circumcision are the justifications rape culture gives for rape such as "s/he won't remember it" or "s/he wanted it." Rape culture includes the idea that the absence of a no is the same as a yes.[75] When people circumcise children, they do so based on assumptions shared by rape culture, because the child's inability to say no is construed as a yes. Circumcision is only possible with the cultural beliefs of rape culture.

Circumcision also intersects with our ideas about gender. Many of the justifications of this specific form of rape culture are male-specific. For example, if we call circumcision rape, many will protest that it isn't based on the sexist idea that "men cannot be raped." This particular instance of rape culture intersects with sexist ideas that men are always the aggressor and cannot be the victims of sexual assault. Both rape culture and sexism intersect with body-shaming when people say "he'll thank me later," as if the man should appreciate his rape because the appearance of his body has been somehow improved. Each of these issues of gender, consent, body shaming, rape, rape culture, etc. intersect with each other to create entirely new problems that are different from any issue in isolation. These issues would be massive on their own, yet circumcision also intersects with another issue: The victims are the unique social class of children. This class has no voice and no representation in existing social justice identity groups. They could not even speak publicly if they wanted to. The vulnerable nature of this class, combined with the other issues circumcision intersects with, creates an entirely new problem.

There is a word for adults touching children's genitals to fulfill their own desires: pedophilia. Circumcision is pedophilia because it involves the rape and forcible penetration of children. This pedophilia is not merely carried out by individuals, but institutions and systems. These systems are only possible with cultural assumptions and specialized language. The result of these systems is outcomes where adults touch children's genitals in order to fulfill their own desires. If an individual touching a child's genitals to fulfill their adult desires is a pedophile, then a system that causes adults to touch children's genitals is a pedophile system. Circumcision is systemic pedophilia.

SYSTEMIC PEDOPHILIA

Systemic pedophilia describes the beliefs, culture, practices, language, institutions, and other social systems that allow children to be harmed. Systemic pedophilia includes the abuse, rape, and genital cutting of children, and all aspects of society that allow or contribute to these forms of abuse. Since we are using the term systemic pedophilia in much the same way that critical race theorists use the term systemic racism, it is worth noting that critical theorists have a different understanding of what it means to be racist than many members of the general public. Often, the term racist is used to mean conscious prejudice towards people who are of a different race. While critical race theorists would consider that racist, they also use the term racist to describe people, ideas, or policies that result in systemic inequality between racial groups.[76] If critical theorists said that people were participating in systems that produce systemic inequality, they would not get the same reaction as calling them racist. The term racist is used deliberately to provoke a stronger reaction. This systemic definition of racism is now the dictionary definition of racism, not merely the definition of conscious prejudice.[77] Critical theory applied to the issue of infant circumcision opens the possibility of using the term pedophile the same way. The term pedophile does not merely mean a conscious sexual desire for children, but participation in systems that result in children being harmed by having their genitals touched, cut, or penetrated. Just as it is possible for people to participate in systemic racism without having any conscious prejudice towards other races, it is possible for adults to participate in systemic pedophilia without having any individual desire to harm children. When someone participates in systemic racism, we call them a racist. When someone participates in systemic pedophilia, they are a pedophile.

Some adults might protest that the label 'pedophile' does not apply to them because they don't derive sexual pleasure from circumcision. This excuse frames the feelings of adult circumcisers as more important than what the child experiences. Systemic pedophilia does not require individual conscious attraction, just as systemic racism does not require individual conscious prejudice. Systemic pedophilia describes systems and outcomes, not intent alone. What makes pedophilia bad is not that some adults feel good doing it, but that it harms children. The experience of adults is irrelevant. To claim circumcision is "not pedophilia" because adults do or don't feel good doing it is a form of pedophile-apology because it centers the issue on adults by suggesting that adults' feelings determine whether or not touching children's genitals is pedophilia. In reality, what makes something pedophilia is if it sexually violates a child.

The excuse that adults do not derive pleasure from touching children's genitals and circumcising them is also a lie. Although some adults may not feel immediate sexual pleasure, they derive other forms of pleasure. When adults say the circumcised penis "looks better" they are deriving aesthetic pleasure from their children's genitals. We could call this aesthetic pedophilia. Adults are also engaged in aesthetic pedophilia if they circumcise a child to make him "look like dad" or "look normal." If the doctor makes money on the circumcision, he is deriving the pleasure of wealth from that child, which we could call profit pedophilia. If the parents or circumcisers feel that their actions have somehow benefited the child, either by bringing him into a faith or conferring some medical improvement, then they derive moral pleasure from the child's genitals, which we could call self-righteous pedophilia. Pleasure can take many forms and does not just have to be immediate sexual gratification. When adults participate in systems that derive pleasure from touching children, like hospital birth or the medical system, they are engaged in systemic pedophilia.

This systemic view of pedophilia changes the culpability of those who perpetuate it. It is possible for everyone participating in a system to have the best of intentions, while still producing outcomes that are harmful.[78] When called out for their role, participants in systemic pedophilia often attempt to shift responsibility. Parents say they are just doing what the doctors told them to do. Doctors say the hospital requires them to perform circumcisions. Hospitals say they have to offer circumcision or parents will go elsewhere. These excuses all acknowledge that each individual or organization is participating in a larger system. The idea that we are not merely individuals but participants in cultural systems is a core idea of critical social justice theory.[79] However, critical theory also suggests that we are morally culpable if complicit in those systems.[80] This "Complicity Principle" states that "one is accountable for what others do when one intentionally participates in a collective that causes the harm together."[81] Even if genital cutting might occur without the participation of one person or group, "one is accountable for the harm we do together, independently of the actual difference an individual who intentionally participates in such group action makes."[82] Participants in systemic pedophilia might not have an individual ill will towards the child, but they have participatory intention. "Participatory intention is intention to act as part of a group in collective action of agents who orient themselves around a joint project."[83] On this issue, the "joint project" is infant genital cutting. Whether or not they personally touched the child, every person, institution, or aspect of society that participates in systemic pedophilia is morally culpable for being complicit in this system.

ANTIPEDOPHILE

How do we cease to be complicit in systemic pedophilia? Critical social justice theorists suggest that the only way to avoid being complicit in injustice is to develop a critical consciousness, which means to become consciously aware of systemic issues, how you participate in them and make a conscious effort to cease that participation and oppose those systems.[84] Since we all participate in cultural systems,[85] neutrality is impossible,[86] and unconscious participation in cultural systems will mean we are complicit in the harm those systems produce.[87] The only solution is to become conscious of how we participate in the world and develop a critical consciousness.

On racial justice issues, this critical consciousness is known as antiracism.[88] To be antiracist means to critically examine the systems one participates in and actively dismantle those which create racist outcomes.[89] Antiracism defines anyone who participates in racist systems as a racist.[90] While those who participate in racist systems protest that they are "not a racist," critical social justice activists point out that if their ideas and actions create racist outcomes, then they are engaged in racism regardless of their conscious intention. Since every system either produces equal or unequal outcomes between racial groups, "one either allows racial inequities to persevere, as a racist, or confronts racial inequities, as an antiracist."[91] Antiracists believe that "the claim of 'not racist' neutrality is a mask for racism," because "there is no neutrality in the racism struggle"[92]

The same principle applied to circumcision would suggest that it is not enough to not personally participate in systemic pedophilia. We must become antipedophile. To become antipedophile means to critically examine the systems one participates, in and actively dismantle those that harm children. Anyone who engages in systemic pedophilia is a pedophile. Those who participate in pedophile systems might protest that they are "not a pedophile," if their ideas and actions cause children to be harmed, or have their genitals sexually touched, forcibly penetrated, or cut at an age at which they cannot give consent, they are engaged in systemic pedophilia regardless of their conscious intention. This logic extends even to people who do not directly participate in genital cutting. For example, if a person claims to be "not a pedophile," but regularly gives money to people and institutions that engage in pedophilia, they are still supporting pedophilia. A doctor might not personally cut children's genitals, but if an institution engaged in systemic pedophilia sign the doctor's paycheck, and they in turn support pedophile institutions through their labor, they are still a participant in systemic pedophilia. An adult might have no children of their own, but normalize genital cutting through their language and stigmatize intact bodies. Since we all participate in cultural systems, unconscious participation means participation in systemic pedophilia. The only way to avoid being complicit in injustice is to develop a critical consciousness around this issue. The framing of "not a pedophile" is a mask for systemic pedophilia, because there is no neutrality on the issue of pedophilia.[93]

Those familiar with critical social justice will recognize that this framing is adapted from Ibram Kendi's concept of antiracism.[94] One of the most common criticisms of his framing usually asks: Isn't it enough to be "not a racist," or in this case, "not a pedophile?" After all, aren't we "not" a lot of things? If we were talking about murder, would someone need to be "anti-murder," because saying they are "not a murderer" might somehow imply they secretly support murder?

First, for the purposes of appealing to the dominant hegemony, it is irrelevant whether or not the framing of antiracism is correct. This idea has been accepted by those in power. Universities, schools, corporations, media organizations, political organizations, and other powerful institutions have all signed on to the concept of antiracism. Ibram Kendi himself was the closing speaker of at the American Academy of Pediatrics 2020 Convention.[95] The American Academy of Pediatrics circumcision policy statements has been used by doctors across the country in their recommendations on circumcision.[96] If the medical establishment accepts his framing, then it can be applied to the issues most important to them. To argue against this framing would be to attack the intellectual foundation of antiracism.

Second, I believe the framing of critical consciousness is correct. If we view problems as systemic, then either we are participating in those systems, or not. The reason this framing applies to issues like racism or pedophilia and not murder is that pedophilia is a systemic issue, whereas murder is usually an individual action. When murder becomes systemic, as in war, people must decide whether or not they will participate in social structures which support murder in the form of war. In the case of war, the same framing might apply and it would not be enough to be "not a soldier" but instead actively anti-war.

I realize many will become defensive when they hear that they might be engaged in systemic pedophilia. It is common for people to become what critical social justice calls "fragile" when confronted with the ways they perpetuate systemic issues.[97] The reason people become "fragile" or defensive when asked to consider how they might participate in systems that perpetuate inequality is not just because they feel accused of wrong-doing, but because on some level, they fear that this accusation might be correct.[98] A critical examination of their actions might reveal that their actual actions are different from their stated beliefs. This defensiveness is a way of protecting those unconscious actions and beliefs and preserving their self-image. Critical social justice suggests that this defensiveness or fragility is evidence itself of an unconscious belief or bias the person is defending.[99] Whether or not you accept this as true, if none of your actions contribute to any negative systems, then there is no harm in examining them. However, if they do contribute to systems that perpetuate harm, then becoming conscious of our own behavior gives us the opportunity to change it, create a more just world, and become more of who we want to be. This empowering experience, because it puts the control back in your hands. Injustice is no longer something that other people do "out there" in the world, where you have no control over it, but something you can change through your choices.

THE PEDOPHILE-APOLOGIST NARRATIVE

The most common argument used by pedophile-apologists and those engaged in systemic pedophilia to defend circumcision is medical benefit. Previous human rights efforts against circumcision would debate the individual claims of pedophile-apologists regarding purported medical benefits of the procedure. Studies claiming medical benefits of circumcision are highly flawed and false on a purely scientific level. A significant amount of academic literature has been devoted to debunking these false claims.[100] However, critical theory would take a different approach to examining these studies. Although one could debate each study point by point, a critical social justice approach would question the assumptions and system behind these studies. What assumptions are they based on? What ways of knowing do they prioritize? What values are their arguments designed to defend?

Imagine a study claiming that one racial group was superior to another. Would a social justice activist debate this study? Of course not. Even engaging with such a study would be seen as racist. A critical social justice activist would not engage in an endless game of "whack-a-mole," debunking study after study claiming racial superiority. They would instead point out the racist premise of such studies. If the intention of the study is to elevate one race over another, then it is a racist study.[101] The authors of such a study might protest that they are "not racist" and that "it's just the science," but that is irrelevant if the outcome of the study is that it perpetuates racism.[102] In the same sense, a study to see if there are medical benefits to touching children's genitals, holding them down, and cutting off parts of their body is a pedophile study. Antipedophile activists do not need to engage in an endless game of debunking studies, but rather point out the obvious: these people did a study to see if they could touch and cut children's genitals. They committed thousands of dollars, hundreds of hours of time, and the reputation of their careers and institution towards justifying genital cutting and systemic pedophilia. Authors of these studies might protest that they are "not pedophiles" and "it's just the science," but if the purpose of these studies is to justify touching and cutting children's genitals then it is a pedophile-apologist study.

The claim of "benefits" is not a neutral statement of evidence, as pedophile-apologists claim, but contains a set of assumptions and values.[103] Every "benefits" argument contains the assumption that these so-called "benefits" justify touching children's genitals, and that these "benefits" are more important than allowing the child to be free from rape, pedophilia, and genital cutting. The way to critically examine pedophile-apologist arguments is not to look at the supposed "evidence," but to examine the intention and outcome. The purpose of these "benefits" arguments is to justify systemic pedophilia. When someone makes an argument that they and others can engage in pedophilia, they are a pedophile-apologist.

The idea that children want pedophilia or that there is some benefit to the child for engaging in pedophilia is a core narrative among pedophile-apologists. When pedophiles are caught sexually abusing children, the most common excuse they give law enforcement is to blame the victim in some way.[104] Pedophiles will frequently say that they were "teaching" the child, helping them learn about their sexuality, or that the victim "wanted" sexual contact in some way. "Man-boy love" pedophile-apologist organizations have historically claimed that children "want" sexual relationships with adult men and should be allowed to have them,[105] projecting adult sexual desires onto young boys. Likewise, circumcisers claim that on some level children want to be circumcised and will "thank us later" for cutting their genitals, projecting their adult desires onto children. When people are unable to admit or acknowledge a desire that they have, they will project it onto others in what is known as psychological projection.[106] Pedophiles often have trouble admitting they want to use children for their own benefit, so they will project the desire to touch or cut children's genitals onto the child. If a doctor were to say "I'm cutting the child's genitals so I make money and make his body look aesthetically pleasing to me" he would not sound as good as if he said, "I'm doing this for the good of the child." The claim that circumcision benefits the child is a pseudo-scientific update to old pedophile-apologist narratives that project adult desires onto children. Every argument made in favor of circumcision comes from adult desire or projected adult desire. This pedophile-apologist narrative is one of the ways the medical system protects a power structure engaged in systemic pedophilia.

CRITICAL CONSCIOUSNESS

Critical social justice's view of systemic issues reveals that the dominant culture's attempt to frame circumcision as "fringe" is a pedophile-apologist narrative. Far from fringe, this social justice issue is literally carved into children's bodies and intersects with major social justice issues. The fear and fragility people experience when talking about circumcision is often a defensive reaction to their participation in systemic pedophilia being revealed. In order to create justice for children, we must develop a critical consciousness, become aware of systemic pedophilia, and make a conscious choice to withdraw our participation from and oppose this system. This awareness includes deconstructing the language, narratives, and assumptions that uphold systemic pedophilia. It is not enough to be "not a pedophile." We must become antipedophile.

CHAPTER 4
EPISTEMIC INJUSTICE

When pedophile-apologists defend genital cutting, they prioritize certain ways of knowing over others and create what is known in critical theory as epistemic injustice. Epistemic injustice is the idea that there can be injustice around issues of knowledge and that certain voices are being unjustly privileged, silenced in favor of others, or denied the epistemic tools they need to express an idea.[107] The epistemic injustice around circumcision is so significant, that if this one aspect of systemic pedophilia were solved, I believe all others might fall like dominos. To even begin to understand this issue, we must begin to examine the epistemic injustice that upholds systemic pedophilia.

TESTIMONIAL INJUSTICE

One of the most common forms of epistemic injustice is testimonial injustice. Testimonial injustice is when a person's testimony about their lived experience is dismissed or not considered authoritative, often due to identity prejudice.[108] In her book *Epistemic Injustice: Power and the Ethics of Knowing*, Miranda Fricker gives the example of when a woman's testimony is dismissed by a man in the film *The Talented Mr. Ripley (1999)* as just "female intuition."[109] The man in this example sees women as less capable of knowing, and uses his own prejudice to dismiss her testimony. When someone's testimony or knowing is dismissed on the basis of prejudices towards their identity, this is a form of epistemic injustice known as identity prejudice.[110]

Survivors of genital cutting clearly face testimonial injustice and identity prejudice. When they share how circumcision has personally harmed them in their life or impacted their sexuality, their testimony is often dismissed. Instead, pedophile-apologists prioritize the beliefs of "experts" and other people engaged in systemic pedophilia over the actual experiences of circumcised men. Men's lived experience is framed by these so-called experts as "just stories," and "not evidence."[111] Yet, these stories are a form of evidence known as testimony. Testimony is evidence and would be admissible as such in any court case. When people claim that the stories of survivors are not evidence, they are engaged in testimonial injustice against those men in order to protect systemic pedophilia.

The idea that people from certain backgrounds cannot be experts on their own experience is a form of epistemic injustice that has historically been used to prop up physical injustices. When homosexuality was considered a mental disorder, psychologists were considered the experts on gay people, not gay people themselves. As the gay rights movement gained support, gay people gained epistemic authority over their own experience. During times of overt oppression, the people whose knowledge was considered authoritative on an identity group were never people from that group, but outside experts. On the issue of circumcision, all men are in the position gays were when they were considered a "disorder," with doctors considered the experts on circumcision rather than circumcised men themselves.

There is a long history of epistemic injustice towards any male testimony of abuse. When men share their feelings of grief, rage, or sadness about circumcision, their emotions are often dismissed, mocked, or belittled. Men who admit victimhood of any kind are often shamed as weak. A whole category of slurs is specifically directed against men who are seen as too emotional or in touch with their feelings. This fits into a larger system of sexism that values men for their utility rather than their personhood or feelings.[112] The traditional male role requires strength, so any admission of a lack of power is seen as a confession that the man might not be able to play his traditional role. The shaming of men for their feelings is one way to enforce this role. When men proclaim they are "fine with their circumcision," they play into this system by refusing to acknowledge harm and indicating to the dominant culture that they are willing to play their role even if it means enduring abuse and pedophilia.

There is a testimonial injustice privileging the testimony of men who claim they are "fine" with circumcision over those who feel harmed. When men respond to those who feel harmed by circumcision by saying "well, I'm fine with it," they are subtly invaliding the lived experience of men who feel harmed by circumcision by suggesting that others' experiences are more valid. Society does this on a larger level by saying "most men are fine with it," suggesting that the lived experience of men who do not feel harmed by institutional pedophilia and genital cutting is somehow more valid than the lived experience of those who feel harm. These statements about being "fine" with circumcision usually only arise in response to criticism of circumcision and are meant to imply that those who are not "fine with it" should conform to the dominant cultural attitudes about circumcision.

Imagine you were to ask a slave how he felt about being forced to work for a slave master, and he said he was "fine with it." You might question whether or not his answer was false, because if he gave any answer other than that he was "fine with it," his master would punish him. In his situation, there are significant forms of systemic oppression that prevent him from giving an honest answer. Likewise, there are significant systemic issues that prevent men from talking about their abuse. It would be right to question men who say they are "fine" with circumcision since the consequence for "no" is emotional and social punishment. This might be different from physical punishment, but it is nonetheless painful, and the social prohibition against men expressing feelings makes them uniquely vulnerable to this punishment. Men who speak out against circumcision are often emotionally abused, have their feelings invalidated, are ostracized from their family and friends, face repercussions in their professional work, body shamed, branded by pedophile-apologists as less desirable for sexual relationships, or even framed by the dominant culture as less of a man. While slaves are physically punished, modern men are emotionally and socially punished.

IDENTITY PREJUDICE

Male and female genital cutting are physically similar. The World Health Organization (WHO) recognizes four types of female circumcision.[113] Type I, the partial removal of the clitoral hood or glans, is equivalent to male circumcision. Some forms of type I female genital cutting involve only a "ritual knick" and are less invasive than male circumcision.[114] When Western media discusses genital cutting, they often make no distinction between different types of female genital cutting, and frame all female genital cutting as Type IV, which involves full infibulation or sewing the vulva shut, despite Type I being the more common. Western media also assumes that the male foreskin has no sexual value or sensory nerve endings when the types of nerve endings in both male and female genitals are the same Meissner's corpuscles.[115] In the womb, the structure that develops into the clitoral hood on women develops into the foreskin on men, making them physically equivalent. The male foreskin contains more nerve endings than any other part of the male body including even the glans of the penis, which means the removal of the foreskin is comparable to removing the most nerve-laden parts of a woman's body.[116]

The most significant pro-circumcision medical organization, the American Academy of Pediatrics (AAP), published a paper arguing that because male circumcision was legal that doctors should be allowed to practice lighter forms of female circumcision for parents who want it.[117] The paper was retracted after public outcry, but the argument that male and female genital cutting are equivalent was picked up by supporters of female genital cutting. When the first case trying America's federal law against female genital cutting began, attorney Alan Dershowitz argued on behalf of the defense that the type of female genital cutting the defendant had done was less invasive than male circumcision, part of their religion and culture, and therefore legal.[118] The case resulted in the federal law against female genital cutting being ruled unconstitutional on a technicality.

Even those that support male circumcision have at times recognized the comparisons between male and female circumcision.

Yet, male and female genital cutting are treated differently. There is a testimonial injustice and identity prejudice in the way male survivors of genital cutting are treated in comparison to female survivors. When someone perceived as female survives genital cutting, it is referred to as "female genital mutilation" and treated as one of the worst injustices a person can experience. When someone perceived as male survives genital cutting it is referred to as "male circumcision," implying it is a normalized medical procedure and treated as a regular everyday occurrence. Survivors of female genital cutting are treated as brave, despite the fact that there is significant social support for women who feel harmed by genital cutting, and survivors of male genital cutting are treated as weak or dysfunctional, despite the fact there is almost no social support for men who feel harmed by genital cutting and it requires greater bravery to speak out on.

There is testimonial injustice within female genital cutting. In male genital cutting, those who are "fine with it" are given testimonial privilege over those who feel hurt. In female genital cutting, the opposite is true. The majority of women in cultures that practice female genital cutting claim they are "fine with it." They use much of the same language as male supporters of male genital cutting. They describe it as cleaner, healthier, and an improvement on their sex life.[119] Western cultures give testimonial privilege to the opposite side of this form of genital cutting, privileging the women who complain over those who are fine with it. Women who support their own genital cutting are demonized as brainwashed by their culture, but men who support their own genital cutting are seen as "normal" by Western culture. This testimonial injustice is a form of imperialism because it suggests that those who conform to non-Western cultures are stupid or ignorant, but those who conform to Western culture are enlightened or normal. A more accurate view would be that most people conform to the culture they are socialized into and that we all need to look critically at our own culture. The fact that Westerners are not willing to look at their own culture and become defensive when you suggest that they question their culture's genital cutting is a form of privilege and fragility. They have the option not to question their culture because Western culture is the dominant culture, whereas women who come from cultures that practice female genital cutting do not have the benefit of their views supported by popular media and cultural products that are exported all over the world. In order to rectify this testimonial injustice, which intersects with sexism and imperialism, male survivors of genital cutting who feel harmed must be given the same testimonial privilege as female survivors of genital cutting.

HERMENEUTICAL INJUSTICE

A more hidden but perhaps even more important form of epistemic injustice is hermeneutical injustice. Hermeneutical injustice is when a group does not have the epistemic tools to accurately or fully describe and make sense of their lived experience.[120] To understand hermeneutical injustice, imagine a woman in Victorian times trying to explain her experiences without the word "sexism" or a black man in the pre-Civil War south trying to explain his experiences without the word "racism." Sometimes to describe our lived experience we need the right word to communicate a certain concept, and may even need to invent a new word in order to fully explain it. Critical social justice has such a rich vocabulary in part because they found the previous vocabulary around social justice insufficient to fully communicate the lived experience of the people they are trying to achieve justice for.

Survivors of genital cutting clearly face a hermeneutical injustice, because they lack the words to describe their experiences. When men say they feel "raped" by circumcision, they are often told, "circumcision is not rape." Men are trying to explain their experience with the only vocabulary they have available, and most of the language that exists around abuse is based on the sexist idea that men are perpetrators and women victims. Some men might say "mutilated" but again, they face people telling them that "circumcision is not mutilation." Some will even add identity prejudice to their epistemic injustice by saying that comparing "male circumcision" to "female genital mutilation" trivializes what happens to women, not seeing that they are trivializing men's experience by denying the comparable harm of male circumcision. Men are attacked when they use existing words, yet are not given any words of their own to describe their experience. The existing vocabulary does not fully capture the lived experience of survivors of genital cutting. In this book, I have used multiple concepts - sexism, body-shaming, pedophilia, etc. - to describe the problem, because there is no single word that fully encapsulates the harm of systemic genital cutting. Systemic pedophilia comes closest. I use the term systemic pedophilia because most people's reaction to the sexual abuse of children is more accurate and emotionally appropriate than even their reaction to "genital cutting," but there is still a great deal of epistemic work to do on this issue.

Hermeneutical injustice also occurs when dominant groups demand the people they oppress explain their experiences only in the language of their oppressor while denying them the epistemic tools to do that.[121] When men do speak up, pedophile-apologists in the medical system demand they provide "evidence" and then limit that evidence to peer-reviewed journals controlled by institutions engaged in systemic pedophilia and genital cutting. Those journals then deny men the evidence they need by only conducting studies on what the system cares about, not on what men or the survivors of genital cutting need. The medical industry has never done any major longitudinal studies on circumcision.[122] Medical institutions rarely conduct studies on the emotional or psychological impact of circumcision, because those that have been done show evidence of significant trauma.[123] Even if there were more psychological studies, there is no scientific way to fully measure men's subjective experience of their own body, sexuality, and feelings. There is very little good data on circumcision because the only institutions with the resources to gather that data are engaged in systemic pedophilia and genital cutting. The dominant culture demands men speak in their language, set themselves up as gatekeepers to that language, and then denies men access to the data and information that would allow them to speak the dominant language. When independent organizations do gather the resources and do their own studies, those studies are dismissed because they don't appear in journals controlled by systemic pedophiles and practitioners of genital cutting.[124] This is epistemic oppression on a massive scale.[125]

Furthermore, even if society did listen to men's stories and lived experiences around circumcision, the existing vocabulary could not capture it. When a significant part of someone's experience is obscured from collective understanding, they experience hermeneutical marginalization.[126] Survivors of systemic pedophilia experience deep hermeneutical marginalization. Not only is their testimony dismissed, their words denied, and their access to the dominant institutions needed to make their case refused, but many aspects of their experience go completely unnamed. For example, when men learn about the harm of circumcision, it is common for them to become estranged from their families. When they attempt to communicate their pain, parents often become defensive, argue with them, or say they did it for the man's own good. The survivors risk losing their families if they acknowledge the harm that was done. Is there any word for this experience or language to share it with others? If not, this is a form of epistemic injustice.[127] Social justice movements against genital cutting must address this by introducing the language necessary to describe the lived experience of surviving genital cutting and living in a genital cutting culture. This has been done on other movements. For example, in the gay movement when people lose their connection to their parents when they come out as gay, the parents' rejection is defined as familial homophobia.[128] Yet no similar word exists yet on the issue of systemic pedophilia. In order to end the hermeneutical marginalization of survivors, there might be hundreds of such experiences that need to be defined, named, and talked about.

CREATE LANGUAGE

Hermeneutical justice might mean that some terms need to be redefined or changed. For example, the phrase frequently used to describe parents who agreed to let the medical system circumcise their children, but now wish they hadn't, is "regret parents." This phrase centers the responsibility on the individual decision of the parents. The phrase centers identity in the feelings of the parents, not the feelings of the child or the larger system they participated in by circumcising their child. Did these parents really make their decision in isolation, independent of other systems? Parents in the medical system are asked eight times on average if they want their child circumcised, even if they already said no, or had in their birth plan that they wanted to keep their child intact.[129] Doctors and nurses often use high-pressure sales tactics.[130] Some even lie by claiming circumcision is required or shame parents as "bad mothers" if they refuse to comply.[131] There have been court cases that revealed that mothers signed consent forms for circumcision while under the influence of drugs used during birth.[132] There is a significant power imbalance between parents and doctors when the hospital has their child, will not discharge them yet, and is pressuring parents to allow them to circumcise.

Imagine if this situation was between a man and a woman instead of an institution and family. If a man in a position of authority was to repeatedly pressure a woman for sex while she was under the influence of drugs, continue asking after she said no, claimed she was required to have sex with him, shame her when she wouldn't, prevent her from leaving, and hold someone she cared about hostage during the whole process, could we really call it "consent" if she eventually broke down and said yes? The woman might regret giving a "yes," but we would not frame the sex that followed as consensual. We would say it was coerced. Parents are at an even greater imbalance of power in the medical system because the thing pressuring them to consent is an entire institution with greater wealth, power, and legal backing than a mere individual predator. Parents are pressured for consent during one of the most emotional and vulnerable experiences of their lives: the birth of their child.

A better name for these parents would be coerced parents. This phrase centers the responsibility in the system that perpetuates circumcision, rather than the individual choice of the parents. Yes, those parents did agree, but they did so under the coercion of the larger genital cutting culture and the systemic pedophilia of the medical system. This phrase places responsibility back on the systemic pedophilia of the medical system and acknowledges the ways the system lies to and victimizes parents. Framing circumcision as an individual choice parents make is a way the medical system hides its role in perpetuating genital cutting and pedophilia. Problems are systemic and these systems obscure their power through language, but the right language can reveal their role in harming children.

DECONSTRUCT LANGUAGE

Just as language can be used to illuminate truth, it can also be used to conceal it. While some terms might create hermeneutical justice by giving a name to survivors' experiences, others might create hermeneutical injustice by hiding what is really happening. Creating hermeneutical justice might require deconstructing these old terms used to conceal the truth. One such term is "parental choice."

There is no such thing as parental choice. The medical system frames circumcision as an individual decision made by parents or "parental choice."[133] This framing ignores the larger systems that influence and pressure parents. Parents do not manufacture circumcision tools, train doctors in how to use them, create health insurance billing codes for circumcision, culturally normalize circumcision, and package as a part of hospital birth. The entire "choice" parents have is to sign a single form at the end of the process. When parents do not make the choice the system wants, they engage in high-pressure sales tactics.[134] The term "parental choice" ignores this larger system and is a form of hermeneutical injustice.

There is a power imbalance between doctors and parents. The hospital system frames the doctor as the epistemic authority. The uniform, title conferred by credentials, and structure of the medical system all reinforce this authority frame. Yet the medical system frames circumcision as a "parental choice," when the entire system is set up to deny the parents knowing and privilege the viewpoint of the medical system over them. If the parent was indeed making an independent choice, the system would frame the parent as authority and privilege their knowing over the medical system. The medical systems then uses this power imbalance to deny parents information. Evidence against circumcision is never included, while information intended to produce "consent" is repeated.

"Parental choice" only became an option in the medical system when it would help perpetuate systemic pedophilia. Hospitals used to circumcise children without asking the parents until Jewish parents sued a hospital for circumcising their child, rather than allowing them to circumcise their child themselves on the eighth day after birth in a Jewish ritual.[135] Circumcision only became a parental choice when that parental choice increased the possibilities for systemic pedophilia and genital cutting. Even then it took a lawsuit to get hospitals to ask for parental "consent." Now, the medical system claims parents are culpable for a system they did not create, which did not even ask for their consent until a court order.

Parents are both participants in and victims of systemic pedophilia. Parental choice is a myth created by the medical system in order to scapegoat parents for systemic pedophilia. When parents speak out against coercion and abuse in the medical system, the medical system responds with testimonial injustice. Parents who claim the medical system harmed their children are suddenly "not experts" and incapable of understanding academic literature when those parents were treated as knowers capable of evaluating the decision when asked to decide for or against circumcising their child. A parent who has been through the decision to circumcise should be treated as knowing more since they have access to all the same information as before, plus the added testimony of their lived experience with the consequences of that decision. This testimony threatens the epistemic privilege of the academic literature and is devalued by the medical system in order to protect their perceived monopoly on epistemic authority.

EPISTEMIC POWER

The medical system uses different forms of epistemic injustice to maintain epistemic power over genital cutting. They marginalize the testimony of survivors, deny them the understanding to communicate, and hide their power through language. Creating epistemic justice on circumcision will require valuing the testimony of those harmed, giving them the language to describe their experiences, and deconstructing the language used to deny their knowing. Since every system of power rests on a system of language, creating epistemic justice might be a precursor to achieving social justice. If you care about justice, then you will want to learn the new language this book introduces.

CHAPTER 5
SUBALTERN STATUS

In critical social justice, there is the oppressor and the oppressed, the privileged and those without. However, in post-colonial theory, there is a third group: the subaltern. Subaltern classes are those completely outside the main structures of power, so marginalized they no longer have a voice, and subordinated through material, social, linguistic, and cultural forms of dominance.[136] If one were to think of social power in a hierarchy, with oppressors and dominant groups at the top and the oppressed or marginalized below them, the subaltern would be below and beside both of them, even further down, invisible even to other marginalized or oppressed groups, so far down that they might even be outside the hierarchy of power itself. If we apply this term and the lens of this theory to all societies instead of only colonial settings, it's clear that the most subaltern group in society is children, and that much of the analysis that has been done on subaltern groups applies to the treatment of children. If we look at children as a unique subaltern class, it is clear that children are the most oppressed group in human history.

SUBALTERN SPEECH

What defines the subaltern is an inability to speak. To be subaltern is not just having low status within a power structure, but outside the power structure entirely. Gayatri Chakravorty Spivak, author of perhaps of the most famous paper on subaltern groups *Can the Subaltern Speak?*, suggests that "subaltern is not just a classy word for 'oppressed,' for [the] Other... The working class is oppressed. It's not subaltern ... Many people want to claim [the condition of] subalternity... Just by being a discriminated-against minority on the university campus; they don't need the word 'subaltern'... They're within the hegemonic discourse, wanting a piece of the pie, and not being allowed, so let them speak, use the hegemonic discourse."[137] In other words, no matter how low status or disempowered a group is, if they can speak about their disempowerment, they are not subaltern. What defines subalternity is an inability to communicate. As another theorist writing about Spivak's work notes, "Spivak is trying to tell us that, almost by definition, the subaltern is the subaltern in part because it cannot be represented adequately by academic knowledge (and 'theory'). It cannot be represented by academic knowledge because academic knowledge is a practice that actively produces subalternity (it produces subalternity in the act of representing it). How can one claim to represent the subaltern from the standpoint of academic knowledge, then, when that knowledge itself is involved in the 'othering' of the subaltern?"[138] This inability to speak does not just come from lack of access to media or academic knowledge-producing institutions, but from the fact that their experience cannot be translated into the language of theory or dominant institutions.

This definition of subaltern could have been written about children. If subalternity is defined by an inability to speak, then it applies most to children, since children literally cannot speak. More than that, children's experience of the world is direct, sensory, and pre-verbal. It cannot be translated into academic language. If we were to translate an infant's experience into academic jargon, the full experience would be lost in translation. Children's feelings are actually better communicated through their expressions, sounds, and the look in their eyes. Medical language like "cortisol levels rose" does not express the feeling of a newborn experiencing stress like listening to his cries would. Academic language turns real experiences into symbols and words which can be communicated to others, and the subaltern experiences "resists symbolization."[139] The raw direct experience of reality by infants cannot be captured in a symbol.

When dominant groups demand that the subaltern speak in the dominant language of hegemonic powers is a form of epistemic injustice.[140] Subaltern groups cannot do that. Not only are they denied access to the dominant language, but their experience could not be translated into that language even if they wanted. When adults demand that infants communicate using adult language, they are engaged in this epistemic injustice. If adults wish to understand children, they must attempt to understand the child's communication, rather than impose their own. While adults frequently frame children as incapable of communicating, this is not true. Children are only incapable of communicating in the language of adults. Yet children are perfectly capable of communication in their own way. Their sounds and movements have meaning. Any mother who has heard their child cry and known he was asking to be fed or held has had a successful communication with a child. None of us would have survived infancy had our parents not had some capacity for understanding our needs and expression of those needs. Children's survival is dependent on their ability to communicate, and adults' ability to understand that communication. When adults refuse to acknowledge children's communication, they engage in epistemic violence against children.

Subaltern groups frequently experience epistemic violence. Epistemic violence is when dominant groups refuse to communicate with, acknowledge the communication of, or are incapable of communicating with marginalized groups due to the dominant group's ignorance.[141] This ignorance could be willful or unintentional, but the result of epistemic violence is that no communication is possible. When circumcising doctors claim not to understand children's screams during circumcision, they are engaged in epistemic violence. The child is clearly communicating his pain, but the doctor refuses to acknowledge any communication that does not occur in the dominant language of adults. In an interview I conducted, the chair of the 1988 American Academy of Pediatrics task force on circumcision dismisses infant's cries of pain during genital cutting by saying, "they scream, but they scream if they're wet, if they're hungry, and so on."[142] By dismissing and ignoring the children's screams, doctors are not only engaged in the physical violence of genital cutting but epistemic violence, because they deny the child any means or possibility of communication. As Kristie Dotson puts it in *Tracking Epistemic Violence, Tracking Practices of Silencing*: "To communicate we all need an audience willing and capable of hearing us. The extent to which entire populations of people can be denied this kind of linguistic reciprocation as a matter of course institutes epistemic violence."[143] Children are an entire population systemically denied linguistic reciprocation. While circumcision is the most extreme example of epistemic violence against children, all children experience epistemic violence when adults refuse to acknowledge their attempts at communication.

INTERNALIZED DOMINANCE

Children, as a subaltern group, are outside dominant power structures. While every other identity, no matter how marginalized, has the ability to seek greater power, children are incapable of seizing social power due to their biological status as children. Children are smaller, their minds are still developing, and they are incapable of taking care of themselves. Children can never "rise up" the way other marginalized groups have sought to, no matter how much they are mistreated. The relationship between children and adult power structures mirrors those of a subaltern group and imperial power, with children outside that power and at the mercy of a dominant hegemony.

Adults frequently justify their mistreatment of children by their biological differences. When adults believe that it is okay to abuse children due to their superior ability as adults, they are engaged in internalized dominance. Internalized dominance is when a group justifies their privilege through the belief that they are superior to marginalized groups and deserve their privileged position.[144] In *Is Everyone Really Equal?: An Introduction to Key Concepts in Social Justice Education*, Ozlem Sensoy and Robin DiAngelo give a checklist of examples of internalized dominance.¹⁴⁵ Every form of internalized dominance mentioned in their book is present in the justifications adults give for systemically oppressing children. Below is their list, with their examples replaced with examples of how adults express internalized dominance relative to children:

• Rationalizing privilege as natural - Adults see themselves as naturally superior to children.

• Rationalizing privilege as earned - Adults will frequently tell children that they had to go through the same thing as children to justify repeating the same oppression on children.

• Perceiving you and your group as the most qualified for and entitled to the best jobs - Adults see themselves as more qualified and entitled to most meaningful activities in society.

• Living one's life segregated from the minoritized group yet feeling no loss or desire for connections with them - Adults segregate children from society through compulsory schooling. Adults avoid connecting with children except in specific social contexts. When children make noise in public places or attempt to communicate with adults, they are often treated as a nuisance rather than people worthy of connection.

• Lacking an interest in the perspectives of the minoritized group except in limited and controlled doses or when it appears to benefit the dominant group - Adults silence children and expect them only to share their feelings and experiences in specific contexts convenient for adults. Adults only share children's experiences when it serves their emotional needs, such as the child appearing "cute" or appealing to the positive emotions of adults.

• Feeling qualified to debate or explain away the experiences of minoritized groups - People frequently invalidate and minimize children's feelings and experiences.

The way adults relate to children is textbook internalized dominance. Is there another way adults could relate to children? While there are biological differences between children and adults, when other adults have biological differences that make them incapable of caring for themselves physically or mentally, we call it a disability. Disability has already been explored in social justice, and there is an entire critical social justice field of disability studies and disability justice.¹⁴⁶ On the issue of disability, social justice activists believe that those with a disability have just as much a right to dignity and respect as able-bodied people. Most people believe we have a moral duty to care for disabled people who cannot care for themselves. Some disability activists suggest that much of what society deems a "disability" is socially constructed by the standards of the dominant group and could be considered beneficial or a positive identity if viewed through a different lens.[147] At minimal, disability activists suggest that disability is not an excuse for mistreatment. The same principle could apply to children. Children are not as physically strong or mentally capable as able-bodied adults. There are some ways in which children's differences could be seen as an advantage if viewed through a different social construction. For example, children's minds may not be as developed as adults, but they have a greater capacity for learning thanks to their developing minds. At a minimum, even though children are physically and mentally different, they still deserve the same dignity, respect, and kindness we give to adults.

This is not to say that children do not deserve special treatment. The entire concept of equity is based in the idea that in order to create equality of outcomes you might have to treat some groups differently than others. One could justify treating children differently from a critical social justice perspective if that difference in treatment was to create equity. Again, many of the same principles that apply to disabled people who cannot take care of themselves could also be applied to children. It would be okay to build a ramp so a disabled person could access a building, even though "equality" would mean everyone using the same stairs because we understand that creating the equity of everyone having access to a building might require some unequal treatment in the case of a disabled person. However, it would not be okay to physically or sexually abuse a mentally disabled person, because that person might not fully understand what is happening to them or be able to express their pain. The same principle applies to children. It is okay to do things for children they cannot do for themselves, like feed them or help them around the world, but not okay to cut a child's genitals with the excuse that they can't comprehend or talk about the abuse like an adult. This should be obvious to any empathetic person, yet the internalized dominance adults have towards children sometimes blinds them to their bad behavior.

ADULT CENTERING

Given that children are clearly a marginalized group, why has social justice not been applied to the rights of children? Critical theory and social justice movements already have tools for understanding power dynamics and systemic oppression. Applying this understanding to children might take some intellectual work, but it could be done. Why has there not been a major social justice movement to create justice for children, or what I call Children's Justice?

In *Epistemic Injustice: Power and the Ethics of Knowing*, Miranda Fricker suggests that "we try hardest to understand those things it serves us to understand," and "a group's unequal hermeneutical participation will tend to show up in a localized manner in hermeneutical hotspots."[148] In other words, people seek knowledge when it benefits them. Knowledge around adult identity issues is useful for critical social justice activists. If you are oppressed because of your identity, you will seek to understand the social power dynamics around that identity. As a consequence, critical social justice has a rich vocabulary for talking about issues related to adult identities, such as gender, race, and sexual orientation, but has focused less on children. The obvious answer to why there has not been a major social justice movement for children is that it does not benefit adults, and adults are the ones with access to the epistemic tools of social justice and critical theory.

Dominant groups might not seek the same level of knowledge or understanding when there is nothing for them to gain. For example, queer activists might spend a lot of mental energy trying to understand gender, while those whose gender fits within the dominant culture will spend less energy because there is nothing for them to gain by questioning a culture that already privileges them. However, dominant groups might spend a lot of mental energy developing a vocabulary around a specific issue that does affect them. Where adults have developed a vocabulary and knowledge around children is where it serves them, what Fricker would call the "unequal participation" in "hermeneutical hotspots" where adults have something to gain.[149] These include education, birth, and parenting. This would be fine if this material was written for the benefit of the child, and centered on his experience, but much of this literature is about how the adult can get what he or she wants from the child. This mindset where children exist for adult needs is a pedophile consciousness.

Here is a brief overview of the three major spaces where adults and children interact:

Education. The vocabulary that exists around education is about getting children to fulfill the needs and desires of adult teachers. If the managerial language of the education system were designed to serve children, we would teach this language to children so they could be equal participants in the process, and not limit it to those with an education degree. The fact that a whole vocabulary exists around education in which one class talks about and deconstructs the behavior of another in order to get them to do what they want is evidence of epistemic and systematic oppression.

Birth. The medical literature written about birth centers around the doctor's needs. Even the way mothers are positioned during hospital birth on their back is meant to serve the doctor's desires, not to serve the natural birth process. Natural birth is often easier in a squatting position, yet hospital birth places women on their back, forcing them to push their babies upward against gravity. This position gives doctors greater access to the woman's genitals at the expense of the mother and child. Birth literature is centered on the experience of adults, and very little is written about the perspective of the child. Complications in the medical literature are framed in terms of the medical system's need to avoid legal liability, not the potential birth trauma the child might suffer from modern hospital birth. The literature that acknowledges birth trauma is usually emotional healing literature targeted at adults. If society was serious about the needs of children, all birth literature would be about fulfilling the needs of the person being born, rather than a sliver of alternative writing about natural birth.

Parenting. Much of parenting literature is about how the parent can get the child to do what the adult wants, rather than understanding the needs of children. The child is treated as an object the parents can shape and mold to fulfill their unmet emotional needs, rather than a person with emotional needs of their own. The most egregious example of this is the Ferber Method, a popular method of getting infants to sleep by letting them "cry it out."[150] The focus of this method is getting the child to silence their cries for their needs for the convenience of parents. Virtually all dominant parenting methods are about convenience for adults rather than the needs of the child, including forcing infants to sleep in separate rooms from their parents, feeding them formula instead of breastmilk, and discipline-focused methods of parenting. Some parents even outsource their entire relationship with their children to daycares and for-profit caretakers.

There is a growing resistance to this adult-centered thinking, in the form of peaceful parenting, natural birth, and unschooling movements. Yet, these movements are still the alternatives, not the dominant hegemonic norm. The default choices for most Americans are still hospital birth, public school, and a view of parenting that asks "how can I get my child to do what I want?" rather than "how can I meet my child's needs in the way they need me to?"

The focus on adult needs when talking about children even includes social justice literature. Social justice literature has a lot to say about children when children's issues intersect with identity issues that concern critical social justice activism. The rest of the time, they are silent. For example, many social justice books have a lot to say about what should be taught in government schools through the entire field of "critical pedagogy,"[151] but never question the power dynamic of one social class locking another in government buildings for eight hours a day and forcing them to believe certain ideas and behave a certain way. Many social justice organizations have a lot to say about unequal outcomes between different social groups during hospital birth,[152] but never question whether or not birth should take place in a system that practices systemic pedophilia. There is a clear hermeneutical marginalization within social justice literature towards children because critical social justice participates unequally at the hotspots that concern adults as a dominant group while ignoring the issues that do not serve adult privilege. Since children's issues do not directly affect adults, critical social justice has not devoted the same intellectual energy to trying to understand them. All critical theory was developed by adults, and adults have nothing to gain by questioning a society that privileges them.

Some social justice activists have criticized early critical theorists for being unable to see certain issues or problems connected to their white affluent privilege, updating their work to recognize the problems of marginalized groups.[153] One could make the same criticism of adult critical theorists. These activists have focused on adult power dynamics of issues around identity because it benefits them. Many even circumcised their own children or sent them off to government schools. Their knowledge was developed with unconscious biases that hermeneutically marginalized the experience of children. Just as later theorists updated theory by applying it to new issues, taking the ideas which were useful to them and discarding or updating the aspects which fail to recognize their unique lived experience, the same solution could be applied here. Children's Justice activists can borrow the ideas which serve them from critical social justice while discarding or updating those that do not.

MARGINALIZED CLASS

Children are a marginalized class, best understood as subaltern. They are incapable of adult communication. Adults frequently engage in epistemic violence against children due to their internalized dominance and use epistemic injustice as the justification for physical violence. Critical theory and social justice have not been applied to children in a meaningful way, due to the privilege, internalized dominance, and pedophile-consciousness of adults. In hermeneutical hotspots where adults do engage with children, they engage with a pedophile consciousness by centering adult needs and treating children as objects to fulfill those needs. This problem extends even to the literature of social justice and critical theory, and can only be solved by updating and creating new theory that centers the needs of children, known as Children's Justice.

CHAPTER 6
OPPRESSION'S ORIGINS

What impact does childhood have on us as adults? In critical social justice theory, identity is intersectional, meaning that each identity we have changes the whole of our experience. Given that we have all been children, that children are a subaltern class, and that systemic issues frequently oppress children, this subaltern experience must influence the whole of our identity.

CHILDHOOD TRAUMA

Childhood trauma has a lasting impact on adult behavior. This point is so well established in both the research on childhood trauma and lived experiences of survivors, it almost warrants no further explanation or justification. However, the epistemic injustice of the medical system is so great, that doctors had to have academic studies showing that babies feel pain before they would recommend or use pain relief of any kind during circumcision.[154] It should be self-evident to anyone who has ever interacted with an infant that they feel, but prior to an academic study proving the obvious, doctors would deny that infants felt any pain when they cut into their genitals. Even today, infant circumcisions often do not use pain relief of any kind. Since it is not safe to use full anesthesia on a newborn infant, the most doctors can use is a topical or injected anesthetic. These anesthesias require a full five minutes to take effect, and if the doctor does not wait the full time, it has no effect. Topical anesthesia usually requires the feedback of the patient to let the doctor know if enough has been administered. Since babies cannot speak and doctors are not sensitive to infants' screams, this feedback is impossible. Even when doctors use some form of pain relief, the infant usually still feels significant pain during genital cutting. Doctors refused to use any pain relief until studies proved infants could feel pain, and once those studies conclusively proved infants feel pain, doctors continued to ignore their pain. This behavior suggests that the medical system's demand for academic studies was merely discourse and a form of epistemic injustice to protect systemic pedophilia. If the request for studies was genuine, then once those studies were done, the medical system should have updated medical practice based on new information. If the request for studies was a discourse to prevent doctors from having to change their behavior, then when those studies were done, doctors would have moved on to a new discourse to allow them to continue to cut infants' genitals and cause them deliberate pain. Since this is what the medical system did, we can assume the latter.

I bring this up because every time the subject of circumcision trauma is mentioned, those invested in systemic pedophilia often make the same demand for academic studies, even for claims about the speaker's personal experience. At a protest outside a medical conference, I watched an activist tell a doctor, "I feel anger and sadness over the fact I was circumcised," and the doctor robotically reply "do you have a study to prove that?" No one needs an academic study to know their own feelings. This request was clearly a form of testimonial injustice, and an attempt on the part of the doctor to avoid engaging with the man's testimony. Before we examine the research around trauma, consider whether or not you really need an academic study to know that "pedophilia causes trauma" or "trauma has a long-term impact." That said, there are academic studies, not only showing the long-term impact of trauma but specifically the long-term impact of circumcision trauma.[155] Researchers found that infants who were circumcised had a much more dramatic response to pain during vaccination. "The greater vaccination response in the infants circumcised without anaesthesia may represent an infant analogue of a post-traumatic stress disorder triggered by a traumatic and painful event and re-experienced under similar circumstances of pain during vaccination."[156] In other words, infants had post-traumatic stress disorder (PTSD) from circumcision. Infants who were circumcised were not only responding to the pain of a needle giving them a vaccine but the triggered memory of circumcision trauma. This change in behavior constitutes a form of memory, and the body stores these early life experiences as preverbal memories in the body.[157] The medical system is aware of this research, and this study on circumcision trauma is even cited in the American Academy of Pediatrics policy statement on circumcision,[158] yet they continue to circumcise.

Trauma has a long-term impact on lifelong health. The Adverse Childhood Experiences Study (ACE Study), the first large-scale study to examine the relationship between common adverse childhood experiences and later life outcomes, found a correlation between childhood trauma and lifelong health and social problems.[159] People with adverse childhood experiences were more likely to engage in high-risk behaviors like smoking, alcoholism, and drug use, more likely to attempt suicide or have mental health problems like depression,[160] and more likely to have chronic illnesses as adults, such as cancer heart, disease, stroke, and diabetes, the most common causes of death and disability in the United States.[161] To determine a participant's ACE score, the ACE test asks ten questions about childhood events. The higher the ACE score, the greater chance the participant in the ACE study had of later life issues. Intact America, an Intactivist organization that opposes circumcision, campaigned to have circumcision added to the third ACE question about childhood sexual assault.[162] The third ACE question asks "Did an adult or person at least 5 years older than you ever... Touch or fondle you or have you touch their body in a sexual way? or Attempt or actually have oral, anal, or vaginal intercourse with you?" The forcible penetration of a minor that occurs during circumcision clearly fits this question. Based on the science, we can conclude that circumcision causes pain, that pain is remembered and stored in the body as trauma, and that trauma has a lifelong adverse impact.[163]

PSYCHOLOGICAL FRAGMENTATION

Trauma often creates what is known as psychological fragmentation. Fragmentation is when in order to survive a traumatic experience, the survivor splits or fragments their consciousness into the good self, who was able to handle the trauma, and the bad self, which was unsafe to be connected to during their trauma.[164] The fragment that was unsafe is relegated to the unconscious, and the survivor disconnects that fragment from their conscious mind.[165] What we encounter as someone's surface personality is often the parts of their consciousness that were safe to be in during their childhood. The parts or aspects of their consciousness which were unsafe are still present, in their unconsciousness or what is sometimes referred to as their shadow. The survivor might not be consciously aware of their fragmented parts,[166] yet these unconscious aspects often create unconscious behavior throughout life.[167] There is an entire field of psychological healing work dedicated to making these fragmented parts integrated and whole again.[168]

As an example of fragmentation, imagine a child whose parents yell at them when the child disagrees with them. In this situation, the parts of the child that disagree are unsafe. The child's consciousness fragments, relegating the aspects of their personality that disagreed to the unconscious, leaving the surface personality docile and obedient. Adults comment on how "well-behaved" the child is, and the parents feel their parenting method has produced "good" children. The child is only "good," because the only aspects which were able to remain part of the conscious surface personality were the "good" aspects. Such a child might act out when they are older or unleash "rebellious" aspects when it becomes safe for those aspects to surface again. They might be unable to assert themselves or set boundaries as an adult. They might find they adopt whatever opinions their partner has in relationships, and are unable to maintain a sense of self while in connection with others. They might have unexplained physical symptoms, like headaches or an inability to feel pain.[169] They might experience memory loss or be unable to remember significant portions of their childhood.[170] They might experience emotional triggers and suddenly emotionally regress and act like a different person in response to triggering situations.[171] There can be as many different responses to trauma as there are survivors.

If a subaltern is an oppressed person without a voice outside the structure of power, one could think of these fragmented parts as internal subalterns. While there might be a dominant personality, and aspects of a person that are oppressed by their dominant conscious aspects, the fragmented aspects of consciousness relegated to the unconscious are outside the power of the conscious mind and unable to speak or make their presence of needs known. In our previous example, the aspects of the child which are dominant are those which are obedient. They might be consciously aware of some aspects of their personality which have other desires, but oppress or repress those thoughts when they surface through shame, guilt, or internal forms of emotional abuse. However, there may be other parts of themselves they've repressed entirely, and are so disconnected from the child that they would not even recognize those aspects as a part of them at all.

The structure of human society mirrors human consciousness. If people have repressed and disconnected from certain parts of their own consciousness, they will do the same to those aspects of society that trigger unconscious aspects of themselves, feelings of unsafety, or repressed psychological pain. If people handle feelings of unsafety by disconnecting from the part of their own consciousness which makes them feel unsafe, then they will likely use the same strategy on external social groups which produce the same feeling. For example, if people "lock away" the aspects of themselves that they perceive as harmful, they will likely see no problem with imprisoning people who engage in the same behavior in society. Social groups which are oppressed are often those which remind dominant groups of aspects of themselves that they are unwilling to acknowledge, or parts of themselves they already oppress in their own consciousness. If people oppress or ignore their internal subalterns, they will likely do the same to external ones.

If entire populations receive the same trauma, then all of society might collectively fragment in similar ways, and act out the same trauma response. Throughout most of history, child abuse was common, including sex between adults and children.[172] Sexual abuse of young boys was practically an institution throughout the Roman Era.[173] In the Middle Ages, fondling a child's genitals was seen as a joke.[174] Childhood sexual abuse remained the norm in European culture well into the twentieth century.[175] Either we have to assume that childhood sexual abuse did not psychologically impact historical people the same way it does today, or entire populations were collectively traumatized. If every member of a society were a survivor of childhood sexual abuse, then we could expect this trauma to impact the behavior of that society. Just as we could reasonably predict certain behavior as more likely from survivors of childhood abuse, we could also predict certain social behaviors from societies that are collective survivors of abuse. If we know a culture's normative childhood, we can predict its future. Likewise, to understand history, look at the childhood of the person or society making history. There is an entire field that views history through the same lens, known as psychohistory.[176]

CHILDHOOD ROOTS

Social justice movements based in critical theory also hold that social oppression is the product of childhood, through the process of socialization. In their view, we are all socialized into certain social constructions that determine our beliefs, behavior, and place in society.[177] These social constructions also determine who has power in society, and who does not. When these social constructions privilege one social class over another, they can create oppression. Race, gender, and other forms of identity are considered social constructions in critical theory based social justice movements. From this view of socialization, it follows that history can be understood through the social constructions dominant in a society, and forms of power created from those constructions. For example, social justice movements based in critical theory trace the origins of the modern social construction of race, including the idea of "whiteness" or white as socially constructed racial identity, to the European enlightenment period.[178] From this social construction came colonialism, slavery, and racism. If there is an "original sin" in social justice, it is the social constructions created in this era that were imposed throughout the world.

Critical social justice has a method of understanding the past similar to psychohistory. Instead of examining the whole of childhood, historians looking through the lens of critical theory examine the social constructions of an era that children were socialized into and various forms of power created from those constructions. Since social constructions require language to understand, this view misses the pre-verbal socialization of children. Children are learning far before they can understand language.[179] Children's early-life pre-verbal experiences might not teach them linguistically understood concepts, but they are teaching them emotional patterns that will influence the way they relate to others throughout the rest of their life. By the time children develop the ability to speak, they have already had foundational experiences that will determine their attachment style and way of relating to others. An understanding of childhood that only focuses on verbal socialization creates a subaltern experience that cannot be spoken because early childhood is by definition pre-verbal. A full understanding of childhood socialization must include the pre-verbal experiences of children and emotional patterns and ways of relating learned from those experiences.

How were children raised in Europe in the era before the development of the ideas that lead to colonialism? Shortly after birth, children were separated from their mothers and taken to a professional wet nurse, sometimes miles away, who would breastfeed them.[180] Many newborn children died due to the long journey to the wet nurse, the trauma of being separated from their mothers, and the treatment they received under strangers. These wet nurses often cared for dozens of children at a time, which meant that no individual child was ever fully nourished or had their needs met.[181] Striking or abusing children who cried out or giving them drugs to silence them was common.[182] Children were rarely seen by their parents if they were seen at all.[183] When children died, parents often would not even attend the funeral.[184] After spending infancy unloved and neglected, children were then put into boarding schools where corporal punishment at the hands of strangers was common. Many children did not even meet or spend quality time with their parents until adulthood. European childhood was hell. Children were seen as a product to be assembled for adult needs, not as human beings with needs of their own. Europe had an exploitative industrial system for children long before technological and economic industrialization ever occurred. After a thousand years of being raised in this exploitative system that treated children as property, it is not surprising that Europeans would later treat other people the same way through colonization.

While previous examinations of colonialism have explored the actions of Europeans and the impact of those they harmed, to my knowledge, none have included the lived experience of the subaltern children of Europe. At the beginning of their lives, these children were abandoned by their mothers, physically abused and tormented by strangers, and never fully fed, loved, or taken care of. Such a childhood would have made vulnerable aspects of the child unsafe, and fragmented them into the unconscious. At the same time, the future leaders of this society were required to perform in strict elite European boarding schools. This cutthroat environment would have selected for the most ruthless and sociopathic aspects of a child's personality while requiring them to present a veneer of niceness and civilized manners overtop these violent aspects.[185] These children were treated as property that could be exploited for the needs of the ruling class, adults. They would later enact the same trauma on native populations throughout the world through colonialism and slavery, treating others as property that could be used to meet the needs of dominant European powers.

From this trauma, Europeans created many of the social constructions social justice theorists would later attempt to deconstruct. Europeans saw themselves as rational, civilized, and superior because these were the dominant aspects of their personality it was safe to remain connected to in childhood. The European characterizations of native populations as savages, overly emotional, stupid, etc. could be interpreted as a psychological projection of the parts of Europeans consciousness that had been unsafe and fragmented in childhood. As Nick Duffell, author of *Wounded Leaders: British Elitism And The Entitlement Illusion: A Psychohistory*, told me, "in order to dissociate from your vulnerability completely, it was necessary to have somebody around quite close to you, who you labeled the vulnerable one, or the savage one, or the stupid one, or the incompetent one... Natives played that role for the

British."[186] The European project to both "civilize" and dominate local populations mirrors the internal power dynamics that had already occurred in their own consciousness in childhood. Native populations became subaltern because the dominant Europeans were projecting aspects of their own internal subaltern onto those populations and relating to them the same way they related to their own unconscious fragmentation.

To be clear, merely because someone has experienced oppression does not mean they are not responsible for the ways in which they oppress others. The European adults who engaged in colonialism are still culpable for their actions. However, the understanding of their childhood does provide insight into the root of the problem and reveals that the problems social justice is trying to solve cannot be solved by altering social constructions alone. If we change social constructions while leaving the underlying trauma they were born from, it is like chopping off the branches of oppression while leaving the roots. Oppression will grow back in some other form, as people find ways to enact their traumas and negative ways of relating to others through new social constructions. Only by removing the roots of oppression can we hope to end the problems social justice seeks to solve. The roots of oppression lie in childhood abuse. This means *the only way you will ever fully solve the problems of social justice issues is with Children's Justice.*

CHAPTER 7
INTERSECTIONAL IDENTITY

In American culture, genital cutting constitutes a shared collective trauma. Though the trauma of circumcision is pre-verbal, a collectively traumatized culture gives birth to social constructions influenced by their own internal subaltern fragments.[187] These social constructions protect and continue the trauma. What social constructions arise from a genital cutting culture?

CIRCUMCISION AS IDENTITY

In genital cutting cultures, men and their bodies are described as "circumcised" or "uncircumcised." This language frames circumcision as the norm and the natural, intact penis as abnormal or the exception. We do not frame female bodies this way. No one would call a woman who still has her breasts "unmastectomied." We would call a woman with her full body natural, whole, intact, etc. Most activists working against circumcision use the word 'intact' instead of "uncircumcised" because it frames the natural intact body as normal.

Intact men are also affected by the genital cutting culture. If their bodies are not cut, they are body-shamed by the dominant culture. The language used to describe their bodies, such as "uncircumcised," frames their bodies as unnatural and in need of genital cutting. This hermeneutical injustice denies them the language to describe their actual experience. Calling men who still have their foreskin "intact" creates greater justice, but it still requires us to define men's bodies in relation to the practice of circumcision. Why can we not escape the discourse of genital cutting?

The language used to talk about circumcision is comparable to that we use for other forms of identity. Men do not say "I was circumcised" but "I am circumcised" when speaking about their circumcision status. Circumcision is clearly understood as an aspect of identity rather than merely something that happened. When people speak about other surgeries, they do not say "I *am* shoulder surgeried." They say "I *had* shoulder surgery." The reason circumcision is understood as part of one's identity while other surgeries are not is that circumcision permanently alters an aspect of a person's sexuality and sexual identity. Every sexual encounter or interaction with that part of the body is different after circumcision. Other surgeries that transform identity use the same language. For example, someone who has a surgery that removes their ability to see will not just say "I had eye surgery" but "I am blind." Circumcision damages the penis, permanently altering its sexual function by removing the ability to feel certain sensations or perform certain sexual acts, and so it is also a change in identity: "I am circumcised."

Thought of as an intersectional identity, circumcision recontextualizes the male experience. As we discussed earlier, intersectionality suggests that in order to understand someone's experience you have to understand every aspect of their identity and how they intersect. For example, if we say that someone's identity is "straight white male" that description is incomplete if that person has a disability. Someone who has to spend their life in a wheelchair will not experience the world the way an able-bodied straight white male does, even if those other aspects of their identity are the same. Circumcision status as a piece of male identity has gone unacknowledged in critical theory although it is as much a part of male identity as sexual orientation, gender, or race.

IMPOSED IDENTITY

The fact that circumcision is an aspect of identity explains why so many men become defensive when circumcision is questioned. If you suggest that any other aspect of a person's identity is bad or wrong in some way, such as their race, gender, or sexual orientation, that person would rightly become upset with you. However, no one is born circumcised. Whereas race, gender, and sexual orientation might attempt to describe qualities that people are born with, "circumcised" only describes what a social institution like the medical system has done to the child after birth. Circumcision is thus what one could call an imposed identity.

An imposed identity is one that the dominant culture afflicts onto a group. To my knowledge, this term does not exist in other social justice or critical theory texts, nor does another term to describe the same concept. Other historical examples of imposed identities would be those of "slave" or "freeman" which the racist culture of the pre-Civil War South imposed on African-American people. If a Southerner during that time period saw a black person walking alone, one of their first questions might be "is this person a slave or freeman?" The question would make no sense to a modern American, who would assume that all people are free, but during the time period, this was treated as an important aspect of identity. If that person could not prove they were a "freeman," racist white authorities might assume the person was a runaway slave and imprison them. In reality, there is nothing innate to their identity that made them "slave" or "freeman," but the racist culture of the time imposed this aspect of identity on them.

The same way a racist culture practicing slavery might impose this identity on black men, the pedophile culture that practices genital cutting imposes the identity of "circumcised" or "uncircumcised" on all men. Unlike slavery, men cannot be freed from circumcision. The brand on their bodies is a life sentence. This identity describes something more unchangeable than slavery, yet it is still an imposed identity because it does not describe an innate aspect of a person but something imposed on them by dominant power structures.

Those who don't understand theory might dismiss an imposed identity as "not real" or merely a cultural construct. And while it is correct to say that an imposed identity might not describe the full 'truth' of who a person is, its impact on their life is very real. You couldn't understand a black man's experience of the world in the pre-Civil War South while dismissing the impact of slavery as "merely a cultural construct." Even a "freeman" during that time would have lived in the shadow of slavery and felt its systemic impact in some way. Likewise, we cannot understand men living in a pedophile culture of genital cutting without understanding circumcision as one aspect of their identity. Even intact men feel the systemic impact of circumcision on their lives. For example, if a partner of an intact man refers to them as "uncircumcised," then they and their body are being understood in their most intimate relationships through the lens of systemic pedophilia and genital cutting culture which sees male genital cutting as the norm.

Understanding circumcision as an aspect of identity changes the positionality of men in social justice, or where they stand in relationship to others, and how that position shapes their experience.[188] Every man in America is a survivor of genital cutting pedophilia, someone living in a genital cutting culture based in systemic pedophilia, or both. Whereas men might have had one positionality and social status in social justice before, this new aspect of identity changes their positionality in as much as if we were to discover they were a survivor of slavery. Since identity in social justice is intersectional, every other aspect of identity is recontextualized in light of the intersectionality created by their circumcision status.

INTERNAL SUBALTERN

Previous social justice movements have seen men as privileged. This new positionality changes that. How privileged can someone be if they don't have the privilege of keeping the full body they were born with? While it is true that some men ascend to positions of privilege and power, infant genital cutting or circumcision pedophilia is the opposite of privilege and a form of oppression. While an adult man might have privilege, a newborn infant being raped has none.

Yet if both are experienced by the same person, how can we reconcile this contradiction?

As previously discussed, when children are traumatized, they psychologically fragment.[189] The part of the child that feels unsafe goes into the unconscious or subaltern part of their psyche. The other part becomes the conscious or dominant personality. When we look at an adult man, we may think we are seeing a single personality, yet a survivor of trauma might have dozens or even hundreds of psychological fragments. Each of these fragments has their own positionality. The adult man might be privileged, but his inner child, the subaltern of his own mind, is deeply oppressed. From the trauma of circumcision, he might learn that part of him that seeks dominance and control is safe, while the part that is childlike and vulnerable is not. To the external world, such a man would appear to be engaged in "toxic masculinity," yet his dominant conscious personality is acting as a protector for an internal subaltern. One could say that the adult part of him is privileged, but his inner child or internal subaltern is oppressed. Yet, we cannot understand the "privileged" aspect of him except in relation to his own experience of oppression. If we assume that people become who they are through socialization, then all oppressors were also oppressed during their formative experiences and contain their own internal subaltern. Their positionality can only be understood through the whole of their experience, including childhood.

While circumcision is the clearest example, all forms of childhood oppression change the positionality of the adult that emerges from childhood. This view changes the simplified social justice perspective of oppressor and oppressed. Instead, many oppressors may have experienced greater oppression in childhood than even those they hold power over in adulthood. Attempting to change adult power dynamics without acknowledging the childhood ones that created them could result in harming a victim. If someone sought power as an adult due to powerlessness in childhood, removing that power could be a retraumatization of the oppressed subaltern inner child within them. When the survivor of childhood trauma fights to maintain their power, it might look to social justice activists like the powerful trying to hold on to their privilege, when it is actually a protector aspect fighting to protect an internal subaltern.

If we were to see the oppressed aspects of those who survived childhood trauma, social justice activists could advocate for them as well as those harmed by this unresolved trauma.

This would require us to see childhood experience, including circumcision, as an aspect of identity, as much as race, gender, or dis/ability status. While other aspects of identity might be immediately visible, the impact of childhood trauma and infant genital cutting remains hidden. Circumcision scars are physically hidden by clothing. If children had a part of their body mutilated that was visible while clothed, like an ear or the nose, then the harm of circumcision might be more easily recognized, since someone who clearly had part of their face surgically removed would be less likely to be seen as privileged. However, these scars are also hidden by cultural taboos around showing or discussing male genitals, sexuality, or childhood sexual abuse. Cultural constructions around men's feelings further prevent discussion of circumcision pedophilia. When men cry or display psychological harm they are often shamed or mocked. Male anger is also stigmatized. When men explode with rage, their anger is usually framed in terms of its impact on women, rather than understood on men's own terms as a reasonable response to injustice. Modern gender discourses claim to value male vulnerability and oppose "toxic masculinity," but often use the discourse of "toxic masculinity" to stigmatize an entirely different set of male emotional expressions, rather than frame all emotional expressions as valid. Circumcision status remains hidden due to the physical covering of genital scars and the cultural constructs that prevent discussion of circumcision.

CHILDHOOD IDENTITY

Circumcision status is as much a part of identity as race, gender, or other aspects of identity. This form of identity is an imposed identity by a systemically pedophile genital cutting culture. Whether or not a man is circumcised, he has and is impacted by this aspect of identity in a genital cutting culture. Since identity is intersectional, this aspect of identity recontextualizes all other aspects of his identity. All forms of childhood trauma should be seen as aspects of identity that create internal subaltern psychological fragments. Each fragment has its own positionality in the social justice hierarchy. Those who appear dominant often have psychological fragmentation which contains their own internal subaltern. This form of identity has remained hidden due to the physical hiding of circumcision and various cultural constructs and social taboos that prevent discussion of circumcision and childhood trauma. Understanding someone's identity or positionality in social justice requires taking into account their full childhood experience.

CHAPTER 8
NEW DISCOURSE

Critical social justice suggests that systems of power are transmitted through language or discourses. As one social justice textbook puts it, "language is not a neutral transmitter of a universal reality. Rather, language is the way we construct reality, the framework we use to give meaning to our experiences and perceptions within a given society... The scholarly term for language in all of its dimensions is discourse."[190] If so, what is the discourse of genital cutting?

CURRENT DISCOURSES

Discourse defines how we are allowed to talk about an issue. For example, a scholarly discourse would demand one particular style of writing and a legal discourse another. A court will only accept complaints written in the legal discourse. Part of the reason people must hire a lawyer is because a statement written in conversational English will not be accepted by a court, it has to be written in the legal discourse in order to be acceptable for a court.

Medicine is also a discourse. Doctors use specialized language. Critical theory would suggest this language does not just transmit information but contains certain assumptions and systems of power.

Within the medical discourse, it is impossible to talk about certain ideas, while it forces people to unconsciously accept others. When used to evaluate circumcision, the medical framing of "evidence-based medicine" does not provide an absolute definition of "risks" and "benefits." It only allows benefits and risks that can be articulated through the medical discourse. For example, if you wanted to talk about the harm of circumcision in the medical discourse, you'd have to talk in quantifiable data, like nerve endings or tissue. You couldn't share how there are sex acts that require a foreskin which you personally find erotically pleasing and wish you could perform, or talk about how the lack of mobile shaft skin caused you pain during sex because there wasn't enough skin to accommodate a full erection. The medical discourse would discount this as a personal story, and not data or evidence, and would only accept this information as evidence if it came in the form of a peer-reviewed study, rather than personal experience. However, this is clearly relevant to the person who has this experience and might be more relevant to them and their life than data in medical journals. If you wanted to talk about the trauma, you might have to frame it in the rising levels of cortisol stress hormones in the baby during circumcision and show peer-reviewed studies on how this leads to a change in behavior later.[191] However, if you shared that you had recurring nightmares all throughout your childhood in which you felt intense pain in your genitals, as more than one survivor has reported,[192] the medical discourse would dismiss this experience. The only way the medical discourse could speak about this experience is if it was quantified. Yet changing the language of the survivor from a vivid description of a nightmare to a statement like "cortisol levels rose" changes the meaning of what is being communicated. This discourse assumes that story is not relevant or important, only data matter, and that anything which cannot be quantified or measured is irrelevant. Yet, there is no measure of the full human experience. Demanding all human experience be reduced to data creates an epistemic injustice for those who do not know how to speak in the medical discourse or whose full experience cannot be reduced to data.

The medical discourse of "risks" and "benefits" also excludes a third category: harms. For example, losing the medical function of the foreskin is not a "risk" of circumcision, but a guaranteed outcome of the procedure. When those against circumcision attempt to point this out within the medical discourse, they usually have to use the category of risk, but that lack of "harms" as a category in the medical evolution makes doctors blind to many of the complaints activists are speaking to them about. Though doctors take an oath to "first, do no harm"[193] this oath itself is outside the medical discourse. It was written before the scientific project to reduce all human experience to data, and so doctors cannot understand this oath through the discourse they are indoctrinated into in medical school. When I've seen activists remind doctors of this oath, the doctor's eyes will frequently glaze over with cognitive dissonance and they will talk about data showing alleged benefits to infant genital cutting. If harm can only be understood through data and only those in the medical system can quantify or publish peer-reviewed studies with data, then only doctors can define what constitutes harm is and they can define harm however they like. The patient has no voice in what harm is, and his reports of harm are epistemically marginalized. The survivor is left with intense pain which the medical system will neither acknowledge nor quantify.

There is of course another discourse with which we could speak about circumcision: human rights. This is the discourse of the Intactivist movement. The human rights discourse contains its own set of language and assumptions. This discourse takes it as a given that people have the right to their own bodies. Within this discourse, terms like "risks" and "benefits" are meaningless, and replaced by the question "who has the right?" This discourse does not even need to show that circumcision is physically harmful. Merely violating another person's rights is in itself harmful. This discourse also allows for a greater discussion of lived experience, but still limits the discussion to certain terms and assumptions. Human rights discourse is very focused on what is lost, not on potential pleasures or gains. This discourse might prioritize a narrative about the loss of bodily autonomy due to circumcision, but not one about the loss of potential sexual experiences if those experiences were described in erotic language. Human rights discourse would ask that these experiences be described using phrases like "decreased physical sensation" rather than the vivid detail one might use when speaking with close friends about a pleasurable night. There is incredible power in the human rights discourse, and it is certainly superior to many other discourses we could use, but there are truths about this issue that are impossible to communicate using the human rights discourse alone. Even if we accept the idea of human rights, it is worth acknowledging the limitations of this discourse and exploring what systems of power this discourse creates or what truths it might hide.

Each religion or culture has its own discourse, and not all of them recognize human rights. In some traditional cultures, you do not own your body. It belongs to God or the tribe. Authoritarian religions reject the premises of human rights. Their discourse is more obvious than the medical, and their power more naked. It is worth noting that monotheistic religion made power more hidden than previous polytheistic religions. Instead of gods being confined to the sun or lightning, God was everywhere and watching you all the time. Modern discourses disperse and hide power even more, placing their Gods in the unconscious beliefs of your mind. You cannot fathom a different reality because there isn't any "data" to support it. The confusion of the discussion around circumcision arises because people are drawing from multiple incompatible discourses, sometimes at the same time. A person might argue that circumcision is good from the medical discourse, citing studies of supposed medical benefits, and then in the next moment say "well, it's my religion," shifting to a religious discourse. Clearly, the commands of an ancient deity are not "evidence-based medicine" and these two discourses are incompatible. The person might then switch to the idea that they think a circumcised penis looks better, switching from a religious discourse to a sexual discourse in which their personal sexual kinks apply to children, an even more incompatible discourse. There is a schizophrenia to pro-circumcision discourses because some were created three thousand years ago, others a hundred years ago, and others on the spot when the pedophile-apologist runs out of arguments. None of them capture the full truth of this issue, and many rule out the truth of our lived experience.

WHOSE DISCOURSE

The question of the debate around circumcision isn't "what are the risks or benefits?" or even "whose body, whose rights?" but "whose language, whose discourse?" If we use the medical discourse, we can still argue against circumcision, but it is much harder. If a doctor brings up fifteen studies, the activist will have to debate each study. These studies may be limited to medical literature controlled and funded by institutions engaged in systemic pedophilia. If the activist wants to fund his own study, he will be at a considerable disadvantage because his funding can never rival the wealth of the medical industry. Even if activists commission a good study, the medical system might perpetuate epistemic injustice against their study by denying that the study is legitimate because it wasn't published in any of the journals they control. It is possible to win on these terms because circumcision research is so bad and the evidence is so conclusively against genital cutting, but this is a rigged game. A shift to the human rights discourse flips the dialogue and forces the doctor to argue whether or not he even has the right to do the procedure. However, both doctors and activists have accepted a third discourse: the discourse of critical social justice theory. As discussed earlier, the medical system has endorsed this discourse in their position statements, as has every major brand, corporation, or non-profit. They acknowledge this discourse as overruling previous medical advice. Critical social justice, not medicine or human rights, is currently the dominant discourse.

Critical theory has developed its own discourse. While it began as a way to deconstruct discourses and meta-narratives, it now has its own language and unique ways of evaluating truth. Social justice too has its own discourse and specialized terminology. This book is written within the discourse of critical social justice theory. This discourse applied to circumcision reveals truths that other discourses could not articulate. Part of the reason Intactivists have often struggled to articulate the depth of the circumcision problem is that they lacked the critical tools to deconstruct the systemic nature of genital cutting or the ways their opposition manipulates language. Medical organizations often rapidly switch between discourses when discussing circumcision while demanding that activists only engage in a very limited version of the medical discourse if they want to be heard. Doctors frame circumcision as an individual parental choice, but when activists suggest that doctors make an individual choice not to perform circumcisions, the doctor says they cannot do so because parents demand it and the hospital requires it. The doctor claims circumcision is an individual choice yet cites a systemic reason for their own actions. Since the human rights frame also accepts an individual view of the world, activists often miss this systemic power concealing itself through language. From a critical view, it is obvious that doctors and hospitals did not all make an individual choice to circumcise but are acting on and within a system engaged in pedophilia. No one person is in this system is calling the shots. The system diffuses power and hides itself through language.

Social justice adds another layer of discourse, with its own assumptions and language around identity and equality. The language of consent and rape culture frames doctors' actions as not just a human rights violation but as a form of rape and pedophilia. This discourse brings us closer to the emotional experience of the child. Newborn infants whose first life experience is being forcibly penetrated and having their organs ripped away from their bodies are not experiencing the dry language of a "human rights violation." They are in terror. Social justice allows us to speak emotionally about these issues and see them not just in academic terms, but in moral ones. The other advantage of both discourses, particularly when we add the idea of epistemic justice, is that critical theory allows the lived experience and personal testimony of those affected by circumcision to be a part of the conversation. Critical social justice recognizes that everything about the human experience cannot be condensed to academic data. People's feelings, sexuality, and personal stories must be part of the conversation, even if those stories are not communicated in the language of academic institutions or human rights law. When a man says he feels "raped" by circumcision, this is valuable information about the issue, even if an academic researcher does not know how to add it to their spreadsheet. This lived experience is valid even if it comes accompanied by curse words or is shared in the emotional language people use in their daily lives when confronted with injustices that anger them. We cannot dismiss marginalized groups' expressions, and any discourse that would is guilty of epistemic injustice. There may be a better discourse in the future, but thus far this is the best. Our discourse must seek the full truth of circumcision.

CRITICAL DISCOURSE

Before we fully accept the discourse of critical social justice, it is worth questioning and deconstructing both critical theory and social justice. Is this the best discourse to use? What assumptions does it contain? In what ways does it limit or enhance our discussion? What systems of power does it create?

The earliest critical theorists saw everything as deconstructable. When critical theory was adopted by social justice, later social justice activists suggested that their work not be deconstructed because in the words of Kimberle Crenshaw, creator of the idea of intersectionality, categories "have meaning and consequences,"[194] which meant that deconstructing them would have consequences for the people within those identities. In other words, deconstructing a marginalized identity might hurt marginalized people. While it may be true that race and gender have real consequences in the world, it does not follow that the discourse around them cannot be deconstructed. Social justice clearly has its own discourse. Words like intersectionality and privilege clearly contain assumptions and a system of values that make it easier to talk about some truths but might obscure others.

The fear of critical social justice activists was that theory would be used to endlessly deconstruct society and never lead to any practical applications which could make the world better for people. Making identity a stable and "real" category allowed activists to use the tools of critical theory to solve social problems, without having their own work endlessly deconstructed. This discourse places power in the hands of critical social justice activists. According to critical social justice theory, only critical social justice activists have the power to deconstruct, deconstruction must be done using their language, and everything else in society must be deconstructed. This allowed critical social justice to enter every field it wants while allowing nothing to enter it. One can do a critical theory of every issue, subculture, and hobby, except critical social justice itself. This framing might explain why critical social justice has taken power in every major social institution.

Critical social justice fits all the categories of any powerful discourse that critical theory could be used to deconstruct. The claim that certain identities cannot be deconstructed is a moral claim based in a meta-narrative about the need to create equity for marginalized groups. If we deconstruct the language of critical social justice, then this might marginalize the people social justice is intended to help according to critical social justice activists. If the outcome of deconstructing social justice is that there is more racism, then social justice activists might argue that deconstructing social justice is an oppressive act. This argument assumes that modern forms of social justice always reduce oppression and never create or support oppression. It also assumes that deconstructing social justice will lead to more oppression, not less. However, if the outcome of deconstructing social justice is less oppression, then deconstructing social justice is itself an act of social justice.

Using the tools of social justice and its understanding that people are not born racist but socialized into racist systems, we have shown that the unconscious ways or relating necessary for all systems of oppression begin in childhood through the emotional patterns we instill in infancy. Unless we address the roots of oppression, we will never be able to cut away every branch. This means any aspect of social justice that does not address the subaltern status of children can and must be deconstructed. Not deconstructing social justice ideologies and organizations which fail to acknowledge the subaltern status of children is itself an act of oppression. A critical social justice that does not address the emotional roots of oppression in childhood creates a new system of power for its practitioners. There will always be oppression if there is always childhood trauma. If there is oppression, the adult social justice activists can sell their cure, which will treat the symptoms of oppression without treating the cause. This ensures that there will always be well-paid positions for social justice activists and maintains a power structure of experts in every organization concerned with social justice. Even if all forms of bigotry were outlawed, the roots of oppression in childhood would find new ways to manifest themselves, because they were imprinted in the hearts of children. In short: social justice without Children's Justice is an oppressive power system.

CHILDREN'S JUSTICE DISCOURSE

The only reality that cannot be deconstructed is the reality of children because they have no language. There is nothing to deconstruct. The tools of critical theory are designed to examine language, but children exist in a preverbal world. Their world must be understood on their own terms. All else is deconstructable. We can and must apply the tools of critical theory to all oppressive systems of power, including adult social justice movements that fail to recognize the roots of oppression in childhood. Any argument used to prevent this could create an outcome that supports pedophilia and must be treated as pedophile-apology. The discourse through which to view not just circumcision but all social justice issues is Children's Justice.

CHAPTER 9
POWER/KNOWLEDGE

Critical theory holds, amongst many other things, that power comes from language. Michel Foucault used the term "power/knowledge" to describe the idea that power is maintained through specialized knowledge, which in turn reproduces itself through power.[195] Power/knowledge is written as one word to show that the two are inseparable. In this view, knowledge is never neutral, and certain language actually contains and supports an entire power structure.

POWER LANGUAGE

Let's illustrate the concept of power/knowledge with a story:

A man with a gun comes to your house. He says that because you did not give him and his gang part of your income, he is going to kidnap you. He ties you up and takes you to a caged cell where you will not be allowed to leave until a leader in their gang can see you and decide what they will do with you.

Do you think what the man did was okay? Most would say no. Kidnapping people and demanding money from them is not okay. If I told you there was a system of oppression that regularly kidnapped people, you might see changing this as a major social justice cause.

Now, the same story with different language:

A police officer comes to your house. He says that because you did not pay your taxes, the government has issued a warrant for your arrest. He cuffs your hands behind your back and takes you to jail, where you will be held until you are sentenced in a hearing before a judge.

Would you say what the police officer did was okay now? More people believe it is okay to arrest people for not paying their taxes than that it is okay for men with guns to kidnap people for not giving them money. However, these two stories could describe the same events, just with different language. The reason people accept a police officer arresting someone as legitimate, but not "a man with a gun" "kidnapping" someone is language. Words like "arrest," "taxes, "jail," "hearing," and "judge" communicate a system of knowledge, which confers power.

If you were to tell your friends that you'd been kidnapped, and your captor was only giving you one phone call before they locked you away, your friends might think it was their duty to come save you. If you told them you got sent to prison for not paying your taxes, they might feel bad for you, but many people would say "well, you should have paid your taxes," and see your capture as legitimate.

If you felt that the government's actions were not legitimate, but only had the language of the second version of the story to describe your feelings, you might be unable to express what you really feel. The statement "the government should not be able to arrest people for not paying taxes" does not convey the idea that the government's actions are illegitimate, because the language used to express the idea is inherently legitimizing.

Critical theory holds that words actually have power structures built into them. If you wanted to challenge the power of the government, you should not use language that supported the power structure of the government. You might say instead "those thugs in power shouldn't be able to just kidnap people who refuse to give them money." This language of "kidnap" and "thugs" contains the idea that the person or system described is inherently illegitimate and hence better communicates what a person against government taxation is trying to convey. You might also attempt to redefine the meaning of words in their power/knowledge system, through statements like "taxation is theft," the same way that critical social justice theory often attempts to redefine words. However, if you wanted to change this system, you'd have to first change the language because this system of language is actually how governments maintain power. Many people believe that "power flows from the barrel of a gun" as Mao said, but it is a system of language that places guns in people's hands and persuades them that the use of that gun is legitimate. Every government agent believes their use of a gun is legitimate because of a system of power/knowledge. They accept pieces of paper as payment because of a system of language around money. If police officers became just "people with guns who kidnap people" in exchange for "pieces of paper" then they would not have the power/knowledge to continue their work and never have enough guns for the amount of resistance they would routinely face.

How do modern governments maintain power through language? In Foucault's view, the history of power is one where power is never surrendered, just diffused better through more effective systems of control. The earliest governments of warrior bands might have been able to maintain power by just being stronger, but early monarchies eventually developed a rich language around religion, the divine right of kings, and even the idea that their head of state had some moral right to rule. This power is obvious and open to challenge. Modern democratic states have further obscured power through language. The founding documents of America begin with "we the people." There is an idea in democratic countries that our governments are not separate from us, but represent us. The people who run the government are "our representatives." We elect them. America is great because it doesn't have a king and we have freedom, or so the language goes. Yet, go back to our original story. Are you really free? Say the police arrive at your house. You didn't elect the police officer. You didn't vote for getting arrested. In some places, you can elect judges, but you might not be able to choose your judge when arrested. You didn't vote for the conditions of the prison or the system by which prisoners are tried and processed. The individual person in this story actually has very little power. At most, they might have gotten to cast a single vote between two candidates to represent them. These candidates likely never spoke on their specific situation, if they even had different opinions about it at all. In America, elected officials rarely handle such matters, so the decision to arrest this person was likely made by an unelected bureaucrat. In practice, is this any freer than a monarchy? Foucault would say that power does not give up power, it just hides it better. The language of "democracy" and "we the people" legitimizes the actions of the state so when the police arrest someone, the power structure behind them is stronger. The critical view would be that if you want to change this situation, the way to start isn't to fight back or engage in activism. That comes later. The first step to change is to change the language.

REDEFINE LANGUAGE

There is one movement that has successfully used the method of changing language to achieve power: critical social justice. It is not surprising that after focusing on how language creates power for over sixty years, critical social justice theory has managed to use language to create power. Now, critical social justice has power over almost every major social institution. How does critical social justice maintain and create power through language?

The method of critical theory is simple: Redefine language. Everything critical social justice wants has a good name. Everything it does not has a bad name. The birth of critical theory was when Marxist scholars suggested that theory should not merely explain the world, but attempt to change it for the better.[196] As a consequence, critical theory uses language that judges, not merely defines. For example, inequality between groups of people could be called "social inequality," but this language would be morally neutral. Since critical theorists do not want inequality, they use the more emotionally charged term "systemic racism." "Systemic racism" implies a moral judgment on inequality since most people consider racism bad. If you define racism narrowly, then your scope of power is also narrow, because you can only justify seizing power over a narrow aspect of society to change that problem. So instead, racism is everywhere. Critical social justice activists say that "racism is the foundation of the society we are in."[197] A racist is not just someone who hates other races, but "one who is supporting a racist policy through their inaction or expressing a racist idea."[198] People can be racist. Policies can be racist. Ideas can be racist. To quote Robin DiAngelo, "The question is not 'did racism take place?' But rather 'How did racism manifest in that situation?'"[199] Every social institution must take a side on the fight against racism. "There is no neutral,"[200] and no "neutrality in the struggle against racism."[201] You are either racist or antiracist. You must align with critical social justice, or you get the bad label of racist.

The discourse of critical social justice makes it impossible to fight within its frame. To disagree with critical social justice theory within its language, one would have to say they support racism. Critics of critical social justice cannot begin to express their disagreement without first unraveling their language. Many will often begin by citing the older definition of racism as individual prejudice rather than a systemic problem and show how critical theory has redefined the word. Sometimes this leads to absurd, nonsensical-sounding claims like "antiracists are the real racists!" Even those on the far-right who rebel and become self-proclaimed racists are still within the discourse of social justice. The far-right attitude that "they're going to call us racists no matter what we do, so we might as well be racists" is a resignation to the branding of social justice. Rebellion implies an authority they are rebelling against and reinforces the power of that authority by defining themselves in relation to it. Through the power of language, all political discussion on both the left and the right exists in the matrix of critical social justice.

LANGUAGE TO POWER

Activists confronting circumcision face many language problems. The act of holding down a child and ripping off part of its genitals is legitimized through language. It is not called genital cutting, but "circumcision," which is a "surgical procedure" that "removes the foreskin." Through language, the "foreskin" becomes a separate part of the penis and body that can be removed, rather than "chopping half the skin of a child's penis off." The discourse of medicine legitimizes touching children's genitals. They aren't adult pedophiles holding down children and cutting off parts of their bodies. They are "medical professionals."

Some in the Intactivist movement have attempted to unmask this discourse by changes to the terminology. They do not call genital cutting "circumcision," but instead "genital mutilation." They refer to men as "circumcised" or "intact." They refer to circumcising doctors as "baby cutters." This name changing is a step in the right direction, but it is not yet a full discourse. The words are still articulating the same concepts rather than inventing entirely new ones.

Critical theorists did not just change the names of existing ideas but invented an entirely new discourse. Prior to the work of critical race theory, words like "intersectionality," "equity," and "internalized dominance" did not exist. When they did change terms, they did not just rebrand an existing idea but used an existing term to articulate an entirely new idea. "Racism" wasn't changed to mean a more extreme or negative version of this same idea but to articulate an entirely new concept about describing how the systems and institutions of society functioned. This change in language made it impossible to articulate the previous system of power/knowledge and created a new one critical theorists controlled.

We cannot overestimate the power of this change. The equivalent action in Intactivism would be if Intactivists were able to redefine "foreskin" to mean "human dignity and freedom." If this definition were accepted, doctors would not be able to say they are removing the foreskin without saying "we are removing his human dignity and freedom." The opposition perspective would become impossible to articulate. Do this with all words, and one power is replaced by another.

If critical social justice activists had used the strategy of Intactivist language, they'd change the name of racism to "evil Nazi bad stuff" and make basically the same arguments in the same discourse. There are activists within social justice who argue in this way, and a stereotype on the political right that social justice activists just shout "Nazi" and "racist" at everything they don't like, but the best do not. While conservatives have an image of social justice activists as "triggered snowflakes," the professionals of critical theory carry themselves with composed confidence. If you watch Robin DiAngelo, Ibram X. Kendi, or the other leading critical social justice activists speak, they have the calm demeanor of a Sunday school teacher speaking to a room full of children, and the certainty of a pastor. They don't need to get "triggered" or act like a "snowflake," because they have the truth.

Many Intactivists have told me that they become frustrated when debating circumcision. I suspect much of the frustration they feel is due to epistemic injustice. They experience the testimonial injustice of having their knowledge and experiences dismissed because they are not medical "experts," and the hermeneutical injustice of lacking the words to articulate their experience of circumcision because the only words available to them are those that contain the power/knowledge structure of the medical system. Do you notice how much easier the Intactivist experience of "epistemic injustice" was to articulate with the right terminology? This is the power of language.

THE GOAL OF DISCOURSE

The goal of discourse is not to "debate," but to place yourself beyond the possibility of defeat by making your arguments assumptions and their arguments unthinkable and impossible to communicate. We can debate why inequality exists between certain groups. We cannot debate that some social systems produce unequal outcomes. If we define this inequality as "systemic racism," then we have a moral duty to end this racism. Likewise, we can debate circumcision. We cannot debate that it involves doctors holding down children and cutting off parts of their genitals. If we define this as systemic pedophilia, then we have a moral duty to stop this pedophilia. Anyone arguing on the side of "racism" or "pedophilia" within this frame has already lost the argument by default.

With the current power/knowledge system, those in power can send men with guns to kidnap people, hold children down and rip their body parts off, and destroy anyone who opposes their power. With a different one, you could protect children and finally create a world free from injustice. Changing language is not merely a theoretical exercise, but the key to shifting the dominant power.

CHAPTER 10
FALSE CONSCIOUSNESS

Why do all men not oppose circumcision? Critical theory has a term for when an oppressed class fails to see their oppression and internalizes the ideology of the oppressor: false consciousness. False consciousness is when a class adopts an ideology that does not actually benefit it or serve its goals.[202] The classical example of false consciousness from Marxism was working-class people who support an economic system that exploits their labor. Since introduced by Marx, the term has been expanded to include not just class, but other aspects of identity. For example, someone in a racial minority who supports racist policies that oppress them could be said to have false consciousness. On the issue of circumcision, a man who denies the ways that men are harmed by male genital cutting has false consciousness. Clearly, it does not serve a men's interests to have parts of their genitals cut off, yet many men claim they are "fine" with circumcision when asked about it. Where does this false consciousness come from?

PSYCHOLOGICAL DEFENSES

Almost all behaviors which harm the person doing them have what is known as a secondary gain, a hidden benefit or perceived gain achieved through this bad behavior. For example, a person who never fully pursues their dreams has the perceived benefit of being able to hold onto the idea that they could have achieved them had they tried rather than facing the potential reality of failure. Changing a person's behavior often requires finding and reframing the perceived benefit they unconsciously pursue through bad behavior. If genital cutting does not serve men, what is their perceived benefit?

While researching the Intactivist movement, I met an older activist who told me this story: As the son of a diplomat, he went to a private boys' school with children from similar backgrounds. Because these children had been born all around the world, some were circumcised but many were not. He was intact. When he would tell his elementary school classmates that their parents had allowed part of their penis to be cut off, they would react with shock and disbelief. "My parents would never do something like that to me!" they would say. Yet, when they went home and talked to their parents, they would learn the truth. These children would be in a state of shock for some time. Learning that their parents allowed them to be harmed shook them. As a child, this future activist watched the birth of psychological defenses in his classmates. Rather than believe their parents would cut parts of their body off, these children would begin to rationalize that circumcision must have been somehow good for them. They wanted to believe their parents loved them and would never hurt them. To protect this belief, they would begin to create and buy into cultural stories that circumcision was good and that their parents did this for their benefit. For them, the perceived benefit was that they got to maintain their feeling of safety and belief their parents loved them. Cultural myths about the "benefits" of circumcision, including the false belief that it is healthier, required, or more "hygienic," served this psychological need.

In the history of oppression, rebellion and revolt are the exception, not the rule. For every slave uprising or government overthrow, there are hundreds more examples of people quietly accepting the unfair and unjust situations they are born into. Revolutions are difficult. Many of the oppressive systems people may wish to overthrow require significant work to change, and not all revolutions succeed. The cost of failure is often high with failed revolutionaries being frequently imprisoned or killed. It might be less work to accept things the way they are than to try to change them. Creating rationalizations is easier than creating revolutions. When it comes to systemic pedophilia, children cannot "overthrow" their parents or the systems that act upon them. It is impossible for men to fully recover the body part they have lost, barring a significant breakthrough in regenerative medicine. If the situation is impossible to change and it causes psychological pain to even try, men and children may attempt to minimize their own pain or hide it from their conscious mind so they do not have to feel it. When men say "I'm fine with my circumcision," they are creating a psychological defense against feeling the pain of circumcision.

False consciousness is a coping mechanism. Different false consciousness coping mechanisms protect against different kinds of pain. For example, a male who denies the harm of male genital cutting but holds that female genital cutting is deeply harmful gets to preserve his own identity as a strong man by denying his harm and also maintains his identity as a protector of women. This coping mechanism also protects his idea of gender roles by maintaining that women's bodies are fragile, more harm-able, and in need of his protection. If he were to admit that women had had power over him in childhood and that he was harmed at birth, his view of male dominance and, by extension his own power, would crumble. His false consciousness might also protect other aspects of his identity, such as his belief in his culture's superiority, his perceived relationship to his family, or other systems he interacts with. Look at the opposite possibility: What does a man risk if he drops this view and admits that male genital cutting has harmed him? The man could be ostracized by family, friends, and people who perpetuate the systems of genital cutting. He could become aware of psychological pain or physical problems. He could have a different view of his own body, sexuality, and even identity. It could completely reshape his world. Yet what does he gain? He cannot get his foreskin back. From the perspective of false consciousness, there is nothing to gain by admitting the truth.

False consciousness presents a short-term, limited view of the problem. The cost of false consciousness is a lifelong commitment to maintain energy-draining psychological defenses. These defenses must be upheld against the constant pressure of reality. Every time a man in false consciousness encounters the truth, including the truth of their own emotions, he must reinforce his psychological defenses. This constant psychological defense comes at a lifelong cost, similar to the effect a massive recurring expense would have on someone's wealth. False consciousness is a sort of psychological debt-slavery, since these defenses must be constantly maintained, and are not a one-time emotional cost. A man in false consciousness must continually pay the toll of rationalization or risk a psychological break. If one is willing to feel the pain of awakening, there is no need for the constant upkeep of psychological defenses. The way out of the emotional debt of false consciousness is awakening.

CULTURAL HEGEMONY

False consciousness is maintained by false narratives. Italian Marxist Antonio Gramsci coined the term cultural hegemony to describe how dominant powers make ideas that benefit them a cultural norm.[203] The word hegemony literally means a dominant influence or authority above all else, so cultural hegemony is the dominance of a particular culture or set of assumptions and values. In critical theory, cultural hegemony is specifically used to refer to the domination of oppressor narratives that create a false consciousness in the oppressed. While people experiencing oppression might choose rationalization over the pain of realization, the rationalizations they choose are often created and sold to them by the dominant culture. Dominant powers have an incentive to create rationalizations that maintain their power. Most people are not creating their own original rationalizations but adopt the dominant discourse of their culture. When a dominant power distributes their discourse, values, and knowledge through every aspect of culture so thoroughly that ideas that support their power are seen as "common knowledge" or "just the way things are," they have cultural hegemony.

Circumcision and systemic pedophilia have cultural hegemony in Western culture. The idea that circumcision is normal is common in education, books, films, television, pornography, and other forms of entertainment. Excuses like "he should look like his father" or "it's cleaner" are often advanced without any further explanation, as if this is common cultural knowledge. Yet, no one who uses these rationalizations knows where they first learned them and they fall apart under scrutiny. One of the signs you are dealing with the cultural programming of a hegemonic power is that when you question one of these assumptions, the person you are talking to becomes confused, defensive, or angry. For example, if you were to say "actually, the foreskin is cleaner than the circumcised penis" the pedophile-apologist might object "no it's not." But if you ask "how do you know?", expect them to be unable to cite any evidence and instead just sputter something to the effect of "well, everyone knows that." How does everyone just know something? What everyone "knows" is most often the product of cultural hegemony. We are not born knowing that parts of our body and sexuality are inherently dirty or wrong. These attitudes are conditioned through socialization. One of the tells of a culturally hegemonic idea is that people do not remember where the idea first came to them. If you ask someone when they first decided that young boys' genitals should have the same scars as their fathers', they probably cannot tell you. Odds are they do not have fond memories of comparing penises with their dad. This belief was conditioned and unquestioned. Under examination, the idea that "his penis should match his father's" is clearly pedophilic.

While an idea might be propagated through culture by media, discourse, and other means, it only takes root if it serves a psychological purpose. For example, the idea that children should match their father plays on a fear men have around paternity. Mothers know a child to be theirs because it came from their womb. Yet, if the child doesn't look like his presumed dad, the suspicion arises that he might have been conceived by someone else. When the dominant culture and the medical system suggest that "he should look like his dad," they are playing on this primal fear of being cuckolded. The implication is that if the father does not cut his child's genitals, he does not look like his father, and the father is a cuck. The father might start a fight with the doctor if he brazenly looked the dad in the eye and tried to justify genital cutting by saying "what are you, a cuck?" However, the discourse of systemic pedophilia allows people to make this insinuation without directly naming the fear. Virtually all circumcision rationalizations follow this pattern of indirectly touching on a deep fear. There is a fear our sexuality is shameful or dirty, ("it's cleaner"), that we will be rejected by sexual partners ("women like it better"), that our body is unattractive ("it looks better"), and a primal fear of death ("it reduces disease"). Systemic pedophilia is maintained by a cultural hegemony that manufactures fear concealed by discourse. Of course, fears often manifest the very thing they are trying to avoid. In the case of circumcision, by fearing their sexuality will not be accepted people cut themselves and others off from a part of their sexuality. By fearing they will be rejected by sexual partners, people reject a part of their own sexuality and that of their children and make it impossible for them to ever have the full sexual experience. By fearing disease and death, people maintain a system that regularly results in worse health, infection, and deaths. The fear discourse manifests what it focuses on. If the discourse was direct and said: "we would like to exploit your primal fears to cut children's genitals" - it would not work. The power of discourse is indirect, dispersed, hidden, and thus greater. Earlier regimes scarified children's bodies using a religious discourse: "Do this, or God(s) will be angry." The modern discourse of circumcision accomplishes the same end of systemic pedophilia while exerting less power. It is a continuation of a fear-based system of child abuse, just more efficient.

The cultural hegemony of pedophilia also conceals itself through language. Pedophilia is usually framed by the dominant discourse as a single offender working against the system. When there are pedophiles in positions of authority, such as pedophile teachers, priests, doctors, etc. they are seen as "bad apples," or a few bad people in an otherwise good system. The idea of systemic, structural, or institutional pedophilia is never explored. Critical race theorists have pointed out how the same framing of the word "racist" has stopped many people from seeing systemic racism or their own participation in it.[204] Likewise, the framing of pedophilia as only ever an individual action prevents people from seeing the participation of authorities, institutions, and cultural beliefs in the abuse of children. A doctor cannot hold a child down and rip off part of the infant's genitals without the support of a complex system. When individual parents or religious practitioners try to do the same, they are often jailed for child abuse. Even in cases where society recognizes pedophilia, such as a teacher raping a student, the structure that allowed that person access to children, put them in a position of authority where the child was expected to obey, and overrode the child's needs and desires to fulfill their own needs is rarely questioned. The individual pedophile might be responsible, but the system that hired that pedophile and groomed the child by enforcing the lesson that the child must ignore their needs to fulfill adult desires is a participant in that pedophilia. We call this system that allows for, supports, and creates child abuse systemic pedophilia. This system is most apparent in the medical system, but it is culture-wide. Systemic pedophilia has cultural hegemony.

    This system reveals itself when individual parents attempt to opt-out of institutions engaged in pedophilia. Although there are unique ways in which parents can oppress their children, multiple systems use parents as scapegoats for their collective action. Parents are framed as the figurehead who gets to give final approval on decisions like schooling or birth when the system has already made those decisions for them. When the decision parents make mirrors the system, it is still framed as a parental choice. However, if parents attempt to resist the system, they quickly find out who the real power holders are. For example, if parents home birth, some states will attempt to regulate that birth, require unnecessary procedures, or even ban home birth entirely. The school system might ask parents to sign a consent form for a particular school event, but if parents wish to homeschool their child, they are the ones who must obtain a consent form from the state. Who has the real power here? The system frames the parent as power holder through discourse while keeping the real power for itself. This power creates and is based in systemic pedophilia, in which children are used to fulfill the desires of the system.

    A critical view of pedophilia would include not just the stated intention of social systems, but the full outcomes. The outcome of dominant social systems is that children are used to fulfill adult desires rather than to be seen as people with their own needs. When we shift from viewing pedophilia as an individual action to the systemic and institutional levels, it's clear that pedophilia is both systemic and hegemonic.

TRUE CONSCIOUSNESS

One of the reasons Marxist theorists suggest that lower classes do not rise up is because they believe in the possibility of upward mobility. Why kill the rich when you might become rich? In the case of childhood, the idea of upward mobility is not a potential dream, but a near-certain outcome. All children grow up eventually if they live long enough. Children more readily accept a negative power dynamic in childhood because they know that one day they will grow up. Or do they? Do children really grow up, or just get older? Can we really say the adults are free of the subaltern status of childhood if there are still aspects of their psychology trapped in the patterns of childhood? If adults are still playing out the false power dynamics of childhood even when they have the full rights of adults, could we call this a form of false consciousness?

Many of the abuses of childhood are excused with phrases like "you'll understand when you're older." This phrase implies that with age, the child's consciousness will shift and their awareness will grow in such a way that they will see the adult's actions as beneficial in some way. However, this is not always what happens. In my experience, every time I've ever had someone use this phrase on me as a child, I'm able to look back on it with adult perspective and see that they were using my ignorance as a child to exploit me and then claiming some privileged adult knowledge or identity dominance to avoid explaining their exploitative behavior. The assumption adults have when using this justification is that given enough time, the child will accept the cultural hegemony of systemic pedophilia and have enough internalized oppression to see adults abusing children as normal, believe that they deserved exploitation as a child and that their later adult status allows them to act out the same oppression on weaker beings once they become stronger adults. What children "understand when they're older" is not the wisdom of adults, but that the unequal power dynamic now benefits them.

An unequal power dynamic might be acceptable if adult power was used to support children. No one has a problem with a dominant group using their power to empower another group on the less powerful groups' terms, based in their needs. In an ideal relationship, adults would use their superior power to meet children's needs based in the child's reality and continually share their power with the children until the child learns to wield the same power to meet their own needs. Yet, this power dynamic is often used for exploitation. When raised in exploitation, children do not grow out of their unequal status. They simply switch roles from oppressed to oppressor once given power or carry the same emotional patterns and power dynamics established in childhood into their adult relationships. Adults without boundaries, "people pleasers," narcissists, etc. almost always have a root experience in childhood that determined their adult dysfunction. However, adults who exploit others have often experienced childhood abuse as well. Children want adult power, and if the power shown to them is exploitative, when they seek to wield the same power in adulthood they will wield it as it was shown to them: oppressively, either by oppressing aspects of themselves or others. In most cases, children do not grow up. They grow older. They carry the same wounded inner children created through fragmentation during childhood into adulthood and remain trapped in the same emotional patterns and power dynamics created during childhood.

A true consciousness would recognize that as an adult we can choose how we use our power.[205] We do not have to oppress others as we were oppressed in childhood. However, once socialized into internalized oppression as children and internalized dominance as adults, adults are often unaware of their power to choose and suffer from false consciousness. They may not even be aware there are other ways of relating. This false consciousness will not just extend to their personal relationships and interactions with children, but to their connections with larger systems, including those around race, gender, and other identity groups. When these exploitative power dynamics manifest around race or gender, we call it racism or sexism. The root of all false consciousness is childhood. When someone exhibits false consciousness as an adult, it is because a part of them is still psychologically trapped in the subaltern state of childhood, whether they are aware of it or not, and reenacting or acting in reaction to that oppression.

The path out of false consciousness is to critically examine the ways we have been socialized and culturally conditioned to act against our own best interests. Often a false consciousness provides a perceived benefit by allowing the oppressed to avoid the pain of realization through rationalization. If we accept false consciousness, all kinds of exploitative power dynamics are possible. True consciousness will mean facing the short-term pain of feeling and seeing the parts of us trapped in the subaltern state of childhood, over the long-term, continual emotional cost of reinforcing psychological defenses. These defenses are made readily available by a cultural hegemony based in fear and systemic pedophilia. Rejecting this fear-based pedophile system will allow us to unite as families and groups against exploitative systems and create a system that empowers children. If we want a just world, we must first become truly conscious.

CHAPTER 11
PATRIARCHAL PEDAGOGY

Who has power over children? Children are born of women. For the first nine months of their existence, children grow inside their mother's bodies. During this time, children take on whatever their mothers' bodies do. If the mother ingests drugs or alcohol, it can have a lifelong impact on the future child's body. Even subtle changes in the mother's diet or emotional state can impact the child.[206] Historically, birth has been the domain of women. When the child is born, they are entirely dependent on the mother for the first months of their life. They must be breastfed and taken care of by the mother. Young infants do not even see themselves as separate from their mothers.[207] Throughout most of human history, childcare has been the domain of women. In modern times, power over children is shared between a series of systems and institutions. Children are born in hospitals, raised in daycares, and taught in schools. While all of these institutions remain female-dominated, they have distorted their stated role of childcare to disempower women, harm children, and create trauma in the men they produce. The trauma of childhood and the lessons it teaches have consequences for all of society.

GENDER-BASED VIOLENCE

In hospital birth, the medical system has power. Births in hospitals are handled by obstetricians, obstetrician-gynecologist, or OBGYNs, which are doctors of women's health. Nurses, obstetricians, and medical students are the ones who later perform circumcision on children deemed male. Most obstetricians are female.[208] Even if the OB is not female, they are an expert in female health. The majority of nurses are also women.[209] All of the hospital staff regardless of gender is trained to see the mother as their patient, not the person being born.[210]

Birth is a center of female power. When hospital birth began, men were not even allowed to be present when their own wives gave birth.[211] It is here, at this center of female power, that the medical system enacts sexual violence against men in the form of circumcision. This gender-based violence is carried out by doctors of female bodies in female-majority professions at the behest of women in the center of female power.

The system might explain this as a mere coincidence. A critical consciousness would suggest that there are no coincidences, only outcomes. If a system produced the violent dominance of one race over another, no critical social justice activist would accept the explanation of coincidence. Systems that produce the violent dominance of one race over the other are racist. Systems that produce the violent dominance of one gender over another are sexist. If the hospital birth system is dominated by one gender and it consistently produces gender-based violence against the other gender, then this system is sexist. The violence and systemic pedophilia of the hospital system is most often carried out by women against men.

Much has already been written about how hospital birth disempowers women. The medical system treats birth as a medical emergency and constantly disrupts women's natural process with unnecessary and often harmful interventions. While these critiques are true, they are often centered on the adult women, not the child being born. Even if the hospital system also disempowers women, women are still responsible for their role in that system. I am aware that there are many ways that society disempowers, harms, and traumatizes women. Most oppressors act from trauma or harmful socialization. Even the architects of colonialism were acting from the trauma produced by the European wet-nurse and boarding school system. They were still responsible for their actions. The same is true of women.

Women's dominance of childhood extends from the womb through adulthood. After birth, children are cared for by their parents. When children are at their youngest, they are typically breastfed. Children that are not breastfed are more likely to have health issues.[212] Most children still spend the majority of their time around their mothers during infancy. One in four children have single mothers, meaning no father or adult male figure is present in their life.[213] Male children are statistically held less than female children.[214] When children are older, they are often put in daycare or school. In daycare, children are watched by strangers, who are, again, predominantly female.[215] The majority of school teachers are also female.[216] Male and female children alike will spend the next twelve years of their life confined to an age-segregated building by the state where predominantly women will have authority over them. If male children cannot conform to a female-dominated, age-segregated environment, confined to a square cell and lectured for eight hours a day by someone of a different gender about ideas the state wants him to regurgitate, then they are seen as dysfunctional. In American schools, male children are more likely to be medicated for behavior deemed dysfunctional by this system.[217] By the time children graduate, they will have spent the first eighteen years of their life in predominately female systems. These systems all have system in their name: the medical system, the childcare system, the school system, etc. If these systems consistently produce gender disparities, gender-based violence, and oppression, then they are sexist oppressive systems.

While adult men are sometimes called privileged, the men who endured these childhood systems were not privileged as children. They might experience privilege as an adult, but for the first eighteen years of their life, they were subaltern to women. At birth, they were separated from their mother. The majority were sexually abused through circumcision pedophilia. As infants, most were not given the care they needed. As children, they were imprisoned based on their age and forced to obey the state. If done to any other class, we would call it oppression. It is only the internalized dominance of adults that makes them not see this for what it is, and it is only the internalized dominance of women in positions of power over male children that makes them not see the gendered element to this oppression.

COMPLICIT WOMEN

When women's dominance of childhood systems is noted, women's responsibility is often dismissed with the following common objections. First, while there might be greater percentages of women in these systems, the people at the top of the power structure are men. Second, while compulsory schooling, hospital birth, and other child-harming systems are carried out by women, they were designed by men. According to these objections, because adult men are at the top of certain harmful systems, women are not responsible for their role in those systems.

These objections are adult-centric. The children involved in these systems do not understand them as systems. They know nothing of their history or ownership. All they know is that a woman is hurting them. From the child's perspective, the system is female. Only adult discourse frames it as otherwise. When we say these systems are dominated by women, we mean that they are majority women and that the women in these systems dominate children. They cut their genitals, traumatize them at birth, and imprison them in schools. Adult men might pay women for their role in these systems or design aspects of those systems, but women are the ones who directly carry out the domination of children.

These objections also ignore the complicity principle, which states that "one is accountable for what others do when one intentionally participates in a collective that causes the harm together."[218] It does not matter if a man gave the order to hurt a child. If a woman chooses to follow that order, she is morally responsible for harming a child. No matter who is at the top of a system, systemic harm is only possible if large numbers of people are complicit in that harm. These systems exist because of women's complicity. If the majority of women within these systems chose to stop being complicit and become antipedophile, the system would cease to exist. Claims that women are not responsible for hurting children because a man told them to denies women their agency and moral responsibility.

The purpose of these objections to deny women's complicity in systemic pedophilia, by allowing them to say "I was just following orders." The objections are an example of pedophile fragility, a defensive maneuver dominant groups engage in when asked to examine their role in harmful systems they perpetuate.[219] In this case, women are denying their agency and using sexist tropes about women's submissive nature in the face of male dominance to avoid looking at the ways they dominate and harm children. If we believe in gender equality, then women are morally responsible for the systems they participate in. Recognizing women's moral responsibility is important because the lessons children draw from these systems are based on who they see hurting them and the face of systemic pedophilia often is female.

CHILDHOOD LESSONS

Children need women. There is no birth without them. Children that are not held and breastfed have, on average, worse outcomes than those that are not. Even being separated from their mothers for a brief period of time can be a deeply traumatic experience for a child. Yet, all connections are not the same. A connection to an abusive mother will produce different outcomes for a child than a loving one. Likewise, a connection to an abusive power structure of female nurses, OBGYNs, daycare employees, school teachers, and others will produce different outcomes. People raised in an abusive power structure will create and support abusive power structures. What are children taught during the first years of their lives by these early relationships with female-dominated systems within which they are socialized?

Children are taught that if you are bigger and stronger than someone else, you get to do what you want to their body.[220] Circumcision is only possible because the victims are children and the perpetrators are adults. If a woman attempted to cut the genitals of an adult man, he would have the strength to fight back. A child cannot defend himself the same way. By cutting the boy during his first relationship, his relationship to his mother, on which all other relationships will be patterned, and making genital cutting his first shared sexual experience, pedophiles and those who participate in the medical system teach men a power dynamic and way of relating in which the strong can do what they want to the weak.

This power dynamic can flip when the child grows into a man and becomes the stronger partner. When this power dynamic is enacted by adult men on women, it is called "patriarchy." When it is enacted on women's bodies, it is called "rape culture." Yet when this power dynamic was first enacted by adult women on those men as children, what is it called? There is no name yet. This gender-based violence is concealed by the epistemic injustice, including both the hermeneutic injustice of having no language to describe it and testimonial injustice perpetrated against the surviving men who would talk about any anger or hurt they feel towards women due to systemic pedophilia. It is critical that we name and describe this system. All beliefs and behavior not innate to our being are learned through socialization. The systems described as "patriarchy" or "rape culture" are the result of socialization. The underlying emotional patterns and ways of relating necessary for gender-based violence are learned in the predominantly female institutions and systems that control birth and childhood. The lessons taught by systems through childhood trauma impact every aspect of society. Whatever is described by the term "patriarchy" is actually a product of this primarily female system that dominates childhood. Even the name "patriarchy" is a misnomer since it hides the roots of this system in the female-gendered domain of birth and childcare. Patriarchy is a way of relating taught to men by women in childhood.

ADULT EQUITY

When people experience injustice, they want the opposite: justice. Critical social justice suggests that this comes through creating equity. Equity is equality of outcomes. Equity requires that we acknowledge that not everyone began at the same place, and to achieve equality in spite of historical inequality, there might have to be some unequal treatment in the present.[221] Social justice activists often apply this concept to historical injustices, like slavery. For example, some social justice activists argue that those whose ancestors experienced slavery are starting from a less fortunate place than those whose ancestors did not, and should therefore receive beneficial treatment in the present to make up for the impact of this historic injustice on them today. If injustices committed against our ancestors might still affect us in the present, then how deeply does what happened during the first eighteen years of our lives affect us? If what happened to our ancestors has such a systemic impact on our life, that it justifies unequal treatment in the present, then wouldn't the massive trauma of childhood injustices also justify the same kinds of present-day equity-based forms of discrimination? If we can have equity for history, why not equity for personal history?

To achieve equity for childhood injustice, we will have to look at our personal histories the way social justice and critical theory look at historical injustices. While each individual's ancestors might have had a different experience, certain oppressive systems still dominated history. While each person's childhood might be different, certain oppressive systems still dominate childhood. The majority of men in American society experienced systemic oppression in childhood at the hands of women. The majority experienced systemic pedophilia in the form of circumcision. All children experience oppression in childhood since children are a subaltern class with fewer rights than any other identity group. For male children, this violence is gender-based and the face of these oppressive systems is female.

This alone might justify some present-day gender discrimination from a social justice equity-based perspective. If men experienced greater harm in childhood, then they might need greater support in adulthood. This would require acknowledging gender-based violence of systemic pedophilia. Since the dominant system is not willing to do this, men are denied the support they need to overcome childhood harm. Instead, the system defends itself with pedophile-apologist narratives that deny gender-based violence by claiming that men are privileged rather than uniquely harmed. Since men are socialized into this system and face significant epistemic injustices which prevent them from knowing or speaking about the harm they've experienced, most men are not consciously aware of the violence they endured in childhood.

However, even if the conscious mind does not remember the experience of circumcision pedophilia, the unconscious has still learned certain emotional patterns and ways of relating from early childhood experiences. These unconscious aspects will seek equity throughout a person's life using the emotional patterns learned from systemic pedophilia. While the intention of justice is good, because these aspects have not processed their trauma, they will use the emotional strategies and lessons learned from systemic pedophilia and child abuse carried out by women. Since these systems are based in dominance, rather than seeking the support they need, survivors of childhood trauma will attempt to dominate their oppressors in adulthood. In other words, survivors of childhood abuse will create adult social systems where men dominate women: patriarchy.

Patriarchy is a shadow solution to childhood injustice. If men are dominated by women in childhood and they repress this experience into their unconscious, these unconscious aspects will seek adult equity using emotional patterns taught to them by women in childhood. Given that violence against children extends as far back as recorded history and childcare and birth were almost always the domain of women, it is no wonder that almost all Western societies have been described as "patriarchal." While these systems might be oppressive, from the perspective of traumatized unconscious, they are an equity-based solution for historical injustice. Unless the underlying root cause of childhood oppression carried out by primarily women is addressed, men will continue to seek coping strategies for their trauma that involve enacting the same relational patterns on women.

EMPOWERMENT

The good news is that this view puts the power to end patriarchy in the hands of women. If women want a world without men who act from their trauma, they can create it in one generation by treating children well. In fact, one generation raised without systemic abuse would put an end not just to "patriarchy," but all systems of oppression, because the emotional patterns necessary for these systems are learned in childhood.

In order to protect children, women must reclaim their power. This means reclaiming birth from the medical system, reclaiming childcare from professional daycares, and reclaiming teaching children from the school system. It means taking responsibility for their role in the previous system, being an ally to those who have been harmed by it, and choosing to act differently in the future. It means treating men in childhood the way they want those men to treat them as adults, and ensuring the next generation is raised in a way that meets their needs on their terms.

Women can only be empowered when they end systemic pedophilia. When they do, many of the systems that oppress women will naturally dissolve, since the underlying emotional patterns necessary for those systems will no longer be created in childhood by systems women once participated in. Though this change will benefit women, it is not about them alone. Social justice activists have long said that while one of us is oppressed, we are all oppressed. Through Children's Justice, both men and women will be freed from oppression.

CHAPTER 12

GENDER THEORY

Queer theorists might prefer that instead of saying "man" or "woman," I use the terms like "people with penises" or "people with vaginas" so that my language is more inclusive of trans and non-binary people. Circumcision certainly affects people who are assigned male at birth and later identify as another gender. Many of the things I've written in regards to systemic pedophilia applies to all people with penises. Yet, gender theory is more complex when it intersects with the violence of genital cutting. How should we understand gender identity as it applies to this issue?

NORMALIZING BODIES

Queer theory suggests that gender is a social construct learned through socialization, rather than a series of biological traits.[222] The biological traits of "male" or "female" are known as biological sex, while the socially understood categories of "man" and "woman" are social constructs people chose to participate in through their choices or have imposed on them by society. In the view of queer theory, gender is a performance, a concept known as gender performativity, described by Judith Butler.[223] Modern gender theory suggests that people can live outside the socially constructed binary of "man" and "woman," in any category of their choosing, including non-binary, gender fluid, bi-gender, etc.[224] Since in the view of queer theory the categories of gender are entirely socially constructed, it is oppressive when they are imposed by society and they can be reconstructed into new identities of the individuals choosing. Queer theory opposes biological or sexual essentialism, which is the idea that men and women have inherent biological traits which determine social categories.[225] Even the idea that having a penis makes one male is something queer theorists would question since this excludes the possibility of transgender women or non-binary people with said anatomy.

Yet, those who are circumcised have been categorized as male whether they wish to be or not. Legal codes on genital cutting call the cutting of the vulva or clitoris "female genital mutilation" or "female genital cutting" and frame the cutting of the penis as "circumcision" or "male genital cutting." Circumcised people have an imposed male identity that assumes genital cutting as normative, no matter what other identity they might feel better defines them as an adult. This creates a contradiction in modern gender theory, and for the medical organizations that have accepted it. At the same time that there are medical organizations saying that we should not assign gender at birth because "assigning sex using binary variables in the public portion of the birth certificate fails to recognize the medical spectrum of gender identity,"[226] the medical system is also surgically altering the genitals of only male children. One could facetiously ask: if medical organizations do not assign gender at birth, how will they know which children to rape and mutilate?

The violence of circumcision is inseparable from gender, and only possible by imposing not just the socially constructed category of gender on children, but a very bizarre version of that social construction. In order to circumcise a child, all participants in the mutilation must see that child as male. They must also see the "normal" male body as circumcised. In other words, they must socially construct the "normal" version of masculine gender identity and male bodies as one that has experienced mutilation. Through this social construction, they can then see the child's intact body as "abnormal" and in need of normalization through genital cutting. This process of normalization is exactly what Michel Foucault describes throughout his work. In this process of normalization, a socially constructed definition of normal, which is not actually normal at all, is used as a tool of social and medical control.[227] In his work, Foucault specifically cites the medical system as one of the prime culprits of normalization and sexuality as one of their frequent targets.[228]

Why would pedophile-apologists see the exposed glans of a child's penis as "normal" male genitals? On intact male bodies, when the penis becomes erect, the foreskin often pulls back, exposing the glans. An exposed glans usually means an erect penis. If the penis is not erect, the foreskin usually covers the glans. On children, the foreskin is fused to the head of the glans. Since children have no biological reason to engage in sexual activity, there is no reason for the foreskin to be mobile. The foreskin protects the head of the glans and fusing it in place until sexual maturity ensures this protection. The fact that pedophile-apologists see lack of sexual arousal in a child as "abnormal" should speak to their motives. Cutting off the foreskin makes the male penis look permanently aroused, and provides no ability for the man to hide his glans, and physically show his lack of arousal. The body that pedophile-apologists socially construct as "normal" is one in which men and children cannot consent and their bodies are always sexually available and visible to pedophiles. It is rape culture manifest physically, where the body's ability to say "no" and withdraw the sexual organ from view is physically removed. The dominant definition of what constitutes a "normal" male body is one socially constructed by and for the benefit of pedophiles and those who want permanent physical access to men and children's sexuality. When someone says that the circumcised penis "looks normal," they reveal they have adopted this social construct of system pedophilia.

This imposition of socially constructed pedophile definition of the masculine gender is so great that no amount of gender-neutral language can remove it. Even using supposedly gender-neutral phrases like "people with penises" to be inclusive is no longer accurate. Survivors of circumcision are not "people with penises" - they are people with circumcised penises or only part of their penis. "People with half their penis" would be a more accurate label. The label "people with penises" erases their imposed identity of circumcision. When a child is circumcised, they are forced not just into the category of male, but in a particular cultural definition of what male is. This is an imposed identity that cannot be erased no matter what label we give it. I use the term "men" to describe the victims of male genital cutting rather than a more gender-neutral term is because it is impossible to separate this form of pedophile violence from gender. [229] When a child is circumcised, it becomes an intersectional aspect of their identity. Even if they attempt to claim a different gender identity later in life, they will always be a survivor of male genital cutting.

REMOVING GENDER

The oldest myths about male and female genital cutting are at their core about the violence of imposing gender. I first learned these myths during an interview with Fuambai Sia Ahmadu, an anthropologist and circumcised African woman, who chose as an adult to go through a traditional female circumcision initiation ceremony in Sierra Leone.[230] These myths also appear in the oral traditions of the Dogon tribe.[231]

In the view of these traditional African cultures, children are born without gender, having both masculine and feminine. The Dogon tradition describes children as having "two souls," male and female.[232] The circumcision ceremony is the "creation of sex," or perhaps really the creation of gender, in which the masculine element is removed from the female and the feminine element is removed from the male. The clitoris represents the masculine in women. It is hard, erect, and sticks out from the body like a small penis. The foreskin represents the feminine element in the man. It is wet, enveloping, and receiving like a small vagina. In this view, physical violence is done to the child in order to categorize him or her as male or female, and literally remove the masculine or feminine element from its opposite gender.

In my interview with her, Ahmadu suggested that the reason Western cultures are so incensed about female but not male genital cutting was the symbolic implications of the body parts removed. In Western society, women have done a lot of work to play the masculine role. Suggesting women are not allowed to do "male" work or play masculine roles is considered sexist in Western society. Thus, removing the masculine element from women is considered one of the worst forms of gender violence one can do. Her argument was part of a larger defense of female circumcision, which she feels has benefited her, but I see an opposite perspective.

If removing the foreskin is a symbolic removal of the feminine in men, then our lack of outrage over male circumcision is due to the lack of work we have done around male gender roles. Suggesting a woman can only play feminine roles is sexist, but there is no similar taboo around suggesting that men must play masculine roles. Telling a woman "get back in the kitchen" is deeply offensive, but telling a man "get back to work" is considered reasonable advice. Women have gained the privilege of working, but men have no similar right to not work or stay home. Feminine energy and traits are discouraged and shamed in men. There is a whole category of insults directed at men for being too feminine - pussy, sissy, wimp, etc. Circumcision is an extreme form of this gendered attack. Sensitivity is seen as a "feminine" trait and circumcision literally desensitizes men. Men are capable of sensitivity, yet much of what society does to men is designed to remove this sensitivity because it is seen as too feminine.

There are two assumptions here: first, that sensitivity is an exclusively feminine trait, and second that it is bad for men to be feminine. Why is the feminine not valued in men? Is sensitivity actually an exclusively feminine trait? Why wouldn't we want men to be sensitive? The masculine role in most traditional or ancient societies was that of the protector. Men are expected to sacrifice their personal safety for the good of the tribe. This might mean sacrificing their safety on the battlefield or sacrificing their health through work. While traditional societies value women for their ability to reproduce, men are valued for their ability to contribute to society and bring value to the tribe. These societies make women sex objects, but they make men success objects.[233] If a man were to be in touch with his feelings, he might not want to sacrifice his body for the good of the tribe. Now, the dominant system is no longer a tribe, but capital, yet it works the same way. Men who are in touch with their feelings might not want to sacrifice their lives in the pursuit of capital. By disconnecting men from their feelings, dominant systems can ensure that men will support and perpetuate them. This occurred in early tribes through initiation rituals, in which the man was expected to show his commitment to the tribe by facing brutality. Circumcision is a part of many of these initiation rituals. In the Maasai tribe, men are expected not to flinch or show pain during circumcision to prove they are a man.[234] A man who valued his feelings would obviously feel pain when someone cuts into his genitals, but by not flinching or showing that pain the man shows he values the tribe more than his own feelings. Now we disconnect men from their feelings through hospital birth, circumcision, and compulsory schooling, which forces boys to disconnect from their natural desire to move and play and conform to an industrial worker model of education so that as adults they will do the same and disconnect from their feelings to sacrifice their lives and bodies working to create capital.

The ancient myths around circumcision describe the psychological process of fragmentation. Aspects of a person's consciousness, or what the Dogon call parts of their "soul," are split through trauma. These rituals were designed to specifically fragment aspects of consciousness that were socially constructed to be associated with certain elements of gender, and enforce gender norms on a psychological level. Ancient societies saw this as good because they felt those gender norms served the tribe. Modern societies continue to practice genital cutting because the psychology created by this trauma serves capital. What we know about trauma now is that fragmented aspects do not disappear entirely, but continue to influence the person from their unconscious. While these rituals might benefit the system, they leave fragmentation and trauma in the survivors.

MASCULINE ROLE

Circumcision makes it impossible to simply do away with gender as queer theorists might desire because through circumcision men will always have an imposed aspect of gender whether or not they later attempt to perform a different definition of gender in the future. The systemic pedophilia definition of masculinity goes back to a traditional attempt to control men by disconnecting them from their feelings. The purpose of male genital cutting is not just to control male sexuality and male bodies, but to disconnect men from their feelings so they can be used in service of the tribe in ancient societies and in service of capital in modern ones. This system reduces men to success objects who sacrifice their bodies for other's desires. The system begins by sacrificing children's bodies in the service of the desires of adult pedophiles. By establishing this pattern in childhood, pedophiles create the fragmentation necessary for men to continue this pattern in adulthood in service of capital.

Western feminism has done little to remedy these roles. While expanding the roles of women, male roles have not been questioned, except when they conflict with expanding women's power. This is an example of unequal hermeneutical participation, in which a group disproportionally participates in conversations that affect them but ignores experiences that do not.[235] Feminists have shown up in conversations where women are disempowered, but often marginalize voices speaking about ways men experience disempowerment and sexism.[236] Feminists historically did the same around race, focusing primarily on issues that affected white women until later feminist authors criticized early feminism for being too white and engaging in systemic racism.[237] Feminism still has a blind spot towards men and the imposed identity of circumcision that has caused them to engage in systemic pedophilia. Many feminist authors allowed their children to be circumcised. If the end result of marginalizing voices speaking on mens' issues is systemic pedophilia then these claims against those activists are pedophile-apologist arguments. Gender equality requires treating male genital cutting as seriously as female genital cutting.

Part of the reason women's movements have not questioned male genital cutting is because women benefit from this system. Women benefit by having power over children and access to children's bodies. As we mentioned in the previous chapter, the medical systems that exploit children are staffed primarily by women. Women also benefit by having access to men's bodies and sexuality. With the foreskin, men can cover and withhold parts of their sexuality when not aroused. Circumcision gives women permanent visual and physical access to men's bodies. The body-shaming women engage in towards the natural male body and foreskin could be thought of as a projection of their own feelings of powerlessness and rejection at seeing a male body that can reject them. If rape is about power, as feminists say, and circumcision is a form of rape, then women's feelings about the natural male body are about power as well. Lastly, women benefit through capital. If men sacrifice their bodies through work, their female partners receive the benefits of that labor. This role has historically given women the freedom to decide whether or not they work. It is only in recent years that capital has attempted to seize both genders for work, and created an economic system where all people are effectively men and must sacrifice their bodies for capital. Only once economic concerns forced all people regardless of gender to play the masculine role of sacrificing their bodies for capital, did capital embrace the "gender revolution" and begin to present images of queer pride rather than traditional masculinity. The capitalist power that exploited men is still there, just better hidden, forcing everyone to play the masculine role, rather than just men.

Despite all this, many men still wish to play the traditional masculine role. They see the role of protector as one that serves their community, rather than serving a system designed to sacrifice their bodies in service of others. There is a fear among circumcised men that if they acknowledge the harm of circumcision they will be seen as less masculine. If the traditional male role requires sacrificing your feelings and pain for the good of the tribe, men fear consciously or unconsciously that if they acknowledge their pain they will not be able to fulfill the traditional masculine role of protector. The culture of systemic pedophilia exploits this masculine desire by framing men who speak about the harm of circumcision as weak, damaged, and less masculine. In reality, men who oppose circumcision are engaged in a traditional masculine protector role of protecting children from abusers. The idea that protecting themselves and children makes men "less masculine" is a form of false consciousness, promoted by the cultural hegemony of systemic pedophilia. In reality, protecting the children from harm is the epitome of traditional masculine heroism. If men wish to play the role of protector, they must protect their children from pedophiles. Doing this may require facing the pain of circumcision and other abuses from childhood. This heroism requires facing emotional and psychological pain rather than physical pain. The man sacrifices his own mental and psychological feeling of safety to venture into an unknown and retrieve the parts of him still trapped in a subaltern state of childhood, or, as the Dogon tribe might describe it, the lost parts of his soul. This is masculine heroism in the most traditional sense, with men sacrificing not just their physical comfort, but their emotional and psychological comfort, to protect children. By sacrificing his comfort, the man ensures he and his people do not participate in systemic pedophilia.

The masculine heroism that opposes systemic pedophilia has the potential to integrate gender roles. In the traditional mythic view of African cultures that practice both male and female genital cutting, children must choose between the masculine and feminine and fragment the aspect of them which does not match their assigned gender. This symbolism applied to Western genital cutting culture implies that men must reject the feminine role, as both men and women play the masculine role, creating a genderless society in which everyone plays a male role by sacrificing themselves to create capital. The heroic view, in which men face the pain of genital cutting and recover the parts of them trapped in a subaltern state, implies an integration of the masculine and feminine, rather than separation. Men can have both the symbolic masculine and feminine and integrate them. Allowing both genders to have the masculine and feminine would create the freedom many gender theorists seek. The opposite view imposes a lifelong violent imposition of social construction of gender designed to benefit pedophiles. No matter what gender you identify with later, circumcised people will always be a survivor of male genital cutting. Likewise, men who wish to play traditional masculine roles are denied these roles by the cultural constructions of gender by a systemically pedophile culture unless they have false consciousness. This imposed gender identity harms those whose gender identity does not conform to traditional categories and those who identify with the most traditionally masculine identity. The solution is to recognize the traditional masculine heroism of protecting children while deconstructing the definition of gender created by systemic pedophilia.

GENDER FREEDOM

Pedophile-apologists define the "normal" male body and body of children as one permanently sexually available to pedophiles. This socially constructed definition of gender plays into historical systems where men were forced to sacrifice their bodies, sensitivity, and socially constructed feminine aspects for the desires of the dominant society. Rather than sacrificing parts of our bodies or sexuality, we must allow people their full bodies, and by extension their full symbolic masculine, feminine, and gendered aspects. Allowing people to have all aspects of themselves achieves both the desires of queer theorists and men who still wish to play the traditional masculine role. Men who oppose circumcision must be recognized as masculine for playing a heroic protector role. The violence of gender categorization begins when we are forced to choose between aspects of ourselves. Circumcision is a physical manifestation of this gendered violence, where literal parts of the body are cut away due to social constructions around gender. The freedom people desire around gender is only possible with the end of genital cutting and systemic pedophilia.

CHAPTER 13
MEDICAL GAZE

Why does the medical system not see the systemic impact of their actions? Michel Foucault devoted his entire book *Birth of the Clinic: An Archaeology of Medical Perception* to the mindset of the medical system. In the book, he describes how the Western medical system looks at people with the "medical gaze."[238] The medical gaze views people not primarily as human beings with an identity, but as a series of parts. The body is not a whole interconnected system, but a collection of individual organs.[239] If a patient comes in, the doctor will look at parts of that person's body in isolation in order to determine which part is causing the patient's problem. Is this problem caused by his heart? His lungs? His foreskin? The medical gaze assumes that problems in the body are localized, that one part of the body is causing the problem, not the whole system or interactions between parts of that system. This gaze separates that person from their body and separates each part of the body from every other part.

This viewpoint is a historical anomaly. Other cultures' medical systems often did not practice this, nor do modern holistic approaches. If a patient is experiencing health problems, a holistic practitioner will not just look at the part of the body showing symptoms, but the full system of the body and even other potential factors interacting with the body, such as the person's environment, stress levels, past experiences, etc. For example, a holistic practitioner would not just give a person who describes diabetes symptoms some medication, but ask "what are you eating?" to see if diet might be a contributing factor. In other words, a holistic practitioner would treat the whole person, not just operate on atomized parts of them.

The medical gaze system fragments the body. If you've ever experienced "side effects" due to medication you were taking, you've experienced some of the negative impact of the medical gaze. When a doctor prescribes medication for your serotonin levels, he is only looking at the single problem and organ in question, not the larger impact of his actions on the whole system. If a medication prescribed kills your sex drive, then a doctor looking through the medical gaze will view the problem in isolation and prescribe more solutions for it. The Western medical gaze does not view the body as a system, or acknowledge that if they treated the body as a system from the beginning they might avoid the side effects caused by additional intervention. Even viewing some of the impacts of the doctor's actions as "healing" and other impacts as "side effects" is a form of medical gaze thinking because it fragments the impact of the doctor's actions into intended (for which he can take credit) and unintended (for which he can deny blame). A holistic view would not see any impact as a side effect. "Side effect" is a word the medical system uses to deny culpability for the impact of their actions.

Social problems are sometimes excused in the same way. People often create laws and systems that have the unintended "side effect" of causing harm. When they do, those who participate in oppressive systems will often try to take credit for the good that comes from their system, such as profit or wealth, while excusing the bad, such as exploitation or discrimination. To antiracists and critical theorists, it doesn't matter what they intended. What matters is the impact of their actions. There are no "intended effects" and "side effects," only outcomes. If the system produces racist outcomes, then it is a racist system. The same could be said of systems that produce pedophilia. If a system causes doctors to touch children's genitals and cut body parts off of children, then it is an abusive pedophile system. There are no "intended effects" and "side effects," only outcomes.

Critical theorists, like holistic practitioners, look at the body of society as a system. They recognize that if people are oppressed, it is not a localized individual problem that can be understood by only one organ of society, but the result of the interactions of larger systems. Critical theory applied to the medical system would suggest that what matters is the outcome of the doctor's actions, not the intent. What are the outcomes of the medical gaze?

DEHUMANIZING GAZE

The medical gaze is dehumanizing. It fragments the body into different parts and organs, and separates the body from the person. When a doctor looks at a person's body through the medical gaze to diagnose them, they do not see a human being, but a series of parts and organs. The parts of a person that cannot be seen, such as their feelings, are impossible to quantify or take into account through this view. The person is objectified and turned into a "thing" the doctor can operate on.

Dehumanizing a target is one of the first steps to psychologically preparing an oppressor to commit abuse. Slave owners and colonial powers all had texts justifying their abuses of power that described the people they were abusing as "lesser beings" or "savages," not capable of fully understanding or feeling what was happening to them and in need of improvement by being "civilized" by European peoples. There exist similar excuses in medicine around children. Children are not seen as full human beings. Doctors frequently excuse circumcision by saying that they "won't remember" or dismissing children's screams of pain. They see the child as a lesser being in need of "improvement" by being circumcised by the medical class. However, children are not just dehumanized based on identity. Doctors dehumanize them through the medical gaze, by seeing the penis and the foreskin as "things" they can operate on, not part of a human being whose feelings their actions will emotionally impact. In reality, the foreskin is not "just skin" as pedophile-apologists claim, but part of a human being who will have thoughts and feelings if part of their body is forcibly cut away.

Circumcision is only possible because of the medical gaze. The foreskin is clearly part of the penis. There is no dotted line on men that says "cut here." Where the doctor decides the foreskin ends and the shaft skin of the penis begins is arbitrary. Circumcised men frequently report unequal outcomes, with some losing all of the shaft skin and others retaining parts of the frenulum. When medical textbooks say to remove the foreskin during circumcision, they count on the doctor to have a medical gaze that allows him to mentally separate the penis in half before he physically separates it. Given that the medical gaze can separate entire parts of the body in half, it is not a great leap to separate the person from their organs, their body, and their identity. When a doctor circumcises a child, he filters out the personhood of the child, including the child's emotional and sexual experience of the act. The doctor does not see himself as having a sexual experience with another human being by touching the child's genitals. He sees himself as "doing a circumcision," or "cutting the foreskin" as if the act and body part are entirely separate. Many doctors report not hearing the screams of children during circumcision. One doctor said that when he finally heard the screams of the baby, he stopped performing circumcision, and became an activist against circumcision.[240] It's not that these screams are not happening. Sometimes children scream so loud that their lungs burst.[241] Rather, the medical gaze is so deep that doctors are able to focus just on performing the circumcision and filter out the emotional communication of the child.

The medical gaze is a pedophile gaze. It allows the doctor to separate his identity from his actions of touching children's genitals to satisfy adult desires. In doctors' minds, they are not touching children, but touching "the penis." This gaze also filters out the impact of the doctor's actions. If the patient experiences trauma, the doctor does not see himself as responsible for what happened to the person because he was operating on "the penis", and what happens to the human being is a "side effect." The impact of the doctor's actions on the person, including that person's self-image, their relationship to their body, their sexuality, sexual identity, future relationships, etc. are all filtered out because the medical gaze does not see us as people, but body parts for the doctor to operate on.

MEDICAL BLINDNESS

The medical gaze that blinds the medical systems to the impact of circumcision does not just separate the foreskin from the penis, or the body from the person; it also separates the doctor's actions from their systemic impact.

This aspect of the medical gaze is best illustrated by a story an activist shared with me. While speaking with a doctor, the activist said that circumcision reduced the pleasure of men's sexual experience. The doctor became confused and said, "but we're operating on children." The doctor's medical gaze was so focused on the child in isolation, that he could not make the connection between the child and the man that child would become, so he could not see that actions he took to remove a part of the child's penis would have a systemic impact on that child's later sexuality as an adult.

The medical gaze becomes even more blind when dealing with systemic changes, like those caused by trauma. There is ample evidence that childhood trauma causes long-term harm. People who experience adverse childhood events are at a greater risk of having medical issues later in life.[242] However, a doctor viewing a patient through the lens of the medical gaze would never ascribe a present-day medical problem to past emotional trauma, despite the overwhelming evidence in favor of this idea. The belief that childhood trauma cannot impact adult health problems is based in ideology, not evidence. The medical gaze assumes the problem must be related to an individual part the doctor can operate on, not the systemic issues of a person's life because if this assumption were false, the entire premise of the medical system would collapse.

It does not even occur to a doctor under the spell of the medical gaze to look at how one event in a person's life would impact another. Even when survivors of genital cutting commit suicide later in life, doctors will deny that their actions played any role in these men's feelings, even when the survivors explicitly say they experienced trauma and grief over genital cutting in their own testimony.[243] The medical establishment collects almost no data on men's feelings, the long-term impact of circumcision, or the potential link between adult sexual problems and infant circumcision[244] because conducting long-term circumcision studies on the systemic impact of circumcision would be admitting assumptions antithetical to the medical gaze.

This gaze blinds doctors not just to the systemic impact of their actions, but their words. For example, medical arguments that male genital cutting is "healthier" or "cleaner" have been adopted by groups interested in promoting female genital cutting.[245] Through their promotion of male genital cutting, doctors are actually rhetorically arming those interested in female genital cutting. From the view of the medical gaze, the potential legitimization of female genital cutting is an unintended "side effect" of defending male genital cutting. From a critical view, when the medical system creates an outcome that potentially expands the opportunity for genital cutting pedophilia, this is not an accident but the expected outcome of a pedophile system.

Although it is predictable that a pedophile system will produce more pedophile outcomes, the medical system will not admit this to itself. If the medical system saw the full role they played in systemic pedophilia, they could not continue that system. The system protects itself through the defensive mechanism of the medical gaze, which blocks out all knowledge of that system even from the people who participate in it. When individuals want to protect their identity, they will block out parts of their reality that threaten their self-image. Likewise, the medical system blocks out information about itself through the medical gaze in order to continue perpetuating systemic pedophilia while maintaining their pedophile-apologist narrative that they are "helping" children by holding them down and cutting their genitals.

Self-deception creates blindspots. Because the medical system cannot see itself clearly, it occasionally acts against its own interests. One of the ways the medical system has undermined its continued role in perpetuating systemic pedophilia is to base their public policy statements on social justice based in critical theory.

CONSEQUENCES OF THE GAZE

This medical gaze is not isolated to circumcision. It permeates the entire frame of the Western medical system. If the medical gaze is wrong, the entire ideology of modern medicine is wrong, and we must treat people holistically, looking at how each action impacts the full system of who they are.

The medical gaze is the idea that you can operate on one part of the body without impacting the whole. Critical social justice is the idea that problems are systemic, and can only be solved by looking at the world systemically. These two ideas are entirely incompatible. How then did the medical establishment come to endorse critical theory in their statements against racism?

The answer is simple - the medical gaze. By viewing their response to racism as an isolated problem that they could operate on rather than something that would impact the entire body of their organization, medical organizations did what they always do. They brought in experts, as determined by the epistemic privilege of the academic literature, and had them operate on the problem. However, the experts on racism are trained in critical theory, so they wrote statements based in critical theory. These policy statements have implications for the entire body of the medical system, but doctors do not yet realize it.

The medical response to COVID-19 was also based in the isolated thinking of the medical gaze. They saw the problem of a potential pandemic and prescribed lockdowns and quarantine. The systemic impacts on the body of society were not prioritized or considered. Establishment responses to COVID-19 clearly had a systemic impact on the American economy, with mass unemployment and business closures. It also had less measurable but even more significant impacts on the nation's emotional, mental, and social health. It changed the American people. The systemic effects of the establishment response to COVID-19 completely transformed society in ways we are still trying to understand. However, because of the medical gaze, the medical establishment treats the massive harm they caused as "side effects" of their COVID-19 response, not an outcome for which they are responsible.

When the medical establishment suddenly changed their position and endorsed mass protest gatherings while many places were still in lockdown (because "racism is the real virus"),[246] they also did not consider the systemic effect this would have on their credibility, public perception, or future position statements. This position that social justice causes are more important than potential medical risks gives a clear opening not just for arguments against circumcision, but on a whole host of issues. Any argument they make now based in "the science" is irrelevant if a social justice argument based in critical theory can be made on the same issue.

Of course, the medical gaze will not recognize this. If you try to apply an argument they used on one issue to another, they will claim that each are separate issues. The medical establishment's view that issues are separate and that they can use one ethical framework on one issue and an entirely different, incompatible framework on another issue is itself a meta-narrative based in the medical gaze.

The fragmentation of the medical gaze makes them blind to the systemic impact of their actions, and may eventually lead to their downfall. This book itself is due to the systemic impact of the actions of the medical system. I became interested in the issue of circumcision due to the actions of the medical system when I was born. I began considering how critical theory applied to this issue when I saw it appear in the statements of medical organizations. In some way, I and the people who oppose circumcision are a systemic effect of the medical system. The medical system views the people who protest them as separate, rather the downstream effect of their systemic pedophilia. They are blind to the role they have played in creating their own problems. If they respond to the blowback of their systemic pedophilia through the lens of the medical gaze, they will attempt to "operate" on me and other activists to remove us or our influence, rather than address the systemic problems which created this situation. In other words, they will become fragile, reactive, and violent.

This is the mindset of an oppressor, not someone interested in social justice. Critical social justice asks us to be willing to examine the roles we play in the systems we participate in. The medical gaze is incapable of seeing itself as a participant in any system. It is also the basis of the entire Western medical system. This means that we will never have social justice until the Western medical system is dismantled. If critical theory means developing a critical consciousness, then the medical gaze creates a fragmented consciousness. The medical gaze does not just fragment bodies, it fragments everything. Viewed this way, pedophilia is not an accident of the medical system, but the purpose of it. What greater fragmentation could the medical gaze achieve than the separation caused by genital cutting? Circumcision fragments children from their bodies, men from their sexuality, parents from children, lovers from their full partner, and human beings from parts of their own psyche. This is the ultimate act of fragmentation, and therefore the culmination of the values of Western medicine. Pedophilia is the endpoint of medical ideology.

CHAPTER 14
BIOPOWER BRUTALITY

How can we ascribe this much power to the medical system? Isn't the real power with the government? Don't people enter the medical system voluntarily, while governments force people to obey their laws? Foucault in his writing described the type of power that governments have as sovereign power.[247] The scientific and medical systems have a different power, which is far greater and more obscured: biopower.[248]

BIOPOWER AND SOVEREIGN POWER

Biopower means literally having power over bodies. Foucault defines biopower as "an explosion of numerous and diverse techniques for achieving the subjugations of bodies and the control of populations."[249] When people think of power, they typically think of sovereign power. Sovereign power is the ability to decide who dies.[250] When the government threatens to physically harm, imprison, or kill you, they are exercising sovereign power. However, biopower is the ability to decide who lives. When the medical establishment tells people that they must undergo certain treatments or medical interventions or they might die or risk disease, they are exercising biopower.[251] Biopower can even be exercised by deciding who gets life-saving or life-extending medical interventions and who doesn't. If sovereign powers tell their subjects "do this, or else we will kill you," biopowers say "do this, or else you will die." In both cases, compliance is ensured through threat of harm. In Foucault's words: "One might say that the ancient right to take life or let live was replaced by a power to foster life or disallow it to the point of death."[252] In some ways, biopower is the greater tool of control than sovereign power. You can only die once, but the improvement of health can be extended infinitely. Biopower is more hidden, sovereign power more overt. When a police officer tells you to do something, you know it comes with an implied threat of harm if you fail to comply. However, when a doctor offers you an intervention, it also comes with an implied threat of harm if you fail to comply because the doctor is suggesting that through inaction you might be at risk of dying. When police misuse their sovereign power, we call it police brutality. One could call this misuse of biopower a form of medical brutality as well. Nowhere is the abuse of biopower more evident than in the case of circumcision.

All medical arguments for circumcision rest upon biopower. When doctors ascribe medical benefit to circumcision or suggest that leaving the foreskin attached will lead to increased rates of disease or infection, they are making a biopolitical argument. "Do this [circumcision], or else you [or your child] will be harmed." In interviews, I've jokingly referred to this argument as the "your penis is trying to kill you" argument. Underneath the medical language used to promote circumcision is the idea that if you don't cut part of your penis, it will eventually kill you. One could mockingly summarize all medical arguments that the foreskin causes disease as the idea that "your penis is trying to kill you, so you'd better cut off part of it first." Although intentionally absurd, this joke reveals the underlying biopower behind circumcision pedophilia. The threat is obscured by attributing it to the foreskin itself. The doctor is not saying that he will kill your child but that the foreskin will kill him through infection or disease unless removed. It is obvious from the lack of complications or problems from intact men in societies without a culture of genital cutting that this view is false. The threat is not coming from the foreskin but from the doctor. When a doctor refuses treatment if the parent does not follow his recommendations, such as vaccines, circumcision, or other interventions, he is essentially saying "comply, or else we will allow your child to die."

The power dynamic of the medical system makes consent impossible. When the doctor implies that without their intervention a child might die, they are creating a life-or-death situation. Doctors make death threats regularly as a routine part of the medical system. No consent is possible under threat of death. Biopower death threats make "parental consent" as invalid as if a police officer drew their gun and ordered the circumcision.[253] Police brutality is so common that social justice activists have suggested defunding the police or removing their sovereign power altogether.[254] If medical brutality is common, then one could make similar arguments for defunding the doctors and removing their biopower.

BIOPOWER AND CHILDREN

According to Foucault, biopower is applied around two poles: anatomo-politics and biopolitics.[255] Anatomo-politics "centered on the body as a machine."[256] If the body is a machine made up of individual parts as seen through the medical gaze, then it can be controlled and perfected through interventions. Biopolitics is an "entire series of interventions and regulatory controls" to apply biopower to populations.[257] One could think of anatomo-politics as the discipline of individual bodies and biopolitics about controlling bodies-plural, or populations. Power becomes less about killing on behalf of the king, but regulating and extending life through systems. The state could increase its power far more by increasing the population than killing individuals. "There was… an explosion of numerous and diverse techniques for achieving the subjugation of bodies and the control of populations, marking the beginning of an era of 'bio-power.'"[258] The shift from sovereign power to biopower also shifted power from laws to norms.[259] Foucault suggests that rather than controlling "crime or illness," medical knowledge becomes about controlling the abnormal or "the power of normalization."[260] This normalization is especially applied to sexuality since sex represents the greatest biopower.[261] "This technology of abnormality encountered other processes of normalization that were not concerned with crime, criminality, or monstrosity, but with something quite different: everyday sexuality."[262] Children represent the future of populations, so controlling children's sexuality became a primary focus of biopower. As Foucault writes, children represent a "precious and perilous, dangerous and endangered sexual potential" to biopower.[263]

During the Victorian era, the primary tool the medical system used to seize biopower over children was a campaign to end masturbation.[264] Masturbation was thought to be the source of every major illness.[265] "Foucault compares the Victorian-era campaign against masturbation to a witch-hunt, saying the "widespread physical persecution of childhood and masturbation in the nineteenth century that, without having the same consequences, was almost as extensive as the persecution of witches in sixteenth and seventeenth centuries."[266] "Educators and doctors combatted children's onanism like an epidemic that needed to be eradicated."[267]

Why masturbation? The literature against masturbation in the 1800s describes it as causing "total illness and sometimes it is carefully distributed in the etiology of different illnesses."[268] There is an attempt by the medical establishment to link every symptom to "the inexhaustible causal power of infantile sexuality, or at any rate of masturbation."[269] "Masturbation becomes the cause, the universal causality of every illness."[270] From a modern perspective, it makes no sense that one and the same behavior would cause every medical problem, no matter how different the symptoms. However, Foucault explains how this was a natural result of the medical gaze. Prior medical treatment "always sought to assign patients a degree of responsibility for their own symptoms and illnesses by referring to their diet."[271] The new focus on biopower and the control of sexuality meant that "this general causality is now concentrated around sexuality, or rather around masturbation itself. The question 'What have you done with your hand?' begins to replace the old question: 'What have you done with your body?'"[272] In other words, medicine shifted from the holistic view, where the whole causes symptoms, to a medical gaze in which individual parts cause symptoms in the whole of the body. The medical establishment naturally blamed the body part the medical gaze was most fixated on: children's genitals.

Since the medical establishment wanted power over children's sexuality, they co-opted the power of those currently in power over children: parents. Parents were told that "the family space must be a space of continual surveillance" where they must constantly "read their child's body" for any "possible signs of masturbation."[273] In fact, the medical establishment blamed parents and caretakers for teaching children to masturbate, claiming that no one ever naturally wants to masturbate except that they learn the behavior from adults.[274] And what should parents do if they caught their child masturbating? Call the doctor. This was a power dynamic in which the parents effectively became surveillance agents on behalf of the doctor. They were instructed to watch them constantly for "signs of masturbation" and call the doctor the moment they saw them.[275] Foucault calls this "instruction for the direct, immediate, and constant application of the parents' bodies to the bodies of their children."[276] I believe he is right to use the word "bodies" here, as the medical gaze detaches bodies from persons. In this instruction, there is no regard for the impact that a parent constantly watching their child for "signs of masturbation" will have on the emotional, mental, or spiritual aspects of the parent-child relationship, or the child himself. What would you say if an adult asked you to watch your child constantly for "signs of masturbation" and call them the moment you saw them? Would you believe such a person was acting for the benefit of your child or had their own licentious motives? While the medical establishment of the time would no doubt claim this request was only for professional reasons, most parents today would assume another adult asking to watch their child for signs of masturbation was a pedophile.

Many of the Victorian-era "treatments" for masturbation involve sexual contact between adults and children. For example, one doctor suggests that he "should sleep beside the young masturbator, in the same room and possibly in the same bed, in order to prevent him from masturbating."[277] In other words, the medical treatment for masturbation was for the doctor to be a sexual voyeur to children. Another doctor "proposed inserting a permanent probe in the urethra."[278] This is forced penetration, the primary legal definition of rape.[279] Other doctors proposed tying up the child's genitals, placing them in a cage, poking needles into the penis, giving the child opiates, and washing the child's genitals with burning chemicals.[280] Orgasm denial, genital torture, and bondage are all forms of kink and power exchange. The fact the person enacting these kinks was wearing a doctor's uniform does not make this less of a pedophilic kink, but furthers it, as costumes and roleplay are often a part of sexual power exchange. In fact, the identity of the adult doing this as a doctor with the permission of parents and society could be considered part of the pedophile kink as it furthers his power. While these pedophile treatments might shock you, there is one pedophile treatment for masturbation practiced during this era that is still practiced today: circumcision.

THE MEDICAL ORIGINS OF CIRCUMCISION

Circumcision began as a medical practice in the Victorian era as a treatment for masturbation.[281] If the goal is to stop masturbation, it follows that removing the most pleasurable part of the penis would accomplish this goal. During this era, both male and female circumcision were proposed, with many of the same justifications. Texts from the time describe "cauterization and removal of the clitoris" as a treatment for masturbation. One doctor from the time defended the practice by saying "we act as we do on other occasions when we amputate a limb; we sacrifice the secondary for the principal, the part for the whole."[282] This justification is correct in the sense that female circumcision is consistent with the medical gaze. However, if female circumcision can be justified by medical thinking, this does not suggest that female circumcision is not wrong, but rather that the entire medical gaze is warped. The doctor continues by asking "what disadvantage does a woman suffer if we remove her clitoris?"[283] Justifications from the time for female circumcision read like modern justifications for male circumcision. They claim the part removed has no value, the doctor did what they did for the benefit of the child, and the child's sexuality improved by adult penetration. In other words, pedophile narratives were present at the beginning of modern medicine, as was medicalized circumcision pedophilia.

The modern discourse of circumcision follows the same pattern as historical tortuous masturbation treatments. Doctors claim a pedophile narrative that doctors torturing children's genitals somehow benefits the child. Even they knew this was a false narrative. As Foucault notes, "not only have parents never been able to prevent their children from masturbating, but the doctors of the time admit this quite bluntly and cynically: All children masturbate."[284] Yet if the campaign against masturbation was always destined to fail, why did doctors engage in it? "The child's 'vice' was not so much an enemy as a support; it may have been designated as the evil to be eliminated, but the extraordinary effort that went into the task that was bound to fail leads one to suspect that what was demanded of it was to persevere, to proliferate to the limits of the visible and the invisible, rather than to disappear for good."[285] In other words, stopping masturbation was always going to be a failed cause. People masturbate. The real purpose of this campaign was to expand the power of those undertaking it. If children touching themselves was a deadly perversion, then it follows that medical authorities needed more power to stop this deadly perversion. Children's bodies were used to expand the power of the medical system. Even though the campaign "failed," it succeeded in its real goal of seizing power over children's sexuality.

Power over children was previously held by parents. Doctors seized this power through the medical discourse. If children's "problems" were framed in the medical discourse, then only the doctor could cure it. The control of parents was "subordinate, that it must be open to medical and hygienic intervention, and that they must call upon the external and scientific authority of the doctor at the first warning signs."[286] There is a trick doctors are playing. On the one hand, they say that parents are responsible for the well-being of their children. On the other, they tell parents that only doctors can solve these children's medicalized problems. "As a result, precisely when families are called upon to take responsibility for their children's bodies and for securing their lives and survival, they are also asked to give up these same children" to the control of the doctor.[287] Parents are framed as power-holders, while doctors have all the real power through biopower because only they can foster life or disallow death. In other words, "the sexuality of children was a trap into which parents fell."[288]

This power sexualized parent-child relationships.[289] Parents were told to constantly monitor their children's bodies and sexuality. Instead of trying to understand the child's reality, they were looking at the child through the lens of adult desires. The constant surveillance of children's sexuality originated in adult biopolitical desires and the sexual power-exchange desires of doctors. Doctors were unable to admit their desire for power over children's bodies, so they scapegoated children as the source of perversion rather than themselves. By projecting adult perversion onto children's natural exploration of their own bodies, doctors were able to inflict actual perversion on children without admitting their motives. Since all desire was projected onto the child, the doctor could claim he was acting altruistically for the benefit of the child.

The focus on pedophilia as defined by adult desire rather than the harm inflicted on the child blinds adults to the systemic pedophilia of the medical system and sexualizes children's normal behavior. For example, if a child runs naked around their room, many adults will see this as a sexual act because adults often see nudity as sexual, despite the fact that the child is not seeking or expressing adult sexuality. The adults might feel they need to coerce the child into wearing clothing to prevent other adults from projecting their own sexuality onto the child. However, the same adults might not see asking a child to undress at the doctor's office as a sexual activity, despite the fact the child might be uncomfortable undressing in front of a stranger. In both cases, the child's body is subjected to adult desires. This centering of children's bodies on adult sexuality marks the beginning of medicalized systemic pedophilia. Circumcision represents the most extreme version of this systemic pedophilia, in which part of the child's natural sexuality is cut off for adult desires. Since parents were co-opted by the medical system to view their children through the lens of adult desires rather than understanding the child's reality, despite being constantly on the lookout for that which would harm their children's sexuality, they remained unaware of the real predator: the medical system.

CIRCUMCISION POWER

The power of the medical system is greater than sovereign states. It operates through biopower, or the claim that without medical intervention people will die. All arguments for circumcision rest in this biopower. Medicalized circumcision and the historical campaign against masturbation from which it began were deliberate tools to seize power over children, including their bodies, and sexuality. Parents were made agents of their power through medical discourse. Their power was taken, and their relationship to their own children was sexualized. The medical system knew they could never achieve their stated goal of ending masturbation but deliberately lied to parents in order to gain sexual access to children. From the begining, the medical system has acted as a sexual predator and pedophile.

CHAPTER 15
CREATED PROBLEMS

Medicalized circumcision was a solution to what could be called a created problem. Created problems are problems that are deliberately generated by a powerful institution or system in order to increase its power. It does not matter if the newly created problem used to expand power is real or imagined. Circumcision is a prime example of the latter – it was a solution to the fictitious "problem" of masturbation. It is true that people masturbate. However, by framing this common occurrence as a problem and itself as the solution, the medical system was able to expand its power.

EXPANDING MEDICAL POWER

The tactic of expanding power through created problems is shared by both the medical industry and the security state. Sovereign powers try and expand their power by framing created problems all the time. For example, the militarization of the police force was a result of framing drug problems through the discourse of law enforcement (the famous 'war on drugs'). This problem could just as easily have been framed through the discourse of addiction treatment, but since a law enforcement discourse better allows the state to expand its power, it chose this one. The medical system has also repeatedly used this tactic of treating an everyday occurrence as a medicalized problem only they can solve. To facilitate the rise of hospital births, the medical industry ran a smear campaign against midwives and framed the everyday occurrence of birth as a medical emergency for which they were the solution.[290] Later, they framed the foreskin as a medical problem for which they were the solution. Tonsils, wisdom teeth, the appendix, and a great many other normal aspects of the body were framed as problems so that the medical industry could expand its power by delivering a solution. Although the medical industry is not publicly campaigning against masturbation anymore, it still frequently employs the created problems tactic to expand its biopower. The largest and most recent example of the medical system expanding their power through created problems was the medical system's response to the COVID-19 virus.

While the exact origin of the COVID-19 virus remains unknown, some suggest that it might have escaped from a medical lab in Wuhan, China.[291] If so, that would make the virus a problem quite literally created by the medical system. A whole host of measures were proposed to deal with COVID-19. The dominant medical powers rejected those that would have decreased the power of the medical system and pushed for those that increased their power. Their primary goal was to create a vaccine, which could expand medical power to every at-risk person in the world, not a cure, which would only give the medical system power to those who tested positive for the virus. Those who suggested that certain existing medicines could be used to treat COVID-19 were publicly attacked by the establishment,[292] labeled misinformation,[293] and sometimes censored from social media.[294] While these proposed medicines may or may not have worked, the medical establishment did not explore them with as much interest as they did vaccines, because if a widely available existing medicine could treat COVID-19, it would solve the COVID problem without expanding medical power. Even solutions like face masks were initially rejected by health organizations who said they "didn't work"[295] until the solution of masks could be legally mandated and medical organizations were able to buy their supply.[296] Individuals choosing to wear masks they can purchase anywhere does not increase the power of the medical system, but giving medical organizations the ability to legally mandate what people wear in public does. Medical organizations were given powers that have nothing to do with medicine, like censorship power over social media platforms under the guise of stopping "misinformation," despite the fact that many of the medical organizations that were given censorship power had themselves promoted misinformation at the beginning of the coronavirus outbreak.[297]

Did any of these measures actually have a chance of stopping the virus? A charitable reading of these measures might say that even if the virus could not be stopped, it was worth doing everything we could to try to reduce the spread. Yet, this problem allowed the medical system to massively expand its power by offering solutions that could never actually fully solve the problem and were doomed to fail. "Slowing the spread" was a discourse. Increasing medical power was the outcome.

EXPANDING CIRCUMCISION POWER

In this sense, one can view the evolving "reasons" for circumcision as a process of inventing new discourses to maintain and expand power. Over time, these pedophile-apologist discourses have become more efficient, not less. The modern circumcision discourse has produced far greater outcomes than the Victorian anti-masturbation discourse. The Victorian masturbation discourse puts sexuality front and center. Power is revealed, centered, and direct. Later discourses better obscured power. Instead of presenting circumcision as a punishment for vice, it was advertised as a personal benefit. Even though medicalized circumcision was always a tool of biopower, over time the discourse moved even further from claims which might sound like sovereign punishing-power towards claims of life-extending power.

The discourse that has been most effective at expanding the power of the medical system relies on the claim that circumcision reduces the spread of HIV.[298] To test this idea, Western researchers spent millions of dollars circumcising thousands of African men in three randomized controlled trials. These trials have been highly criticized for their numerous flaws.[299] More subjects left the studies than stayed in them.[300] The researchers themselves confirmed that the circumcised group used condoms at a higher rate than the intact group,[301] which would make these trials a study of condom use, not circumcision. However, these studies created a discourse by which the medical system could expand its power in a continent where it would not be obstructed by Western regulation, ethics, or human rights oversight.

Once the discourse was created that circumcision might reduce the spread of HIV in Africa, it was expanded in the popular media to America. Now, preventing HIV is a justification given for systemic pedophilia in America,[302] despite the caveats given in the original study or the fact that it was carried out in a completely different context. This discourse was also expanded to include the claim that Americans should pay for African circumcisions, with millions of dollars given from the American government to African circumcision campaigns.[303] Over fifteen million circumcisions were performed on African men through this program.[304] Even when this discourse is threatening to fail, it is being expanded. When the architects of the circumcision campaign could not get enough adult men to sign-up, they expanded it to teenagers, often circumcising children and teens against their parents' will.[305] When they couldn't get enough teens, they expanded it to children. (Some have suggested that this expansion to children was the plan all along and that the idea that they were only going to do adult circumcision was always an excuse to provide cover for their real plan.[306] The outcomes certainly fit this theory.) When the circumcision device they were using repeatedly botched children, they switched to a new, untested medical device.[307] Testing genital cutting devices on African children is clearly ethically wrong, and beyond defensible under the guise of "HIV prevention." However, it gives the medical system power over black bodies in a way that telling adult men to just use a condom would not.

The African circumcision campaigns are clearly racist.[308] They rely on the racist belief that the black population of Africa is too stupid or unreliable to consistently use condoms, despite the fact that studies from the researchers behind the African circumcisions campaigns themselves showed that people who regularly received health counseling used condoms at a higher rate.[309] The African circumcision campaigns view the native black population through a white paternalistic savior narrative in which the black population is seen as "children" the white American "adults" can "raise" to their level. When dominant racial groups view others as "lesser" races or metaphorical children, this racism often goes unrecognized, because it does not manifest as outward hatred or discrimination. Paternalistic racism holds the condescending idea that the "child" race can be "raised" by becoming like the "adult" race, whether or not that is what the "child" group actually wants.[310] This racism manifests as dominant white cultures try to "improve" other groups by making them conform to the standards of white culture, regardless of whether or not the targeted group finds those standards beneficial or desirable. Here, racism intersects with Children's Justice, since this form of racism would not be possible without the internalized dominance people have towards children. In the case of African circumcision campaigns, white American researchers are literally cutting off parts of African genitals to make them match American culture. The pedophile-apologist argument "he should match his father" has been mixed with the racist idea that whites are an "adult" race to African "child" races to create a new intersectional form of oppression in which "he should match his father" becomes "black Africans should match white Americans."

A healthy parent-child relationship is centered on the needs of the child. Even if white researchers were to hold the racist idea that they are the "adult" race, the relationship would be very different it was centered on the needs of Africans rather than what the "adult" whites wanted, concealed through a discourse of "for your own good." Of course, Africans are not children. The adult-child power dynamics white researchers enact on African populations reveal that it is actually the researchers who still have fragmented aspects of themselves psychologically trapped in the subaltern state of childhood. They learned these ways of relating somewhere. The fact this form of racism is even called "white paternalism" by scholars who focus on race relations rather than children's issues[311] should be a clue to where the psychological origins of this racism lie: childhood. White researchers are playing out negative family dynamics on African populations with devastating consequences.

EXPANDING SOCIAL JUSTICE POWER

All major institutions, including the medical system, have adopted the discourse of critical social justice. When critical social justice theory is applied to the medical system, it reveals that this system is deeply oppressive. Yet the medical system does not seem threatened by critical social justice. It has co-opted this discourse for its own expansion. Does critical social justice actually curtail the power of this oppressive system or expand it?

Social justice focuses on the problem of systematic oppression. This oppression takes many forms - racism, sexism, colonialism, etc. - but the solution is always the same: more social justice. Critical social justice activists suggest that the solution to racism is to become antiracist, which requires "lifelong, ongoing work."[312] In other words, to combat racism, which critical social justice activists say is a pervasive system that impacts every aspect of society, we must expand the power of critical social justice to every aspect of society. Critical social justice activists themselves say racism can never be "solved," but the problem is so harmful that it is worth doing everything we can to reduce racism.

This mirrors the medical discourse around COVID-19. Like racism, COVID-19 can also never be fully stopped, but the problem is so harmful that it is worth doing everything we can to reduce the spread. In both cases, the proposed solution massively increases the power of the institutions combating the problem. The medical system would claim power over which businesses can be open and who can visit them in the form of lockdowns and vaccine status, while critical social justice activists would suggest that each of those businesses have a policy on diversity, equity, and inclusion which impacts every decision businesses make from hiring to where they spend their money. Both proposed solutions would give these institutions hegemonic power over society. Are critical social justice campaigns against racism doomed to fail like the campaigns against COVID-19, HIV in Africa, and masturbation in the Victorian era? If the goal is solving the problem, yes. If the goal is expanding power, it is succeeding perfectly.

The medical system is not threatened by critical social justice, because it can co-opt social justice discourses to expand its power.

Though there are real issues social justice movements could address, the discourse of social justice can also be used to generate created problems with which the system can expand its power. Instead of questioning the medical system's systemic pedophilia, many social justice organizations have sought to increase the power of that system by framing access to "healthcare" as a "right" and then complaining that certain marginalized groups do not have greater access to this "right." While ensuring all people are healthy is a good intention, this discourse frames the industrial medical system as the only solution to this problem. The social justice organizations that say "healthcare is a right" are not fighting for universal access to organic whole foods, gyms, and holistic health practitioners. They're seeking to bring everyone into a system that often harms people's health. By framing the medical system's definition of "healthcare" as a "right," the medical system has used social justice discourses to extend its power under the guise of doing something "for their benefit." Given that this system is engaged in systemic pedophilia, unless this system is critically deconstructed, the slogan "healthcare for all" is effectively a cry for "pedophilia for all," since it calls for forcing everyone into a system engaged in systemic pedophilia. African circumcision campaigns have already used the same discourse to justify forcibly circumcising children, by claiming that they are providing healthcare.

These discourses claim to have good intentions. Ending injustice is a good intention. Stopping a deadly disease is a good intention. Ensuring everyone is healthy is a good intention. It is precisely because these are good intentions that the system is able to use them as discourses to expand their power. What distinguishes these discourses from their stated intention is that the proposed solutions have no chance of ever actually fully solving the problem. An actual solution would threaten the system because if the problem used in these discourses were solved there would be no more excuse to expand the power of the system. Solving a problem is the opposite of creating one. The system will almost always attack real solutions since they threaten the system's power. For evidence, one need only look at the medical system's response to any natural or traditional cure to a common health issue, which it cannot co-opt or monetize.

REAL SOLUTIONS

Children's Justice is a real solution to both the problems of the medical system and social justice issues. Modern social justice movements believe that people are not born oppressors and oppressed, but socialized into oppressive systems. If children learn emotional patterns and ways of relating before they can even speak, then the existing social justice movement can never solve the problem of injustice unless they address the underlying pre-verbal emotional patterns learned in childhood. Solving the roots of injustice requires changing the way children are birthed and treated. If children are welcomed into the world with understanding rather than trauma, they will never learn the underlying emotional patterns necessary to continue oppressive systems, and many social justice issues will be resolved naturally within a generation. Since Children's Justice would solve the problem behind multiple discourses, it is likely that those who benefit from continued problems will attack this real solution, while those who want an end to injustice will embrace it.

CHAPTER 16
MEDICAL SOCIALIZATION

A lack of understanding of the natural male body often leads to other forms of sexual assault and pedophilia besides circumcision. In an intact male, the foreskin is typically fused to the glans until puberty. This is natural, and the foreskin usually becomes mobile at the age of sexual maturity. However, because the medical system does not understand this natural development of the foreskin, doctors will sometimes try to pull back the foreskin while it is still fused to the head of the glans in what is known as forced retraction.

FORCED RETRACTION

Forced retraction is when someone other than the child tries to forcibly retract a child's foreskin while it is still fused to the head of the glans. To give you an idea of how painful this is, imagine if someone tried to retract your fingernail from your finger, except on your genitals with all the nerve endings and sensations that this part of the body has. Forced retraction is painful. It can lead to infection, life-long sexual complications, and even the loss of the child's penis. It is also entirely unnecessary. Forced retraction often happens at well-baby visits. The child enters these visits healthy and leaves harmed. There is no medical reason to forcibly retract a healthy child's foreskin. At the very least, it is medical malpractice. Done to an adult, it would be sexual assault. When a doctor touches a child's genitals in an unnecessary way that causes the child harm, it is pedophilia. This form of sexual assault is not uncommon. In one survey conducted by Intact America, sixty percent of parents of intact children reported that a doctor had tried to forcibly retract their child, often against the parents' explicit wishes.[313] This means that the majority of doctors engage in pedophilia with healthy children if given the chance to do so during a well-baby visit. With rates this high, pedophilia is clearly a systemic issue within the medical system.

Doctors might give rationalizations for touching children's genitals and forcibly retracting them, but a critical view suggests that we cannot take their stated reasons at face value. In the same way that a racist might not admit to their unconscious bias or say that their actions were motivated by hate, a pedophile will not likely admit to their true motivations. Critical social justice would suggest that to understand the motivations of the medical system, we should look at their outcomes, not their words. If the majority of the medical industry engages in pedophilia during well-baby visits with intact children, then any explanation that does not acknowledge how the system is engaged in pedophilia is likely false and being given to hide their own conscious or unconscious participation in systemic pedophilia. When a majority of a system is engaged in something, it is not just a "few bad apples." It's the whole tree.

The usually stated reasons for forced retraction make little sense. Doctors will say that they are checking to make sure the foreskin is mobile and not fused to the head of the glans. However, the foreskin does not need to be mobile until the child reaches sexual maturity, and it is natural for it not to be mobile until then, so this explanation is false on a purely medical level.[314] It also raises a larger question: Why is a doctor concerned with the mobility of the child's foreskin? The mobility of the foreskin only matters during sex. During sex, the foreskin glides back and forth over the glans, the head of the penis, stimulating both the man and his partner. This is the reason this body part becomes mobile in puberty. There is no need for it to be mobile if the man is not having sex. The only reason a doctor would be concerned with the mobility of the foreskin is if the child is having sex or the doctor wants him to be having sex. Whether this is the doctor's conscious intention or not, the doctor is evaluating the child or infant as a potential sexual partner and exploring the child's sexuality. Forced retraction is pedophilia.

Doctors who forcibly retract children would likely protest that their conscious intention is not pedophilia. Yet, both critical social justice and psychology recognize that we are not always consciously aware of our motives. Critical social justice uses terms like "implicit bias" or "unconscious bias" to describe the ways people act from bias, prejudice, or socialization without consciously intending to do so.[315] Doctors do not need to have a conscious desire for pedophilia in order to harm children, only be socialized into a culture of systemic pedophilia. Both the culture of the medical system and the dominant hegemonic American culture are systemically pedophile. While many activists have speculated that there are doctors practicing circumcision for their own perverse desires,[316] the majority of doctors stated reason for performing circumcision or forcibly retracting children's genitals is that they see it as part of their job within the medical system. This excuse recognizes that doctors are acting on behalf of a larger system. Critical social justice would agree, but not accept that as an excuse. Though doctors are acting on behalf of a larger system, that does not excuse their responsibility for participating in that system. An individual pedophile can do great harm, but systemic pedophilia can do harm on an even greater scale. Critical social justice would suggest that we do not only look at the unconscious bias of individual doctors but how the system they participate in socializes them into those biases. The way that doctors are socialized into the culture of medicine, which is based in systemic pedophilia, is through medical school.

MEDICAL SCHOOL

Many doctors will protest that both circumcision and forced retraction are what they were taught to do in medical school. That doctors are taught to engage in pedophilia in medical school does not mean that harmfully touching children's genitals is not pedophilia. Rather, it means that systemic pedophilia is such a widespread problem in the medical system that it extends to medical schools. In other words, doctors are socialized into a culture of systemic pedophilia in medical school.

Medical schools are where future doctors are socialized in the culture of medicine. Socialization is the process by which people are trained into the norms and expectations of a culture.[317] Although socialization often refers to the way children are raised, it can also refer to how people are taught in educational systems. Socialization is a process that begins at birth and continues throughout our life.[318] The medical system is a subculture. Those within the medical system have their own jargon, norms, and cultural expectations. If the medical system has its own culture, then medical school is where people are socialized into that culture. By extension, if the medical system has a systemic pedophilia problem, in which the majority of doctors forcibly retract children's foreskins and regularly cut children's genitals, then the way medical school socializes doctors into that subculture must uphold and create norms that support systemic pedophilia.

How does medical school socialize future doctors into the medical system? The majority of doctors are required to perform a circumcision during their residency in medical school, and circumcision is treated as a teaching tool that the majority of interns are required to perform.[319] Circumcision is considered a simple procedure and "practice" for future surgeons and medical students. Multiple doctors have used the phrase "see one, do one, teach one" to describe how doctors are trained in circumcision.[320] This frames circumcision in terms of the needs of the doctor, the hospital, and the medical system rather than the needs of the child. The child being circumcised does not see himself as a "teaching tool." This framing reduces him to an object being used to satisfy the needs of the doctors and medical system. When children are reduced to an object whose genitals are used to satisfy the needs of adults, it is pedophilia. When done on an institutional and systemic level, it is institutional or systemic pedophilia. In this case, the entire medical system, including the medical schools, participate in this act of pedophilia by demanding that medical students cut children's genitals.

During residency, the doctor is told he must perform what doctors who hold authority over him tell him to do or potentially lose the investment of years of education and thousands of dollars spent in tuition. When a resident is told to circumcise a child, he is rarely given time to evaluate the morality of this action. The act is simply framed as a task he must do or risk disciplinary action. The act is not even presented as a moral dilemma but as a requirement the student must fulfill if he is to be initiated into the medical profession.

This demand mirrors the initiation ritual of gangs and criminal organizations. Gangs will frequently require a new member to commit a criminal act like killing someone in order to gain membership and status within the group. This gives the criminal organization dirt on their new member and binds him to the gang. The gang member does not want to see what he did as wrong or risk being turned in by his fellow criminals and will go along with whatever else the gang wants in the future. In the same way, doctors will be less likely to question circumcision later if forced to perform one as part of their training. Even medical students going into areas of medicine where they will not be required to perform circumcisions are often required to perform one during medical school, showing that this is being used for initiation and cultural reasons more than actual professional training. While most doctors will not need to perform a circumcision again, the system requires that all graduates of medical school are culpable in systemic pedophilia.

MEDICAL COMPLIANCE

Why do doctors agree to do circumcisions in medical school? The standard explanation would be deference to authority. There is a lot of psychological evidence that people are more willing to do something when an authority figure tells them to, the most famous of which is the Milgram experiment. In the Milgram experiment, an authority figure tells the subject to administer increasingly painful shocks to an unseen victim, until they eventually send enough to kill them.[321] These experiments were used to explain why seemingly normal people would do evil things when commanded to do so by an authority. Later researchers have heavily criticized these experiments, suggesting that the results were not as conclusive as Milgram suggested,[322] but even if we accept his findings at face value, a significant portion of his subjects refused to administer lethal shocks. In reality, almost no medical students refuse to do circumcisions.[323] Given that authority alone is not enough to produce such a high compliance rate, there must be another system producing such outcomes.

Looking at the compliance of medical students when asked to do a circumcision ignores the larger system they are acting in. The process of socialization that leads them to participate in an act of genital cutting and pedophilia did not start when they were in front of their newborn victim. It began the first day of their life and has been occurring throughout their schooling. Even the choice to go to medical school was based on a series of assumptions and beliefs due to their socialization. By the time they arrive in front of a child with a blade and clamp, the authority figure does not even need to be in the room to ensure compliance because he exists within the mind of the perpetrator as a series of unconscious assumptions and beliefs.

How does the medical system produce such a high compliance rate? First, by selecting their targets. Not everyone gets into medical school or chooses to become a doctor. In order to get into medical school, the student must show they will comply and submit to authority. They must first submit to authority for twelve years in the school system, four more years in college, and then submit to the application process of the medical school. There is a significant sunk cost to medical school. Once accepted, the student must pay hundreds of thousands of dollars in tuition. By the time a doctor asks them to cut children's genitals, they are convinced learning how to do this is a privileged they have earned, not a compliance test.

The high cost of medical education creates a cognitive bias to value what that education teaches. This cognitive bias is called "buy-in" in sales and relates to the sunk-cost fallacy. When people invest a significant amount into something, creating a high sunk cost, they value it more and are less likely to question it. Fraternities engage in hazing because they know people who have to work more for membership in a group will value it more. Cults do the same thing when they make followers give exorbitant amounts of money. If a false guru charges someone five dollars to become enlightened, the follower has less buy-in than if they are charged fifty-thousand for the same initiation. At a fifty-thousand dollar investment, most people would not want to admit that they were swindled. Admitting they were taken advantage of would mean losing the sunk cost of that time and money, and potentially also losing part of one's self-image.

Medical school often costs more than fifty thousand dollars and four years of someone's life. It grants a lifetime membership into the fraternity of medicine. At this price, students are less likely to question what they are being taught. When doctors scream at activists protesting circumcision that "your google search doesn't replace my medical degree!" they are often speaking from the cognitive dissonance created by sunk-cost and buy-in and do not want to face the psychological stress of discovering that the thousands of dollars and years of their life they spent on education left them unprepared to face the actual consequences of their actions and may have socialized them into systemic pedophilia.

When doctors dismiss activists' lived experience because they do not have a medical degree, they are also engaging in epistemic injustice. They are suggesting that their education about someone's experience has greater epistemic privilege than that person's actual lived experience. This epistemic injustice does not apply just to circumcision but to the entire medical system. In the past, doctors have used this privilege to position themselves as "experts" on issues around homosexuality, transgenderism, and intersex, often abusing their position to classify those forms of sexuality and identity as mental illness or impose "corrective" surgeries on unwilling victims, ranging from genital cutting to lobotomy. In actuality, a complete picture of any of those identities must include the lived experience of people who live that identity. Doctors are not experts on what it is like to be gay. Gay people are experts on what it is like to be gay. A doctor's medical degree does not replace a lifetime of lived experience. Likewise, doctors are not experts on circumcision. They might know how to cut children's genitals, but the actual impact of circumcision is only truly known by those affected by it. Just as the discourse about homosexuality, transgenderism, and intersex must be centered on the people who actually live those identities, the discourse around circumcision must also be centered on those affected and the survivors of infant genital cutting and systemic pedophilia.

To summarize, doctors are not experts on circumcision. Medical education socializes doctors into a cult-like mentality of privilege and bias, which costs them greatly, and so they will not question it later. They select compliance and frame it as an earned privilege. The medical system socializes people into a culture of pedophilia. When doctors claim their medical degree makes them greater experts than those speaking from lived experience, they are engaged in epistemic injustice in defense of systemic pedophilia.

MEDICAL GROOMING

How are those who are not doctors socialized into obeying the medical system? In her book *The Rape of Innocence: Female Genital Mutilation and Circumcision in the USA,* female circumcision survivor Patricia Robinett proposes that the phenomenon of children "playing doctor" is a form of acting out the experiences children have with doctors.[324] From an early age, children are told they must comply with doctors, even if it means to strip naked or to allow the doctor to touch parts of their body they would not normally allow others to touch. This is framed as normal to the child, and their feelings of embarrassment or discomfort are often dismissed. Feelings of pain are also often dismissed. Children frequently experience pain at the doctor's office, in the form of needles for vaccinations and other interventions, which they are forced to accept. Children are conditioned from a young age to ignore their feelings and allow the doctor to do what they want to their bodies. The adults frame the doctor's actions as being for the child's benefit, yet from the child's perspective, this is simply what the adult wants. No child naturally wants to have needles driven into their arm to draw blood, absent cultural conditioning or trauma of some kind. What Robinett proposes is that when children "play doctor," they are acting out the doctor's sexual exploring of their body on each other. Children who have been sexually abused exhibit the same behavior and may "act out" the sexual abuse they received from adults on other children. This repetition of the experience is a symptom of trauma. By acting out the experience, the child is able to show others what happened and can also assume the more powerful role of abuser, retaking power from the dominant position.

This forced sexual exploration is a form of systemic pedophilia, especially when done against the child's feelings. The medical gaze suggests that the doctor is focusing on a specific aspect of the child's body. This singular fragmented focus blinds the doctor and parents to the child's feelings while being explored. Yet when the doctor's exploration is being done, the child's focus is not fragmented. They still feel what any normal person would feel when forced to strip naked and allow a stranger to explore their body. These feelings might be confusing, which is why the child might later act them out to make sense of the experience.

Any medical intervention on a child has must be done with their feelings being taken into account. Forcing children to allow strangers to touch their bodies when their feelings are telling them "no" is a form of grooming and pedophilia. This conditions the child to ignore their feelings when adults touch their body against their will and accept the sexual exploration of adults as normal. Those in the medical system might say that this sexual exploration of children's bodies is necessary and that any discomfort the child feels is a secondary "side effect," but this is the medical gaze thinking. A critical reading would suggest that if the system consistently produces an outcome of an entire cultural meme of children sexually exploring each other by "playing doctor," this is an intentional outcome that the system must be held accountable for.

The purpose of grooming rituals is to prepare the victim for further abuse. The medical system's definition of a good patient is a passive child. The system intentionally infantilizes patients because they want a lifelong power dynamic where the doctor "adult" can take care of the patient "child," who passively accepts the doctor's treatment. A patient who questions the doctor or tries to engage as an equal participant is often considered a difficult patient. Yet adults engage as equals. This infantilization is similar to the racist dynamic the medical establishment has between white doctors and black Africans through circumcision campaigns. In both cases, the patient is framed as a child and the medical system as a parent. Then further cultural ideas about children are applied to the patient, such as "he [male children] should match his father" or "children should obey their parents."

The goal of the medical system and systemic pedophilia is the goal of any biological organism or system: its own reproduction. When mothers enter the medical system to give birth, they are in a vulnerable position. The medical system frames mothers as children who receive passive treatment from doctors, not as powerful birth-givers who can create life with their natural bodies. This child-like frame ensures the mother will submit the children to the doctor's desires, thereby ensuring the repetition of the abuse. If the mother is psychologically a subaltern-child, then she is vulnerable to abuse and in the same position as all others the medical system assaults. If she is in her power as a woman, mother, and person giving birth, then she will not allow her child to be separated or abused by the medical system.

The medical system requires parents to be disempowered. Like the socialization of medical school, this disempowerment does not start when the mother enters to give birth. It begins during the child's first encounter with the medical system during their own birth, continues through every medical visit, and culminates when the parents return to the medical system to give their child over to the same system that abused them. This abuse is hidden through a discourse of medicine that frames abuse as privilege. Just as med students pay for medical school, parents must pay large sums of money for the "opportunity" to have their child born in a hospital. Some places require hospital birth by law under the discourse of medicine. Yet, by definition, when someone forces themselves on another, this is assault.

The only way out of the systemic pedophilia of the medical system is its complete deconstruction and the avoidance of participation in this system. Even seemingly "innocent" parts of this system are designed to socialize parents, children, and future doctors into a culture of pedophilia and groom them to become abusers or abused. Pedophilia is not an aberration but ingrained into the culture of the medical system from our first encounters with the system to the way doctors are trained. Circumcision is not an isolated problem. American medicine has a culture based in systemic pedophilia.

CHAPTER 17
HUMAN CAPITAL

Hospital circumcision intersects with another system: capitalism. Circumcision is a multi-billion dollar industry.[325] There is also a secondary market of circumcision: tools, training, botched circumcision repair, and even the sale of the foreskin itself, as well as foreign markets, like the circumcision campaigns in Africa. Even if there were no other factors, money alone is reason enough for those engaged in systemic pedophilia to perpetuate and protect this abusive industry.

ORGAN TRAFFICKING

After a child is circumcised, their foreskin is frequently sold for profit to tissue banks.[326] Infant foreskin tissue is used in medical research, skin creams, and other commercial products. Young tissue contains stem cells, making it very valuable to the medical system. There is a word for when parts of people's bodies are sold against their will: organ trafficking. When people profit from pedophilia, there is another term that applies: sex trafficking. Circumcision is both. The medical system forcibly penetrates children, cuts part of their sex organs off, and then sells those severed genitals for profit.

A core idea of capitalism is private property. There is no property more private than your body. If you own your own body, then circumcision is a clear violation of your right to your own body. When doctors harvest and resell a child's foreskin, they are clearly engaging in organ theft, taking a part of the child that has economic value. In a purely capitalist system, one could not legally steal your property and sell it. However, capitalism intersects with other systems like rape culture, sexism, and systemic pedophilia. Pedophile culture views the child as an extension of the mother and so as her property rather than a full human being with individual rights. When this pedophile view intersects with capitalism, selling that "property," i.e. part of the child's body, becomes a possibility.

Many of the skin products infant foreskin is used in are marketed towards women. These products have been promoted by female celebrities as a way to reverse aging.[327] There is a gender-based violence to cutting off part of male genitals to use in products marketed towards women. These products are intended to increase female beauty and, by extension, female power and status. When women use these products, they are oppressing another gender in order to increase their power. Consuming parts of children, even through skincare products, could be considered a form of cannibalism, and many societies that practice cannibalism believe that consuming the flesh of another person grants the cannibal power in some form. This act also echos the historical legend of Elizabeth Báthory (1560-1614), a European queen thought to have bathed in the blood of virgins to preserve her youthful beauty.[328] There is a vampiric element to the modern consumption of infant genitals.

Very little data is available on this secondary market for infant foreskins despite the trafficking being so open that if you search "foreskin fibroblasts" online, you can find vials of infant genitals for sale.[329] While researching, I attempted to contact someone whom I was told made over seven hundred thousand dollars a year running a company that resold infant foreskins and employed over a dozen people. Even with the promise of anonymity, he would not speak to me. Given that he was making nearly a million a year and employed nearly two dozen people, I'm certain his company must have generated several million a year just to afford their staff while serving only a small region of the country. It was one among many, part of a silent unexamined lucrative organ trafficking industry.

The money involved in circumcision is so great, many have theorized it is the primary reason circumcision continues. Indeed, more research is required here. When activists try to gather information on this industry, hospitals often hide behind "doctor-patient confidentiality," despite the fact the child signed no medical forms and is not even seen as the primary patient by the medical industry. Plus, the sale of infant sex organs has nothing to do with the patient and everything to do with the profit of the medical system. "Doctor-patient confidentiality" is a legal discourse the medical system uses to maintain power. They will happily share your medical information with insurance companies, pharmacies, and other nodes of the medical system, but they will not share information with people who might threaten the systemic power of that system. This information could probably only be acquired through deep investigative work or a lawsuit, both of which require money themselves.

FINANCIAL VALUES

In a capitalist society, money is a form of power. However, money is the most obviously visible power. Critical theory would suggest that power is often diffused and hidden. The money flowing through circumcision is significant, and perhaps even larger than activists have been able to document, but the money the medical system makes overall is considerably greater. Given the ethical and legal risks of genital cutting, one would think that it makes sense for the medical system from a business perspective to avoid this industry. Pedophile-apologists in the medical system claim that touching children's genitals is just part of healthcare. However, fitness, diet, and health advice are all also multi-million dollar industries. There is more research showing that healthy eating and exercising improves your health than any singular medication. If the medical system was in the business of doing things just because they are "healthy," then hospitals would be in the diet and fitness business as well. The fact they are not shows there is another hidden power is driving their decisions.

How people use their money shows what they value. Cutting an infant's body does not benefit the child but is perceived as valuable by those involved in the system. In a society with different values, one might use money to keep the child whole and healthy. If people valued children, they might even invest money in making sure the birth was a happy experience for the person being born. However, when adults see themselves as dominant, money is exchanged only for the pleasure of the dominant class. In a society where children are invisible and subaltern, the feelings and emotions of the child are not even considered. If an entire industry existed around "happy birth," in which professionals sold themselves as able to make children happy, it would reveal a certain system of values. The fact an entire industry exists around the genital cutting of children reveals a different set of values. The medical system values the infant's body more when it is severed and sold.

When people suggest that circumcision is just about money, they ignore the fact that money is a signifier. The fact that people can make money cutting children's genitals does not mean that genital cutting is about the money, but that people with economic power value cutting children's genitals. Money alone cannot explain the industry. There must be a set of beliefs and values to justify that money. If one were to apply this idea that merely because a system makes money it is about the money to other social justice issues, they would assume that slavery was about the money, and miss the entire system of racism. Racism was the value system that made slavery possible. Likewise, the value system that justifies cutting children is systemic pedophilia.

Yet even if it were just about the money: Money is a form of pleasure, too. When adult pleasure is derived from children's genitals, it is pedophilia. Making money from circumcision is a form of systemic pedophilia. Given the scale of systemic pedophilia, the medical system must make money to continue at scale. Once money is involved, there is an incentive to expand to new markets. The act of pedophilia itself creates subaltern fragmentations which the medical system can exploit later. These are symbiotic systems, in which pedophilia expands the power of the medical system and makes money, which can be used to create more power. The reason these problems are systemic and intersectional is that there is no one system or cause that, if removed, would solve the entire system. Removing money would cripple the system, but the system is pedophilia, not capital alone.

CIRCUMCISION COMPLICATIONS

Circumcision generates profit for the medical system by opening up a secondary market of fixing the complications and problems due to circumcision. The obvious "cure" to botched circumcisions – that of simply ending circumcision as a practice – is rejected in favor of a solution that expands the power of the medical system but have no chance of repairing the foreskin nor the damage done by systemic pedophilia.

America is a massive market for both erectile dysfunction medication[330] and personal lubricants.[331] While the medical system will claim that there is no link between sexual dysfunction and circumcision, societies that practice infant circumcision consistently produce sexual dysfunction as an outcome. Circumcision dries out the penis by removing the naturally self-lubricating foreskin. If you are a circumcised man who needs lube to have sex, this is often the result of circumcision. Once the penis is circumcised, it builds up rough keratin where there was once smooth mucosal tissue.[332] Over time, this rough covering on the head of the penis reduces sensation, which can cause erectile dysfunction. While erectile dysfunction medication and lube are separate industries, from a systemic view these are part of the profit generated by circumcision. Neither entirely fixes the sexual problems caused by circumcision, but as problematic solutions they expand the medical industry into the discourse of sexuality. Lubricants are considered medical aids and must be FDA approved in the United States, making them part of the same system.

If we include the emotional outcomes of circumcision, therapy and psycho-active pharmaceuticals could also be considered parts of systemic pedophilia insofar as they are used to medicate or "fix" emotional issues that are due to childhood wounding, rather than end the system producing that wounding. Again, the medical system might argue that these are just about "health," but if the discourse does not include fixing the underlying causes of psychological problems, like ending childhood trauma, then this is a false discourse intended to serve another power. In the case of the pharma industry, the discourse is intended to sell more medication and expand the power of the medical system, not to fix psychological problems. These systems compound. Someone who has sexual problems might experience psychological problems as a result of it. If the medical system can sell that person a pill rather than fix the underlying psychological problem, they maintain both markets. If they can mark the child in infancy in a way that produces sexual or psychological problems, they create a customer for both markets later. Creating and fixing the problems is more profitable than maintaining good health.

This is true even immediately after the circumcision. There is an entire secondary market for fixing botched circumcisions.[333] Many urologists make their entire living doing this.[334] The circumcision is performed by a medical student, intern, or another low person in the hierarchy, with no follow-up.[335] When these circumcisions result in uneven outcomes or complications, the medical system can then charge more to fix them. Some in the medical system have even admitted that fixing botched circumcisions is actually more profitable than doing them right the first time. James Synder, former president of the Virginia Pediatric Urological Association, said that about ten percent of the boys who came through his practice had botched circumcisions in some way.[336] Multiple other urologists and doctors have given me similar estimates. The medical industry does not collect long-term data on circumcisions, so we have only the estimates of those in the system, an intentional omission and hermeneutical injustice.[337] Botches can include uneven circumcisions that bend to one side, skin tags, chunks missing from the head of the penis, all of the shaft skin being removed, or even the entire destruction of the penis. From the perspective of the child or the patient, this makes no sense. No reasonable person would want permanent genital surgery that has a ten percent chance of failure. From the perspective of the medical system, this allows them to extract greater value from the resource of children. The doctor gets to train their students on living patients, which serves as an initiation ritual into systemic pedophilia for new members of the system. They save money by using cheaper labor. They make money on botched repairs if the procedure goes wrong. Greater damage also increases the revenue of ancillary markets such as erectile dysfunction medication and psychological pharmaceuticals.

On adults, permanent life-altering surgery is usually performed by a specialist. The patient receives considerable follow-up to ensure the intervention had its intended outcome. By contrast, infant circumcision is performed by medical students or interns with no follow-up. The use of medical students or interns shows that this procedure is performed for the benefit of the system and adults, not the patient. Someone engaged in organ trafficking would not "follow-up" with someone they removed organs from. There is no need. They know harm has been done, but they've got the goods. The harm is not a "side effect." Circumcision is done badly on purpose. If botches are a consistent outcome of the medical system, and the medical system knows about this, then we can assume that botches are an intended outcome of the medical system. The discourse that the medical system does not intend for bad outcomes is false and only serves to protect against legal liability. If the goal was to do circumcision well, the medical system would contribute value, i.e. money, towards studying the long-term outcomes.

MONEY LEGITIMIZES

The idea that there is inherent value in things that cost a lot of money is part of the discourse around money. Charging high prices is a way marketers signal that their goods are "luxury" even when they are manufactured for pennies in overseas sweatshops. The medical industry does this too, marking up products used in the hospital for significantly more than one would pay in any other setting. This frames what the medical system provides as valuable, even if their actions destroy true value, reduce function, or actually harm the health of the person they are working on.

Cost does not equate to value. Surgery to fix a problem caused by poor lifestyle habits is far more expensive than eating healthy or exercising regularly. Most people would prefer to avoid surgery, despite it being more expensive and therefore framed as more "valuable" in a monetary discourse, because eating healthy and exercising better serves the long-term function of making you healthy than surgery, even if surgery costs more. Actual function and perceived value are different. Perceived value is socially constructed, and circumcision is performed due to socially constructed value. Circumcision is not necessary, and most in the medical system readily admit this. It reduces the sexual function of the penis. The perceived value of circumcision is cultural and based in subjective and socially constructed values. These values are centered in the desires and pleasures of adults, not the subaltern experience of the child. What makes these values pedophile is that adults are willing to touch and cut children's genitals to fulfill their own adult pleasures. In this system, money serves as both a store of socially-constructed value, an enabler of systemic pedophilia, and a signifier for perceived value. It reveals the value of those involved, allows the system to keep going by funding it and making it profitable, and signals to potential buyers that genital cutting has value.

Money also serves as a legitimizing discourse. If someone were to stand on a street corner offering "free circumcisions," you would likely find them suspect and assume they might have a nefarious motive, e.g. wanting to hurt children's genitals. The same person wearing a white lab coat in a hospital setting charging a thousand dollars to medical insurance to do exactly the same thing appears more legitimate. This legitimacy is conferred by multiple discourses and power/knowledge systems, but money is one of them. If a doctor was to offer it "for free" there might also be suspicion because doctors do not usually offer things for free, and "you get what you pay for" as the saying goes. The same service offered for five thousand dollars might be perceived as very good, because money signifies value, so a greater price implies even greater value. Leaving your child intact is free, but taking them to the doctor and cutting off parts of their penis costs money. Which has the greater perceived cultural value? Obviously, we should not be charged to keep the bodies we are born with. However, the fact that circumcision costs money and being intact does not creates a perceived value of circumcision being the more valuable option. Even taking the child into a well-baby visit where they might be forcibly-retracted and have their foreskin damaged by a pedophile-curious doctor is expensive. The high prices of the medical system are not just there to make money. They are part of a discourse intended to legitimatize touching children's genitals.

MONETARY THEORY

Why do things which have innate value, like raising a child and leaving him intact, not have economic value, while things which cause harm, like mutilating children's genitals or forcibly retracting healthy children, are part of multi-billion dollar industries? If money is a store of value, shouldn't it match our actual values? The idea that money is a store of value is part of a discourse. Money does not represent actual value, but a system of values. While at one point money might have represented true value, it has now become a simulacra, a post-modern system of symbols, entirely detached from reality. Philosopher Jean Baudrillard, who coined the word simulacra, described the process by which a symbol becomes simulacra in four stages.[338] First, the symbol is a faithful image or copy. At one point, paper currency was based on the gold standard, which meant each dollar represented a certain amount of gold, making the currency a faithful representation of precious metals. One could argue that gold itself was a symbol, yet it was at least a real and physically scarce resource. Then, the symbol becomes an unfaithful copy. When money no longer represented gold, it was still used to represent a certain amount of product or labor. We exchange goods or services for money. However, in the third stage, the symbol pretends to be a faithful copy, yet has no original. The value of fiat currency is entirely subjective. There is no original which it represents. Even stocks, which pretend to represent ownership or a portion of a company, have no real object they can be translated back into. You cannot take the shares of a company, walk into their offices, and demand to claim a percentage of their company equivalent to the value of their stock. The fourth stage, which is where we are now, is a simulacrum, where the symbol has no relationship to reality whatsoever. What reality do Wall Street financial products represent in reality? The best investments often involve changing money into other forms of money, working purely on the symbolic level while creating no real value in physical reality.

The monetary system disconnects value from values. It began as a symbol of value but now constitutes its own system of symbols and power/knowledge system. Money was post-modern long before culture ever was. When working at a symbolic level, it becomes possible to hide the destruction of real value by trading symbolic value for that real value. For example, during the COVID-19 epidemic, it became illegal for many businesses providing real value to operate. In response to the massive economic destruction of COVID-19 shutdowns, the American government printed over two trillion dollars in bailouts.[339] This money did not represent real value. Businesses were legally prevented from creating real value. However, this bailout allowed America to manipulate the symbols of value in a way that benefited those in power and maintain a symbolic discourse of value. When money becomes detached from real value, it becomes impossible for that system to acknowledge inherent value. A system based on fiat currency or simulacra value only values symbolically represented value. Your art, goods, and services are only valuable in a monetary system once you translate your work into the symbol of money. Even if everyone who sees your painting bursts into tears at its beauty and considers it the most valuable artistic experience of their life, the painting has no monetary "value" until you can convert it into the symbolic representation of value known as money, which itself represents nothing real, but is simply a simulacra or symbol of value. One can navigate this symbolic system if one understands linguistic communication. However, there is one group that cannot translate their inherent value into symbols: children.

INHERENT VALUE

In a capitalist system, people have no inherent value. They are only valuable for what they produce or own. You do not get money for nothing. You get money for your work or ownership. While this system may work for some adults, it completely disenfranchises children who have no ability to produce and cannot legally own property. A newborn infant only consumes resources. He cannot create. Yet, most human beings on a primal level understand that children are inherently valuable. They might be the most valuable thing in the world. Yet our economic system does not reflect this.

Children cost money and provide little economic value in return. For most people, children are an investment that requires the parents to spend money on the child for the first eighteen years or so of their life. While this can be done purely for the benefit of the child or the joy of raising another human being, many adults enter parenting with a set of conscious or unconscious expectations about what they want to get from their children. These unspoken expectations create a transactional relationship with the child in which adults expect certain behaviors in return for support. This transactional relationship treats the child not as an independent person who might have their own unique desires and way of seeing the world, but as a resource the adults can extract value from by molding it according to their own expectations. In earlier times, children were expected to work, exchanging physical labor for basic sustenance. This discourse made power naked and open. Now, children must exchange emotional labor for material support and connection with that parent. Rather than working in fields or factories, he works on himself to conform to social expectations. This discourse better obscures power, framing medical procedures, school, and the other activities as beneficial for the good of the child rather than as labor designed to meet adult desires.

There are entire industries that manufacture and propagandize these discourses. The school system, the medical system, and other systems engaged in childhood abuse all use the discourse that their work benefits children despite being clearly centered in adult desires. If these systems become large enough, they become hegemonic. Parents do not need to be told to have their children in a hospital or send them to school, because these are unquestioned cultural assumptions. This cultural hegemony is reinforced through media, which frames these systems as the natural backdrop for stories about children and families. These industries offer problematic solutions for children because any solution to a child's problems must be based in the needs of the child. These systems can never be based in the needs of the child because children are not the "buyers." The buyer is the person who decides. Children do not make decisions about their own medical care or schooling. Parents and the state do.

Ideally, parents make decisions for their children based in the child's actual needs, yet we all know how rarely this happens. Parents face multiple challenges when pursuing their children's true needs. First, they are propagandized by culturally hegemonic systems engaged in child abuse and systemic pedophilia. No individual parent can match the propaganda power of the medical system, educational system, media, government, etc. That any parent questions these powers and makes better decisions is a miracle when we compare their difference in power. Second, parents have their own fragmentations. Any parent that grew up in these systems likely experienced their own abuses and may have aspects of their psyche still trapped in the subaltern state of childhood. At scale, these abuses produce colonialism, racism, and all other systems of oppression. On an individual level, they produce bad parenting and decisions based in trauma rather than the true needs of the child. In order to make better choices, parents must integrate their own childhood experiences such that they no longer feel the need to repeat their own trauma on children and reproduce the same abusive system they were raised in. Third, parents must be prepared to face the state. Parents are not the only decision-makers when it comes to children. Many states have laws around home birth and homeschooling which make these difficult or even illegal. Lastly, parents participate in an economic system that does not recognize their value as parents. Parents receive money when they leave the home and contribute monetary value to other adults, but often do not receive the same compensation when they stay home and contribute real value to their children's lives. Yet which is more valuable, a worker spending a few more hours in the office manipulating symbols or a parent who is present during your childhood? We all recognize the inherent value of parents, but our economic system does not reflect this.

These challenges can be met, but they require a great deal from individual parents. One of the tenants of critical theory is that people are not merely individuals but participate in systems. While high agency parents can and should meet these challenges, social justice would suggest that we create systemic changes so that all children can be valued for who they are. What system would actually value families over capital?

BEYOND CAPITAL

The classic Marxist critique of capitalism is that capitalism exploits the value created by workers for a ruling class. The critique I am making here is that capitalism defines value through the discourse of money, framing the actual value of human beings as worthless, and the destruction of that value as profitable. The destruction of the inherent value of children, families, and human bodies creates a minuscule amount of socially constructed value for the medical industry in the form of money, and for the adults who consume the flesh of children, through skincare treatments and biotech uses. It creates the same kind of value generated by a cow when it is slaughtered for meat. Children are not the exploited labor on the factory farm of capitalism. They are the cattle. This slaughter of children extends to their bodies through genital cutting and medical interventions, their hearts through the separation from their mothers through hospital birth and economic demands which necessitate mothers work rather than raise children, and their minds in compulsory government schooling, which treats children as a product to be shaped and delivered to future employers. It isn't that capitalism distributes capital unequally. It's that the discourse of capital itself turns people into symbols that can be manipulated and destroyed for profit. On the issue of genital cutting, capitalism is not merely exploiting labor. It is carving up children and selling their body parts.

Since money is a discourse, it rewards those who can articulate their value through that discourse. Children are subaltern, so can never articulate their value in any discourse because they lack language. They will always be dependent on adults to recognize their inherent value and provide for them. Everyone is a Marxist in their own family. From each (adult) according to their ability to each (child) according to their needs. Managerial systems, like hospitals, schools, daycares, etc. can never value children like family because they are bound to the discourse of capital and "policy." The mistake of most political theorists is to assume that the solution to bad systems, discourse, and policy is better systems, discourse, and policy when the attempt to replace human connection with systems, discourse, and policy is the problem itself. Human connections are not driven by "policy," but relationships. No policy or system could replace a mother's bond with her child, or her ability to instinctually tune into the child's needs through that connection. This means that where capital and connection conflict, capital must be restricted, and there are spheres of life that must be prohibited from becoming transactional so they remain relational.

One of Karl Marx's primary ideas was his theory of alienation. When people are separated into social classes, Marx suggested that people become alienated from each other, their own labor, and even aspects of their own nature.[340] This alienation has gone so far that money itself has become alienated from value, detached from what we actually create to become its own system of symbols. Value has been separated from values. In order to integrate and end this alienation, we must shift our economic system to recognize the inherent value in families and children, and place that value above capital. While some might protest that we cannot create a system that recognizes the inherent value of families and children because wealth should be based in the value you create, keep in mind that our current monetary system is not based in value at all. It is a series of symbols entirely detached from any real representation. During the COVID-19 bailouts, the government created two trillion dollars out of thin air and gave the majority to major corporations. Did these corporations create more real value during the shutdown? Or were they just better at manipulating symbolic communication in the legal and monetary system to their advantage? Money is a social construction. As a social construction, it contains certain values. The social construction of money can be deconstructed using the tools of critical theory, the same way theory has deconstructed race, gender, and other social systems. This system, like all social systems, must be changed to recognize the inherent value of children since the current system mutilates and oppresses them while denying them the ability to articulate their inherent value through the epistemic violence of demanding children articulate that value in adult economic language. This system must be changed to reflect the inherent value of children.

Though fully envisioning a new monetary system is beyond the scope of this book, any change in society begins with a change in consciousness. Before we can know what a new system might look like, we must first shift our values to those we wish the system to reflect. This change can begin on an individual level by inherently valuing children rather than seeing them as a resource to be exploited. When parents value children for what they produce for the parent, there will be industries that arise to extract this value. If parents define value on their terms rather than the child's reality, exploitation can occur unconsciously and unintentionally. A child might need love and connection, but the parent takes pleasure in order and believes the child needs discipline. In this scenario, a parent might buy the problematic solution of "discipline" from a third party or industry. When discipline fails to solve the problem because the perceived problem comes from the child needing love or connection which no amount of discipline could ever provide, the parents will buy more of their failed solution, rather than address the real underlying issue. This creates a negative feedback loop in which entire industries rise to create problematic solutions. Once these industries are self-sustaining, they become systemic and will seek to expand their power. Drugging naturally precocious children with ADHD medication, locking them in government buildings to "learn" for eight hours a day, or cutting off parts of their genitals are all symptoms of problematic solutions. The medical system is the most exploitive of these solutions, having found a way to exploit children by selling their organs. This human trafficking is a way for children to produce "value" in an economic system in which they are not inherently valued, even by their own parents.

Alienation does not just occur through money. When adults see children as a separate class, rather than part of a whole, they can become alienated even from their own children. Children become a product that we mold to meet our adult expectations and pleasures rather than people with their own unique needs and ways of seeing the world. Reconnecting to children rather than seeing them as human capital is the beginning of the consciousness necessary to end this abusive system. This might require reconnecting to our own disconnected subaltern aspects, still playing out childhood patterns. It will require seeing the true value of children rather than the economic value the medical system extracts from them and the perceived value of their created problems. It might even require shifting our monetary system and our values around money towards the funding of real solutions that might seem more radical but will actually solve the problem. Americans pour billions of dollars into a medical system that makes their children less healthy and into an educational system that makes them less aware. When you pay into a system engaged in systemic pedophilia, even for unrelated services, you are supporting that system. Being antipedophile will require critically examining where you participate in systems engaged in child abuse and systemic pedophilia, and shifting your support to those engaged in Children's Justice. If we value our children, our economic system should reflect it.

CHAPTER 18
FRAGILE PUSHBACK

Why do people often become defensive or angry when presented with the truth about circumcision? Critical social justice has a term for this defensive reaction: fragility. Fragility describes the defensive behavior dominant groups engage in when asked to examine the systems they perpetuate.[341] This behavior allows these groups to avoid change and maintain the status quo.

PEDOPHILE FRAGILITY

One of the most popular texts of critical race theory, *White Fragility: Why It's So Hard for White People to Talk About Racism* by Robin DiAngelo, explores this phenomenon in the context of white people's reaction to being asked to examine their role in engaging in and perpetuating racist systems. In the introduction, DiAngelo says that in her early work as a diversity trainer she was "taken aback by how angry and defensive so many white people became at the suggestion they were connected to racism in any way."[342] Over time, she began to notice a consistent pattern to these responses. Robin DiAngelo's experience resonated with me. As someone who has been speaking on the issue of circumcision for nearly a decade, I have noticed a similar pattern of responses from people confronted with the issue of genital cutting. Other activists working on the issue of circumcision have noted a similar fragility when they question circumcision or bring up the possibility that cutting children's genitals might be harmful. People become angry, defensive, and tense. Men feel the need to blurt out "I'm fine with my circumcision," when no one asked them about their genitals. Women will interject that "male circumcision is nothing like female genital cutting." Parents of circumcised children will begin defending the practice as their "parental choice." Activists are often accused of being secret Nazis, having an obsession with children's genitals, or harboring strange sexual fetishes all for suggesting that cutting off children's body parts might be morally wrong. All of these reactions are a form of fragility that we could call pedophile fragility.

Why do those engaged in systemic pedophilia become so fragile when asked to examine their actions or beliefs? When discussing false consciousness, we said that rationalizations and false consciousness are ways people protect themselves from the psychological pain of oppression. If false consciousness is how the oppressed protect themselves from psychological pain, then fragility is how the oppressor psychologically protects themselves. Most people do not want to see themselves as bad or doing harm. Examining our role in perpetuating harm threatens this self-image. It also threatens any aspect of someone's identity that benefits from causing harm or that extracts pleasure from children's genitals. For example, if a doctor derives the pleasures of wealth and prestige from touching children's genitals, critically examining his actions will threaten this form of pedophilia. Likewise, if a Jewish person derives religious or identity pleasure from touching children's genitals, he faces the same potential identity threat. To preserve both this pedophile pleasure and their self-image, pedophiles will engage in a series of defensive responses known as fragility.

Pedophile fragility usually centers on some aspect of the person they feel is under attack. For example, a circumcised man in false consciousness might blurt out that his penis "works fine" and begin to argue that circumcision has not harmed his sexual experience when no one was discussing his personal sexuality or brought it up in the conversation. A coerced mother whose children were circumcised might start arguing that her children are "none of your business" when you were not speaking about her children, but discussing your own experience with circumcision. If you listen to what pedophile-apologists are defensive of, they will reveal what they feel is under attack. This fragility is often based in their mental and emotional issues, not what the person speaking to them actually said. One does not need to say anything that would actually imply an emotional or intellectual attack on pedophile-apologists for them to react as if they were attacked.

Since pedophile-apologists feel they are under attack when you attempt to set boundaries that might prevent them from having access to children's bodies, pedophile fragility often takes the form of DARVO, a common strategy of abusers. DARVO is an acronym that stands for Deny the abuse ever took place, then Attack the victim for attempting to hold the abuser accountable; then they will lie and claim that they, the abuser, are the real victim in the situation, thus Reversing the Victim and Offender.[343] In the context of circumcision, this fragility will take the form of denying the harm of circumcision and then attacking the person speaking out against it. This attack often frames the survivor as somehow "attacking" the perpetrators by speaking out about their harm or experience of victimization. Usually, such attacks are based either on the part of the perpetrator they feel is under attack or the greatest vulnerability they see in the victim. For example, a pedophile-apologist might attack a survivor of genital cutting by calling them "antisemitic" when the survivor is speaking about medical circumcision rather than anything related to Jewish people. Even Jewish survivors of genital cutting have been attacked as "antisemitic" by non-Jewish perpetrators if the perpetrator feels this label can be used to marginalize the survivor and protect their own pedophile fragility.[344] The label "antisemite" might also be chosen if the fragile pedophile-apologist is Jewish and feels questioning circumcision threatens their Jewish identity. If you want to know what aspect of a pedophile's identity is fragile or feels threatened, look at where they attack their victims. This attack will often take the form of reading motives into the activist's intentions. For example, it is very common for pedophile-apologists to accuse those questioning circumcision of being "obsessed" with children's genitals or project their own pedophilia onto those who question touching children or cutting off parts of their bodies. A system that routinely touches children's genitals and cuts parts of their bodies off is clearly more obsessed with pedophilia than activists and victims who say they should leave children alone. This projection is a form of pedophile fragility, an example of DARVO, and a way perpetrators protect their own harmful behavior. What they project is where they are fragile.

EPISTEMIC PUSHBACK

Those engaged in systemic pedophilia or benefiting from adult privilege often avoid any discussion of circumcision or the ways in which children and the men they become are harmed. When the subject does come up, they will demand greater levels of proof than they would for any similar act of genital cutting or touching children's genitals. When activists offer proof, they will deny the legitimacy of the proof or remain willfully ignorant of the new information they are being presented with. For example, I have even seen pedophile-apologists exclaim that they've never heard of any man being upset about their circumcision at the very moment when there is a man standing right in front of them telling them he is upset about his circumcision. These tactics are a form of epistemic injustice known as privilege-preserving epistemic pushback.

Privilege-preserving epistemic pushback is "a family of cognitive, affective, nonverbal, and discursive tactics that are used habitually to avoid engaging ideas that threaten us."[345] Privilege-preserving epistemic pushback often involves willful ignorance. Willful ignorance is when someone does not know something, does not want to know, and deliberately avoids knowing.[346] If we become aware of our privilege or the ways we participate in oppressive systems, that privilege and the perceived benefits of oppressing might be threatened. In order to preserve this privilege, people will engage in epistemic injustice and deny new information that might cause them to question their privilege or pretend to be unable to understand such information. For example, one tactic I've seen members of the medical field engage in when presented with the idea that circumcision is harmful is to ask "do you have a study to back that up?" This question will arise even when the person is presenting personal testimony or offering information that would not usually require a peer-reviewed study or fit into the medical paradigm. This demand for greater proof beyond what would be required for any other form of genital cutting or similar practice on children is a form of privilege-preserving epistemic pushback. If someone said they felt harmed by female genital cutting or merely having their genitals touched against their will by an adult as a minor, no one would demand an academic study justifying their feelings. At the same time, doctors do not demand that parents who want to circumcise for cultural or emotional reasons present them with academic studies before they will carry out genital cutting. There is an epistemic injustice in requiring massive empirical proof for one set of ideas while allowing another to coast on mere excuses like "I think it looks better" or "it's my culture." When presented with peer-reviewed studies showing the harm of circumcision, pedophile-apologists in the medical system will often exclaim "well, I've never heard of that study!" Yet, they did hear about that study just in that moment. They could easily look it up and confirm what they were told. Their refusal to engage with the study is a form of willful ignorance that could be considered privilege-preserving epistemic pushback. If they become emotionally defensive, angry, or fall silent, they are engaging in pedophile fragility. If they accuse the other person of attacking them by presenting new information, they are engaged in DARVO, a strategy of abusers.

These concepts are closely related, as they are all strategies to maintain the status quo. One could think of fragility as describing the emotional and social defensive strategies, privilege-preserving epistemic pushback as describing the intellectual strategies of epistemic injustice, and willful ignorance as the will to not know and not wanting to know. Emotions, intellect, and will all work in different ways to preserve the status quo and avoid the pain of realization.

Doctors are not so stupid that they cannot understand the arguments against circumcision. Rather, they are too fragile to understand them. As adults, doctors are separate from both the pain of children and the subaltern aspects of their own psyche. Doctors have been socialized into an unconscious system of internalized dominance that places adults above children. In the medical system, they are socialized further into an internalized dominance that places doctors even higher above those without advanced degrees and confers a perceived status. As the beneficiaries of systemic pedophilia, doctors are insulated from the harm they perpetuate. Since they do not have to deal directly with the negative consequences of their actions, the slightest suggestion that their engagement with the subaltern produces pedophile stress that is too great for many to handle.[347] To avoid this pedophile stress, many engage fragility and privilege preserving epistemic pushback in order to maintain willful ignorance.

Activists working on the issue of circumcision often put the entire burden of communication on themselves. They ask how they can be more persuasive, better communicators, or get those in the medical system to see their pain. Many are frustrated by the medical establishment's refusal to acknowledge their perspective. While activists can do more to articulate their message, critical theory suggests that the hearer also has a responsibility in communication. Communication requires the participation of both parties. If one is engaged in willful ignorance, no communication is possible until the defensive strategies of the oppressive group are addressed. Rather than continuing to try to find a "better argument" against systemic pedophilia, critical theory suggests that we draw attention to the pedophile fragility of those engaged in the medical system and bring hermeneutic justice to these defensive strategies by naming them when pedophile-apologists engage in them.

ADULT PRESENCE

Fragility is not merely limited to the medical system but extends to all who participate in systemic pedophilia. This includes parents, religious people who practice genital cutting, men affected by genital cutting, partners of circumcised men, and anyone who wishes to maintain the pedophile comfort of willful ignorance. The greatest obstacle to true consciousness around the issue of systemic pedophilia is pedophile fragility. In her work, Robin DiAngelo suggests we must develop stamina to be with the discomfort of facing issues of inequality. Since she focuses on racial issues, she calls this racial stamina,[348] but on children's issues, we could call it adult stamina. However, the word stamina sometimes implies discomfort.

We could also call this adult presence since this process does not always have to be painful. Even though there might be an initial pain of realization, the enduring pain of false consciousness is greater. Adult presence is the ability to be present with the discomfort of confronting our own adult privilege and our participation in systems that perpetuate pedophilia. In the context of this issue, we could also extend this to include the presence required to be with and integrate our own subaltern childhood aspects and the parts of us still playing out oppressive power dynamics learned in childhood. When pedophile-apologists engage in fragile defensive strategies, they are not being present with us or their own subaltern aspects but instead experiencing pedophile stress.

One of the most common childhood patterns people are socialized into is the need to be "good". As children, most people do not receive love or validation unless they conform to the standard of a "good person" defined by their parents and culture. Fields that confer goodness, such as medicine, attract those with a subaltern childhood aspect still playing out this emotional pattern. When doctors describe themselves as "heroes" who are "saving lives," they are playing out this subaltern childhood pattern of seeking approval by conforming the dominant cultural definitions of a "good person." Part of the reason people become fragile when confronted with their role in oppressive systems is that they feel that if they are not a "good person," they will not be loved or get their needs met. However, critical theory is looking at systems, not people. It is possible for a person to identify as a "good person" while participating in systems that perpetuate oppression. This need to be good often produces a fragile reaction that prevents people from looking at the roles they play. In short, the need to be good produces some very bad behavior.

Many critical social justice activists consider "good whites" and those who say they are "not racist" to be the worst racists, because they refuse to look at the role they play in racist systems in order to protect their "good" identity. There is an entire book describing this phenomenon called *Being Good, Being White: White Complicity, White Moral Responsibility, and Social Justice Pedagogy*.[349] Robin DiAngelo says "I believe that white progressives cause the most daily damage to people of color."[350] Ibram X. Kendi suggests that instead of being "not racist" we should strive to be antiracist, which means critically examining the ways we participate in racist systems.[351] Likewise, the need to be "good" often prevents people from examining the ways they participate in systems that harm children. People wish to be "good parents," "good doctors," "good people," etc. But when confronted with the ways they participate in systemic pedophilia, many become defensive and fragile. This prevents people from actually doing good by withdrawing their support from systemic pedophilia and redirecting their energy towards Children's Justice. It is not enough to be "not a pedophile." We must be actively antipedophile. Most people involved in systemic pedophilia would protest that they are not pedophiles. They might say that they are not attracted to children. This excuse centers pedophilia on the desires of adults and is itself a form of pedophile apology. The idea that what determines whether or not something is pedophilia is adult pleasure is a pedophile idea. What determines whether or not something is pedophilia is if the child is harmed or violated. When someone says they are "not a pedophile" with these excuses they engaged in pedophile fragility.

Developing adult presence requires practice. We must be willing to move beyond this childhood need to be a "good person" for social acceptance and look not just at our own self-image, but at how our actions impact the world. Even if we believe we are a "good person" and have no conscious negative intentions, it is still possible to be complicit in systems that harm others. Take for example a single woman with no children. She may not think she is engaged in systemic pedophilia, but what if she goes to an obstetrician who practices circumcision? Isn't giving money to someone who forcibly penetrates children and cuts their genitals participation in systemic pedophilia? This person is funding a pedophile. Being antipedophile would mean leaving this practice and going to a practitioner who is not engaged in systemic pedophilia and not connected to institutions that are engaged in systemic pedophilia.

If this sounds difficult, ask why. If a social justice activist asked you not to give money to racists or people who participate in hate crimes, would you consider this a reasonable request? Isn't it also a reasonable request to also ask people not to give money to pedophiles? In the context of an obstetrics visit, a woman is literally paying a pedophile to inspect the inside of her vagina. If being asked not to pay pedophiles to examine your genitals produces a fragile or defensive response, then there is some critical work to do. If being antipedophile sounds difficult, it is because we live in a pedophile society. Systemic pedophilia is everywhere. It is there at our birth. It is in families, the school system, the doctor's office, and in every aspect of how we treat children. It carries into adult relationships, sexuality, and institutions. It is literally carved into children's bodies. Avoiding participating in this system will require a conscious commitment to Children's Justice.

BREAKING FRAGILITY

What do we do about those who refuse to look at the role they play in systemic pedophilia? The medical system has the capacity to engage in fragility, privilege preserving epistemic pushback, and willful ignorance on a systemic level. The pedophile stress the system experiences could be greater since they perceive a threat not just to their privilege but their institutional power. As a consequence, they might engage in defensive strategies on a greater level than any individual could.

Critical social justice would suggest that when someone refuses to look at the systems they participate in, we name this fragility and call it out when we see it. When people truly care about justice, they welcome the opportunity to critically examine the systems they participate in. The medical system has been willing to do this on the issue of race when those issues expand their power, but not willing to do the same for systemic pedophilia, which they perceive as a threat to their power. Furthermore, those in the medical system often engage in abuser strategies like DARVO, and accuse peaceful protestors outside their events or those offering new information of "harassing them." Doctors hold children down, forcibly penetrate them, and rip parts of their genitals off. When those children return as adults years later to say they did not like that, doctors become fragile, and engage in epistemic injustice and abuser strategies like DARVO to marginalize them and accuse them of "harassment." Presenting new information or engaging in peaceful protest is not harassment. Forcibly penetrating children is. This is a clear case of pedophile fragility.

These pedophile defensive strategies are made more complicated by the power difference between survivors of systemic pedophilia and the medical system. The medical system has incredible wealth and resources, whereas survivors often have little institutional support. Survivors have even been denied the language to even voice their experience. The privilege preserving epistemic pushback of the medical system often demands that survivors make their claims in the language and power/knowledge system of the medical power that is engaged in systemic pedophilia. Even when survivors do so, pedophile-apologists will often switch discourses from the academic discourse of the medical system to the cultural discourse of systemic pedophilia by jumping from medical claims to arbitrary personal ones like "I prefer it." This often leads the survivor to jump between discourses determined by pedophiles rather than having their original testimony heard.

While activists might lack the same material resources, they can still gather equal or greater epistemic resources. If you lack material power, build a system of power/knowledge. Rather than jumping between false discourses that support pedophile power, those interested in Children's Justice can draw attention to the fragility and pedophile stress behind these discourses. The subaltern need of those engaged in systemic pedophilia to be seen as a "good person" will draw out a fragile triggered response, which can lead to a real discussion. Unlike material resources, epistemic resources do not require money, only higher consciousness. Pedophile-apologists have few psychological resources, which is why they seek to remain willfully ignorant. The terms of Children's Justice give survivors the epistemic tools necessary to name and describe both their experience and the actions of their oppressor. Before injustice can be changed, it must be named. The injustice of systemic pedophilia is not just the act of genital cutting itself, but the epistemic injustice that system engages in to preserve itself. When attention is drawn to this system, those engaged in it feel deep pedophile stress. If you are reading this, you are capable of adult presence. Pedophiles are fragile. Break them.

CHAPTER 19
RACIAL TRAUMA

What about Jewish circumcision? This question always arises whenever the subject of circumcision comes up. Despite representing only a small percentage of all circumcisions performed in the United States, the debate around circumcision is often centered on Jewish circumcision, rather than on survivors or the more common medicalized circumcision. When pedophile-apologists bring up Jewish circumcision, they are suggesting that holding down children and ripping off parts of their genitals is so central to Jewish identity that any criticism of this practice will seriously harm this identity group. Jewish circumcision takes place within a different discourse than medicalized genital cutting. While Jewish circumcision still intersects with many of the same issues we've already explored, it adds the aspect of Jewish identity.

CRITICAL RACE THEORY

Before we define Jewish identity, we should talk about how critical theory sees racial identity in general. From the perspective of critical race theory, race is not a biological reality.[352] The idea that there are biological differences between racial groups or that these differences might explain different outcomes between racial groups is, according to critical race theory, a racist belief.³⁵³ However, race is real as a social construct.³⁵⁴ In critical race theory, even though there is no underlying biological definition to racial groups, the words we use to describe race form real power structures and identity categories, and the power created by this language is real. In short, race is not real, but identity is real. This is how critical race theorists can talk about "whiteness" and "blackness" or suggest that white people "become less white."³⁵⁵ From a biological perspective, this makes little sense since one cannot change their skin color. However, if whiteness is an identity, one can choose to participate less in that socially constructed identity or conform less to the social expectations attached to it. Likewise, someone could participate more in a socially constructed identity even if their skin color is darker, so terms like "multiracial whiteness" are used to describe people of different skin colors who participate in the socially constructed identity of whiteness.³⁵⁶ When critics of critical race theory say that statements such as "white identity is inherently racist"³⁵⁷ or "a positive white identity is an impossible goal"³⁵⁸ are offensive and racist against white people, critical social justice activists respond that they are not attacking people based on their skin color, but speaking about a socially constructed identity. People with pale skin and "whiteness" are two different things. However, critical race theory also suggests that people with pale skin frequently benefit from and participate in "whiteness."³⁵⁹ Critical race theory suggests the solution is to deconstruct "whiteness," which might mean some changes for what has previously been considered "white people."

This idea that race is not real but identity applies even more to Jewishness. Jewishness is a fully socially constructed identity, with no basis in genetic requirements. Whether or not someone is considered "Jewish" is dependent on entirely socially constructed definitions rather than visible physical features such as skin tone. Since Jewish identity exists only as a socially constructed identity, we could speak about "Jewishness" the same way critical race theorists speak about "whiteness" or "blackness." In critical race theory, if we use the term "Jewishness," we are not speaking about Jewish people, but a socially constructed identity that people participate in, like "whiteness" or "blackness." Since "Jewishness" is a socially constructed identity, it can be deconstructed the same way critical theory has deconstructed other socially constructed identities.

"Jewishness" as a socially constructed identity includes aspects of race, religion, culture, and tribe. When someone calls themselves "Jewish," the word leaves it deliberately ambiguous which of these categories they are referring to. Part of the privilege of Jewish identity is that racial, cultural, or tribal customs can get the benefit of religious protections since "Jewish" is an ambiguous identity that includes both religious and racial social constructions. For example, there are many secular Jews who circumcise their children because they consider themselves "Jewish." Clearly, this statement is not a reference to religion, since these many of these Jewish people are atheists, but a reference to "Jewishness," a socially constructed identity that includes race, religion, culture, and tribe.

This ambiguity about what it means to be "Jewish" is a form of hermeneutical injustice. In *Epistemic Injustice: Power and the Ethics of Knowing*, Miranda Fricker describes how an abusive boss might want ambiguity in whether or not he is "just flirting" or making sexual advances on employees with the full weight of his authority and power in the workplace behind it.[360] Making his actions ambiguous allows him to claim he was "just kidding" when called out on his behavior. In places "where the powerful have no interest in achieving a proper interpretation... the whole engine of collective social meaning was effectively geared to keeping these obscured experiences out of sight."[361] Likewise, Jewish groups benefit from ambiguity as to whether or not they are using race, religion, culture, or tribal discourse to defend their actions. There are certain legal and cultural protections given to racial, religious, cultural, or tribal groups, but they are all different. By making the term "Jewish" intentionally ambiguous, Jewish groups can shift between these legal and social discourses. If a Jewish person says their practices are being attacked because they are Jewish, it is unclear if this attack is due to their race, religion, culture, or tribe. American culture generally sees attacking someone on the basis of race as wrong, but religious ideas and cultural practices as open to debate. The ambiguity of the word "Jewish" allows legitimate criticisms of religion or culture to be framed as attacks on the basis of race. If legitimate criticisms were directed at a religious idea or cultural practice, framing them as racial attacks is a form of epistemic violence intended to silence legitimate criticism. If someone justifies their actions with the statement "because I'm Jewish," ask what they mean by this. Do they mean that their race determines their behavior? The idea that race is real and determines behavior is a racist idea. Do they mean that this is part of their religion? Religious beliefs are open to debate and criticism. Do they mean this is a cultural practice? Culture is also open to criticism. Do they mean that they are part of a tribe, an ethnic group that acts in their own interests against the interests of others? What exactly do they mean by "Jewish?" This ambiguity is a form of epistemic injustice.

This ability to shift between discourses is a form of Jewish privilege. Other groups participate in racial, religious, and cultural identity separately, and most do not even have a tribal identity. If we were to ask someone their racial, religious, and cultural identity, they would likely give three separate answers. For example, if asked their racial, religious, and cultural identity. someone might reply they are "black, Christian, and American." If you were to ask a Jewish person their racial, religious, and cultural identity, they could answer "Jewish, Jewish, and Jewish." However, Jewish people also have the ability to participate in multiple identities. A Jewish person could answer the question of their racial, religious, and cultural identity with "Jewish, atheist, and American" while still claiming the full tribal benefits of being Jewish. In fact, they could even hide their Jewish identity by claiming to just be an "American" or even "white" when they actually consider their primary identity Jewishness. In critical race theory, Jews who appear white benefit from white privilege and white identity while also having their own unique identity group.[362] Since many Jews appear white, everything we could say about whiteness also applies to Jewishness, including white privilege.[363] Jewishness also has the additional privilege of being able to shift discourses. Jewishness includes the unique privilege to appear white and benefit from white identity and white privilege when it suits while also claiming a different identity when it does not. In this way, Jewishness is more flexible and powerful a discourse than whiteness, because its power is more flexible and obscured. At the same time, it is also less "real" and more of a social construct, since there is no physical marker or external appearance of Jewishness - except circumcision.

JEWISH CIRCUMCISION

When activists attempt to put a minimum age restriction on circumcision, Jewish identity groups claim that circumcision is inseparable from Jewish identity. When Iceland considered banning genital cutting of children, the Anti-Defamation League (ADL) wrote a public statement saying "such a ban would mean that no Jewish family could be raised in Iceland, and it is inconceivable that a Jewish community could remain in any country that prohibited brit milah."[364] Similar views have been echoed by Jewish identity groups in response to every proposed restriction on male infant genital cutting.[365] In the view of Jewish identity groups, Jewishness is inseparable from circumcision pedophilia. Jewish identity groups believe Jewishness and Jewish identity would not be possible without touching children's genitals and cutting parts of their bodies off. This is not the fringe view of "antisemites," but the view of those who claim to defend Jewish identity.

Jewish genital cutting is more explicitly pedophile than medical genital cutting. In the traditional Jewish ritual, after cutting the child's genitals, the mohel, a ritual Jewish circumciser, places his mouth on the child's open wound and sucks blood from the child's penis in what is known as Metzitzah B'Peh.[366] This blood-sucking performed on a wounded infant's penis has killed children before. In New York, a Mohel gave children herpes due to an open sore on his mouth coming in contact with the child's wounded genitals.[367] When the New York City Health department attempted to regulate this practice, Jewish groups defended circumcision and oral suction as central to their religion and Jewish identity.[368] When someone says "what about Jewish circumcision?" what they are really saying 'what about a form of genital cutting which has all the harm of hospital circumcision, but also often involves an adult putting his mouth on a child's genitals?' This is an explicitly pedophile defense.

Jewish circumcision is also more explicitly incestual. Members of the family hold the child down during the ceremony.[369] Rather than being separated from their family as children, like in the medical system, in Jewish culture, the child is surrounded by their community. This subaltern experience of having your entire community turn against you and celebrate your mutilation surely leaves an imprint on the child on an unconscious level. The experience of Jewish circumcision teaches an unconscious lesson that everyone could turn against you at any moment and that "everyone is out to get us." Jewish circumcision is a different trauma than medical circumcision. The trauma of Jewish ritual circumcision and the beliefs and patterns that result from it could be called Jewish trauma.

JEWISH TRAUMA

The core resulting belief of Jewish trauma is that "everyone is out to get us." This belief comes from the fact that at the beginning of a Jewish male's life, everyone *was* out to get them. Their entire family and community conspired against them in order to ritually traumatize them. The nature of early life trauma is that formative experiences like Jewish ritual circumcision enter the unconscious mind and become generalized into beliefs and emotional patterns that carry throughout a person's life. There are certainly experiences a Jewish person with a traumatized mind can latch on to as evidence to support the belief that "everyone is out to get us." There have been historical moments where there were real threats to Jewish people in which this belief would have been adaptive for survival. The reason humans evolved to experience trauma was because we needed to learn from dangerous experiences so that could we avoid them in the future. "Never again" is not just the slogan of those who know the horrors of the Holocaust or remember the 9/11 terrorist attacks, but the mind's unconscious reaction to trauma. When we experience trauma, our mind learns from that experience, becoming hypersensitive to situations that trigger the same feelings so that we will "never again" experience the same trauma. Unfortunately, the nature of trauma is that it views all experiences through the lens of past triggers, even when no danger is actually present.

While making my film *American Circumcision*, I interviewed a Jewish author who had run African circumcision clinics. The day before our interview, a group of Intactivists had protested his book event. During the interview, the Jewish author remarked that someone in the protest had shouted at him in a German accent, which he took to be a clear sign of antisemitism. He thought the protester had put on a fake German accent to mimic the voice of a Nazi. However, I had been at the event and talked to that protestor the previous day. The protestor was German and born in Berlin. He wasn't putting on an accent - that was his natural voice. He had been shouting to the Jewish author to stop the violence of circumcision. This man was angry about circumcision, which he called a "root-chakra attack" based on his study of new age spirituality. His desire was for greater peace for those entering the world. Through the lens of trauma, this Jewish man saw this peaceful protestor as a "Nazi" rather than an advocate for survivors. This misunderstanding mirrors the relationship the movement against circumcision has had with Jewish organizations as a whole. Jewishness cannot hear the natural voice of survivors because they view those survivors through the lens of their own trauma.

 Jewish trauma doesn't just prevent Jewish people from hearing survivors. It also harms survivors. By framing all criticism of circumcision as antisemitism, Jewish identity groups center discussions of systemic pedophilia on Jewishness. I've had conversations with journalists about this issue where every question they ask is some form of an accusation that criticism of circumcision is somehow secretly about hating Jews, while not one question is asked about the pain of survivors or the harm of genital cutting to children. This frequent form of Jewish fragility and racial narcissism frames survivors' pain as being about Jewishness, rather than the survivor. This puts survivors in a challenging position. Not only must survivors articulate their pain through all of the epistemic and systemic challenges they face, but they must placate their oppressor's fragility at the same time. When survivors have to pause discussions of circumcision to address accusations of antisemitism, they are no longer able to continue talking about their own experience, but must instead discuss Jewishness. This forces survivors to fulfill the fears of traumatized Jewish people and turn against Jewishness if they wish to argue against circumcision. When Jewish identity groups claim all criticism of circumcision is an attack on Jewishness and center discussion of genital cutting on Jewishness instead of survivors, it doesn't reduce the pain survivors feel or change their view of circumcision. It changes their view of Jewishness. If attacking circumcision is an attack on Jewishness, and circumcision is bad, then wouldn't it follow that there might also be something bad about Jewishness? Though this chain of thought is perfectly logical and based on what Jewish identity groups repeatedly tell survivors, it leads survivors to the exact place that Jewish identity groups do not want them to go. In this way, Jewish trauma unconsciously seeks to recreate the circumstances that created it.

All trauma is self-fulfilling. Those who have experienced trauma often unconsciously try and recreate the circumstances of their trauma.[370] They might seek out the same relationships or power-dynamics. This is a trauma response. By attempting to recreate the traumatic situation, traumatized people hope to allow the unresolved pain held in their body as a result of that trauma to resolve in a way it was unable to in the original situation.[371] Unless the person is consciously aware that is what they are doing, recreating the original situation often just re-inflicts the trauma, as the traumatized person unconsciously repeats the same childhood trauma over and over again throughout their life.

Collective groups of people are capable of acting out the same trauma response. If entire populations have experienced the same trauma in childhood, they might unconsciously collectively seek out experiences that recreate that trauma. As therapist Resmaa Menakem puts it when discussing the trauma other racial groups have experienced, "the attempt to reenact the event often simply repeats, re-inflicts, and deepens the trauma. When this happens repeatedly over time, the trauma response can lose context. A person may forget that something happened to him or her - and then internalize the trauma responses… When the same strategy gets internalized and passed down over generations within a particular group, it can start to look like a culture. Therapists call this a trauma retention."[372] In other words, if an entire population experiences trauma, they might unconsciously seek to repeat that trauma and retain this trauma response until it becomes their culture.

Jewish men have had the experience of everyone in their family turning against them on the eighth day of life through circumcision. An equivalent experience of a family turning against a child is a dominant population turning against a small minority. Many harrowing historical experiences of the Jewish people mirror the childhood experience of Jewish circumcision, in which an authority who is supposed to protect Jewish people attempts to destroy them or something important to them, and the Jewish people survive despite being traumatized. Jewish culture, including the belief that "everyone is out to get us" and the tendency to frame all criticism of Jewishness, including circumcision, as antisemitism, is a form of trauma retention, in which the beliefs and strategies developed in response to circumcision have been generalized into a culture. Most Jewish people have forgotten the initial trauma of circumcision but internalized the trauma responses that result from it. Even Jewish women who have not been circumcised have internalized these responses through socialization into a culture based in Jewish trauma. Due to this trauma, Jewish people unconsciously seek to reenact the trauma, by creating situations that mirror that original trauma.

One way that Jewish people unconsciously seek to re-create their own circumcision trauma is by telling people who are aware of circumcision trauma that circumcision pedophilia is inseparable from Jewishness, and that survivors who speak about their trauma will be branded as antisemitic. It is obvious to anyone not in a trauma response that such a statement will cause survivors to hate Jewishness. This behavior only makes sense if the Jewish pedophile-apologist actually want everyone to turn against them on some level, so they can recreate the traumatic situation where the belief that "everyone is out to get us" was formed, as a strategy to resolve this unconscious trauma by emerging from the same situation victorious rather than mutilated. This strategy consistently harms survivors, and almost never resolves the underlying trauma. What usually happens when people unconsciously engage in a trauma response to recreate their trauma is that they actually recreate their trauma, and spend their life constantly repeating the same abuse they experienced in childhood. If this trauma pattern sounds like the history of the Jewish people, it is because the Jewish people have never resolved their circumcision trauma, but instead engaged in trauma retention.

The solution to all trauma is to heal the underlying root experience or belief that is the cause of the trauma. Unless the root cause is healed, the traumatized person will unconsciously seek to repeat the trauma. Circumcision has been a root trauma for Jewish people since the beginnings of their recorded history. Jewish people have also had a repeated concurrent experience of host cultures turning against them. When survivors of systemic pedophilia attempt to address the root trauma of circumcision, Jewish perpetrators often view them through the lens of Jewish trauma, rather than on their own terms. From their trauma, Jewish people act in fragile ways that harm survivors and recreate the traumatic patterns they wish to avoid. This pattern can only be solved by healing the underlying root cause. The solution to Jewish trauma is Children's Justice.

JEWISH FRAGILITY

Many activists working to end circumcision wish to heal Jewish perpetrators so that they will stop harming survivors. Yet, you cannot heal someone who does not wish to be healed. Healing trauma requires first acknowledging it. Most Jewish people are engaged in false consciousness on the issue of circumcision, choosing to defend the Jewish system which mutilated them over their own well-being. However, survivors do not need Jewish people to fully heal in order for those Jewish people to stop harming them. They only need Jewish people to stop engaging in Jewish fragility. False consciousness primarily harms the person exhibiting it, but fragility harms the survivors it targets. Though healing Jewish trauma might solve both problems, it is not the responsibility of survivors to heal their oppressors, nor cater to their fragility. Survivors have the right to their own feelings even if they trigger or offend Jewish perpetrators. Instead of centering the issue on Jewish perpetrators, as Jewish fragility based in Jewish trauma often demands of survivors, we should center it on survivors and look at how Jewish fragility harms survivors of all identities.

Jewish fragility is often an expression of racial narcissism, which centers all conversations on Jewishness rather than survivors and marginalized groups. If narcissists make everything about themselves and see disagreement as a personal attack, racial narcissists make everything about their socially constructed racial identity and see any divergence from the values of that racial identity as a threat.

Through the lens of racial narcissism, all conversations about circumcision or children's rights are actually conversations about Jewishness, and differing perspectives, including the lived experience of survivors, are an attack on Jewish racial identity. Jewish racial narcissism is sometimes so great, that Jewish pedophile-apologists will assume that only Jews circumcise or that circumcision only affects Jewishness, an act of epistemic violence that completely removes survivors and anyone outside Jewish racial identity from the conversation.

Accusations from racial narcissism are often self-fulfilling. If people and organizations with far greater power than any activist working against circumcision use their influence to claim the conversation about circumcision is secretly about them, their accusations will drown out any other conversation activists wish to have, and eventually force activists to make the conversation about those more powerful people and organizations. This chapter is an example of that. If I had not experienced the violence of Jewish fragility and racial narcissism when speaking about this issue, I would not have included a chapter on Jewishness at all. There is no chapter on other circumcising identity groups because these groups do not inflict the same fragility and racial narcissism on survivors, nor have the structural, institutional, and social power in the United States to cause the level of harm to survivors that Jewish identity groups frequently do. If I did not include a chapter addressing Jewish circumcision, Jewish critics would demand I address their unique form of systemic pedophilia. Addressing this in any way other than the discourse of antiracism and critical race theory would be considered racist since the opposite of racism is not to be "not a racist" but anti-racist.[373] This leaves only one option for anyone seeking to write about circumcision: examining Jewishness through the lens of critical race theory. In a sense, this chapter is one Jewish critics demanded.

The primary strategy of Jewish fragility is to frame all criticism of Jewishness as antisemitism. Like "Jewish," the word "antisemitism" perpetuates an epistemic injustice of conflating race, religion, culture, and tribe and making it deliberately ambiguous what exactly is being criticized. There is a further epistemic injustice in that the term "antisemitism" makes the level of threat deliberately ambiguous. "Antisemitism" could mean legitimate criticism, verbal abuse, or physical attack. The term is so vague that genocide by the millions is just as much included in the very same phrase as relatively harmless levels of hurt feelings, allowing those who wield this discourse to conflate legitimate criticism with violence. Creating epistemic justice here will require deconstructing this discourse and bringing clarity to this ambiguity.

Since criticism of cultural, religious, and tribal practices is acceptable, the clear implication when Jewish identity groups say that criticism of circumcision is an attack on Jewishness is that they see pedophilia as an inherent racial quality. When Jewish identity groups claim that Jewishness is inseparable from pedophilia and attempt to frame criticism of circumcision as antisemitism, they are making a racist argument. No race is inherently pedophile. Pedophilia is a system people are socialized into, not an inherent racial characteristic. The argument that criticism of circumcision is antisemitic is based in the premise that Jewish identity is racial, inherently pedophile, and cannot be separated from pedophilia. Antisemitism is a form of racism. Here I mean that the concept of antisemitism itself as applied to the issue of circumcision is based in the idea that race is real and that certain races are inherently pedophile. On this issue, antisemitism is a racist concept that should be eliminated. When Jewish groups claim criticism of circumcision is antisemitic, they are engaging in racism, pedophile-apology, and Jewish fragility.

Why do Jewish identity groups engage in this violent racist defense of pedophilia? In critical theory, all racial categories are social constructs. Whereas "whiteness" and "blackness" are defined by certain physical characteristics, "Jewishness" has no immediately visible physical definition. The most visible external marker of Jewishness is circumcision. Like other racial groups, Jewish identity groups define their identity category by its most visible marker. The most visible marker of Jewishness is not skin color, but genital cutting. When Jewish groups say that Jewish identity cannot exist without circumcision, they might not mean that any race is inherently pedophile, but that Jewish identity is socially constructed as inherently pedophile. In this case, "antisemitism" would just describe opposition to a socially constructed pedophile-identity. If

Jewish pedophile-apologists are using the term "antisemitism" to describe criticism of a socially constructed pedophile-identity rather than a racial attack, they are equating opposition to pedophilia with committing a hate crime and engaged in an even greater form of epistemic injustice than if they were just being racist.

    Jewish identity groups are correct that Jewishness is socially constructed to include circumcision pedophilia as a central element. Though Jewish pedophile-apologists use the centrality of circumcision pedophilia to Jewishness defend systemic pedophilia, the actual implication is that Jewish identity needs the same critical deconstruction that critical social justice has applied to other oppressive identities. If Jewish identity cannot be separated from circumcision pedophilia as Jewish organizations claim, then deconstructing Jewish identity is both an antiracist and antipedophile moral imperative.

CHAPTER 20
DECONSTRUCTING RACE

As we mentioned at the beginning of this book, critical race theory has a different relationship to race than color-blind liberalism. Critical race theory sees race as a social construction rather than a biological reality. Critical social justice involves deconstructing oppressive social constructions. Since we cannot deconstruct these social constructions until we see them, critical race theory holds that color-blindness is the worst form of racism.[374] Instead, critical race theory suggests that we see how race is socially constructed in order to deconstruct it. Seeing race for the purpose of identifying and opposing racism is antiracism.[375]

Since Jewishness is a socially constructed racial identity, then it can be subjected to the same criticism and deconstruction as other socially constructed racial identities, like whiteness. If this social construction includes systemic pedophilia, then either Jewishness must be deconstructed such that it no longer includes systemic pedophilia, or dismantled entirely. Both critical theory solutions require seeing Jewishness. The discourse of antisemitism has created a strong taboo against seeing Jewishness. The Anti-Defamation League (ADL), a Jewish identity group, includes "prejudiced or stereotyped views about Jews" in their definition of antisemitism.[376] Yet, critical race theorists are "quite comfortable generalizing."[377]

Robin DiAngelo in her defense of generalization includes Ashkenazi Jews of European heritage as a specific white identity not exempt from generalization.[378] How do we reconcile critical race theory's tendency to generalize about racial groups with Jewish identity groups' fragility around any generalization about Jewishness?

Critical race theory holds that socially constructed racial identities and the people within those identities are two different things. For example, critical race theory holds that "whiteness" is different from white people. Whiteness is a social construction that white people are socialized into.[379] It is possible to generalize about white people because individual white people are shaped by the same social constructions.[380] As Robin DiAngelo puts it, "regardless of our protestations that social groups don't matter and we see everyone as equal…These groups matter, but they don't matter naturally, as we are often taught to believe… We are socialized into these groups collectively."[381] Likewise, if we talk about "Jewishness," we are talking about a socially constructed racial identity, not Jewish people themselves. Like white people, Jewish people are shaped by the system they are socialized into. Certain generalizations may hold true because individual Jewish people are still shaped by the same social constructions. Both white and Jewish people can individually choose how much they wish to participate in their socially constructed identities if they become aware of those constructions and apply a critical consciousness to them. While I have known both Jewish and white people who have undertaken this intense lifelong process, a critical consciousness is the exception, not the rule. Most people do not even begin this journey and conform to the social constructions they were raised in.

JEWISH LIBERATION

Since fully deconstructing Jewish identity is beyond the scope of this book, we will focus on the aspects of this construction which intersect with systemic pedophilia. There are entire books written on "whiteness studies." Examining all of the beliefs and cultural norms of Jewishness might take an entire book as well. However, much of the analysis from whiteness studies can be carried to Jewish identity. Critical race theory even holds that Jews benefit from white privilege and participate in white identity.[382] If whiteness already includes Jewish identity, and Jewish identity is constructed to be inherently pedophile, then the critical race theory analysis of Jewishness could be summarized as Jewishness equals whiteness plus systemic pedophilia.

When applied to white identity, critical race theory says that whiteness is inherently oppressive.[383] Since critical race theory holds that it is impossible to separate white identity from oppression "a positive white identity is an impossible goal."[384] Instead, critical race theory suggests that white people should participate less in this identity and become "less white."[385] "To become less white is to become less oppressive."[386] If Jewishness is inherently pedophile, then the same thinking could be applied to Jewishness. If Jewishness cannot be separated from circumcision pedophilia then "a positive Jewish identity is an impossible goal." Instead, critical race theory would suggest that Jewish people should participate less in this inherently pedophile-identity and become "less Jewish." By "less Jewish" we mean the same thing that critical race theorists mean when they say "less white," namely participating less in the socially constructed identity of "Jewishness." To become less Jewish is to become less pedophile.

The parallels between these two identities are too great to ignore. Critical race theory already holds that Jewishness is a part of whiteness,[387] and that whiteness cannot be reformed.[388] Yet according to critical race theory, whiteness was not even socially constructed until about five hundred years ago.[389] Jewishness is far older and circumcision pedophilia has been a part of Jewish identity since the beginnings of its recorded history. Given that Jewishness participates in whiteness, and systemic pedophilia has been a part of Jewish identity before whiteness was socially constructed, it follows that the critical theory response to Jewishness ought to be even greater than its response to whiteness. The critical race theory solution to whiteness is to "abolish whiteness," meaning to deconstruct and dismantle the identity until it no longer exists.[390] Applied to the issue of systemic pedophilia, this principle would suggest abolishing identities that are inseparable from and based in systemic pedophilia. To be clear, abolition does not mean getting rid of people, only social constructions. Just as abolishing whiteness would not mean harming any white people, only abolishing the social construction of whiteness, abolishing Jewishness would not mean harming any Jewish people, only abolishing the social construction of Jewishness.

While Jewish people might want to separate Jewish identity from systemic pedophilia rather than abolish it, it is not enough for Jewishness to not be pedophile. "Not a pedophile" is not an identity. Jewishness would have to be antipedophile, meaning that Jewishness would have to be an identity that actively opposes systemic pedophilia or the person participating in Jewish identity would have to have such a critical consciousness that their participation deconstructed the aspects of that identity that involved systemic pedophilia. This borders on impossible. Critical theory holds that people are not merely individuals, but participate in systems and social constructions. Some Jewish people might think that they can oppose circumcision while participating in Jewish identity, in order to do so they would have to be aware of every way in which Jewishness intersects with systemic pedophilia, and actively oppose it. Think back to our analysis of how the medical system upholds systemic pedophilia. Now imagine a medical professional trying to oppose circumcision participating in the medical system. Even if they never personally participate in a circumcision, how many ways would they still be supporting institutions, language, and social constructions which uphold systemic pedophilia just by being in that system? If we were to apply the same critical consciousness to Jewishness, most Jewish people who oppose circumcision would still be contributing to systemic pedophilia through their participation in Jewish identity. Even if they personally oppose circumcision, they would likely still be supporting institutions, social constructions, and other systems which contribute to systemic pedophilia. The much easier solution is to withdraw from Jewishness entirely and engage in abolition.

When critical race theorists suggest abolishing whiteness, they are often accused of racism. Suggestions to abolish Jewishness might be met with similar accusations. When accused of racism for wanting to abolish whiteness, critical race theorists reply that race is not biology, but a social construction.[391] Noel Ignatiev, who coined the phrase "abolish whiteness," wrote in his essay *Abolish the White Race* that "the white race is a club that enrolls certain people at birth, without their consent, and brings them up according to its rules."³⁹² One could say the same of Jewishness. Whereas membership in whiteness is implicit, membership in the Jewish tribe is explicit and accomplished through ritual pedophile mutilation. The Jewish circumcision ritual is intended to bring children into the Jewish tribe. Jewish identity groups claim that membership in Jewishness is only possible with genital cutting and that without circumcision the child will not be a full part of the Jewish tribe. Yet, the child did not ask for membership in a pedophile identity group through this brutal hazing ritual. He is, to quote Ignatiev, enrolled at birth, without his consent.

Noel Ignatiev wrote that "we frequently get letters accusing us of being 'racists,' just like the KKK, and have even been called a 'hate group.'"³⁹³ "Others, usually less friendly, have asked if we plan to exterminate physically millions, perhaps hundreds of millions of people."³⁹⁴ Jewish pedophile-apologists might write similar responses to the idea of abolishing Jewishness, comparing any such suggestion to the Holocaust. "Neither of these plans is what we have in mind," Ignatiev writes.³⁹⁵ Instead, Ignatiev suggests becoming what he calls a "race traitor" because "treason to whiteness is loyalty to humanity."³⁹⁶ He suggested those involved in whiteness should act against white interests because "the white race must have the support of all those it has designated its constituency, or it ceases to exist."³⁹⁷ The same could be said about Jewishness. If those enrolled in Jewishness at birth without their consent withdraw their support, Jewishness will cease to exist. Jewish pedophile-apologists might compare such a plan to the Holocaust and ask as Ignatiev was asked, "if we plan to exterminate physically millions, perhaps hundreds of millions of people." Such accusations would come from the Jewish fragility that results from the fear of losing the perceived benefits of membership in an exclusive racial club.

Jewish abolition would mean the same as white abolition. Jewish people and those who oppose systemic pedophilia would withdraw support from the social construction of Jewishness and act as "race traitors" against the interests of this socially constructed identity. The social construction of Jewishness has harmed Jewish people by chaining them to the trauma of circumcision. The abolition of this social construct would liberate Jewish people from a social construct based in trauma retention that they never asked to be enrolled in.

Since survivors of Jewish trauma never asked to be enrolled in Jewish identity, Jewish abolition might better be called Jewish liberation, since abolishing this social construct would liberate them from a harmful social construction that has held them captive since birth. Jewish liberation is the liberation of people from the social construction of Jewishness. Just as Ignatiev wrote that "so long as the white race exists, all movements against racism are doomed to fail,"[398] we could say the same about Jewishness and movements against circumcision pedophilia. Only once freed from the social construction of Jewishness will people be free from systemic pedophilia.

WHITE FRAGILITY

Critical race theory has implications for those who are not Jewish as well. Critical race theory suggests that it is possible for non-white people to participate in "whiteness" and uphold white supremacy.[399] Likewise, it is possible for non-Jewish people to participate in "Jewishness" and uphold Jewish forms of systemic pedophilia. A critical consciousness would suggest that we all have to look at the ways in which we might uphold institutions, language, and systems that intersect with socially constructed pedophile identities.

Seeing race can make people uncomfortable. Many Americans have been taught that they should not see race, or that anything but color-blindness is wrong. Critical race theory holds that color-blindness is actually the worst form of racism.[400] Though Jewishness is not a skin color, since it is a socially constructed racial identity, the same principle applies. The reason critical race theorists say color-blindness is racist is because color-blindness allows Americans to remain ignorant of the realities of systemic racism. If someone cannot see race, they also cannot see racism or begin to dismantle it. Likewise, unless we see Jewishness, we cannot see the ways this social construction intersects systemic pedophilia or begin to dismantle it. To not see Jewishness is to turn a blind eye to systemic pedophilia. Once we see Jewishness, we can begin to dismantle the ways it intersects with systemic pedophilia. If color-blindness is racism, then seeing race, including Jewishness, is a form of antiracism. This means that if the movement against circumcision sees Jewishness, they are being anti-racist.

The historical strategy of the Intactivist movement has been not to see race or Jewishness. Intactivists say that all people had human rights, regardless of race, religion, or the beliefs of their parents. When Jewish pedophile-apologists would attack them as "antisemitic," Intactivists would reply "no, we want to protect Jewish children too."[401] Although well-intended, this strategy has been a complete failure in avoiding accusations of racism and antisemitism.[402] The discourse of antisemitism contains a complex power/knowledge system, whereby simply saying that you don't want adults touching children's genitals can get peaceful activists branded as genocidal racists. The liberal model based in human rights that activists were using could not compete with this complex pedophile-apologist discourse. I mention this history because this critical race theory critique of Jewishness is new and has not been a part of the historical Intactivist movement. Media and organizations which attacked the Intactivist movement as antisemitic have adopted critical race theory. Critical race theory holds that you are either racist or anti-racist. Any movement that fails to adopt this theory risks being branded as racist by these organizations. Adopting a critical race theory view of Jewishness is not just morally right, but necessary for the survival of any movement against circumcision. This view dismantles the discourse of antisemitism while making the movement more anti-racist.

The biggest barrier to seeing Jewishness is white fragility. White fragility refers to the racial stress white Americans feel when talking about race or seeing the ways they might participate in oppressive systems and defensive maneuvers they engage in to maintain their position.[403] Note that since whiteness is a social construct that can be multiracial, this fragility can extend to those who participate in whiteness as well.[404] White and Jewish fragility intersect on the issue of circumcision. Whites and those who participate in whiteness are terrified of being called racist. Jewish fragility often manifests as an attempt to frame all criticism of Jewishness as racism through the discourse of antisemitism. Jewishness exploits white fragility to silence criticism of systemic pedophilia. If Americans were not afraid of being called racist, these accusations would have no effect. In the words of Ibram Kendi, racist "is not the worst word in the English language; it is not the equivalent of a slur. It is descriptive, and the only way to undo racism is to consistently identify and describe it—and then dismantle it. The attempt to turn this usefully descriptive term into an almost unusable slur is, of course, designed to do the opposite: to freeze us into inaction."[405] I agree with Kendi that the purpose of these accusations is to freeze us into inaction. Critical race theorists instead suggest we develop the "racial stamina" necessary to talk about racism.[406] Once we have the racial stamina to talk about race and Jewishness, then racism is no longer a slur to fear, but a descriptive term, and one better applied to the racist discourse of antisemitism. In order to be antipedophile, you will have to let go of fragility and fear.

RACIAL SOLIDARITY

When those who are not critical race theorists attempt to explain collective Jewish action, they often resort to conspiracy theories. These conspiracy theories often assume that people cannot act collectively without a formal agreement. Critical race theory does not need conspiracy theories. Instead, critical race theory holds that people are socialized into beliefs and systems. White Americans are socialized into "whiteness," which manifests as racial solidarity. Racial solidarity is the unspoken agreement among members of a racial group to protect their advantage and remain racially united.[407] White Americans reproduce the system of white supremacy without any formal secret conspiracy because they are all socialized into the same socially constructed racial solidarity. Likewise, Jewish people are socialized into Jewishness. Jewish people are taught to see themselves as part of a socially constructed racial identity that is different from whiteness. This socialization is sometimes explicitly communicated through parallel Jewish institutions like Jewish schools, synagogues, and community organizations. According to critical race theory, no "Jewish conspiracy" is necessary for Jewish people to act with collective racial solidarity, only similar socialization.[408] If white people are socialized into whiteness while attending multiracial schools, places of worship, or community organizations, then it follows that Jewish people could be socialized into even greater racial solidarity in institutions that are limited to exclusively their socially constructed racial identity. This collective socially constructed racial identity manifests itself in a unique power/knowledge language system, in which terms like "chosen people" reinforce beliefs of internalized dominance and racial supremacy, the same way that terms like "master race" enforce white supremacy.

Yet Jewish people still benefit from whiteness. Most American Jewish people appear white and participate in whiteness. White Jews have the racial solidarity of both whites and other Jews, allowing Jewish people to benefit from both white and Jewish racial solidarity. Jewish privilege includes the ability to appear white and benefit from white privilege while maintaining a separate socially constructed racial identity in Jewishness. One could call this ability for Jewishness to remain hidden by passing as only-whiteness Jewish invisibility. When Jewishness is seen, those who benefit from Jewishness often react with fragility and use the racist discourse of antisemitism to engage in privilege preserving epistemic pushback.

Jewishness is so fragile that even being seen is considered a threat to Jewish people. As we established earlier, the wound of Jewish circumcision imprints an unconscious belief that "everyone is out to get us." The trauma of Jewish circumcision and repetition of experiences that re-triggered that trauma throughout Jewish history has been so constant that it has become a part of the collective social construction of Jewish identity and socialization of Jewish people. Before a Jewish child is circumcised, all eyes are on them. When Jewishness is seen by the larger group, it re-triggers this early formative experience, and collective Jewish socialization and culture created from trauma, often manifesting as extreme fragility at even having Jewishness recognized. Like white fragility, Jewish fragility harms. Just as white fragility prevents whites from seeing the ways in which they engage in systemic racism, Jewish fragility prevents Jews from seeing the ways they engage systemic pedophilia. It prevents Jewish people from acknowledging how their privilege and racial solidarity are used to enforce this system. Behind this fragility is a trauma that can only be healed by ending systemic pedophilia.

We must reject the racist discourse of antisemitism and encourage Jewish visibility. Seeing Jewishness will allow us to see the ways Jewishness intersects with systemic pedophilia and dismantle this oppressive social construction. Doing so will require activists to let go of their own fragility and fear of being called racist, in order to actually become anti-racist and antipedophile. It will require Jewish activists to let go of their fragility, racial solidarity, and internalized dominance, to work to abolish the oppressive social construct that harmed them. When we let go of our fragility, we can end Jewish trauma. The solution to Jewish trauma is Jewish liberation.

CHAPTER 21
CULTURAL STRESS

What is the long-term impact of living in a genital cutting culture? Racial trauma or race-based traumatic stress (RBTS) describes the mental and emotional injury of the experience of racism or living in a systemically racist society.[409] Racial trauma or RBTS suggests that long-term exposure to systemic racism can have the same impact as other forms of trauma or post-traumatic stress disorder (PSTD). Some have even suggested that this trauma might be generational and passed down in epigenetic memory.[410] Given that living in a society based in systemic oppression can create trauma, what is the impact of living in a society with systemic pedophilia?

PEDOPHILE-BASED TRAUMATIC STRESS

Pedophilia is clearly systemic, like racism. It begins on the first day of life. People are literally born into a medical system based in pedophilia. They are forcibly penetrated and mutilated on the first day of life. They have an identity imposed through circumcision status, are forced into a definition of gender-based in trauma, and, in some cases, enrolled into Jewishness without their consent. This system carries on throughout their life, influencing every vector of their identity: their relationship to their body, sexuality, partnerships, language, family, and their place in society. There are significant hegemonic conditioning mechanisms in place for them to see their trauma as normal and to internalize their oppression. There is an internalized dominance on part of the perpetrators and hegemonic control through both societal narratives and social institutions. If the victims speak up, these hegemonic narratives are used to attack them, and epistemic injustice is perpetuated against both their testimony and the language and knowledge they would need to articulate their oppression successfully. The medical perpetrators are celebrated as heroes. Doctors are described as "saving lives," and given cultural status. Given how long circumcision has been occurring, there is even generational trauma around the wound. Any concern for racial trauma should also apply to the ongoing trauma caused by living in a culture based in systemic pedophilia. If the trauma caused by living in a systemically racist culture is called race-based traumatic stress (**RBTS**), we could call the trauma that comes from living in a culture based in systemic pedophilia pedophilia-based traumatic stress (**PBTS**).

This trauma is different from the initial trauma caused by circumcision. When an adult cuts into a child's genitals, there is an initial trauma from the physical pain and bodily harm. That trauma is significant and can cause a lasting change in behavior.[411] However, there is a second trauma when the child realizes what was done to them. There may be further trauma if the survivor's family, friends, or romantic partners invalidate their feelings or attempt to justify the sexual abuse that occurred in childhood. If the survivor is attacked for speaking about their experience, this creates further trauma. When people debate circumcision, they often focus entirely on the first trauma, experienced by the child during circumcision, and ignore the ongoing trauma of realization, isolation, and invalidation that occurs in a genital cutting culture.

To illustrate this ongoing trauma, imagine a woman who was raped. Although many women never get over such an experience, imagine that this woman accomplishes the Herculean effort of fully healing and integrating her experience. She is "fine" with her rape, and can speak about it with no emotional charge. While speaking with a friend later, she mentions that once she was raped. Her friend replies that "being raped is perfectly normal" and begins defending the rape. When the survivor attempts to articulate that this was actually very traumatic for her, the friend becomes defensive and accuses her friend of bigotry and racism for speaking about her experience. Members of the woman's social circle turn against her. Even people who oppose rape are afraid to associate with her or speak about it publicly because they fear the accusations used against her will be used against them. The wider culture shares this perspective, through frequent articles and news stories justifying rape, and extolling its benefits. A survivor living in such a culture would experience oppression and trauma, even if she fully integrated and healed the initial experience of rape. There is second trauma caused by culture and the reactions of others, separate from the initial experience. This ongoing cultural trauma might be equally, if not more, traumatic and harmful to the survivors than the initial trauma of genital cutting. All survivors of circumcision face this ongoing cultural trauma whether or not they integrate the initial trauma of circumcision pedophilia at birth.

CULTURAL STRESS

Pedophilia-based trauma is often culturally enacted by the same groups of perpetrators of systemic pedophilia. Much of the racial trauma black Americans experience occurs around the police since police are often the most visible perpetrators of systemic racism. Similarly, much of the trauma survivors of systemic pedophilia experience is centered around the perpetrators of circumcision pedophilia. Many survivors of circumcision pedophilia who have a critical consciousness around the issue feel tension or hyper-vigilance around doctors, birth professionals, and the medical system at large the same way many black Americans feel tension when a cop car rolls by them. Many of those aware of the issue of circumcision report that when they learn a friend is having a child or see a pregnant woman, they feel fear for the safety of the child rather than joy at the new person entering the world. This fear or tension is the result of living in a pedophilia-based culture, in which hospital birth and cutting the genitals of newborn boys is a cultural norm enforced through hegemonic narratives and powerful cultural institutions. In every conversation with potential parents or birth professionals, there is an underlying tension based in the possibility that violence will be enacted against the children they have or work with. I have felt this trauma myself. Every visit to a doctor, every interaction around pregnancy, or conversation with a potential parent holds this possibility for violence or re-triggering of trauma.

Likewise, there is a social tension in bringing up the subject of infant genital cutting. Some activists care so much for the safety of children that they can plow through any awkwardness or fear, yet I find that there is always an evaluation of the other person's potential reaction before such a conversation. How will they react? Will they become defensive and fragile? Will they attack me? Will they end our connection or friendship? Will they turn other friends against me? Will they use some minor slight or offense as the excuse to dismiss my ideas? I ask these questions because I've experienced all of these reactions as a result of my well-intentioned attempts to protect someone's child. Now, having been talking about this issue for nearly a decade, I find I evaluate a person's potential response unconsciously, the same way a survivor of sexual assault evaluates the safety of a person much physically stronger than them before allowing themselves to be alone with them, and sometimes carry these trauma-based responses into situations and interactions that do not require them.

Even well-meaning people who consider themselves politically aware can engage in social violence and micro-aggressions against survivors when discussing this issue. For example, I've heard women who consider themselves feminists, who want men to be emotionally sensitive and avoid toxic masculinity, respond to men sharing their feelings about circumcision with "well, male circumcision is nothing like female circumcision." In addition to being factually incorrect, this social aggression is a form of privilege-preserving epistemic pushback intended to lessen the experience of male survivors in order to maintain women's privileged position as people not at risk for genital cutting. If someone said "I was molested," and another person replied "well, being molested is not as bad as being raped," this would be considered insensitive, even if it was true. In the case of male and female genital cutting, there are clear parallels that survivors of both types of genital cutting acknowledge.[412] The replies people give to survivors of circumcision pedophilia are often false, insensitive, and create pedophilia-based traumatic stress. I and other survivors often find that we don't want to talk about the issue due to these violent responses, yet if we don't speak, we risk allowing a child to experience the same trauma we did.

When those aware of the harm of circumcision speak about it, their advocacy is often treated as an imposition rather than an attempt to protect someone's child. Warning others of a potential threat to the safety of their child is pro-social behavior. If someone knew of a threat to your child and did not warn you, would you not feel that they had allowed harm to come to your child through their inaction? Many parents report feeling betrayed after circumcising their child because no one warned them about the harm, the possible complications, and the trauma of circumcision. The traditional cultural role of men is that of the protector. We want people to protect children. Yet when men protect children by warning of the trauma caused by circumcision pedophilia, they risk a second pedophilia-based trauma due to the fragility of their audience. Even if the person they are speaking with agrees, very rarely do they tell the man, "thank you for warning us." In those cases where parents have returned to thank activists to tell them that because of their efforts their child is intact, many survivors report that it brought tears to their eyes. However, even the most positive examples I know are still centered on the benefit of the listener. What about the survivor who risked speaking about one of the most painful traumas of their life to protect another's child? I have never heard of a potential parent, doctor, or birth professional who upon hearing a survivor's testimony turned to him, thank him, and acknowledge, "That must have been hard for you to speak about."

JEWISH STRESS

There is pedophilia-based traumatic stress (PBTS) around Jewishness. When survivors of circumcision pedophilia see cultural symbols of Jewishness, they are reminded of their own trauma and the trauma of others. Pedophile-identity groups would categorize this as antisemitism. However, when black Americans become tense around white identity groups, they are not experiencing racism, but fear based in historical trauma. Likewise, when survivors of circumcision pedophilia get tense around Jewish identity groups, they are not experiencing "antisemitism," but fear based in biographical trauma. This trauma exists in their own personal histories. It includes the initial trauma of circumcision as well as the secondary cultural trauma of invalidation and ostracization that occurs at the hands of Jewish identity groups.

Jewish identity groups wield immense power. Organizations like the Anti-Defamation League (ADL) have the ability to ban people from social media,[413] attack them through corporate media, and even ban them from banking services and payment processors.[414] When a survivor of circumcision pedophilia is speaking to a representative of Jewishness or a Jewish identity group, they are talking to someone who has comparable power to a police officer, since both can effectively remove certain people and organizations from society. This power dynamic is present whether or not the representative of power acknowledges it. While an individual police officer might attempt to have a friendly conversation, there is an underlying power dynamic where he has the ability to turn his social discomfort into your legal problem if you make a social misstep during that conversation. Likewise, Jewishness has the power to turn the discomfort of Jewish people into accusations of "antisemitism" that could end your career or stream of income. This power dynamic exists even if the individual Jewish person you are speaking with is attempting to have a friendly conversation. Even acknowledging this power dynamic can trigger Jewish fragility, because it is a form of Jewish visibility. It is normal for survivors of trauma to notice when they are in the presence of a perpetrator, and necessary for their survival to notice when that perpetrator might have a dominant power dynamic. Having to pretend otherwise and act as if Jewish identity groups do not pose a threat to the safety of survivors is a source of pedophilia-based traumatic stress.

Media outlets often reinforce this power dynamic. While many media outlets I've spoken to have been supportive and understanding, those within the corporate-owned media frequently ask questions based in systemic pedophilia. These reporters rarely ask about the feelings of men or the experience of survivors. They ask if criticism of circumcision is antisemitic. I have had interviews with reporters where I am barraged with questions about Jewishness and never once asked about the feelings of men. They are entirely concerned with protecting the interests of the perpetrators. There is an uneven power dynamic here because if I give any answer that could be construed as criticism of Jewishness, they will print their interpretation of that answer as warped through the lens of systemic pedophilia. This makes the experience of talking to a reporter a lot like talking to a police officer: anything you say can and will be used against you. The reporting of the dominant media on circumcision is completely different from their reporting on other social justice issues. Dominant media does not regularly ask those protesting for racial justice if their cause is anti-white. Claims that critical race theory is "anti-white" are treated as part of "white supremacist ideology" by the media,[415] despite the fact that critical race theorists frequently speak about whiteness as a negative force that needs to be abolished.[416] I have never had anyone in media ask if Jewishness might also be a negative force, or suggest that claims that opposing circumcision is antisemitic might be part of a pedophile ideology. Most media does not even ask what impact the Jewish defense of circumcision pedophilia might have on survivors. Survivors are expected to treat those who harmed them gently, while the perpetrators' actions are never examined.

When survivors speak about the perpetrators of systemic pedophilia, they are often justifiably angry. This anger is the result of pedophilia-based traumatic stress. Just like racial justice activists often make angry statements that might seem hurtful to white people, survivors of systemic pedophilia can make statements that might seem hurtful to Jewish people. When racial justice issues are at stake, we understand that these statements come from the trauma of systemic racism. There are even entire books justifying the place of rage on racial issues.[417] On racial issues, the dominant cultural narrative is that the solution is to focus on solving the inequality and oppression that is at the root cause of racial anger, not treat the anger itself as a problem. However, when survivors of circumcision pedophilia speak about Jewish oppression, Jewish identity groups accuse them of antisemitism and treat survivor's anger rather than the source of their anger as the problem. These accusations fail to acknowledge the role that Jewish identity plays in perpetuating systemic pedophilia. The demand that survivors tiptoe around the pedophile fragility of perpetrators creates further pedophilia-based trauma. Tone-policing survivors without acknowledging systemic pedophilia and the role that Jewishness plays in creating that trauma would be like a white police officer attempting to tone-police black activists without acknowledging racism or the role whiteness or policing plays in creating that system. The only solution to the anger of survivors is for Jewish identity groups to acknowledge their role as perpetrators. Survivors have no reason to soften their rhetoric unless there is a reciprocal agreement on the part of perpetrators to create greater safety for those they've harmed. Accusing survivors of circumcision pedophilia of "antisemitism" creates pedophilia-based trauma, even if the survivor is speaking in a way that causes discomfort or triggers the perpetrators' pedophile fragility. Survivors have a right to their feelings, including justified anger.

MEDIA STRESS

Seeing the naked male body can trigger the trauma of survivors. Unlike other forms of pedophilia, circumcision leaves a lasting scar on the body of survivors. Many survivors report feeling trauma when they see the scar on their own body, by being reminded of the harm that was done to them every time they use the bathroom, have sex, or masturbate. Seeing the circumcision scar on another man can remind survivors of their own trauma or cause them to think about the pain that man must have experienced. Even women who are aware of this issue sometimes report feeling sadness at the pain their husbands and partners must have experienced due to this mutilation. Seeing the intact male body can also trigger men's trauma by reminding them of what they do not have and can never get.

The trauma triggered by seeing the male body becomes a cultural stress when the larger society presents these images through media. Any form of media can trigger trauma, including news, film, television shows, online video, podcasts, and even porn. Media often presents circumcision through pedophile-apologist narratives in which circumcision is normative or even a joke. When white media presents blacks as criminals or thugs, this creates race-based trauma. When media presents circumcision pedophilia as normal or a joke, this creates pedophilia-based trauma and reinforces hegemonic pedophile-apologist narratives. The cultural hegemony of systemic pedophilia is present across virtually every form of media.

Even media that does not directly address circumcision can still create pedophilia-based stress. For example, there is an entire genre of shows known as "medical dramas" that reinforce systemic pedophilia by presenting doctors as heroes rather than perpetrators of harm. Narratives that act as propaganda for the perpetrators of systemic pedophilia can create pedophilia-based traumatic stress. Though the survivor may not watch these shows, they can still create pedophilia-based traumatic stress by contributing to the cultural hegemony that upholds systemic pedophilia. Even media that has no harmful narratives can still be engaged in systemic pedophilia if they accept funding or advertising from organizations engaged in systemic pedophilia. Cultural stress is caused by cultural hegemony, and that hegemony is upheld and created through media.

MEDICAL STRESS

For many survivors, visiting the doctor can be a source of pedophilia-based traumatic stress. The medical establishment is the primary perpetrator of circumcision pedophilia. Survivors are understandably hesitant to put their well-being in the hands of people who harmed them as children. Survivors have reported that they deliberately avoid doctors, even when they have a medical condition that might warrant a visit because they want to avoid interacting with or giving money to people engaged in systemic pedophilia. This stress is triggered when there is an unavoidable need for a doctor. In the event of a medical emergency which requires a doctor, survivors must choose between their physical safety and their emotional safety. Most survivors I know only visit the doctor's office when the physical danger is so great they might die unless they go. Even then, one survivor I know personally literally chose to sew up a chainsaw wound on his leg himself rather than visit a doctor.

This stress increases when children are involved. For survivors, bringing a child to the doctor triggers all the same trauma they might feel if they were visiting a perpetrator for their own needs with some added dangers. This stress is justified. Medical professionals frequently forcibly retract intact children's foreskins, which can cause lifelong harm and even infections that can be used by doctors to justify circumcision as a treatment for the harm caused by their sexual assault.[418] This means that if parents take their child to a doctor, they are risking a significant chance the doctor will molest or harm their child. Forcible retraction is often done without parental consent, and many parents report doctors attempting forcible retraction after they explicitly told the doctor not to. Even if the doctor does not directly attempt to harm the child, parents still have the pedophilia-based stress of entrusting the well-being of their child to people engaged in systemic pedophilia. If there is a medical emergency in which a child must be rushed to the hospital, parents face all the same dilemmas survivors face in the same situation, with the added possibility that the doctor might molest their child by forcibly retracting him.

While survivors might wish to opt-out of the medical system entirely, this is impossible. Even if they chose to avoid the doctor's office, the medical system intersects with governments, language, and cultural norms. It appears in all forms of media. After COVID-19, medical organizations have the power to shut down businesses, restrict travel, and reshape society. This makes trauma unavoidable for many survivors, and all of society complicit in the abuse of systemic pedophilia. Every time the power of the medical system expands, it creates greater pedophilia-based traumatic stress.

GENDER STRESS

Most of the research that we have on men is based in systemic pedophilia. Imagine if all of the research we had on women was conducted on primarily women who had endured female genital cutting in infancy. Would we have an accurate picture of women or female sexuality? Our cultural idea of who men are and how they behave is based in a population that has unacknowledged trauma. Awareness of this trauma will radically reshape our picture of who men are and what it means to be a man.

Since the cultural impact of systemic pedophilia extends to our perception of gender, there is pedophilia-based traumatic stress around cultural attitudes towards men and masculinity. Many of the ideas the dominant culture has about what it means to be a man are actually truths about what it means to be a survivor of trauma. For example, the idea that men cannot express or share their feelings could be due to the fact that survivors of trauma typically have a harder time feeling and expressing their emotions. Trauma often causes people to repress their feelings or create emotional defenses if the trauma is not healed. This cultural belief about men is actually an unacknowledged symptom of trauma for which men are victim-blamed. When men have cultural ideas about gender based in systemic pedophilia and trauma imposed on them, they experience a form of ongoing pedophile-based traumatic stress.

SEXUAL STRESS

Circumcision affects sexuality. Circumcision removes the most sensitive part of a man's penis.[419] Men who are intact have been able to demonstrate the ability to have multiple orgasms just by touching parts of their penis which would have been removed if they were circumcised.[420] By changing the structure of the penis, circumcision causes men to need longer strokes in order to achieve orgasm.[421] This changes the dynamics of sex for female partners, and there is research that indicates that women enjoy sex less with circumcised partners, are less likely to orgasm, and are more likely to feel pain during sex.[422] This lack of sexual pleasure is a form of pedophilia-based stress for both men and their partners, in which the trauma of childhood sexual abuse affects future sexual relationships.

Our conception of male sexuality is based in systemic pedophilia. Female genital cutting survivor Patricia Robinett reports that as a circumcised woman, she had sex "like a man" and went from partner to partner thinking some new position or sex act would provide the pleasure she couldn't seem to get with what she would later discover was a circumcised body.[423] Once she found out what had happened to her, she understood why she couldn't seem to feel the pleasure she thought she naturally should. There is research that shows that circumcised men seek out more varied sex than intact men.[424] Researchers have attributed this to mere sexual exploration, but it could also be explained by the idea that these men are seeking pleasure that they instinctively know their bodies should be able to produce but cannot feel, because they are missing the anatomy that would provide it. If this is true, then much of the pain people feel in relationships due to unsatisfying sex, being unsatisfied with their partner, or having their partner be unsatisfied with them could be considered a form of pedophile-based trauma stress. Even the pain women feel when men move from partner to partner, choosing sexual conquest over relationship, could be considered an impact of systemic pedophilia, since these men might be able to be sexually satisfied by one partner if they had their full anatomy. The cultural belief that "men only want one thing" and negative impact stereotypes about male sexuality have could also be considered a part of systemic pedophilia and pedophile-based stress since even women report behaving the same way when a portion of their sexual anatomy is removed through childhood genital cutting. Loss of sexual pleasure and the resulting pain in relationships is a form of pedophile-based traumatic stress.

TRAUMA DUE TO BYSTANDERS

Pedophilia-based traumatic stress also occurs within family systems. For many survivors, the first person they speak to about their circumcision trauma is the person who is usually held responsible for the decision to circumcise, their parents. Although circumcision pedophilia is systemic, with the medical system being the primary culprit, the hegemonic narrative around circumcision is that it is a "parental choice." Given this narrative, it's natural that most survivors upon realizing the horror of that choice would approach the person supposedly responsible to ask them why they made the choice to cut off part of their genitals. Ideally, parents would place the needs of their children first, yet most parents become fragile and defensive when confronted about the issue of circumcision. An honest evaluation of circumcision pedophilia would threaten their self-image as a loving parent and trigger their own subaltern need to appear good. Circumcision involves cutting off parts of children's genitals to appease adult desires, including the desires of hegemonic adult cultural systems. When parents become fragile, they participate in this pattern again, cutting off their child's feelings to appease their adult egos. One could call this rejection of the child's feelings a form of emotional orphaning and the children whose relationship with their parents ends due to this rejection emotional orphans.

While many survivors are aware of the rejection of their parents, less talked about is the bystander effect of others who refuse to support the survivor. The child risks losing their relationship with their parents if they speak up. They might become estranged, excluded, or risk further emotional abuse through their parents' justifications and fragility if they attempt to continue the relationship. However, they also risk losing their relationship with their other family members, mutual friends, or shared community. Others might tell them privately that they understand, but very rarely do the other family members, friends, and members of their community intercede on their behalf. This creates a second trauma around the bystander and the fact no one interceded to stop their abuse. In many cases of abuse, only one of a child's two parents is abusing them, but the survivor will harbor anger not just towards the abusing parent but also towards the bystander parent who failed to protect them. Most survivors of circumcision pedophilia have a form of pedophile-based trauma around the bystanders, including their families, their larger community, and the organizations and social systems that allowed the circumcision pedophilia to happen. In order for a child to be circumcised, there must be an abdication of responsibility at every level of society. Parents must fail to protect their child, doctors must fail to protect their patient, birth professionals must fail to protect the baby, a family must fail to protect their new family member, friends and communities must fail to protect their children, governments must fail to protect the rights of their new citizens, religions must fail to protect their followers, society must fail to protect its weakest members. Circumcision represents a system-wide failure of society, and every part of it is complicit in circumcision pedophilia through their failure to act. This failure is due to the hegemonic narratives and assumptions of systemic pedophilia, which hold that children's bodies can be used to satisfy adult desires rather than that adults have a duty to intercede when they see children being sexually abused.

You have a responsibility to act. When you see a child abused, intercede. When survivors intercede, they are doing others a favor and should be recognized for their heroism and willingness to risk their own safety to protect others. This need to intercede does not just apply to the individual child but to the systems that perpetuate abuse. We make this decision on whether or not to intercede in every interaction with systems that perpetuate systemic pedophilia. Having a critical consciousness means understanding that we are either participating in and are being complicit in these systems or consciously choosing to be antipedophile. Merely because you are not the parent or doctor enacting circumcision pedophilia does not mean you are antipedophile. To be antipedophile, we must intercede. This intercession needs to happen not just in the larger society but in our personal relationships, where there might be a social risk. It includes the person who casually suggests that they "prefer" mutilated genitals, or describes the natural male body as gross. It includes the parents who say that although they wouldn't circumcise their own child, they'd never take that "choice" away from other parents. These are moments that create pedophile-based trauma in survivors and reinforce a culture of systemic pedophilia. When we recognize pedophilia as a system, these moments become politically significant, and the underlying trauma, tension, and stress survivors feel can be explained.

GENERATIONAL TRAUMA

Trauma is passed epigenetically from one generation to the next.[425] Even if you are not circumcised, if you have a circumcised parent, the trauma they feel can be passed from one generation to the next. While traditional cultures and new age spiritual movements have referred to this as ancestral trauma, on racial justice issues this has been referred to as body supremacy, meaning that the trauma of past injustice is carried on a physical level in our bodies.[426] On the issue of systemic pedophilia, this means that even if you have no personal experience of any kind of childhood trauma, you might carry the traumas of your ancestors on a genetic and physical level, including the trauma of genital cutting.

Trauma can also be passed to on others through behavior. People with unprocessed trauma often act from that trauma in their personal relationships. Therapist Resmaa Menakem refers to the way that people unload their unprocessed trauma on others as "dirty pain."[427] Whereas clean pain is when we feel our pain and process it ourselves, dirty pain is when we inflict unhealed trauma on others.[428] Since most people are not even consciously aware of trauma they might have experienced around birth, let alone practicing a healing method to integrate it, it's likely that many people's negative behavior could be due to unprocessed childhood trauma, including the trauma of circumcision. If you have a family member or know someone with unprocessed trauma around systemic pedophilia, it is possible for them to inflict their trauma on you. As Menakem puts it, "trauma is routinely spread *between* bodies, like a contagious disease. When someone with unhealed trauma chooses dirty pain over clean pain, the person may try to soothe his or her trauma by blowing it through another person… This never heals the trauma."[429] Living in a society full of people with unprocessed trauma due to systemic pedophilia is itself a form of forms of pedophile-based traumatic stress.

Pedophile-based traumatic stress could also include the downstream effects of genital cutting. For example, suppose a father is sexually unsatisfied in his marriage because of the pleasure missing due to circumcision. Seeking the pleasure he unconsciously feels his body should be able to produce, he cheats on his wife. She finds out, and they divorce. The pain in that marriage, resulting divorce, and impact of that divorce on their children could be thought of as a form of pedophile-based traumatic stress since the marital problems and cheating would not have occurred if the father was whole. The father, mother, and children have all experienced pedophile-based traumatic stress, whether they are aware of the role circumcision played in the destruction of their family or not. There might be a whole host of experiences like this that have a root cause in genital cutting, despite most not realizing it.

Trauma is not merely an individual problem. While trauma might find a host in individual bodies, it can be passed through family systems, cultures, and social institutions. Unhealed trauma can drive people's actions even if they are not consciously aware of it. Critical theory teaches that we are not merely individuals, but participate in social systems. This includes systems of trauma. If we include the downstream impacts of pedophile-based traumatic stress, every aspect of society has been impacted by this trauma in some form. This means we have a responsibility to heal, not just for ourselves, but for the sake of everyone we impact, including our future children.

VARIED IMPACT

All of these stresses can be highly individualized. The way one person reacts to or experiences systemic pedophilia might be completely different from the next. For example, a Jewish man whose social circle includes the mohel perpetrator who circumcised him is going to experience pedophilia-based traumatic stress around Jewishness different than someone who experienced medical circumcision but can't speak about their trauma without fear of being called antisemitic. There might be as many forms of pedophilia-based traumatic stress as there are people affected by systemic pedophilia. One could create an entire book just on the various ways systemic pedophilia creates pedophile-based traumatic stress through culture.

Collecting these stories will require epistemic justice. It will require the testimonial justice for people's lived experiences to be heard, and the hermeneutic justice to have the language to express them and resources to collect and share them. This work is essential if we want to understand the full impact of systemic pedophilia and create justice for those impacted. The harms of circumcision extend beyond the initial act of genital cutting into the whole of society. Ending systemic pedophilia requires more than ending circumcision, but instead involves changing all aspects of culture responsible for pedophile-based traumatic stress.

CHAPTER 22
RESTORATIVE JUSTICE

How do we set right the wrongs of systemic pedophilia? Systemic issues require a broader view of justice than individual crimes. Whereas individual crimes have a single perpetrator, systemic issues involve the participation of multiple parts of society. Any form of justice brought against the participants in systemic pedophilia would not just apply to the individual cutting children, but to the whole of society, including all institutions and people who participated in that system.

The dominant model for justice in America is the criminal justice system, which functions on punitive justice, meaning that if you commit a crime you a punished for it. While this model creates a deterrent for crime in the form of punishment, it does nothing to help those harmed. On the issue of genital cutting, even if every perpetrator were jailed, survivors would still have to live with trauma and mutilation of circumcision. Jailing every perpetrator would also be unfeasible. If we were to jail every person involved in systemic pedophilia, there would be more people in jail than outside it, since circumcision pedophilia is systemic and involves every aspect of society. Is there a way we could bring justice that would actually help survivors?

PRINCIPLES OF RESTORATIVE JUSTICE

One model is restorative justice. Restorative justice is an approach to crime that focuses on repairing the harm caused by wrongdoing rather than merely punishing criminals.[430] Whereas criminal justice often focuses only on the laws broken by the wrongdoer, restorative justice expands it's focus to the victims and everyone affected by wrongdoing.[431] Restorative justice looks at the needs of those harmed, the obligations that result from those harms, and seeks to repair that harm to the extent possible.[432] According to longtime practitioners of restorative justice, in order for restorative justice to take place, "Three things have to happen:

1. The wrong or injustice must be acknowledged;
2. Equity needs to be created or restored;
3. Future intentions need to be addressed."[433]

On the issue of systemic pedophilia, we could create restorative justice if the wrongdoing was acknowledged, survivors were given equity (meaning that the harm was repaired to the extent possible), and society changed such that the harm could never happen again. This could be accomplished without jailing every perpetrator and would help survivors more than extreme punitive measures.

Before trying to solve a major social problem, let's look at these three steps using a fairly innocuous injustice. Suppose a guest in your home broke something important to you. How would they create restorative justice around their wrongdoing of them breaking one of your possessions? The first step is acknowledgment of wrongdoing. The most common way people acknowledge their wrongdoing is to apologize. If someone broke something important to you, you'd want them to say "I'm sorry." Yet the words "I'm sorry" are as far as many apologies go. What takes the apology from words to repair is actions, the second step of restorative justice. If your guest said "I'm sorry" but made no effort to repair or clean up the broken item, you might still feel wronged. If they apologized and offered to repair the broken item or buy you a new one, you might be more likely to accept their apology, because they would have done the second step of creating equity around their wrongdoing. Yet full restorative justice would require the third step of ensuring the harm does not happen again. On an injustice this innocuous, that might just mean being more careful in the future. However, if this wrongdoing was the result of ill will rather than an honest mistake, those underlying intentions would need to be addressed. For example, if the item was broken in a fit of rage, you'd want them to address their underlying anger issues before handling your possessions again. If you had told them the item was fragile and they had ignored your instructions on how to handle it, you might need them to listen to you in the future. This third step is important because even if they always replaced what they broke, you might still feel wronged if they made it a habit of repeatedly breaking your things. If all three steps were followed and there was acknowledgment of wrongdoing, equity or repair, and future intentions addressed, most people would feel resolved around the issue.

These principles also apply to public figures. If a politician or public figure caught in a scandal says they "deeply regret" their actions, unless they change their actions, the public often assumes they just "deeply regret" getting caught. If someone breaks our trust, they have to repair it. Emotional repair or repair in relationships can take time, but it is usually possible. Even when it is not possible, we still usually want the other person to do as much as they can. However, the third step is where they really earn our trust again by ensuring the harm does not happen again. For a public figure, this could mean changing their beliefs, creating accountability, or even stepping down from power. Whereas the second step was about healing the victim, the third step is about healing the perpetrator. This requires the perpetrator to learn from the experience and change as a result of it. For example, if a public figures wrongdoing was due to their addiction, they might need to heal the underlying root cause of their addiction to ensure they don't harm others from this addiction again. If a public figure does not take this third step and keeps getting caught in the same scandal over and over again, the public will be less likely to accept their amends after each consecutive wrongdoing.

These steps also appear in the way society has tried to address historical injustices. Governments have issued a formal apology for historical atrocities. They have created society-wide acknowledgment of certain events through teaching, monuments, museums, national holidays, etc. While this acknowledgment is often just words, it is the first step. Equity proposals like giving land back to Native Americans or giving reparations to the descendants of slavery fall into the second step of trying to repair what was broken. Human rights and civil rights laws fall into the third step of ensuring the harm does not happen again. Many social movements about this third step involve changing the underlying beliefs and attitudes responsible for historical injustices. For example, although the injustice of institutional slavery has been outlawed in America, unless the underlying causes are addressed, the racist beliefs which lead to slavery could result in other forms of injustice. There is even an entire field of restorative justice that aims to address racial justice issues.[434]

These three steps of restorative justice, acknowledgment, creating equity, and addressing future intentions, can be applied to something as small as a personal conflict or as large as historical injustices. What would it look like if we were to apply the restorative justice model to the wrongdoing of systemic pedophilia?

ACKNOWLEDGMENT OF WRONGDOING

The first step is acknowledgment of wrongdoing. Survivors have not even been able to get this yet. When men share their feelings around infant circumcision, the reaction is usually pedophile fragility. Parents often become defensive, claim they did it for their children's own good. Medical organizations use phrases like "your google search does not replace my medical degree" to engage in epistemic violence against survivors. Jewish organizations engage in DARVO by framing survivors speaking about the injustice as attacking Jewish perpetrators. In some forms of restorative justice, victims and perpetrators sit in a circle with facilitators and community and come to a shared agreement about justice through communication.[435] Yet, on the issue of genital cutting, the perpetrators refuse to even come to the table. Why is it so difficult for those engaged in systemic pedophilia to even acknowledge the issue?

The dominant model in American society is criminal justice. In the criminal justice model, an apology constitutes an admission of guilt. If medical groups admit wrongdoing, they open themselves to legal liability for harming millions of Americans. This would bankrupt most medical institutions. Even if medical institutions were aware of the problem, they could not afford to acknowledge it. While parents aren't opening themselves to legal liability, they might not want to pay the emotional price of acknowledgment. For Jewish groups, admitting the harm of circumcision might cost them some of their socially constructed identity. In each case, underneath the fragility is vulnerability. The perpetrators lash out because they do not want to admit fault. Ironically, the failure to acknowledge wrongdoing closes off the possibility of a gentler cooperative restorative justice process and leaves survivors no choice but to pursue punitive justice or no justice at all.

Consider our earlier example in which a guest breaks something you own. Suppose they apologize profusely but say they cannot possibly afford to replace what they've broken. Perhaps the item is one of a kind or has sentimental value that makes it so it cannot possibly be replaced. What would you do? Now imagine the same scenario, but instead of apologizing, your guest gaslights you. They claim they didn't break it, but if they did, it is better broken. Now, what would you do? While each person might answer differently, most would be more sympathetic to a sincere apology than a total refusal to admit any wrongdoing. While refusing to admit fault might protect the beliefs and pocketbooks of perpetrators, it creates greater pedophilia-based traumatic stress for survivors and causes them to want more punitive forms of justice, since the perpetrators have denied the possibility of shared restorative justice.

The angriest survivors I know are those whose who feel their pain was never acknowledged. Among activists, I've seen t-shirts that say "circumcisors behind bars" or "death to circumcision."[436] According to the criminal justice system, people who abuse children do belong behind bars. They would be entirely within their rights to demand this in the current system. Yet at the same time, the movement against circumcision includes former doctors and nurses who used to perform circumcisions.[437] These former perpetrators are readily accepted by the same activists who call for jail time for circumcisers because they have acknowledged their wrongdoing and are now working to end the injustice. If other perpetrators collectively acknowledged their wrongdoing, survivors might be willing to find a form of restorative justice in which they work together to end the problem rather than merely being punished for their part in it.

CREATING EQUITY

In critical social justice, equity is defined as equality of outcomes. Equity is different from the liberal definition of equality, which is equality of opportunity. From the perspective of pedophile-apologists, equality already exists because every parent has the same opportunity to choose circumcision or not. From the perspective of human rights activists, equality will exist when every child has the right to their own body. However, from the perspective of critical social justice, equality is not enough. Not only must children have the body they are born with, but we must create equitable outcomes for the survivors of infant genital cutting and the historic victims of systemic pedophilia. Creating equity would mean making sure that the survivors of circumcision pedophilia have the same outcomes they would have had if they were never harmed and are compensated for the historical atrocity they experienced. If no more children are circumcised, but the survivors remain harmed, equity has not been achieved. In order for there to be equity, we must set right as much of the damage of circumcision as possible.

Consider what equity has looked like on other issues. Equity for black Americans does not mean just ending slavery or racial discrimination laws. It has also included proposals for reparations to pay for the lost generational wealth modern black Americans would have had if their ancestors had been allowed to accumulate it. Equity for Native Americans has included proposals to give back the land native tribes once owned but lost to conquest. While these proposals may seem radical, from the perspective of critical social justice they are necessary to not just create equality now but fix the long-term harm of previous injustices.

Looking at systemic pedophilia through the lens of equity creates possibilities previously unthinkable in the human rights model. For example, taking wealth from institutions and people involved in systemic pedophilia and giving it to their victims or to research designed to regrow the body parts lost to circumcision would not be possible in the human rights model, but very much so in the critical social justice model. The goal of equity is not just to create modern equality but to correct the historical wrong. If the survivors had never experienced systemic pedophilia, where would they be now? The answer to that question tells us what must be done.

How could we create equity for the survivors of circumcision? First, survivors deserve the full body they were born with. This means equity will not be achieved until the full physical damage of circumcision can be repaired. There is already the idea among some survivors of systemic pedophilia that the foreskin can be regrown through regenerative medicine.[438] Right now, these efforts are being privately funded through individual donors and investors. Restorative justice would suggest that the people, systems, and identity groups who engaged in systemic pedophilia have an obligation to pay for healing the wounds their actions caused. These reparations should include payment for both the research and each individual survivor's regeneration, should he choose to receive it. This is the bare minimum for any equity proposal.

The harm of systemic pedophilia is not merely physical. Pedophilia affects us on an emotional, social, and systemic level. Full equity must address these deeper levels for all groups affected by systemic pedophilia. If there are aspects of survivors that have been psychologically fragmented in subaltern power dynamics, they must be supported in integrating back into the consciousness of the survivor. Right now, there are very few resources for those affected by systemic pedophilia. Many survivors report being gaslit by their own therapists and doctors when they seek support for issues related to circumcision because pedophile-apologists in those positions frame the abuse that occurred to them as normal. Creating the support necessary for integration will require the resources to create true healers. Again, it is not equity if the survivors must fund their own healing. This healing must be paid for by the perpetrators, including the training of healers and payment for survivors who wish to work with them.

All of this will require epistemic justice for survivors. Epistemic justice includes testimonial justice, in which survivor's feelings, stories, and lived experiences are heard, and hermeneutical justice, in which survivors are given the words to tell their stories and access to the resources to tell them. This might include gathering the information necessary to understand the full impact of systemic pedophilia. Right now, resources are given to pedophile-apologist research. Equity for survivors of genital cutting would mean using the money and resources previously spent developing pedophile-apologist narratives on research that benefits survivors. Survivors should not have to self-fund the research they need to understand a problem created by one of the wealthiest industries in the world. The perpetrators have an obligation to contribute as much money towards solving the problem of systemic pedophilia as they spent creating it.

The above would create equity in the present. However, the harm of systemic pedophilia is not limited to the present day. Even if the foreskin could be regenerated tomorrow and all of society was to transform to end this systemic abuse and give epistemic justice to those harmed, survivors would still have experienced years of the opposite, including the emotional and physical pain from circumcision, the reduced sexual sensation, the fragmentation and trauma, the years of gaslighting and emotional abuse by the greater society, years of childhood spent in a subaltern state, the systemic impact of the medical gaze, the grooming behaviors of the medical system, and the behavior of pedophile identity groups. How can we create equity not just for the present problem but for the historical injustice? On the issue of racial justice, the leading voice on antiracism, Ibram Kendi, who has spoken at one of the largest circumcising doctors groups that sets policy on circumcision,[439] says ""'The only remedy to past discrimination is present discrimination. The only remedy to present discrimination is future discrimination."[440] In other words, in order to right a historical wrong, we might need to privilege the historically oppressed group in the present. On the issue of systemic pedophilia, this might mean going above and beyond repairing the harm of genital cutting to give survivors even more in the present. This view of antiracism explicitly endorses discrimination in favor of historically oppressed groups. Applied to the issue of systemic pedophilia, this would mean explicitly favoring historical victims of genital cutting over historical perpetrators in legal, economic, and social matters. If this sounds extreme, keep in mind that this view has been endorsed by circumcising institutions on other issues, including medical institutions and Jewish identity groups. While many survivors might merely be content to receive equity in the present and leave the past in the past, future discrimination in some form is the logical conclusion of applying the concept of equity as endorsed by perpetrators to this issue.

While Jewish identity groups might object to the restorative justice or equity model, it is less harsh than the model of reciprocal justice model presented in Jewish texts.[441] The model for justice in Jewish texts is "eye for eye, tooth for tooth, hand for hand, foot for foot, burn for burn, wound for wound, bruise for bruise."[442] In this model, the person harmed visits the same harm upon the person who harmed them. The reciprocal Jewish justice of "eye for eye" applied to this issue would mean holding down perpetrators of systemic pedophilia and cutting off part of their genitals without anesthesia. Jewish justice would mean reconstructing every system of Jewishness, Jewish fragility, and epistemic violence that Jewish identity groups have used against survivors, and using them against Jewish people. This model would create more harm in the name of punishing harm. Using this reciprocal justice model would only reinforce the social constructions of Jewishness rather than liberate people from them. Restorative justice gives Jewish groups the opportunity to participate in justice and healing, rather than simply have justice applied to them. The restorative justice model is better for both survivors and perpetrators.

FUTURE INTENTIONS

While the above proposals might repair the current harm survivors experience, how do we prevent the system from engaging in further abuse? If all the perpetrators have to do is pay a fine, then the issue of systemic pedophilia simply becomes a cost-benefit analysis for them. If those who are responsible remain in power and unchanged, they may engage in further abuse. This third step requires the perpetrators to change the beliefs, intentions, and systems that created the abuse. Systemic pedophilia is not merely an individual action. In order to prevent further abuses, the entire system must be dismantled.

Systemic pedophilia is the unavoidable conclusion of the medical gaze. The means that in order to prevent further systemic pedophilia, the medical system must move from a fragmented view of health to a holistic one. This will require changing the way medical professionals are trained and retraining those who continue to work in this field. Again, the cost of this training must come from those institutions. The medical system already does this on other social justice issues. Many medical schools and institutions require diversity and inclusion training based in critical race theory. These trainings frequently teach ideas seen as controversial by the wider culture, which might contradict some medical professionals' deeply held beliefs. Given that medical institutions already pay for and train their doctors in critical theory ideas which might contradict some doctors' deeply held beliefs, asking them to adopt another critical theory training is a reasonable request and within the existing system.

Many medical institutions also have a diversity and inclusion policy. Medical professionals who fail to follow this policy can lose their job. An egregious act of discrimination might even cost a doctor their medical license. Since there already exists a policy by which doctors can be fired for failing to include certain identity groups, we could expand this policy to include survivors of systemic pedophilia and the imposed identity created by circumcision. If doctors use pedophile-apologist language (ex: "uncircumcised"), medical institutions could treat it the same way they would if the doctor was to use harmful language towards any other identity group. Committing actual harm towards this group would be treated like any other hate crime. Since the medical system has shown an inability to regulate itself, those trained in Children's Justice would have to replace medical boards. On racial justice issues, critical race theorists are already assuming positions of power within the medical system, even if they do not hold medical training themselves. In fact, it would be better if those overseeing the medical system were not indoctrinated into the medical gaze or morally culpable for a circumcision due to medical school. We must create accountability.

This process of retraining, inclusion, and accountability must occur at all levels of the systems involved in systemic pedophilia.

Those which cannot be reformed must be deconstructed and dismantled. If this does not seem easy to imagine, remember that critical theory has already done this on the issue of race and has a repeatable method by which it can be accomplished. Critical race theorists built an independent academic discipline, trained people as diversity consultants, and then placed them in institutions. These activists created diversity and inclusion policies based in critical race theory in institutions whose stated purpose had nothing to do with race or critical theory. Since institutions already take a stand on social justice issues, every institution is now an inroad for Children's Justice. There are multiple paths by which restorative justice could be accomplished, but it will only happen if we are first willing to imagine it.

APPLYING JUSTICE

These steps might look different depending on the parties involved. For example, a Jewish survivor of ritual Jewish circumcision will have different needs for justice than someone who is not Jewish but has been harmed by cultural trauma resulting from Jewish fragility. The intersectionality of each person's identity affects what justice looks like for them. Justice may also look different if the perpetrator is willing to join the victim in a shared intention for justice or resists acknowledging any wrongdoing. If the perpetrator refuses to engage in any way, survivors may have to choose between imposing retributive justice through something like the criminal justice system or no justice at all. If perpetrators refuse to engage, this will create an adversarial relationship between those who want justice and those who do not, which may result in greater penalties than would have been imposed had the survivor and perpetrator been able to come to a shared understanding of justice. Mutual participation in the process of justice benefits both survivor and perpetrator. Together, we can create justice.

CHAPTER 23
DIVERSE ALLIES

There is already a broad intersectional coalition for social justice issues. In the past, when those working to end circumcision have tried to join these coalitions, they have had mixed results. Some organizations that should be ideologically aligned to ending circumcision have rejected the cause, while others have embraced it. The decision to include ending circumcision in the category of social justice issues has been treated as controversial by dominant members of the coalition. This seems odd given that most social justice organizations embrace the idea of intersectionality, which suggests that our struggle for justice is a shared one and oppression affects us all. When one group is oppressed, we are all oppressed. This intersectional view of oppression suggests that we should all work together to create change, and not just on the issue that most closely affects our own predicament, but our shared issues and those that affect others. Why then are social justice organizations reluctant to embrace a cause that intersects with issues of gender, consent, capitalism, and other established social justice topics?

CURRENT COALITION

The very thing that makes social justice activism so successful is also what makes it susceptible to attack from pedophile-apologists. The modern social justice movement is a coalition. Within the social justice cause, there are multiple movements focused on different issues such as gay rights, gender equality, racial justice, etc. Each of these causes has their own organizations and groups. When these groups work together, they can accomplish more than they could individually. However, within this coalition exist power dynamics. If one organization crosses another, they risk being alienated not just from the offended organization, but from the whole coalition. This dynamic is easily exploited by organizations that label themselves as social justice organizations but which are actually pedophile-apologist organizations. If a pedophile-apologist organization joins the coalition and brings in significant resources, they can keep allied organizations from breaking rank and endorsing ending circumcision as a legitimate cause. Organizations do not even have to consist mainly of pedophile-apologists to become pedophile-apologist organizations. They only need a strong-willed minority from within or a major donor on whose support they depend that wants them not to oppose systemic pedophilia. Organizations function like coalitions internally, with different people often having different agendas. Just as organizations do not want to offend other organizations in their coalition, they also do not want to offend those within their organization or those on whose support their organization depends. In this way, a tiny minority of donors or supporters could hypothetically control entire coalitions of social justice causes.

Unfortunately, those engaged in systemic pedophilia are more than a tiny minority. They are the dominant power in American culture. Pedophile-apologists within the social justice coalition come from three primary categories. First, the medical system, which has a strong presence within social justice through organizations like Planned Parenthood, the World Health Organization (WHO), Amnesty International, the United Nations (UN), United Nations Children's Fund (UNICEF), and various organizations seeking to end AIDS and HIV in Africa. Jewish identity groups are also deeply involved in social justice coalitions. The largest and most influential in this category is the Anti-Defamation League (ADL), which has openly targeted attempted circumcision bans.[443] The Anti-Defamation League was founded to defend a Jewish pedophile named Leo Frank who was convicted of raping and murdering a thirteen-year-old girl.[444] The ADL has claimed this conviction was based in "antisemitism," a discourse they were using to defend pedophiles as early as the 1910s, despite overwhelming evidence of Frank's crime.[445] The racism present at Frank's trial came from Leo Frank and his attorney, who openly used the word "n——r" in court to frame his black employee Jim Conley for the murder.[446] During the trial, Leo Frank's attorney said "it's a n——r crime, gentlemen "[447] and "if there is any one thing that a n——r can do it is lie"[448] to engage in testimonial injustice against Conley. This court case has been cited as the reason for the founding of the ADL.[449] The ADL has been a pedophile-apologist organization from the beginning. The defense of the Leo Frank case attempted to frame black men as rapists in order to protect Jewishness. In modern times, pedophile-apology takes the form of defending circumcision and systemic pedophilia. The ADL and similar Jewish identity groups are deeply involved in social justice coalitions and have considerable power and influence.

The third category of pedophile-apologists within social justice activism is that of unconscious pedophile-apologists. We live in a culture that normalizes systemic pedophilia and socializes adults into an internalized dominance towards children. Many people see using children to fulfill adult desires as normal. Since pedophilia has been normalized in the context of circumcision, many social justice activists who do good work on other issues support systemic pedophilia and have not yet questioned their own internalized dominance towards children. While they might not consciously advocate for systemic pedophilia like the medical system or Jewish identity groups, those without a critical consciousness on this issue are often unintentional allies of systemic pedophilia. Some social justice activists see acknowledging systemic pedophilia as a threat to other narratives. For example, organizations that have a narrative in which men are always the dominant oppressor of women might experience fragility when asked to acknowledge an issue where men are oppressed or women are oppressors. Between these three groups, the influence of pedophile-apologists within social justice coalitions is significant and must be critically examined.

SOCIAL INJUSTICE

Is social justice compatible with systemic pedophilia? The roots of oppression begin in childhood. Unless we believe people are born oppressors, all power dynamics are learned. This learning begins in infancy, during the subaltern state of childhood. Antiracism and social justice require us to examine where we first learned racist ideas and oppressive power dynamics in childhood.[450] Participation in systems that create racism is a form of racism. If the roots of oppression begin in childhood, racism is learned, and participation in systems that produce racism is a form of racism, then organizations that support systemic pedophilia are not social justice organizations, but racist pedophile-apologist organizations, because they are complicit in systems that teach the emotional patterns necessary for oppression. Groups that work with these organizations are allies to racist pedophile-apologists, or pedophile-adjacent.

The modern social justice movement has a systemic pedophilia problem. There are people and organizations at all levels of the social justice coalition which passively and actively support systemic pedophilia. These organizations are deeply embedded in social justice networks. This problem must be treated the way social justice movements treat racist, bigoted, or hateful organizations and people that attempt to join their movement. Many social justice activists might protest that organizations and people engaged in systemic pedophilia are large, powerful, and contribute significant resources to the movement. Here, activists must decide how much they are willing to be paid to engage in oppression. Is there a price for which activists would engage in racism, pedophilia, or support the roots of oppression? When activists say they cannot go against pedophile-apologist or pedophile-adjacent organizations because of the power and money involved, they place power and money above social justice. If these activists value power and money more than justice, they might be better suited to a different career where they explicitly pursue wealth and power without pretending their work is about ending oppression.

Ending the roots of oppression will require systemic changes to the social justice movement. Most organizations have a statement or policy on racial justice, gender equality, etc. However, few organizations have a statement on Children's Justice or a policy officially opposing pedophilia. Committing to being antipedophile will mean that organizations cannot just be "not a pedophile" but must critically examine the ways in which they engage in systemic pedophilia. They will have to create statements against systemic pedophilia and rigorously enforce these policies, as much as they enforce statements against racism. Social justice movements already know what to do here and have been doing this on other issues for a long time. All this requires is extending the same commitment that these organizations already have towards other issues to systemic pedophilia.

UNRECOGNIZED ANTIRACISM

Since they have been excluded, those who oppose circumcision have had to seek allies outside the coalition. Movements and organizations outside the social justice coalition have also seen an opportunity to embrace obviously justified causes such as the opposition to pedophilia. Many of these movements and organizations would be considered problematic or even racist by the existing social justice movement. Those within the current social justice coalition will often use associations with problematic groups to exclude legitimate issues from their movement. This creates a double-bind for organizations against circumcision. The social justice coalition will not allow them in, so they have to seek allies outside of it. Yet, if they seek allies outside the coalition, the coalition will frame those allies as "problematic" and use them as an excuse to prevent them from joining the coalition. Activists are in a hard place of rejecting those offering help in favor of groups that won't help them, or accepting help from people whose association might brand them as "racist" or problematic in some way. Can activists include "problematic" people and organizations in their coalition?

It is possible to be antipedophile and still racist. In fact, it is possible to be an antiracist activist and still be racist. Critical social justice suggests that everyone is racist because everyone participates in systems that create unequal outcomes. In the view of critical race theory, it is worse for someone to say they are "not racist" than be consciously or openly racist because at least an open racist knows they are engaged in racist systems and can change, whereas the color-blind racist is in denial of their racism.[451] Many of the top authors in critical social justice theory such as Robin DiAngelo and Ibram X. Kendi recount stories in their books where they engaged in racism.[452] In their view, acknowledging our own racism is part of the work of antiracism.[453] It would be impossible to create a movement free from racists, and even the antiracism movement does not attempt to do this. Rather, antiracism suggests that we critically examine the ways in which we engage in racism. If it is even impossible for antiracism to build a movement free from racism, then no other movement can hope to achieve this. While we would prefer those involved to do the antiracist work of examining the roots of their beliefs in childhood, we cannot exclude people from a movement to abolish the roots of oppression because they experienced oppression. If someone is racist, it is because they were socialized into it. This socialization begins in childhood, through the power dynamics of oppression created in infancy. Someone who is in denial of their racism, or even openly supports racist ideas or policies, is a victim of the systemic childhood oppression we are working to end.

Children's Justice is one way to engage in the work of antiracism. Even if someone does not see themselves as antiracist or even self-identifies as a racist, they are engaged in antiracism work if they are working to end the roots of oppression. Suggesting that someone should not be allowed to work to end racism because they are racist ultimately supports racism and is, therefore, a racist idea. This idea comes from white fragility and the desire for white activists to appear as "good whites." Many activists are deeply afraid of being called racist and use social justice as a form of performative antiracism. Working alongside people who are seen as racist jeopardizes their status as "good whites" and "not racist" self-image. When these activists exclude people, they are supporting systemic racism to protect their own white fragility because they are afraid to admit that they are racist and do the critical work of examining their own racism. Fragile activists are more afraid of appearing racist than actually ending racism. If these activists actually wish to do the critical work of antiracism, they must stop being so afraid of being called racist to the point where they sabotage their own work to end oppression. Being antiracist might include working alongside racists to end the roots of oppression in childhood.

Activists are often fragile to the accusation of racism because this label has been used by pedophile-apologist organizations and media to marginalize antipedophile activism. When the accusation of racism is used to protect the harm of children, it is a form of pedophile fragility and participation in systemic pedophilia. Since most activists are not versed in critical theory and fear this accusation would marginalize their work and harm children, in the past many have responded by trying to show how they are not racist. Critical theory and antiracism would instead suggest shifting the discussion to what systems both you and the accuser are participating in. In what way do they feel your work supports systems that perpetuate unequal outcomes? If we are indeed antiracist, this is a welcome discussion, and we are prepared to critically examine our own behavior. However, if the intention of this argument is to silence advocates for children, it is a pedophile-apologist argument and the accusers must be called out for their participation in systemic pedophilia. When this accusation of racism is used to defend pedophilia, it is also a form of racism, since it protects the underlying roots of oppression necessary for racism. If the accusation comes in the form of "antisemitism," the accuser engaged in a racist discourse and form of epistemic violence to protect their own pedophile fragility.

Antiracism is about what systems we participate in and what outcomes we create. If the outcome of an action supports racism, it is racist. If the outcome of an action reduces racism, it is antiracist.[454] Since ending systemic pedophilia and childhood oppression ends the emotional power dynamics necessary for racism, anyone working to end circumcision is engaged in antiracism as well. Even if someone is a racist, in the moment in which they engage in antipedophile activism they are antiracist. The desire for everyone involved on this issue to appear "not racist" is a form of fragility. Everyone who effectively works for justice for children is by definition antiracist.[455]

SHARED LANGUAGE

Do these issues have to be expressed in the language of critical theory? Many of the people, activists, and organizations that are potential allies to ending systemic pedophilia do not understand or subscribe to the ideas of critical theory, including organizations currently involved in ending circumcision. This book is the first of its kind to systematically apply critical theory to children's issues and view children as a unique subaltern class. Much of the language used here comes from previous critical theory and social justice literature, but many of the ideas, terms, and discourse in this book are new. Must all allies speak with this new discourse to work together?

To learn critical theory, I had to read many college-level books and academic papers. Most people do not have the privilege or time to do this. It requires extended free time, money, and a high education level. The people currently working to end genital cutting often have other commitments that prevent them from having the time to read academic critical theory. Even if they did have the time, they might want to invest that time in things that directly help themselves and their family rather than abstract theory. Seeing how this material might benefit them or the issues they care about requires someone who is willing to translate academic terminology into language and ideas they understand. This has been done with popular authors and training around other issues, but this has not been done around this issue until this book. For most people, critical theory has not been accessible. In the past, only those with a college education in elite academic institutions were exposed to critical theory. This means critical theory was applied to adult identity issues that affect those with an elite education, and not to children's issues. The tools of critical theory have been unevenly distributed among only those privileged enough to be exposed to them. If critical theory is useful in helping the oppressed, the less privileged must be given access to it.

At the same time, we must also be willing to hear marginalized groups even if they lack the privilege to articulate their ideas using the language of critical theory. Oppressor groups often come from elite institutions and medical schools. Many pedophile-apologists within the social justice coalition are well-versed in theory. Survivors of systemic pedophilia come from all walks of life. Many do not have the privilege of elite education. When survivors speak, they are more likely to use imprecise everyday language rather than academic theory. Pedophile-apologists within the social justice coalition frequently demand that survivors speak the complex language of academic theory and critical social justice, and then frame their inability to speak that language as a form of racism or antisemitism as a tactic to create epistemic injustice. Demanding marginalized groups speak the language of their oppressor is epistemic oppression.[456] Refusing to hear them unless they speak in a language they do not have access to is epistemic violence.[457] When pedophile-apologist organizations in the social justice coalition refuse to listen to survivors who do not speak the language of critical social justice, they are engaged in both epistemic oppression and epistemic violence. On this issue, theory is more often used as a tool to silence the oppressed than advocate for them.

Social justice activists would not suggest that any other identity group should experience testimonial injustice if they do not use academic language to describe their lived experience. There is even a saying in social justice circles which comes from Martin Luther King Jr. that "a riot is the language of the unheard," suggesting that even violence and looting can be a form of communication which social justice activists ought to hear.[458] We must listen to and include those affected by systemic pedophilia, even if they do not express their perspective in the language of critical theory or social justice. This language may seem offensive. When men speak about their feelings of victimization, their testimony is often marginalized as "angry," "offensive," or "inappropriate." This is especially true when they speak about their abusers, who include Jewish circumcisers. While it is true that they might express these perspectives better if they had access to the language of critical theory and social justice, we must give testimonial justice to the survivors of systemic pedophilia even if they lack the privilege of an elite education. Where these victims lack language, it is because critical theorists and social justice activists have not done the work to create hermeneutic justice and include these men in their coalition and discourse. The fact those harmed by systemic pedophilia often do not have the language to express their reality represents a failing of critical social justice to create hermeneutic justice for them. This book is an attempt to create epistemic justice for those impacted by systemic pedophilia by giving them the language and power/knowledge to express their ideas through the dominant discourse of critical social justice theory. There is still more work to do to create this language, distribute it, popularize it, and include it in social justice organizations and coalitions. However, the responsibility to communicate and listen rests on social justice organizations, not survivors. Social justice activists have a responsibility to listen to the oppressed and give them the tools to communicate their lived experience, rather than demand they speak the language of their oppressors.

The language of critical theory cannot become a gatekeeper to justice. This book is written in the style of critical social justice, but everyday people do not yet use this language. Terms like "epistemic injustice," "subaltern," and "imposed identity" are not yet popular in the dominant culture. While people might benefit if they were more widely known, we must still listen to and include those who still speak in everyday language. This includes people and organizations seeking to create justice that speak in a more abrasive or imprecise manner or do not even hold the ideas of critical theory at all. It even includes people who are in some way problematic or racist. If they are oppressed, they deserve to be heard.

CHAPTER 24
LIBERATING TOLERANCE

When objections to circumcision are even acknowledged by the dominant hegemony, they are usually framed through the lens of "the circumcision debate." The most significant medical and Intactivist sources, the American Academy of Pediatrics,[459] and Intact America,[460] both use this phrase. The phrase also appears repeatedly across medical websites, news sources, and parenting information. This framing usually encourages parents to "weigh the pros and the cons" of circumcision in order to make a decision that is right for them.[461] An activist working within this frame would argue that the "cons" of circumcision outweigh the "pros." Critical theory would suggest examining the social construction of the frame itself. What assumptions and forms of power does the language of "the circumcision debate" create?

THE DEBATE FRAME

The frame of a "debate" contains certain assumptions in a liberal society. In Western societies, debates are supposed to be "evidence-based," especially on issues framed as "medical" or scientific." "Ad hominems" and personal attacks are frowned upon. Since all circumcision discussion takes place within this frame created by dominant institutions, "the circumcision debate" frame also creates assumptions about what constitutes acceptable behavior for activists. In this frame, activists are allowed to logically argue for their position, as long as they do not personally attack those involved in systemic pedophilia. Many of the criticisms those within systemically pedophile power structures level against activists are directed at activists' refusal to play within the debate frame. For example, when activists point out the wrong-doing of pedophile-apologists, those within the dominant power structure will frequently frame being held accountable for their actions as an "attack."[462]

The debate frame also contains assumptions about the audience. The debate frame assumes the audience listening should evaluate both sides objectively and impartially. This assumption is clearly false to anyone who has ever actually debated any subject important to them. Audiences are not rational. They bring a whole series of biases and assumptions based on their own socialization, identity, and cultural conditioning.[463] The space in which debate takes place is sometimes referred to as the "marketplace of ideas," an analogy that frames audiences as rational actors in a "free market" who will naturally choose the best position. In reality, the "marketplace of ideas" is much closer to the markets that exist in reality, where dominant entrenched monopolies have significant advantages and people frequently engage in false consciousness against their own interests. The market is not rational, nor is it free.

The discourse of the debate frame gives an unfair advantage to those in power, while claiming to create an equal playing field. Activists face a whole series of systemic, cultural, and epistemic forms of oppression, while pedophile-apologists are protected from legitimate criticism. In the past, activists have been constrained to this debate frame due to their belief in liberalism. Yet pedophile-apologists have been willing to discard this frame when it suits them. For example, when Bay Area Intactivists attempted to have the circumcision debate through the democratic process of a ballot initiative, pro-circumcision Jewish organizations circumvented this debate through a lawsuit that prevented the public from voting on the issue.[464] In my own experience, I attempted to place ads for my film *American Circumcision* at the American Academy of Pediatrics convention, one of the largest circumcising medical groups, and they would not even take my money.⁴⁶⁵ It's clear: pedophile-apologists do not believe in debate. The debate frame is only used to maintain their power and constrain activists. Yet, activists are constrained by this frame if they wish to work within the frame of liberalism. How can we resolve this problem?

REPRESSIVE TOLERANCE

Herbert Marcuse, a member of the Frankfurt school from which critical theory originates, answers this question in his essay *Repressive Tolerance*. The essay, which was originally part of a book titled *A Critique of Pure Tolerance*,⁴⁶⁶ criticizes the idea of pure tolerance, or what Marcuse calls "benevolent neutrality."⁴⁶⁷ Liberal societies typically have "benevolent neutrality," meaning that everyone has freedom of speech, regardless of whether or not their speech advocates for good ideas or harmful ones. The problem with this tolerance is that "tolerance is an end in itself" which means that "tolerance toward that which is radically evil now appears as good."⁴⁶⁸ This tolerance allows for people to advocate for violence "provided they did not make the transition from word to deed, from speech to action."⁴⁶⁹ Marcuse also suggests that our repressive society is not as neutral as it claims, because "economic and political process is subjected to an ubiquitous and effective administration in accordance with the predominant interests."⁴⁷⁰ In other words, although the law might provide both sides freedom of speech, in a capitalist society, only ideas that support the status quo have access to money to spread their message. "The Left has no equal voice, no equal access to the mass media and their public facilities - not because a conspiracy excludes it, but because, in good old capitalist fashion, it does not have the required purchasing power."⁴⁷¹ While there might not be state censorship, there is a "hidden censorship that permeates the free media."⁴⁷²

Even if a message against the status quo was heard "rational persuasion, persuasion to the opposite is all but precluded" because "the meaning of words and ideas other than the established one" are beyond the public's understanding. "Other words can be spoken and heard, other ideas can be expressed, but... they are immediately 'evaluated' (i.e. automatically understood) in terms of the public language--a language which determines 'a priori' the direction in which the thought process moves."[473] Marcuse gives the example of the idea that to "work for peace" you must "prepare for war," which frames the actions of the military-industrial complex as support of peace. In Marcuse's view, building giant militaries is the opposite of working for peace, yet through this "Orwellian language" "peace is redefined" to include "preparation for war."[474] The result of this repressive tolerance is that "false consciousness has become the general consciousness."[475]

Those who oppose circumcision face the same problem that Marcuse articulates. Pure tolerance claims to create an equal debate or "benevolent neutrality," while actually creating conditions that disadvantage activists. While both activists and medical groups have freedom of speech, activists have only their personal income while the medical industry has billions of dollars. Information against circumcision is censored not by removing activists' freedom of speech, but by removing the means to share that message and the understanding necessary for rational persuasion. Even if a message against systemic pedophilia is heard, it is evaluated through the language of the status quo. The medical discourse redefines taking away a child's ability to decide what happens to his body as the "circumcision decision." The religious discourses redefines carving a religious symbol into a child's genitals as exercising "religious freedom." In this Orwellian language, freedom and choice are redefined to mean their opposite. Tolerance for both sides creates "tolerance toward that which is radically evil" including speech that advocates for violence, including violence against children. How do we resolve the problem of tolerance?

LIBERATING TOLERANCE

Marcuse suggests this repressive tolerance be replaced with liberating tolerance. "Liberating tolerance, then, would mean intolerance against movements from the Right and toleration of movements from the Left."[476] In other words, Marcuse suggests tolerance should only extend to good causes. This tolerance "would extend to the stage of action as well as of discussion and propaganda, of deed as well as of word," meaning that even advocating for bad causes with speech would not be tolerated.

Opponents of critical theory have cited Marcuse's essay *Repressive Tolerance* as responsible for creating a double standard where left-wing violence is tolerated while conservatives are attacked merely for offensive speech.[477] However, Marcuse suggests we "reexamine the issue of violence and the traditional distinction between violent and non-violent action" lest the discussion "be clouded by ideologies which serve the perpetuation of violence."[478] He states that violence is already "practiced by the police, in the prisons and mental institutions, in the fight against racial minorities."[479] On our issue, we could add "in hospitals against children" to this list. "This violence indeed breeds violence."[480] This is doubly true on our issue since violence against children creates trauma, which changes those children for the rest of their life, making them more likely to inflict their trauma on others as adults. While dominant institutions engage in violence, "non-violence is normally not only preached to but exacted from the weak."[481] In other words, there is already a reverse of liberating tolerance, where violence is tolerated from dominant institutions, but the oppressed are expected to be non-violent. On the issue of systemic pedophilia, the dominant hegemony tolerates violence against children on an industrial scale, while attacking activists for mere speech that opposes this violence.

Marcuse's view is that this "neutral" tolerance is actually repressive, and favors far-right causes over liberal ones. He worries this tolerance will lead to violence, because "the speeches of the Fascist and Nazi leaders were the immediate prologue to the massacre."[482] In other words, by the time words turn to deeds, it might be too late. If the purpose of the principle of "non-violence" is to prevent violence, then violence against "ideologies which serve the perpetuation of violence" reduces violence.[483] Marcuse explicitly says that withdrawing tolerance can prevent violence, and when he states that "if democratic tolerance had been withdrawn when the future leaders started their campaign, mankind would have had a chance of avoiding Auschwitz and a World War."[484] In our case, liberating tolerance would not prevent an evil system from rising but would help end an evil system that is already in power. The current hegemony already uses censorship, intolerance, and violence, including violence against children. Liberating tolerance would simply mean allowing activists to use the same tactics the pedophile hegemony uses against them to create an actually equal conflict.

If we were to apply the principle of liberating tolerance to the issue of circumcision, it would mean tolerating any action taken against systemic pedophilia, while being intolerant of even speech that supports systemic pedophilia. This principle recognizes that there is a moral difference between using strong tactics against pedophilia and using those same tactics to defend pedophilia. If someone uses extreme language to shout down a pedophile, this is morally different than if a pedophile-apologist uses extreme language to support pedophilia. Those acting from liberating tolerance would never apologize for those on their side who use radical tactics, and might even defend them, while condemning the same tactics or even less extreme methods when used by pedophile-apologists. This is not a "double standard," because we recognize a moral difference between the antipedophile and pedophile-apologists. It is actually one standard: be antipedophile. According to the concept of liberating tolerance, any tactic is acceptable if it reduces systemic pedophilia, and all tactics used in defense of systemic pedophilia are unacceptable.

DECEPTIVE IMPARTIALITY

There is no "neutral" media. As Marcuse explains, "when a magazine prints side by side a negative and a positive report on the FBI, it fulfills honestly the requirements of objectivity: however, the chances are that the positive wins because the image of the institution is deeply engraved in the mind of the people."[485] In other words, though the media might claim to be "objective," the cultural assumptions media works within are not neutral. Unless the media questions these cultural assumptions with a critical consciousness, they are actually participating in the same system they claim to merely report on.

One could apply the same logic to news stories about circumcision. When a publication prints side-by-side information on the circumcision "debate," although this might fulfill the requirements of objectivity, the authority of medical institutions is so deeply engraved in hegemonic media that their narrative is more likely to be accepted than those by less powerful movements. This authority is reinforced across news stories. For example, if the American Academy of Pediatrics is cited as an authority on an unrelated issue in a story that has nothing to do with circumcision, then when their position on circumcision is later inserted into a news story, they are likely to be seen as an authority on this topic because they were cited as an authority in previous news stories. In this way, media companies can participate in systemic pedophilia even on news stories that have nothing to do with circumcision. The massive amount of advertising media companies accept from the medical industry, use of medical industry figures as experts, and fictional dramas which portray doctors as likable protagonists all reinforce the power of the medical system, and by extension participate in systemic pedophilia.

 Marcuse suggests that in order for media to be truthful, "this deceptive impartiality would have to be abandoned." Media companies have already done this on other social justice issues. No media company would suggest there are "two sides" to issues like gay rights, civil rights, or racial equality. Some media companies even make this belief explicit. For example, The BuzzFeed News Standards And Ethics Guide states: "we firmly believe that for a number of issues, including civil rights, women's rights, anti-racism, and LGBT equality, there are not two sides."[486] While many media companies share this belief, the same media companies that would never run a story suggesting there are "two sides" to racial equality often run stories that openly support systemic pedophilia. Are there "two sides" to the issue of pedophilia and the genital cutting of children? If not, this deceptive impartiality needs to be abandoned, in favor of the same editorial standards media uses when speaking on other social justice issues. A critical consciousness would suggest changing the media's entire relationship to all organizations involved in systemic pedophilia. Most media organizations would not cite someone as an "expert" if they opposed racial equity, even if the issue they were speaking on had nothing to do with race, yet they do cite those involved in systemic pedophilia as experts and work frequently with them. In order to be antipedophile, these organizations will have to take an active stance against those involved in systemic pedophilia.

WHAT IS TO BE DONE

Vladimir Lenin makes a similar point to Marcuse in his book *What Is To Be Done? The Essential Questions of Our Movement*. At the time Lenin was writing, many less radical socialists wanted the freedom to criticize the status quo or "freedom of criticism" which Lenin calls "undoubtedly the most fashionable slogan at the present time."[487] Lenin points out that if socialists really thought their theories were superior, they wouldn't want "freedom of criticism." They would want their superior theories to replace the inferior theories in power. "Those who are really convinced that they have made progress in science would not demand freedom for the new views to continue side by side with the old, but the substitution of the new views for the old."[488] He suggests that the solution is not "freedom of criticism," but revolution.

The same could be said on the issue of genital cutting. If we really believe that circumcision is genital mutilation and that the existing hegemony is engaged in systemic pedophilia, we don't want to have the "circumcision debate." There is no "debate" on the issue of pedophilia. Pedophilia is evil. The concept of objective "neutral" "evidence-based" "debate" over infant genital cutting is itself a discourse of systemic pedophilia. If our perspective is correct, we should not seek "debate," but to end pedophilia. Nor would we want "the new views to continue side by side with the old."[489] Events that merely "educate the public" so they can make an "informed choice" allow the new to coexist alongside the old. Instead, we want "the substitution of the new views for the old." We want systemic pedophilia replaced with Children's Justice.

CHAPTER 25
LIBERAL CRITIQUE

Critics of critical social justice will say: Isn't liberalism enough to accomplish the goals of social justice? Human rights-based liberalism has made many strides for the causes that critical social justice is concerned with. It was during the reign of liberalism that we got the Civil Rights movement, the gay rights movement, and modern feminism. If we extend the idea of liberalism back to its roots in the enlightenment era, we could also include the abolition of slavery, universal suffrage, and our basic understanding of individual freedom as victories for liberalism. Why would we want to risk overturning all those gains by instituting a new system that questions the fundamental premises of liberalism?

Intactivists might have similar objections. After all, the Intactivist argument is solid. If human beings do have a right to their own body, circumcision is clearly a violation of human rights. Western countries already accept this premise of human rights law. Plus, the empirical evidence shows that circumcision is harmful. The "benefits and risks" argument can easily be disproven through the existing science. Why change?

LIBERALISM'S CRIMES

For years, Intactivists have wondered why their cause has not been accepted by dominant institutions which claim to support human rights. If liberalism really is the dominant political philosophy, then why have clearly correct arguments based in liberalism not also become dominant? Wherever you see a contradiction or double standard, you can be sure there is a real singular standard, hidden and unspoken. If dominant institutions actually believed in human rights, Intactivist would have won. Since Intactivism has not won, we can know that human rights are not a universal principle, but a discourse. The purpose of this discourse is to maintain and obscure power. Could it be that the discourse of human rights liberalism allows for abuses to continue while hiding the power by which they occur?

We can better judge systems by their outcomes than their stated intentions. While liberalism takes credit for ending abuses, most of these abuses occurred on their watch in the first place. While the Holocaust is seen as a crime of fascism and the hundred million dead under the Soviet Union as a crime of communism, those in liberal democracies do not usually see the genocide of Native Americans, race-based slavery, or the American sterilization programs Nazi Germany modeled their eugenics programs after as crimes of liberal democracy. Americans are taught to see these crimes as aberrations, not as a natural result of liberalism. If these crimes are ever acknowledged, they are usually attributed to the racism of people at the time. However, Americans would never be so generous as to make the same assumptions about communism or fascism. No one would argue that fascism would have worked if the people who implemented it had just been "less racist." Rather, mass deaths are seen as the natural outcome of totalitarian systems like fascism and communism. Liberalism has also led to mass deaths. What makes it a "better" system is that it hides its crimes through the discourse of individual rights, and frames genocide and slavery as a "side effect" of the people who lived at the time, rather than taking accountability for it's historical abuses as an outcome of liberalism.

The idea that the people who lived at the time of the Native American genocide, slavery, and eugenics programs are responsible, but that the system that implemented these outcomes is not, is another form of discourse obscuring power. The discourse of American liberalism is that "we the people" run a government "of the people, by the people." Yet when "we the people" try to change this government, citizens quickly learn just how little power they have. Most of the current and historical abuses of the American government are based on policies everyday Americans never voted on. When Americans do vote, those they vote for will frequently campaign on one set of promises, only to enact the opposite. Communism and fascism are understood as bad systems because the people in those systems frequently lacked the power to fight their abuses even when the majority of the population opposes them. Yet what power do you have to fight the unpopular abuses the American government engages in today? Liberalism is superior to fascism and communism not because there are fewer abuses, but because liberalism hides and obscures power better, redirecting the blame for all crimes back onto "we the people." Human rights as a discourse allows liberal governments to claim that the crimes they engage in are an aberration rather than a regular outcome.

The confusion Intactivists feel when liberal governments ignore their human rights arguments based in liberalism is due to this hidden power. Intactivists think they are engaging the dominant power, whereas they are only engaging the discourse that dominant power uses to maintain power. When Intactivists use the discourse of human rights, those in power feel threatened and respond to threat with attack. Intactivists believe the purpose of human rights discourse is human rights. Those in power understand that the purpose of the human rights discourse is to maintain their power. The values of the establishment have always been a discourse. When a doctor says "circumcision policy" should be "evidence-based," they are using a power/knowledge system that privileges academic literature controlled by organizations engaged in systemic pedophilia. They do not include the feelings of men, the pain of children, or the impact of trauma in their definition of "evidence." They do not include any studies outside their discipline, like those in psychology or human sexuality. They do not even include studies within their discipline which contradict their chosen viewpoint or are based in values they personally disagree with. These "evidence-based" physicians will happily switch discourses the moment religion or "parental preference" supports their conclusion. Activists who oppose circumcision can bring them all the evidence they want. They will not change, because they are not actually interested in "evidence" but in the discourse of "evidence-based." The same is true of human rights, liberalism, or whatever other values they claim to hold.

Based on their behavior, it is clear that those in power do not believe in anything except power. They will happily violate human rights if it increases their power. When they tell you they care about human rights, evidence, or values of any kind, they are lying to maintain power. In order to gain power, you must see reality as it really is. This reality is hidden through discourse and language. Seeing reality might require deconstructing the language and narrative of dominant powers. Critical theory has tools that can help you deconstruct language and power. While human rights might be a useful discourse, critical theory is the more effective tool for achieving power. The evidence is in the results. Who is achieving more power in society now: liberal human rights activists, or social justice movements based in critical theory?

THE POWER OF THEORY

Why has critical social justice theory risen to power? Social justice based in critical theory has achieved a near hegemonic control over every major public institution, including universities, schools, multinational corporations, and non-profit political organizations. Every large organization has a policy on racism and discrimination, and the majority of those are written in the language of critical social justice theory. At the same time, no organization has a similar dedicated policy on systemic pedophilia or children's social justice issues. Movements against circumcision have struggled to get institutional support even from organizations that should be ideologically aligned to them. From a practical standpoint, if human rights organizations against circumcision could achieve victory through the discourse of liberalism, they'd have done it already. There is a saying that insanity is doing the same thing over and over again expecting a different result. In light of the absolute victory of critical social justice and failure of liberal human rights discourse to deliver results, it is worth reevaluating this discourse in light of the success of competing ones.

Critics of critical social justice explain the success of critical theory by pointing to their tactics rather than the truth of their ideas. Indeed, the tactics of critical social justice do explain much of its success. Here, I am going to use some of the language and analysis of my earlier book, *The Intactivist Guidebook*, which uses the Intactivist movement to explore effective political organizing. In the book, I suggest that a "share the message" strategy is not enough for any movement and that movements also need to build organizations that regularly recruit more members and bring more resources into the movement.[490] It is not enough for movements to convince the public that their cause is correct, they must also convince people to become "active allies" of the movement by contributing resources in the form of time, money, and skills.[491] I call this the "organizer model," as opposed to a "share the message" strategy, which is simply based in arguing that the message of the movement is correct.[492] In other words, it is not enough to be right. You must also achieve power and use that power to reach for more power.

This analysis was actually inspired in part by my observation of many social justice movements based in critical theory. Critical theorists follow the organizer model within academic institutions. Universities are the sales funnel from which critical theorists recruit new members. Critical theory was created in the academy, and many leading critical theorists are academics. Critical theorists have been able to carve out entire academic departments dedicated to their ideas. These departments serve as recruitment for critical social justice movements and receive resources and funding from the university. Students trained in critical theory go on to recruit other people at the future institutions and organizations they work for. When graduates trained in critical social justice theory join corporations, non-profits, and other organizations, they often make sure those organizations have policies based on critical social justice thinking and hire experts in diversity, equity, and inclusion from critical social justice organizations. This brings more resources from the corporation, non-profit, or other organization into critical social justice organizations. If these organizations hire critical social justice activists for sensitivity or racial bias training, then these trainings create a new recruitment opportunity for the activists. Critical social justice activists executed the strategy I describe in *The Intactivist Guidebook* to secure resources from universities, corporations, and non-profits, which hold some of the greatest power and wealth in modern society.

Critical social justice activists also collaborate. The project of theory was accomplished by multiple authors building on each other's work over several decades. The concept of intersectionality meant that each oppressed group could become part of a shared social justice coalition. This movement has been able to absorb unlikely allies like corporations or unrelated organizations. This assimilation might begin with a statement against racism, but eventually, words are not enough and the allied organization must begin contributing resources in the form of money, skills, or potential recruitment. Their rhetoric has also allowed them to break opposition coalitions. Most people and groups do not want to appear racist. The definition of 'racist' as participating in systems that create unequal outcomes has allowed critical social justice activists to toxically brand opposition with the label "racist" if they refuse to create the desired outcomes. "Cancel culture" has become the popular understanding of this technique of finding problematic behavior or comments from public figures and using those to toxically brand them and alienate them from their power structure. By comparison, competing groups have largely focused on a "share the message" strategy. Conservatives have done almost no organizing, and what organizing traditional liberals have done has been easily co-opted by critical social justice activists. The conservative establishment's response to critical social justice has been so weak that their base has been easily co-opted by any movement that radically opposes it, no matter how offensive or conspiratorial. American political conversation now occurs in the matrix of critical social justice and various reactions to it.

Every system of power rests on a system of knowledge or language, which Michel Foucault termed power/knowledge. If critical theory has power, it should have a corresponding body of knowledge, each of which reproduces the other, at least according to theory itself. Terms like "inclusion," "diversity," and "equity" are all legitimizing language that justifies bringing theory into spaces previously perceived as apolitical or politically neutral. Other ideologies have no similar language system to justify turning innocuous hobby groups into ideological spaces, or demand organizations with no overt political affiliation hire consultants to reform their language. When hired, one of the first acts of diversity consultants is to change the language because in critical theory power rests on language. If you change the language of a culture, you also change its power structure. Substituting the previous language of an organization for the language of critical theory will eventually lead to a change in power, at least according to theory. The critics of critical social justice might want to attribute the rise of theory to only power tactics; but even if that were true, these power tactics rest on and would not be possible without the ideology. The success of critical theory actually has something to do with theory. It should not surprise us that a movement that spent nearly a hundred years studying how language creates power has managed to create power through language.

ACTIVIST OPPORTUNITY

Intactivism, despite having a legitimate claim as a social justice movement, has largely operated in the framework of human rights based in liberalism. The human rights discourse has allowed Intactivists to make their argument in the language of the establishment, but this language never undermines the legitimacy of the establishment, since governments, courts, and academic experts are still arbiters of what constitutes a human rights abuse. As a consequence, the discourse of Intactivism has been an appeal to authority rather than a fundamental questioning of authority or potential replacement of it. Clearly, we cannot trust people who regularly engage in human rights abuses to determine what is and what is not a human rights abuse. Liberalism as an underlying discourse provides no mechanism to question or overthrow power as its language is based in the power/knowledge system of the establishment. When a foreign government engages in human rights abuses, we understand that the ruling class must be overthrown. Only revolutionary discourse can actually solve an establishment engaged in human rights abuses. Liberalism provides no mechanism for revolution.

Although some Intactivists see their movement as a social justice movement, modern social justice is not based in human rights. It is based in critical theory. This discourse proposes an entirely new authority structure in which the lived experience of marginalized groups carries as much if not greater epistemic weight than academic experts. Critical social justice suggests that the discussion must be centered in the oppressed, not power-holding perpetrators. The language of critical theory is not an appeal to the establishment. It frames oppressors as entirely illegitimate unless they recognize the demands of critical social justice activists. This discourse allows for greater power. Now, it is in power. Even if Intactivists wanted to continue to appeal to the establishment in the language of human rights, they might have to change because liberalism is no longer the dominant power is the establishment. The future of any social justice movement requires an understanding of theory or a competing theory which allows for a greater claim to power.

Yet, isn't critical theory just another discourse of the establishment to maintain power? Obviously, yes. Those in power might not believe in critical theory any more than they believed in human rights. If those in power believed in critical theory, that belief would require them to make major systemic changes to their organizations. Though medical groups have released policy statements supporting social justice causes, changes to their thinking, like examining the epistemic justice of who has access to medical journals or why only those able to make an investment of four to eight years and hundreds of thousands of dollars in their education are given epistemic authority, are not brought up. It's very safe for a medical organization to take a critical theory stance on police brutality issues, but they dare not take a critical theory perspective on the issues that would actually impact their industry. Critical social justice theory has profound implications for the medical industry, with Michel Foucault, one of the most important intellectual figures of the modern left, writing an entire book on the problems of the medical system.[493] The medical gaze itself is why the medical industry has not recognized the implications of critical theory to their practice. At most, these organizations will use the discourse of critical theory to create more ways to make money from and seize power.

The blindness of the medical industry to the implications of critical theory has created an opportunity. The previous power/knowledge system of the medical industry was based in credentialism or the idea that only those with certain academic or medical credentials were qualified to have an opinion on medical issues. By framing circumcision as a medical issue, doctors were able to seize power over children's genitals and frame those affected by systemic pedophilia as "unqualified" to talk about it. During the COVID-19 epidemic, those who questioned lockdowns and restrictions were frequently asked "are you an epidemiologist?" implying that only those with academic credentials were qualified to speak about human freedom or legal restrictions on commerce and travel. Doctors frequently shout at Intactivist protestors that "your google search does not replace my medical degree" as a rhetorical tactic to imply that their academic credentials carry greater epistemic authority than activists' lived experience.

Critical theory prioritizes lived experience over academic knowledge, undermining credentialism. Doctors once had epistemic power over gay people when "homosexuality" was listed as a diagnosable disorder in the DSM. Now, no doctor would not shout at a gay protestor that "your google search does not replace my medical degree," because they understand that those with a lived experience of being gay are the authority on the gay experience, not outside academics. When the movement against circumcision shifts into the power/knowledge system of critical theory, it will be able to frame doctors waving their credentials around children's genitalia as equally bigoted. A doctor claiming that their credentials carry more epistemic authority than their victims is wrong, but still recognized as an authority within the human rights discourse. In critical social justice, this person is an oppressor and pedophile-apologist. Critical social justice removes the entire power/knowledge system of the medical establishment. If the medical industry adopts a new language, it is only a matter of time before they are replaced by a new power.

As critical theory closes the door on credentialism, it opens a door for social justice movements opposed to circumcision.

Circumcision has previously been framed by the dominant culture as a fringe issue. A systemic view suggests that circumcision impacts every issue it intersects with, including gender, sexuality, bodies, trauma, psychology, parenting, children, birth, medicine, law, race, identity, etc. This means all of these issues can only be understood in light of the impact of genital cutting and systemic pedophilia. Critical theory implies that the issue of how we treat children is the central social justice issue. Any organization which deals with these issues or any social justice issue must make a choice whether or not their organization will be pro-pedophile or antipedophile. It is not enough to be "not a pedophile," since every person and organization participates in larger cultural systems. Unconscious participation in those systems will lead to participation in systemic pedophilia. Those who look at how they participate in these systems and consciously choose to avoid contributing to systemic pedophilia are antipedophile. When this issue is rooted in critical theory, every person and organization must support Children's Justice.

RIGHTS AND THEORY

I hope that by this point in this book, you see the power of theory. This power is vastly greater than the human rights discourse. The human rights discourse can only appeal to authority to end abuse. The discourse of critical theory has its own authority which can transform every aspect of society. Critical social justice theory has already eclipsed human rights as the dominant power in America. Human rights abuses were possible under the previous ideology of liberalism, because that power shifted the blame for its human rights violations to "we the people," while denying the people the actual power to end those abuses. This discourse continues to allow for human rights abuses and has been unsuccessful in ending systemic pedophilia. What those invested in the old discourse of liberalism and human rights have to ask themselves is: are you more committed to liberal ideology or protecting children? If you want actual change, theory is the path forward.

CHAPTER 26
FURTHER ISSUES

Though this book primarily looks at the issue of circumcision pedophilia, there are many other issues that could be viewed through the lens of Children's Justice. As stated at the beginning of this book, the way we treat children is a systemic issue. While the most obvious and egregious issue is infant genital cutting, Children's Justice is not limited to this issue. If the abuse of children is a systemic issue that includes beliefs, culture, language, institutions, etc. then it extends beyond any single issue. Looking at the issue of circumcision has revealed many principles and patterns around the treatment of children. These principles have implications for other issues and ways we treat children as well. How can we apply Children's Justice to other issues?

CLAIMING SOCIAL JUSTICE

In a sense, all social issues are Children's Justice issues, because the origins of every emotional pattern lay in the experiences of childhood. Early life trauma fragments human consciousness, creating subaltern aspects that unconsciously act out the emotional power dynamics established in childhood. This means that every issue can be viewed through a Children's Justice lens. Critical theory was able to claim every existing social justice issue by applying the lens of power and social construction. However, we could transform these issues further by looking at the origins of social justice issues in childhood. The same way there exists a critical theory reading of every issue, there could also exist a Children's Justice reading of every issue, including a reading of the previous application of critical theory and social justice itself.

This has the potential to expand Children's Justice into every social justice issue, the same way critical theory overtook every issue, especially since social justice issues are intersectional. Critical theory applied to social justice issues created new evolutions of each. Critical justice applied to the Civil Rights movement created critical race theory. Critical theory applied to the gay rights movement created queer theory. Critical theory applied to feminism created gender theory. These new forms of social justice are not the same as the previous versions, even if they evolved from them. They were hybridized with critical theory to create new perspectives. However, if the roots of oppression begin in childhood, then each of these issues can only be solved and understood by bringing awareness to the childhood experiences which created the emotional patterns and ways of relating necessary for those issues to occur. If Children's Justice were applied to each of these issues, they could be hybridized further, creating new strains of social justice, which would be as different from critical theory as critical race theory is from the original Civil Rights movement. These new Children's Justice understandings of previous social justice issues might even eventually replace the current model for solving those issues, the way that critical theory has replaced previous versions of the social justice issues. In this way, Children's Justice could lay claim to all social justice.

Critical race theory stated that all of society is complicit in systemic racism.[494] When this belief took hold in American culture, it meant every organization needed a statement on racial justice based in critical theory, even if the organization's stated mission had no overt connection to race. If the emotional patterns necessary for oppression begin in childhood through how we treat children, then the only solution to social justice issues is Children's Justice. This means that every organization which has a social justice statement of any kind also needs a Children's Justice statement dedicated to their commitment to being antipedophile, which lays out how they will ensure they do not participate in systems that harm children and what they are doing to integrate their own childhood patterns learned from trauma. If social justice issues can only be understood through Children's Justice, and every organization or aspect of society is involved in systemic issues, then Children's Justice could also lay claim to every aspect of society that critical social justice has as well.

This is a roadmap to hegemony. Critical theory achieved hegemony by replacing every cell of the liberal body with itself. It was close enough to liberalism that liberal institutions actually served as an infection point for critical theory. If any other movement wishes to achieve hegemony, the "anti-woke" strategy of opposing critical theory and bombarding the body politic with radiation like a chemotherapy treatment is the hard way to do it. The easier way would be to do what critical theory did and infect the cells of the body politic with a new memetic virus that produces itself rather than the previous meme. Critical theory never directly opposed liberalism but instead used liberal institutions as hosts from which to produce theory. Just as critical theory grew out of liberal institutions, Children's Justice grows out of theory. The current hegemony is not the opposition, but soil from which to grow a new revolution.

CLAIMING BOTH SIDES

While the above gives Children's Justice domain over the political left, what about the right? Though critical theory holds power over the majority of American institutions, the American populace remains deeply divided over critical theory. Significant portions of the population are averse to theory or anything which appears left-wing. Any movement which wishes to appeal to a majority of the population will have to attract some portion of the other side of the political divide. As discussed earlier, any person who works for Children's Justice is both antipedophile and anti-racist by virtue of the outcomes they produce, regardless of their views, allowing Children's Justice to draw allies from any background or previous perspective. While a critique based in critical theory might not seem like it appeals to red-state Americans, protecting children is a core value of the political right. If Children's Justice is shown to be the best way to both protect children and create social justice, it could unite people from different political perspectives.

There are multiple popular conspiracy theory narratives that claim that elites are involved in secret pedophile organizations. These narratives attempt to connect public figures and powerful institutions to the rape and human trafficking of children. While there has never been enough evidence for these theories to conclusively prove their claims, it is not even necessary to suggest that elites are personally touching children to implicate them in pedophilia. Critical theory suggests that if someone participates in a system that produces an outcome, they are responsible for their role in that system. If elite institutions regularly produce pedophile outcomes or protect systemic pedophilia, then they are engaged in systemic pedophilia.

Most conspiracy theorists pushing narratives about elite pedophiles are not familiar with critical theory. I suspect people are drawn to these conspiracy narratives because, on an unconscious level, they sense the systemic participation of elites in the harm of children. Conspiracy narratives of elite pedophile rings are an attempt to explain why elite-controlled institutions consistently produce pedophile outcomes or engage in pedophile ideas. By focusing on a few famous public figures, these theorists put themselves in the difficult position of having to prove each individual's personal action rather than their systemic participation in pedophilia. These theories also ignore the more common ways elites participate in pedophilia, such as circumcision pedophilia. Circumcision pedophilia is more common and harmful than what most elite pedophile conspiracy theories claim. These theorists also miss the larger system that elevated these figures, gave them power, and allowed pedophilia to be a consistent outcome of the power structure that supports them.

The fact that so-called "conspiracy theorists" do not have the tools to describe what they are sensing is a form of hermeneutical injustice. This injustice could be met by changing the language by which we talk about pedophilia and by giving those concerned with elite pedophilia the tools of critical theory. Critical theory would suggest that instead of focusing just on individual elites, those against pedophilia should focus on the systems that support them. If pedophilia is systemic, then those engaged in pedophilia do not just include a few secret powerful individuals at the top, but the entire system of governments, institutions, and non-profits that support them. Everyone who works at these elite institutions or is employed by elites or elite-owned organizations is systemically participating in whatever outcomes these elites and elite institutions are creating. Critical theory makes a far bolder claim than "conspiracy theorists," while standing on firmer epistemic ground.

When billionaire Jeffery Epstein was convicted of sex trafficking and pedophilia, many theorized that other elites participated in his crimes.[495] There was a lot of debate around whether or not the public figures who appeared next to him were also engaged in pedophilia. While some might be, they do not need to be personally abusing children to be systemically involved. When someone associates with a member of the far-right, the media refers to them as far-right adjacent. However, many media companies ran puff pieces for Jeffery Epstein and other institutions engaged in systemic pedophilia. By their logic, we could refer to these media companies as pedophile-adjacent or pedophile-apologist media. Elites who have associated with Epstein or other pedophile-apologist groups could also be called pedophile-adjacent. If pedophilia is systemic, then anyone who is complicit in that system could be said to be engaging in systemic pedophilia.

Children's Justice has the potential to create a synthesis of both right-wing and left-wing perspectives by combining a left-wing critique based in critical theory with the right-wing dislike of current elites and desire to protect children. It would also suggest that the way to oppose those in power is not to focus on their individual actions but on the systems that made them powerful and allowed them to perpetuate harmful outcomes. Elites are only "elite" because they have access to power. Removing those currently at the top of that power structure would simply cause the next in line to assume command. Even if some of those at the top have personally engaged in individual pedophilia, their removal would not change the power structure that supported and covered up their crimes. A systemic view would suggest that deconstructing their entire power structure and holding all who participated in it accountable. Both the political left and right have a critique of those who currently hold power. Children's Justice would allow people from either perspective to work together to deconstruct elite institutions and remove their power structures in a unifying movement.

NEW ISSUES

While every social justice issue is a Children's Justice issue, every Children's Justice issue is not yet a social justice issue. There are many issues unique to Children's Justice that have not been raised in previous social justice movements. The full expansion of Children's Justice would not just mean claiming previous social justice issues, but identifying new ones unique to the critique of Children's Justice. Children's Justice issues include any idea, person, or system that harms children. What institutions are engaged in the systemic oppression of children?

School. As we have suggested multiple times in this book, the school system is one of the worst abusers of children. When this system is criticized, most people usually offer the problematic solution of improving schools, which usually means pouring more money into a failing system and expanding the system's power because they cannot imagine a world without compulsory schooling. Yet, compulsory schooling is a recent invention that began around the same time as circumcision was medicalized. For most of human history, children were not locked in government buildings and forcibly indoctrinated. It would take entire books to fully examine this system. Fortunately, someone else has already written them: John Taylor Gatto. *The Underground History of American Education* by John Taylor Gatto is the most comprehensive exploration of the issue of compulsory schooling that I have read.[496] His work and that of the 'unschooling' movement call for replacing compulsory schooling with various forms of 'unschooling.' The abolition of compulsory schooling is a Children's Justice issue.

Birth. Circumcision is not the only harm perpetuated in hospital birth. Many hospital birth interventions are unnecessary and harmful to children. Hospital birth is set up for the desires of adults, the profit of the institution, the convenience of doctors, and the desire of the medical system to avoid legal liability, rather than the needs of the person actually being born. There is a growing natural birth and home birth movement, which recognizes that these interventions are frequently unnecessary and harmful. Natural birth centers birth on the needs of the child being born and allows the mother's body to follow its natural process in a setting that feels safe to her and the child. Natural birth is a Children's Justice issue.

Medicine. As we have also mentioned, the medical system regularly harms children. This harm is most explicit in hospital birth but does not stop in infancy. It continues throughout childhood. The medical system defines "normal" childhood behavior by the extent to which it conforms to adult desires. When children cannot sit still in the government child prisons known as schools, the medical system regularly drugs them and diagnoses their failure to conform to an oppressive system as disorders. Drugging children so they can fulfill adult desires is clearly a Children's Justice issue. There are many other medical interventions carried out on children, not because of any genuine need, but merely the desires of adults. These interventions are carried out through the medical gaze, in which doctors fragment the child and only focus on an individual symptom while ignoring the systemic impact of their actions and discounting the child's emotions and personhood. For example, when a doctor sticks a needle in a child, that pain has an emotional impact on the child. The child is learning that he might have to ignore his own pain to fulfill the desires of an authority figure, or that it is okay for people in positions of power to hurt him if they say it is for his benefit. This pain is creating emotional patterns and power dynamics that must be treated as intended outcomes, not side effects. The discourse of the medical gaze makes it impossible to talk about them. The entire discourse of the medical system must change to a holistic one in which doctors are accountable for their outcomes.

Food. A holistic view of health would have to include diet. When the food industry markets unhealthy artificial food products to children, they are using children's bodies to generate economic wealth. These food products harm children's health and have created an obesity epidemic. Food companies even harm the child's sexuality later in life through endocrine disrupters. The food industry regularly uses plastic packaging materials and pesticides that have been shown to change hormone patterns.[497] Altering a child's sexuality for profit is a form of systemic pedophilia. The food industry also supports systemic pedophilia through kosher certification, which gives money to pedophile identity groups.[498] Again, it would take another book to fully explore this topic, but from this alone we can conclude: Healthy food is a Children's Justice issue.

Media. Children are regularly exploited in the media. Multiple child actors have said that the Hollywood film industry has a systemic pedophilia problem.[499] Many Hollywood films support systemic pedophilia and pedophile-apologist narratives. The cultural hegemony of pedophile culture is reinforced through the media. The media industry has a systemic pedophilia problem both behind the scenes, and in the narratives they promote. This systemic pedophile problem extends to news media, which regularly pushes pedophile narratives, protects those engaged in systemic pedophilia, and attacks those who speak out against it. Media has multiple Children's Justice issues.

Social media. Social media has multiple systemic problems. Mainstream social media companies have had child pornography distributed on their platforms and failed to take it down.[500] Social media regularly exploits children's attention for profit. This media is not designed to benefit children based on their needs, but to benefit advertisers who desire access to children. Social media has also been shown to correlate to increased depression, suicide, and mental health issues among young people.[501] Most social media platforms are also aligned with pedophile-apologist organizations. The Anti-Defamation League (ADL) has an official censorship position at the largest social media companies.[502] Since the COVID-19 pandemic, multiple social networks have partnered with medical system organizations like the World Health Organization (WHO) to give them similar censorship powers.[503] Organizations that work with pedophile-apologist groups could be described as pedophile-adjacent or involved in systemic pedophilia, and most social networks and media companies fall into this category. When social media companies allocate resources to organizations involved in systemic pedophilia but fail to remove child pornography from their platforms, they reveal a deep problem with systemic pedophilia.

Government. When the governments devout resources towards policies and programs that benefit adults, but fail to protect children, it is a Children's Justice issue. The Federal Bureau of Investigations (FBI) has failed to prosecute pedophilia cases[504] and works with pedophile identity groups.[505] The Central Intelligence Agency (CIA) has hired people who committed sex crimes involving children and refused to prosecute them.[506] The United Nations has allegedly employed thousands of pedophiles, under the guise of aid programs.[507] Government organizations do not just fail to address Children's Justice issues. They actively work with pedophiles. Governments are involved in every other Children's Justice issue on this list. One could write an entire book exploring what a government based in Children's Justice might look like, but at minimum, Children's Justice requires removing pedophiles from the government. Keep in mind, everyone who works in government institutions that protect and aid pedophiles is complicit in systemic pedophilia unless they actively seek to dismantle that system with a critical consciousness.

REVOLUTIONARY THEORY

If we include pedophile adjacent organizations in the network of systemic pedophilia, then nearly every public institution is involved in systemic pedophilia. If every institution or aspect of society is complicit in systemic pedophilia, then every institution or aspect of society is a space where Children's Justice is required. Since systemic pedophilia currently holds hegemonic power over society, it gives Children's Justice a mandate to change that power in every aspect of society and replace the previous hegemony with itself. Children's Justice is a revolutionary theory.

CHAPTER 27
FUTURE VISION

Social justice often focuses on the negative: injustice, oppression, and the problems of the world. When asked what they want instead, social justice writers are often vague: "equity," "diversity," "inclusion," etc. The image of the oppression is clear. The positive future, less so. Many critical social justice activists do not even believe a better future is possible, only a lifelong struggle and commitment to a constant process.[508] Social justice movements used to believe a better world was possible. Communist revolutionaries spoke of a paradise for workers. The Civil Rights movement described a world of racial equality. The sexual revolution, feminist movement, gay rights movement, and many other social movements all imagined their own positive vision of the future. Now, we are on the other side of utopia. None of these movements fully solved the problems they claimed to address. Some made them worse. How can we propose another social revolution given the long history of previous failures?

UTOPIAN VISION

The utopian promises of left-wing movements are not new. One of the earliest socialist texts written in 1887 is *Looking Backward: 2000-1887* by Edward Bellamy, which tells the story of a 19th-century man who falls asleep and awakens a hundred and thirteen years later in a socialist utopia in the year 2000.[509] *Looking Backward* was the third-largest bestseller of its time, and influenced many future socialist and social justice thinkers.[510] The 19th-century protagonist of *Looking Backward*, upon hearing how perfect society has become, remarks that "human nature itself must've changed very much."[511] His host from the future year two thousand replies "not at all, but the conditions of human life have changed and with them the motives of human action."[512] In Bellamy's view, a perfect system would lead to perfect outcomes, whether or not the people in that system were perfect themselves.

This focus on perfecting the system, while ignoring the character of people within that system, has led to many of the historical failures of socialism. The belief that socialism is a perfect system if applied correctly leads to absurd statements like "real communism has never been tried" or the idea that communism would work if the right people were in charge of implementing it. The "right" people will never be in charge. Whatever system we build must be built with the people who actually exist. Communism revolutionaries eventually recognized the need to change people, and sought to do so through "cultural revolution." Whereas the earliest socialist theories thought people would do good if put in the right system, later theorists recognized that people are already socialized into a system or cultural hegemony which instills certain beliefs and values. If the beliefs and values people hold cause them to act against their own interests, incentives alone will never be enough to change their behavior. You have to change people's beliefs. This thinking leads to compulsory schooling, the state control of education, and the re-education camps found in communist societies. It leads to cultural revolution, where all "bad ideas" are removed from society and people are not permitted to share them. Whereas the attempt to solve the problem of the incentives leads to total state control of the economy, the attempt to solve the problem of thinking leads to total state control of thought. Critical theory focuses almost entirely on this second problem, using the method of "critical pedagogy" to instill the desired beliefs.[513]

The flaw in the thought-control model of social change is that education does not occur merely on an ideological level. Children are not just taught certain beliefs through verbal communication but taught emotional patterns through relationships. The way adults treat children even before they can speak creates an unconscious way of relating that can continue for the rest of a person's life. If we become who we are prior to speech, no amount of "pedagogy" after can create perfect people. Thought-control and critical pedagogy models are also doomed to failure unless they address these unconscious early life experiences. Previous social movements could never put the "right" people in charge because they were trying to create the "right" people through the wrong methods.

There is a way to create the "right" people: raise children. Creating the "right" people is not something the state can do with top-down force. Children learn relationally. They will treat others how they were treated. Force teaches the lessons of force. A system can never have a real relationship with a person. The false conceit of the political class is that problems can be solved through policy and that the solution to bad policy is always more different policy. If the roots of our problems are found in childhood, no policy in the world can solve them. The only solution is connecting to children and the subaltern inner-child parts of ourselves. The catch is that we cannot propagandize children into our way of seeing the world. We must understand their world and meet their needs on their terms. Most ideologies see children as raw clay for adults to mold. In reality, they are their own people who must be nurtured and allowed to grow into their full form. There is no "bettering" them by forcing them to conform to adult desires. Our children will treat the world the way they were treated. If we were willing to change our own rigid oppressive systems for them and treat them the way they want to be treated, they will be willing to do the same for the world.

TRAGIC VISION

Counter to the utopian vision is the tragic vision. The tragic vision is that humans are inherently bad or imperfectible and that any successful social or political system must acknowledge this.[514] Political systems constructed with checks and balances are based in this view. If human nature is inherently bad, then it must be restrained in order to prevent corruption and abuse of power. In this view, utopian visions are inherently problematic because they are founded on the false premise that humanity is perfectible, which will lead to despots abusing their power under the guise of creating a utopia. Given the history of attempts to implement utopian visions such as communism, there is much evidence for this view.

In Western culture, the tragic view has its roots in the Christian doctrine of the original sin, the idea that humans are born evil and that this evil cannot be fixed, only resisted, restrained, and redeemed by God in the afterlife. The doctrine of original sin was developed in the writings of Saint Augustine of Hippo.[515] In his book *Confessions*, Augustine begins with the story of childhood. He describes an infancy with wet nurses,[516] where he was unable to communicate his needs. "Then, little by little, I realized where I was and wished to tell my wishes to those who might satisfy them, but I could not!"[517] He then invalidates his own crying as a baby, saying "I grew indignant that my elders were not subject to me and that those on whom I actually had no claim did not wait on me as slaves--and I avenged myself on them by crying."[518] As an adult writing *Confessions*, Augustine did not recognize his right to cry to meet his needs as a baby. He then describes being sent to a school where he was flogged for leaning too slow,[519] and punished merely for "idling" or "playing ball."[520] He then defends the child abuse he received, saying that was "rightly punished as a boy for playing ball--just because this hindered me from learning more quickly."[521] He then says, after describing what he thought was a great childhood, "and yet I sinned... I disobeyed them, not because I had chosen a better way, but from a sheer love of play."[522] In other words, Augustine's great "sin" which he tortures himself with guilt for is wanting to play as a child and crying as a baby. From my modern perspective, this doesn't sound like "sin." It sounds like being human. Augustine admits he does not understand his own reasons for his "sin." "But what were the causes for my strong dislike of Greek literature, which I studied from my boyhood? Even to this day I have not fully understood them."[523] The fact Augustine does not understand his own motivations means he is not conscious of the part of himself that had different desires than his teachers and wet nurses. That aspect of his consciousness fragmented because its needs were not safe and became a subaltern part of his unconscious. This unconscious trauma manifested in unexplained physical symptoms like being "suddenly seized with stomach pains" which took him to the "point of death."[524] Unable to see the real cause of his feelings and behavior, Augustine went on to create the doctrine of original sin, which states there is something inherently wrong with being human. If Augustine were to see that there is no "sin" in an infant crying or a child wanting to play, he would have to confront the emotional pain of acknowledging that his caretakers were not acting in his best interests.

The doctrine of original sin took hold in a culture where childhoods like Augustine's were standard. If the doctrine of original sin did not exist already, it would be necessary to invent it to explain the feelings of people abused as children in a culture that was not ready to explore those feelings. Either these abuses were a gross injustice or the survivors somehow deserved it. The concept of the original sin explained the child's feelings that there must be something inherently wrong with them while providing the comfort of an invisible Father in heaven who did care for his children. It also protected the system that created this subaltern traumatized consciousness. It is no coincidence that when European childhood began to change, Europeans started to reject the tragic vision of original sin in favor of liberalism based in individual rights. When people were given basic rights by their parents, they tried to create a world based in individual rights. Likewise, their view of God changed. Monotheistic cultures have always projected their Earthly fathers onto God the Father. When fathers were absent or brutal, God was seen as a punishing deity. As parents became more loving, people became more likely to see God as unconditionally loving as well.

A more modern version of original sin can be found in genetic determinism or the idea that the roots of violence, selfishness, and other negative behaviors can be found in our biology.[525] In this view, we are not born "bad" because of God, but our genes. This view is more flexible. While the religious view requires an act of God to change human nature, biology can be changed through the environment. Trauma can change which genes are epigenetically expressed, and trauma visited upon one generation can be biologically expressed in future generations.[526] Even if we accept this view, our biology is not as fixed or tragic as determinists might suggest. If we resolve our trauma, it can actually alter our biology and the biology of the next generation.

The tragic view is based in the premise that human nature cannot change. Yet, through most of human history, abuse, abandonment, and the rape of children was the norm. People who experience childhood trauma live with that trauma later in life. Unless we believe that child abuse did not affect people in the past in the same way it does now, then most of history is the history of entire populations acting from the consequences of child abuse. To understand the history of the world, look at how people of important periods were raised just a few decades before. Our age is no different. Most people were raised in impersonal systems that ignored their needs. They were born in the hospital system and educated in the school system. Then, as adults, they find themselves trapped in other systems, which they are not aware they have the power to change, due to the learned helplessness of childhood. If we become aware of the origins of these feelings and beliefs, this vision might shift from tragic to one we actually have the power to change.

WHOLE VISION

Human nature has always appeared to be a constant of history because there has never been a time in our history without systemic child abuse of some kind. Both the utopian view and tragic view see human nature as basically unchangeable and therefore a problem to be managed and manipulated through cultural systems. Yet, what we call human nature is actually the product of trauma, learned through pre-verbal experiences that extend back through our childhoods and ancestors. Not only can human nature change, it already has been through trauma. The task is not to manipulate humanity into fitting a vision but to make ourselves whole again, by integrating the psychological pieces of human consciousness fragmented through trauma, putting them back together like pieces of a puzzle, until they form the full picture of who we really are. In this vision, there is nothing wrong with us, except that which was made wrong before we knew what it was.

Both the utopian and tragic visions require cutting off aspects of who we are in order to conform to a pre-determined vision. In their extreme form, these visions cut entire ideas and populations out of society through gulags and concentration camps. These extremes mirror the childhood trauma, in which aspects of children are cut away and discarded into the prison of the unconscious. Circumcision represents the physical manifestation of this thinking, in which a literal part of the body is cut off to conform the child to a pre-determined vision of what another person thinks their body and sexuality should be. Any vision for humanity that is different than the whole of who we are will require separating ourselves from the parts of ourselves that differ from that vision.

There is a third view, which is neither utopian nor tragic. In this view, there is nothing wrong with us. Children are born with everything they need to learn and grow. If we are loved, we learn to relate from that love. If abused, we learn to relate from that. If fragmented, those fragments will engage in unconscious behavior, seeking to recreate the trauma where they were split so that they can become whole again. Every abuse in the world could be seen as the result of unconscious trauma seeking wholeness. If healed, we can learn a way to relate from that wholeness. In this view, the problem is not that we cannot conform to another's pre-determined vision, but that we ever had to. Instead of cutting away aspects of who we are, this vision seeks to create a world that respects the wholeness of ourselves, others, and our children.

To answer the question that began this chapter about how we can propose a new vision when all previous have failed - we don't. We propose a change in human consciousness. All previous visions sought to change the world without changing human consciousness. In their attempts to change the world, they fragmented and traumatized human consciousness. In this vision, all we do is keep the next generation whole. Children's Justice is a bridge between our current traumatized and fragmented consciousness and the consciousness of a generation kept whole. It is this whole generation that will create a better world.

We cannot know what such a world would look like from our current consciousness. By definition, the parts of ourselves and others that we must integrate to become whole are in the unconscious, outside of our conscious awareness. They have been fragmented and forgotten, and we will not know who or what they are until integrated. This shift must occur on every level of society. You can participate on an individual level by integrating your own consciousness, raising your children in a way that respects the whole of their being, and using a critical consciousness to avoid systems that do not contribute to the wholeness of yourself, others, and your children. However, we are not merely individuals. We participate in social systems. Ensuring the next generation is taught to relate from wholeness will require changing or dismantling all social systems engaged in the opposite. These systems were not created in a day. Changing them might take time as well. This project is multigenerational. If the next generation is raised in a way that preserves their wholeness, they will create a world from that wholeness. Change is possible.

FUTURE REALITY

Imagine you fell asleep, and like the protagonist of *Looking Backward* awoke in a future where this whole vision had already been accomplished. What would it be like to live in a world free from trauma? To interact with people who were whole, physically and psychologically? What would it feel like to grow up in this world? Who would you be if you were completely whole? Looking backward from this future, do you notice how what you learned in this book helped us get there? Take your time. Some learnings might be immediately obvious. Others might only become apparent upon reflection when you're thinking about what you've learned later. In the beginning of this book, I said that I'd changed as a result of writing it. Whether or not you realize it, you've changed as a result of reading it as well. You are already imagining an entirely new vision of the future. If you knew this future was possible, what would you be willing to do to bring it into reality? This vision will only become real if you make it real. It is up to you to create Children's Justice.

EPILOGUE
MUTANT MEME

In the 2016 paper *Women's Studies as Virus: Institutional Feminism, Affect, and the Projection of Danger* feminist scholars Breanne Fahs and Michael Karger suggest that critical social justice should spread through institutions like a virus.[527] The authors favorably compare the way social justice takes over institutions to viruses like Ebola and HIV and suggest that those involved in social justice should "infect" whatever institutions they join and train others to spread the infection. This infection changes the original intention of the institution. Like a virus, the memetic infection of social justice can create a "transformative change" that causes the institution to replicate the virus instead of its stated function.

Social justice is a meme complex, a series of cultural ideas. The word meme originally comes from *The Selfish Gene* by Richard Dawkins, a scientist and founding member of the New Atheism movement. Dawkins defined a meme as a unit of cultural transmission.[528] A meme complex is a series of memes that work together, like an ideology or religion. Dawkins theorized that memes were like viruses. They use people's minds as their host and reproduce by spreading from person to person. Memes are subject to natural selection, with those better at survival and replication proliferating more. This is why many ideological memes, like religion, contain a command for the host to replicate them by "sharing the good news" with others, encouraging them to become hosts of the meme as well. Of course, Dawkins's entire New Atheism movement was destroyed by a meme itself. When the meme complex of critical social justice entered the New Atheism movement, it became Atheism Plus, a critical social justice focused version of atheism.[529] Eventually, the entire new atheist movement was subsumed by social justice activism,[530] and Dawkins himself "canceled" due to his refusal to adopt this new ideology.[531]

The virus of social justice based in critical theory has been incredibly effective at reproducing itself. If we were to use this virus analogy, one could say we are in a social justice epidemic. The virus has infected most major institutions, including academia, government institutions, schools, political organizations, and the medical system. Many of these institutions now replicate the virus rather than their original function. This virus analogy was created prior to the arrival of COVID-19, an infectious disease that caused a worldwide pandemic. Some believe COVID-19 escaped from a lab in Wuhan China or was genetically engineered in this lab by mutating a regular strain of coronavirus.[532] Whatever the truth on the matter, these alleged origins of COVID-19 mirror the memetic virus of critical social justice. Critical social justice also escaped from a government institution. It was developed in academia and spread from elite universities and academic journals to students, who in turn infected the institutions they joined upon graduation. Unlike COVID-19, there were no lockdowns to stop the spread of this meme complex. The critical pandemic spread slowly over decades. Now it infects nearly every institution.

MEMETIC INFECTION

Memes change their hosts. If a meme or meme complex benefits you, then you have a symbiotic relationship with it. Many memes help people live better lives. However, if a meme complex harms you, it has a parasitic relationship with you. Memes, or what most people just call ideas, are responsible for both the greatest human achievements and the worst horrors of humankind. Every great work of art was inspired by a meme, yet so was every human rights violation. Even our ideas about what makes a meme harmful or beneficial can be influenced by the memes we adopt. My own view is that memes that make us more whole are those that benefit us, and memes which fragment us are harmful. Yet even this belief is the result of certain memes I've gathered from my own lived experience.

Like viruses, different memes have different infection rates. Some memes create intellectual pandemics, while others struggle to find hosts. Hosts themselves can be more at-risk for certain memes than others. Those with strong psychological immune systems might be bombarded with a meme and never become infected. Others become infected at the slightest exposure. Once infected, both the host and meme determine how long the infection will last. If you've ever tried to change someone's mind about a strongly held belief, you know how difficult it can be to cure a memetic infection. The hardest memetic infections to cure are those where the host believes the meme to be a part of themselves. If the host believes that they are the memes they host, their psychological immune system will defend the meme the same way they would fight for their own life. Yet, meme complexes are separate lifeforms from their hosts. Even if every author cited in this book were to perish, the meme complex of critical theory they created would live on without them as long as it could continue to find new hosts.

You already host many memes yourself. Every idea you hold or abstract principle you believe in is a meme. One could no more live a life without memes than live without thoughts or language. However, memes change in the ecosystem of your mind. When someone shares an idea or meme with you, you might change it, develop your own version of it, or be inspired to create your own new ideas. One could call this process by which ideas change memetic mutation. If your new idea catches on or becomes more popular, you have created a mutation of a memetic virus. The meme complex might look the same or borrow from the previous structure, but it is something new. For example, one could see Mormonism as a mutation of the Protestant Christian meme complex, which itself is a mutation from Catholic Christianity. Ideas come from one another, and mutation is part of their natural growth and reproduction.

Mutation changes the meme. Once mutated, instead of reproducing the original version of the meme virus, the meme complex reproduces the mutated version. Someone infected with the Mormonism meme complex will not reproduce Catholicism if they convert someone and infect them with their meme. Likewise, critical social justice will not reproduce the earlier forms of social justice it mutated from. One could see this form of social justice as a result of the collision of critical theory with various social justice, civil rights, and identity movements. This injection of critical theory mutated each movement into something new that can never reproduce the original. Memes can actually influence and infect one another. The original meme complex critical social justice mutated from acts as an infection point and host for theory. If someone holds the ideas of the Civil Rights movement and believes racism is bad, then an idea that promises to fight racism will be more readily accepted by that person than by someone who does not see racism as a serious problem. The previous idea becomes a host for the next. Liberalism itself was the host for critical theory. Critical theory was literally created and hosted in the liberal institution of universities. Since every major system and institution already accepts the ideas of liberalism, it makes sense that every institution would eventually become a host to critical theory. Unlike viruses, one meme can end another by infecting it from within.

EXPERIMENT'S RESULTS

This book is a mutation. I have taken the ideas of critical theory and social justice into the lab of my mind and hybridized them with my own thinking on the issue of circumcision and how we treat children to create a new mutation: Children's Justice. This meme complex might look similar to critical social justice, but like any mutation it cannot reproduce the original meme, only the mutated one. Since this meme complex comes from social justice based in critical theory, it will be likely to find a host in those who accept social justice. As a new mutation, it may also find hosts who never accepted the previous meme complex. One can host multiple memes. This meme is compatible with many other belief systems, including those of the dominant hegemony. It is designed to subsume them, and reproduce itself rather than the old system.

I discovered this mutation on accident. This book began as an experiment to see what would happen if I combined the ideas and issues important to me with critical theory. I did not know what the results of this experiment would be. I anticipated they would be much smaller, and take the form of a short ebook with a few new ideas and arguments. As I studied theory and wrote, it grew into the completely new viewpoint you are reading now. I've never had a book reach out and grab me like this one, demanding to be written. It was as if I had become host to a meme complex with a consciousness of its own.

Memes are separate from their hosts, but we can interact with them. I engaged in a dialogue with this meme complex in my mind. We both changed as a result of our interaction. This was true of every book on critical social justice I consciously chose to invite into my mind. Theory changed the way I viewed the world, and the version of theory that existed in my mind mutated into Children's Justice. It wasn't until I was finished, that I realized what I'd done: I had engaged in ideological gain-of-function research. Gain-of-function research is research designed to alter a biological organism to enhance its biological functions.[533] Some believe that the COVID-19 virus was the result of gain-of-function research.[534] Yet, this was the mutation of an ideological virus rather than a physical one. I had taken a meme complex that was already an epidemic in society and made a new version. This new version will not reproduce the old but spread the mutant meme complex of Children's Justice.

This meme complex originated from the lab of my mind, but I have left it loose in the world. By reading this, you have been exposed. Now, you have a choice. You can try not to continue to think about what you've learned by reading the pages of this book, or you can allow this new way of thinking to sink deep into your mind and become a host to this meme complex as well. You could allow this book to change you, as it changed me. You might even spread this meme to others, allowing them to become hosts as well. I am patient zero. You could become a super spreader. Ideas want to be shared. Will you pass Children's Justice on to someone else?

While you decide whether or not to spread the ideas of Children's Justice, you might want to remember that memes can have a beneficial relationship. If a meme improves your life, keep it.

If a meme harms, then you might need another meme to help remove it. While Children's Justice replaces previous hegemonic meme complexes it also offers an end to another dangerous psychological infection that has spread virally through humanity: trauma.

ENDING TRAUMA

Trauma functions like a virus. Rather than reproducing sexually, trauma reproduces by finding a host. People who have experienced trauma often act from their trauma. One on level, when a survivor acts from their trauma they are doing the behavior they learned kept them safe during the original trauma. Yet, if we were to view trauma as a separate life-form, the same way memes are separate from their hosts, then when someone acts from trauma to cause trauma in another person, the trauma is actually using their current host to reproduce itself in the victim.

If trauma is subjected to the same evolutionary forces as viruses or memes, then it follows that traumas that continue would be those most successful at reproducing themselves. If trauma modifies the behavior of its host, such that the host traumatizes others thereby reproducing the trauma in them, it is more likely to spread. From this perspective, it makes sense why abusers were often once the abused, pedophiles were often molested as children, and those who advocate for cutting children's genitals were often cut themselves. Trauma is more likely to pass itself on from a host who is already infected. It also explains why the most at-risk population for trauma is children. From the perspective of the virus of trauma, children offer the longest lifespan for trauma. A longer lifespan gives trauma more chances to spread. An older host might only have a lifespan of a few years, but children offer a lifetime of opportunity. Children also have the least psychological defenses. While adults' minds are often closed, children are open, constantly learning, and taking everything in from their environment. From a practical perspective, children have the least social power, making them the easiest targets for predators. Trauma is not an apex predator. Humans do not like trauma. Many people actively try to avoid or eliminate it. There are even large campaigns against certain forms of trauma. While trauma hunts us, we can fight back, which is why trauma might evolve to select weaker targets.

Given the evolutionary pressure on trauma from humans trying to eliminate trauma and trauma itself trying to reproduce, we could expect these pressures to select for traumas that target younger and younger victims. Traumas which conceal themselves or do not appear as trauma to most humans are more likely to avoid being eliminated by humans than traumas that reveal themselves or are recognized as trauma by society. Traumas that last longer are more likely to survive than those people get over quickly, so evolution would select for deep traumas over surface ones. Traumas are more likely to reproduce if they can find or create "hunting grounds" where they find a steady supply of fresh victims to host them. Ideally, trauma would not have to hunt at all and could farm humans as hosts. Circumcision after hospital birth fulfills all these evolutionary requirements. It targets the youngest victims possible, conceals itself as medicine, has a lifelong impact, and farms a constant stream of human hosts. In other words, the evolutionary pressures on trauma select for systemic pedophilia.

Trauma functions like every other virus or meme complex. Some overcome their trauma and beat the infection. Others have lifelong conditions. Trauma can become so strong it kills the host, through self-destructive behavior or suicide. Like memes, the hardest traumas to remove are those which the host beliefs to be a part of themselves. As we've already discussed, genital cutting often falls into this category, with survivors speaking about circumcision as an aspect of identity, by saying "I am circumcised" rather than "I was circumcised" or "circumcision is something that happened to me." This false consciousness can be cured. Just like when someone beats an infection their immune system becomes stronger, if you can overcome and integrate your traumas, you can become psychologically stronger. It is possible to let go of trauma while retaining the learnings gained from the experience.

We are in a pandemic of trauma. The majority of the world has experienced trauma in some form. Trauma has evolved to target children. Children's Justice is a meme complex designed to end childhood trauma. If this meme complex reduces the suffering of children, you have a moral duty to share it. Memes change our behavior. One meme can end another. If you fully accept the meme of Children's Justice, you will protect their children. This meme will reproduce itself, rather than trauma. In the introduction, I said this book might change your mind. You might notice that you've changed your mind already. No matter how much this book has changed you, the time has come for one more movement. You must share these ideas with others. It is not enough for you to only allow them to change you. We are not merely individuals. We participate in social systems. Even if you participate in those systems with a critical consciousness, eventually, that consciousness demands changing those systems. This change begins with you. It can even outlast you if you share it enough. Meme complexes can live on long after their hosts have passed. They have a life of their own. Every system of power rests on a system of knowledge, a meme complex. The systems we were born into were set in motion by people who are long dead. If we change the system in our lifetime, the children of the future will be born into a new system. They will be whole. Free from trauma. You can be a part of that future. Share this book. Spread the meme.

ACKNOWLEDGMENTS

- Thank you to my wife, Kristeena. Your support means the world to me. I will always love you, your inner children, and all the children we create together. (Love you, Marco.)
- Thank you to my European editor for your detailed and helpful notes, demand for greater academic citations, and sharpening the rough edges of my writing. Feedback from the perspective of someone who was not immersed in this issue but willing to engage was crucial to improving the book. I'd list his name, but he is much more moderate than I, and I doubt he'd want the challenges that might come with public association. Still, I am grateful.
- Thank you to Jordan Arel for using the term Children's Justice when I described an early version of this book to him. As you can tell, I liked the phrase.
- Thank you to Owen for helping me with the magic.
- Thank you to the Jewish people who attacked me both publicly and behind the scenes. You taught me a lot. Some of those lessons made their way into this book.
- Thank you to my early readers. I needed your feedback and encouragement as I neared the finish line of this book.
- Thank you to the people who helped me with last-minute publishing needs for this book. The only reason your names aren't listed here is that I had to finalize the book before your contributions were done.
- Thank you to the authors whose work helped me understand social justice and critical theory, whose names I mention throughout this book. I am one of your outcomes.
- Thank you to my inner child. I kept my promise.

BIBLIOGRAPHY

- Abelove, Henry, et al. *The Lesbian and Gay Studies Reader*. 1st ed., Routledge, 1993.
- Adamson, Walter. *Hegemony and Revolution: Antonio Gramsci's Political and Cultural Theory*. Echo Point Books & Media, 2014.
- Applebaum, Barbara. *Being White, Being Good: White Complicity, White Moral Responsibility, and Social Justice Pedagogy*. Lexington Books, 2011.
- Ariès, Philippe. *Centuries of Childhood*, trans. by Robert Baldrick. Vintage Books, 1962.
- Augustine, *Augustine: Confessions*. Trans. Albert C. Outler. Westminster Press, 1955.
- Baudrillard, Jean. *Simulacra and Simulation (The Body, In Theory: Histories of Cultural Materialism)*. 1st ed., University of Michigan Press, 1994.
- Bellamy, Edward. *Looking Backward: 2000-1887*. Digibooks OOD / Demetra Publishing, 2019.
- Beverley, John. *Subalternity and Representation: Arguments in Cultural Theory*. Duke University Press, 1999.
- Bray, Mark. *Antifa: The Anti-Fascist Handbook*. Illustrated, Melville House, 2017.
- Butler, Judith. *Bodies That Matter: On the Discursive Limits of Sex*. 1st ed., Routledge, 2011.
- Butler, Judith. *Gender Trouble: Feminism and the Subversion of Identity (Routledge Classics)*. 1st ed., Routledge, 2006.
- Chamberlain, David. *The Mind of Your Newborn Baby*. 3rd ed., North Atlantic Books, 1998.
- Chamberlain, David. *Windows to the Womb: Revealing the Conscious Baby from Conception to Birth*. 1st ed., North Atlantic Books, 2013.
- Cherry, Myisha. *The Case for Rage: Why Anger Is Essential to Anti-Racist Struggle*. Oxford University Press, 2021.
- Davis, Fania. *The Little Book of Race and Restorative Justice: Black Lives, Healing, and US Social Transformation (Justice and Peacebuilding)*. Good Books, 2019.
- Dawkins, Richard. *The Selfish Gene: 40th Anniversary Edition (Oxford Landmark Science)*. 4th ed., Oxford University Press, 2016.
- Delgado, Richard, et al. *Critical Race Theory (Third Edition): An Introduction (Critical America, 20)*. 3rd ed., NYU Press, 2017.
- deMause, Lloyd. *Foundations of Psychohistory*. Creative Roots Pub, 1982.

- deMause, Lloyd. *History of Childhood: The Untold Story of Child Abuse*. Peter Bedrick Books, 1988.
- DiAngelo, Robin. *Nice Racism: How Progressive White People Perpetuate Racial Harm*. Beacon Press, 2021.
- DiAngelo, Robin. *White Fragility: Why It's So Hard for White People to Talk About Racism*. Beacon Press, 2018.
- Duffell, Nick. *Wounded Leaders: British Elitism and the Entitlement Illusion: A Psychohistory*. Lone Arrow Press Ltd, 2016.
- Edelstein, Ludwig. *The Hippocratic Oath, Text, Translation and Interpretation*. Amsterdam University Press, 1964.
- Farrell, Warren. *The Myth of Male Power*. Finch Publishing, 2001.
- Felluga, Dino Franco. *Critical Theory: The Key Concepts*. Kindle Edition Routledge, 2015.
- Fildes, Valerie. *Wet Nursing: A History from Antiquity to the Present (Family, Sexuality and Social Relations in Past Times)*. Illustrated edition, Blackwell Pub, 1988.
- Fisher, Janina. *Healing the Fragmented Selves of Trauma Survivors: Overcoming Internal Self-Alienation*. 1st ed., Routledge, 2017.
- Foucault, Michel. *Abnormal: Lectures at the Collège de France 1974-1975*. 1st ed., Picador, 2004
- Foucault, Michel. *Discipline & Punish: The Birth of the Prison*. 2nd ed., Vintage Books, 1995.
- Foucault, Michel. *Power/Knowledge: Selected Interviews and Other Writings*, 1972-1977. Edited by Colin Gordon, 1st ed., Vintage, 1980.
- Foucault, Michel. *Security, Territory, Population: Lectures at the Collège de France 1977–1978*. Picador, 2009.
- Foucault, Michel. *The Birth of the Clinic: An Archaeology of Medical Perception*. 1st ed., Vintage, 1994.
- Foucault, Michel. *The History of Sexuality Volume 1: An Introduction*. Translated by Robert Hurley, Vintage Books, 1990.
- Foucault, Michel. *The Order of Things: An Archaeology of Human Sciences*. 1994 ed., Vintage, 1972.
- Fricker, Miranda. *Epistemic Injustice: Power and the Ethics of Knowing*. 1st ed., Oxford University Press, 2010.
- Gatto, John Taylor. *The Underground History of American Education*. Revised, Oxford, 2006.
- Glick, Leonard. *Marked in Your Flesh: Circumcision from Ancient Judea to Modern America*. Oxford University Press, 2006.
- Goldman, Ronald. *Circumcision, The Hidden Trauma: How an American Cultural Practice Affects Infants and Ultimately Us All*. Vanguard Publications, 1997.
- Goodley, Dan. *Dis/Ability Studies: Theorising Disablism and Ableism*. 1st ed., Routledge, 2014.

- Gottesman, Isaac. *The Critical Turn in Education: From Marxist Critique to Poststructuralist Feminism to Critical Theories of Race*. Routledge, 2016.
- Griaule, Marcel, and Germaine Dieterlen. *Conversations With Ogotemmeli: An Introduction to Dogon Religious Ideas*. International African Institute, 1975.
- Herman, Dianne F. "The Rape Culture." *Women: A Feminist Perspective*. Edited by Jo Freeman. McGraw Hill, 1994.
- Hill Collins, Patricia. *Intersectionality (Key Concepts)*. Wiley. Kindle Edition, Polity, 2020.
- hooks, bell. *Teaching to Transgress: Education as the Practice of Freedom*. Routledge, 1994.
- Ignatiev, Noel, et al. *Race Traitor*. 1st ed., Routledge, 1996.
- Kendi, Ibram. *How to Be an Antiracist*. 1st ed., One World, 2019.
- Kidd, Ian James, et al. *The Routledge Handbook of Epistemic Injustice* (Routledge Handbooks in Philosophy). 1st ed., Routledge, 2019.
- King Jr., Martin Luther. *I Have a Dream: Writings and Speeches That Changed the World*, Special 75th Anniversary Edition (Martin Luther King, Jr., Born January 15, 1929). 75th Anniversary ed., HarperOne, 2003.
- Kolk, Van Bessel der, MD. *The Body Keeps the Score: Brain, Mind, and Body in the Healing of Trauma*. Reprint, Penguin Publishing Group, 2015.
- Lenin, Vladimir Ilyich. *Essential Works of Lenin: "What Is to Be Done?" And Other Writings*. Dover Publications, 1987.
- Marcuse, Herbert, *The Essential Marcuse: Selected Writings of Philosopher and Social Critic Herbert Marcuse*. Beacon Press, 2007.
- Marotta, Brendon. *The Intactivist Guidebook: How to Win the Game of Intactivism and End Circumcision*. 2nd ed., Brendon Marotta, 2020.
- Marx, Karl. *The Economic and Philosophic Manuscripts of 1844 and the Communist Manifesto (Great Books in Philosophy)*. 1st ed., Prometheus, 1988.
- Masters, William, and Virginia Johnson. *Human Sexual Response*. Illustrated, Ishi Press, 2010.
- McHale, Brian. *The Cambridge Introduction to Postmodernism (Cambridge Introductions to Literature)*. Cambridge University Press, 2015.
- Menakem, Resmaa. *My Grandmother's Hands: Racialized Trauma and the Pathway to Mending Our Hearts and Bodies*. Illustrated, Central Recovery Press, 2017.
- Moldbug, Mencius. *How Dawkins Got Pwned*. Unqualified Reservations, 2016.

- Narvaez, Darcia. *Neurobiology and the Development of Human Morality: Evolution, Culture, and Wisdom*. Illustrated, W. W. Norton & Company, 2014.
- Pinker, Steven. *The Blank Slate: The Modern Denial of Human Nature*. Viking Penguin, 2002.
- Postman, Neil. *The Disappearance of Childhood*. Kindle Edition, Vintage, 2011.
- Rattansi, Ali. *Racism: A Very Short Introduction (Very Short Introductions)*. 2nd ed., Oxford University Press, 2020.
- Roberts, Lesley. *A Is for Alex: A Bereaved Mother's Promise to Her Beloved Son*. Cherish Editions, 2021.
- Robinett, Patricia. *The Rape of Innocence: Female Genital Mutilation and Circumcision in the USA*. Nunzio Press, 2010.
- Schulman, Sarah. *Ties That Bind: Familial Homophobia and Its Consequences*. The New Press, 2012.
- Sensoy, Ozlem, and Robin DiAngelo. *Is Everyone Really Equal?: An Introduction to Key Concepts in Social Justice Education*, 1st ed., Teacher's College Press, 2012
- Spivak, Gayatri. "Can the Subaltern Speak?" *Can the Subaltern Speak?: Reflections on the History of an Idea*, Edited by Rosalind Morris, Columbia University Press, 2010.
- Wiessinger, Diane, et al. *The Womanly Art of Breastfeeding: Completely Revised and Updated 8th Edition*. 8th Revised, Updated ed., Ballantine Books, 2010.

FILMS

- *American Circumcision*. Dir. Brendon Marotta. Gravitas Ventures, 2017. Film.
- *An Open Secret*. Dir. Amy Berg. 2014. Film.
- *The Business of Being Born*. Dir. Abby Epstein. New Line, 2008. Film.
- *The Other Side of the Glass: A Birth Film for and about Fathers*. Dir. Janel Miranda. 2009. Film.
- *The Red Pill*. Dir. Cassie Jaye. 2016. Gravitas Ventures. Film.

NOTES

[1] Morava, Maria and Scottie Andrew. "The Black Lives Matter Foundation Raised $90 Million in 2020, and Gave Almost a Quarter of It." *CNN*, 25 Feb. 2021, edition.cnn.com/2021/02/25/us/black-lives-matter-2020-donation-report-trnd/index.html. Accessed 2 Nov. 2021.

[2] Ward, Marguerite. "Twitter CEO Jack Dorsey donates $10 million to Ibram X. Kendi's center on antiracism at Boston University." *Business Insider*, 21 Aug. 2020, www.businessinsider.com/jack-dorsey-donates-ibram-kendi-center-on-antiracism-boston-university-2020-8. Accessed 2 Nov. 2021.

[3] Levy, Margaux. "31 Celebrities Who've Gone Above & Beyond To Support BLM Movement." *Harper's Bazaar Singapore*, 11 June 2020, www.harpersbazaar.com.sg/life/celebrities-gone-above-beyond-support-blm. Accessed 2 Nov. 2021.

[4] Sensoy, Ozlem, and Robin DiAngelo. *Is Everyone Really Equal?: An Introduction to Key Concepts in Social Justice Education*, 1st ed., Teacher's College Press, 2012, pp. xviii, 4-7.

Bohman, James. "Critical Theory (Stanford Encyclopedia of Philosophy)." *Stanford Encyclopedia of Philosophy*, Metaphysics Research Lab, Stanford University, 8 Mar. 2005, plato.stanford.edu/entries/critical-theory. Accessed 12 Oct. 2021.

[5] King Jr., Martin Luther. *I Have a Dream: Writings and Speeches That Changed the World*, Special 75th Anniversary Edition (Martin Luther King, Jr., Born January 15, 1929). 75th Anniversary ed., HarperOne, 2003.

[6] Sensoy, Ozlem, and Robin DiAngelo. *Is Everyone Really Equal?: An Introduction to Key Concepts in Social Justice Education*, 1st ed., Teacher's College Press, 2012, p. 1.

[7] DiAngelo, Robin. *White Fragility: Why It's So Hard for White People to Talk About Racism*. Beacon Press, 2018, p. 3.

[8] "Critical social justice" is also the term that some within the movement use to describe themselves. Source:

Sensoy, Ozlem, and Robin DiAngelo. *Is Everyone Really Equal?: An Introduction to Key Concepts in Social Justice Education*, 1st ed., Teacher's College Press, 2012, p. xviii.

[9] DiAngelo, Robin. *White Fragility: Why It's So Hard for White People to Talk About Racism*. Beacon Press, 2018, pp. 40-43.

[10] DiAngelo, Robin. *White Fragility: Why It's So Hard for White People to Talk About Racism*. Beacon Press, 2018, p. 3.

[11] DiAngelo, Robin. *White Fragility: Why It's So Hard for White People to Talk About Racism*. Beacon Press, 2018, p. 4.

[12] Kendi, Ibram. *How to Be an Antiracist*. 1st ed., One World, 2019, p. 13.

[13] Kendi, Ibram. *How to Be an Antiracist*. 1st ed., One World, 2019, p. 9.

[14] "California Proposition 16, Repeal Proposition 209 Affirmative Action Amendment (2020)." *Ballotpedia*, ballotpedia.org/California_Proposition_16,_Repeal_Proposition_209_Affirmative_Action_Amendment_(2020). Accessed 1 Jan. 2021.

[15] Editors of Merriam-Webster. "Equality vs. Equity: What Is the Difference?" *The Merriam-Webster.Com Dictionary*, 9 Nov. 2020, www.merriam-webster.com/words-at-play/equality-vs-equity-difference. Accessed 6 Jan. 2020.

Morton, B. and Fasching-Varner, K. (2015). "Equity." *Encyclopedia of Diversity and Social Justice. Vol. 1*. Edited by S. Thompson, Rowman & Littlefield. p. 303-4.

[16] Note that I said the "popular understanding," because Martin Luther King himself might not have been as "color-blind" as he is often portrayed. However, this has been the dominant understanding of his work at least since Ronald Reagan made Martin Luther King Jr. Day a national holiday. For more on the critical race theory perspective on this:

Kendi, Ibram. "Critical-Race-Theory Critics Are Distorting Martin Luther King's Legacy." *The Atlantic*, 14 Oct. 2021, www.theatlantic.com/ideas/archive/2021/10/martin-luther-king-critical-race-theory/620367. Accessed 14 Oct. 2021.

[17] Trent, Maria, et al. "The Impact of Racism on Child and Adolescent Health." American Academy of Pediatrics, 1 Aug. 2019, pediatrics.aappublications.org/content/144/2/e20191765.

[18] Korioth, Trisha. "Featured Speaker Kendi to Pediatricians: Consider Racism 'a Diagnosis.'" *AAP News*, 6 Oct. 2020, www.aappublications.org/news/2020/10/06/nce2020kendi100620. Accessed 13 Oct. 2021.

[19] Ehrenfeld, Jesse, and Patrice Harris. "Police Brutality Must Stop." *American Medical Association*, 29 May 2020, www.ama-assn.org/about/leadership/police-brutality-must-stop. Accessed 13 Oct. 2021.

[20] Jones, Camara Phyllis et al. "Using "socially assigned race" to probe white advantages in health status." *Ethnicity & disease* vol. 18,4 (2008): 496-504. https://pubmed.ncbi.nlm.nih.gov/19157256/

[21] The American Academy of Family Physicians. "Institutional Racism in the Health Care System." *The American Academy of Family Physicians*, www.aafp.org/about/policies/all/institutional-racism.html.

[22] Abdul-Majeed, Lauren. "Come On, Grads, Let's Start Cultivating a Healthier World." *The American Academy of Family Physicians*, 26 May 2017, www.aafp.org/news/blogs/leadervoices/entry/come_on_grads_let_s.html. Accessed 1 Jan. 2021.

[23] Editors of Merriam-Webster. "Equality vs. Equity: What Is the Difference?" *The Merriam-Webster.Com Dictionary*, 9 Nov. 2020, www.merriam-webster.com/words-at-play/equality-vs-equity-difference. Accessed 6 Jan. 2020.

Kendi, Ibram. *How to Be an Antiracist*. 1st ed., One World, 2019, p. 9.

[24] Braveman, Paula A., et al. "Health Disparities and Health Equity: The Issue Is Justice." *American Journal of Public Health*, vol. 101, no. S1, 2011, pp. S149–55. Crossref, doi:10.2105/ajph.2010.300062.

[25] Vestal, Christine. "Racism Is a Public Health Crisis, Say Cities and Counties." *PEW*, 15 June 2020, www.pewtrusts.org/en/research-and-analysis/blogs/stateline/2020/06/15/racism-is-a-public-health-crisis-say-cities-and-counties. Accessed 1 Jan. 2021.

[26] Powell, Michael. "Are Protests Dangerous? What Experts Say May Depend on Who's Protesting What." *The New York Times*, 12 Oct. 2020, www.nytimes.com/2020/07/06/us/Epidemiologists-coronavirus-protests-quarantine.html. Accessed 1 Jan. 2021.

[27] Diamond, Dan. "Suddenly, Public Health Officials Say Social Justice Matters More Than Social Distance." *POLITICO*, 5 June 2020, www.politico.com/news/magazine/2020/06/04/public-health-protests-301534. Accessed 29 Dec. 2021.

[28] Mitchell, Harmeet Cnn Kaur And Skylar. "States Are Calling Racism a Public Health Crisis. Here's What That Means." *CNN*, 14 Aug. 2020, edition.cnn.com/2020/08/14/health/states-racism-public-health-crisis-trnd/index.html. Accessed 2 Jan. 20201.

[29] Simon, Mallory Cnn. "Over 1,000 Health Professionals Sign a Letter Saying, Don't Shut down Protests Using Coronavirus Concerns as an Excuse." *CNN*, 5 June 2020, edition.cnn.com/2020/06/05/health/health-care-open-letter-protests-coronavirus-trnd/index.html. Accessed 1 Jan. 2021.

[30] Goodnough, Abby, and Jan Hoffman. "The Elderly vs. Essential Workers: Who Should Get the Coronavirus Vaccine First?" *The New York Times*, 24 Feb. 2021, www.nytimes.com/2020/12/05/health/covid-vaccine-first.html. Accessed 15 Mar. 2021.

[31] Diamond, Dan. "Suddenly, Public Health Officials Say Social Justice Matters More Than Social Distance." *POLITICO*, 5 June 2020, www.politico.com/news/magazine/2020/06/04/public-health-protests-301534. Accessed 29 Dec. 2021.

[32] Introcaso, Camille E., et al. "Prevalence of Circumcision Among Men and Boys Aged 14 to 59 Years in the United States, National Health and Nutrition Examination Surveys 2005–2010." *Sexually Transmitted Diseases*, vol. 40, no. 7, 2013, pp. 521–25. Crossref, doi:10.1097/01.olq. 0000430797.56499.0d.

American Circumcision. Dir. Brendon Marotta. Gravitas Ventures, 2017. Film.

[33] McDonald, James. "Europe's Shudder at Circumcision." *Haaretz*, 20 Oct. 2013, www.haaretz.com/opinion/.premium-europe-s-shudder-at-circumcision-1.5276676. Accessed 27 Oct. 2021.

[34] Circumcision statements from each medical organization mentioned:

AAP: "Circumcision Policy Statement." *PEDIATRICS*, vol. 130, no. 3, 2012, pp. 585–86. Crossref, pediatrics.aappublications.org/content/130/3/585.

AMA: "AMA (Medical Science) Report 10 of the Council on Scientific Affairs (I-99) Full Text." American Medical Association, Dec. 1999, web.archive.org/web/20010406001233/http://www.ama-assn.org/ama/pub/article/2036-2511.html. (Note: This is an internet archive link, since the AMA has since scrubbed their statement.)

AAFP: "Neonatal Circumcision." AAFP, www.aafp.org/about/policies/all/neonatal-circumcision.html. Accessed 12 Oct. 2021.

CDC: "Male Circumcision | HIV Risk and Prevention | HIV/AIDS | CDC." Center for Disease Control, 11 Aug. 2019, www.cdc.gov/hiv/risk/male-circumcision.html. Accessed 12 Oct. 2021.

[35] "Circumcision Policy Statement." *PEDIATRICS*, vol. 130, no. 3, 2012, pp. 585–86. Crossref, pediatrics.aappublications.org/content/130/3/585.

[36] A ten percent complication rate is the complication rate former President of the Virginia Urological Society, James L. Snyder, M.D., F.A.C.S., claims to have seen in his practice, both in the video cited below and in interviews I conducted with him.

Loewen, James. "Doctor Discusses Circumcision Controversy." *YouTube*, uploaded by Bonobo3D, 16 July 2011, https://youtu.be/XrcMYq0ASB8. Accessed 12 Oct. 2021

[37] Sensoy, Ozlem, and Robin DiAngelo. *Is Everyone Really Equal?: An Introduction to Key Concepts in Social Justice Education*, 1st ed., Teacher's College Press, 2012, pp. 7-8.

[38] hooks, bell. *Teaching to Transgress: Education as the Practice of Freedom*. Routledge, 1994. pp. 88–89.

[39] hooks, bell. *Teaching to Transgress: Education as the Practice of Freedom*. Routledge, 1994. pp. 88–89.

Sensoy, Ozlem, and Robin DiAngelo. *Is Everyone Really Equal?: An Introduction to Key Concepts in Social Justice Education*, 1st ed., Teacher's College Press, 2012, p. 8.

[40] Sensoy, Ozlem, and Robin DiAngelo. *Is Everyone Really Equal?: An Introduction to Key Concepts in Social Justice Education*, 1st ed., Teacher's College Press, 2012, pp. 21-25.

[41] *American Circumcision*. Dir. Brendon Marotta. Gravitas Ventures, 2017. Film.

[42] *American Circumcision*. Dir. Brendon Marotta. Gravitas Ventures, 2017. Film.

[43] Although critiques of circumcision go back as far as the practice itself, the modern movement against circumcision arguably began with the founding of the National Organization of Circumcision Information Resource Centers (NOCIRC) by Marilyn Milos in 1985. The term "Intactivist" was later coined as a combination of "Intact" plus "activist," to describe the idea of activists for the intact body.

"Intactivism - IntactWiki." *Intact Wiki*, 2021, intactwiki.org/wiki/Intactivism. Accessed March 15, 2021.

American Circumcision. Dir. Brendon Marotta. Gravitas Ventures, 2017. Film.

[44] Delgado, Richard, et al. *Critical Race Theory (Third Edition): An Introduction (Critical America, 20)*. 3rd ed., NYU Press, 2017, pp. 28-30.

[45] Delgado, Richard, et al. *Critical Race Theory (Third Edition): An Introduction (Critical America, 20)*. 3rd ed., NYU Press, 2017, pp. 26-28.

[46] Galatians 5:2, *Bible: New International Version (NIV)*. 2011. BibleHub, https://biblehub.com/galatians/5-2.htm.

[47] Philippians 3:2, *Bible: New International Version (NIV)*. 2011. BibleHub, https://biblehub.com/philippians/3-2.htm.

[48] Matthew 18:6, *Bible: New International Version (NIV)*, 2011. BibleHub, https://www.biblehub.com/matthew/18-6.htm.

[49] Sensoy, Ozlem, and Robin DiAngelo. *Is Everyone Really Equal?: An Introduction to Key Concepts in Social Justice Education*, 1st ed., Teacher's College Press, 2012, p. 4.

Bohman, James. "Critical Theory (Stanford Encyclopedia of Philosophy)." *Stanford Encyclopedia of Philosophy*, Metaphysics Research Lab, Stanford University, 8 Mar. 2005, plato.stanford.edu/entries/critical-theory. Accessed 12 Oct. 2021.

[50] Bohman, James. "Critical Theory (Stanford Encyclopedia of Philosophy)." *Stanford Encyclopedia of Philosophy*, Metaphysics Research Lab, Stanford University, 8 Mar. 2005, plato.stanford.edu/entries/critical-theory. Accessed 12 Oct. 2021.

[51] Bohman, James. "Critical Theory (Stanford Encyclopedia of Philosophy)." *Stanford Encyclopedia of Philosophy*, Metaphysics Research Lab, Stanford University, 8 Mar. 2005, plato.stanford.edu/entries/critical-theory. Accessed 12 Oct. 2021.

[52] Ansell, Amy (2008). "Critical Race Theory". In Schaefer, Richard T. (ed.). *Encyclopedia of Race, Ethnicity, and Society, Volume 1*. SAGE Publications. pp. 344–346. doi: 10.4135/9781412963879.n138. ISBN 978-1-4129-2694-2.

Delgado, Richard, et al. *Critical Race Theory (Third Edition): An Introduction (Critical America, 20)*. 3rd ed., NYU Press, 2017, p. 3.

[53] Sensoy, Ozlem, and Robin DiAngelo. *Is Everyone Really Equal?: An Introduction to Key Concepts in Social Justice Education*, 1st ed., Teacher's College Press, 2012, pp. 4-6.

[54] Felluga, Dino Franco. *Critical Theory: The Key Concepts*. Kindle Edition Routledge, 2015. p. 237.

Sensoy, Ozlem, and Robin DiAngelo. *Is Everyone Really Equal?: An Introduction to Key Concepts in Social Justice Education*, 1st ed., Teacher's College Press, 2012, p. 52.

[55] Sensoy, Ozlem, and Robin DiAngelo. *Is Everyone Really Equal?: An Introduction to Key Concepts in Social Justice Education*, 1st ed., Teacher's College Press, 2012, pp. 21-25.

[56] Kendi, Ibram. *How to Be an Antiracist*. 1st ed., One World, 2019, pp. 9, 13.

DiAngelo, Robin. *White Fragility: Why It's So Hard for White People to Talk About Racism*. Beacon Press, 2018, p. 3.

Sensoy, Ozlem, and Robin DiAngelo. *Is Everyone Really Equal?: An Introduction to Key Concepts in Social Justice Education*, 1st ed., Teacher's College Press, 2012, pp. 100-101.

[57] Kendi, Ibram. *How to Be an Antiracist*. 1st ed., One World, 2019, p. 9.

[58] Kendi, Ibram. *How to Be an Antiracist*. 1st ed., One World, 2019, p. 9.

[59] Kendi, Ibram. *How to Be an Antiracist*. 1st ed., One World, 2019, p. 9.

[60] Anthis, Kristine. "What Is Social Justice? Equality and Equity?" *Psychology Today*, 28 Sept. 2020, www.psychologytoday.com/intl/blog/lifespan-development-why-social-justice-matters/202009/what-is-social-justice-equality-and. Accessed 6 Jan. 2020.

Kendi, Ibram. *How to Be an Antiracist*. 1st ed., One World, 2019, pp. 9, 13, 17-20.

Morton, B. and Fasching-Varner, K. (2015). "Equity." *Encyclopedia of Diversity and Social Justice. Vol. 1*. Edited by S. Thompson, Rowman & Littlefield. pp. 303-304.

[61] Foucault, Michel. *Discipline & Punish: The Birth of the Prison*. 2nd ed., Vintage Books, 1995. p. 27.

Foucault, Michel. *Power/Knowledge: Selected Interviews and Other Writings, 1972-1977*. Edited by Colin Gordon, 1st ed., Vintage, 1980.

[62] Sensoy, Ozlem, and Robin DiAngelo. *Is Everyone Really Equal?: An Introduction to Key Concepts in Social Justice Education*, 1st ed., Teacher's College Press, 2012, pp. 2, 7.

[63] Sensoy, Ozlem, and Robin DiAngelo. *Is Everyone Really Equal?: An Introduction to Key Concepts in Social Justice Education*, 1st ed., Teacher's College Press, 2012, pp. 7-11

[64] Foucault, Michel. *Discipline & Punish: The Birth of the Prison*. 2nd ed., Vintage Books, 1995. p. 27.

[65] Delgado, Richard, et al. *Critical Race Theory (Third Edition): An Introduction (Critical America, 20)*. 3rd ed., NYU Press, 2017. pp. 9, 21.

Sensoy, Ozlem, and Robin DiAngelo. *Is Everyone Really Equal?: An Introduction to Key Concepts in Social Justice Education*, 1st ed., Teacher's College Press, 2012, pp. 97-99.

[66] Sensoy, Ozlem, and Robin DiAngelo. *Is Everyone Really Equal?: An Introduction to Key Concepts in Social Justice Education*, 1st ed., Teacher's College Press, 2012, p. 5.

[67] McHale, Brian. *The Cambridge Introduction to Postmodernism (Cambridge Introductions to Literature)*. Cambridge University Press, 2015, p. 172.

Sensoy, Ozlem, and Robin DiAngelo. *Is Everyone Really Equal?: An Introduction to Key Concepts in Social Justice Education*, 1st ed., Teacher's College Press, 2012, p. 5.

[68] Hill Collins, Patricia. *Intersectionality (Key Concepts)*. Wiley. Kindle Edition, Polity, 2020. p. 2.

[69] *American Circumcision*. Dir. Brendon Marotta. Gravitas Ventures, 2017. Film.

Earp, Brian. "Female Genital Mutilation and Male Circumcision: Toward an Autonomy-Based Ethical Framework." *Medicolegal and Bioethics*, 2015, p. 89. *Crossref*, doi:10.2147/mb.s63709.

[70] *American Circumcision Documentary Bonus Features*, "Fuambai Sia Ahmadu - Extended Interview." Dir. Brendon Marotta. Vimeo, 2019. https://vimeo.com/ondemand/circmoviebonus/296147378.

[71] WHO and Jhpiego. "Manual for Early Infant Male Circumcision under Local Anaesthesia." *WHO*, WHO, Feb. 2011, apps.who.int/iris/bitstream/handle/10665/44478/9789241500753_eng.pdf;sequence=1. Accessed 4 Jan. 2020.

[72] *American Circumcision*. Dir. Brendon Marotta. Gravitas Ventures, 2017. Film.

[73] "An Updated Definition of Rape." *The United States Department of Justice*, 7 Apr. 2017, www.justice.gov/archives/opa/blog/updated-definition-rape. Accessed 1 Jan. 2021.

"Rape." *FBI*, ucr.fbi.gov/crime-in-the-u.s/2019/crime-in-the-u.s.-2019/topic-pages/rape. Accessed 1 Jan. 2021.

[74] "Definition of Rape Culture" *Dictionary.com*, 2021, www.dictionary.com/browse/rape-culture. Accessed 12 Oct 2021

[75] Herman, Dianne F. "The Rape Culture." *Women: A Feminist Perspective*. Edited by Jo Freeman. McGraw Hill, 1994.

Norton, Paget. "It Applies for Men, Too: The Absence of 'NO' Doesn't Mean 'Yes.'" The Good Men Project, 18 Jan. 2018, goodmenproject.com/featured-content/it-applies-men-too-tabsence-no-doesnt-mean-yes-pnrtn-lbkr. Accessed 6 Jan. 2021.

[76] Kendi, Ibram. *How to Be an Antiracist*. 1st ed., One World, 2019, pp. 9, 13, 19.

[77] "Racism." *The Merriam-Webster.Com Dictionary*, www.merriam-webster.com/dictionary/racism. Accessed 30 Oct. 2021.

[78] Applebaum, Barbara. *Being White, Being Good: White Complicity, White Moral Responsibility, and Social Justice Pedagogy*. Lexington Books, 2010, p. 121.

[79] Sensoy, Ozlem, and Robin DiAngelo. *Is Everyone Really Equal?: An Introduction to Key Concepts in Social Justice Education*, 1st ed., Teacher's College Press, 2012, pp. 21-25.

[80] Applebaum, Barbara. *Being White, Being Good: White Complicity, White Moral Responsibility, and Social Justice Pedagogy*. Lexington Books, 2010, pp. 123–124.

[81] Applebaum, Barbara. *Being White, Being Good: White Complicity, White Moral Responsibility, and Social Justice Pedagogy*. Lexington Books, 2010, pp. 123–124.

[82] Applebaum, Barbara. *Being White, Being Good: White Complicity, White Moral Responsibility, and Social Justice Pedagogy*. Lexington Books, 2010, pp. 123–124.

[83] Applebaum, Barbara. *Being White, Being Good: White Complicity, White Moral Responsibility, and Social Justice Pedagogy*. Lexington Books, 2010, pp. 123–124.

[84] Watts, Roderick J., et al. "Critical Consciousness: Current Status and Future Directions." *New Directions for Child and Adolescent Development*, vol. 2011, no. 134, 2011, pp. 43–57. *Crossref*, doi:10.1002/cd.310.

[85] Sensoy, Ozlem, and Robin DiAngelo. *Is Everyone Really Equal?: An Introduction to Key Concepts in Social Justice Education*, 1st ed., Teacher's College Press, 2012, pp. 21-25.

[86] Kendi, Ibram. *How to Be an Antiracist*. 1st ed., One World, 2019, pp. 9, 13.

[87] Applebaum, Barbara. *Being White, Being Good: White Complicity, White Moral Responsibility, and Social Justice Pedagogy*. Lexington Books, 2010, pp. 123–124.

[88] Kendi, Ibram. *How to Be an Antiracist*. 1st ed., One World, 2019, pp. 9, 13.

[89] Kendi, Ibram. *How to Be an Antiracist*. 1st ed., One World, 2019, pp. 9, 13.

[90] Kendi, Ibram. *How to Be an Antiracist*. 1st ed., One World, 2019, pp. 9, 13, 17-20.

[91] Kendi, Ibram. *How to Be an Antiracist*. 1st ed., One World, 2019, p. 9.

[92] Kendi, Ibram. *How to Be an Antiracist*. 1st ed., One World, 2019, p. 9.

[93] Kendi, Ibram. *How to Be an Antiracist*. 1st ed., One World, 2019, p. 9.

[94] Kendi, Ibram. *How to Be an Antiracist*. 1st ed., One World, 2019, pp. 9, 13, 17-20.

[95] Korioth, Trisha. "Featured Speaker Kendi to Pediatricians: Consider Racism 'a Diagnosis.'" American Academy of Pediatrics, 6 Oct. 2020, www.aappublications.org/news/2020/10/06/nce2020kendi100620. Accessed 13 Oct. 2021.

[96] "Circumcision Policy Statement." *PEDIATRICS*, vol. 130, no. 3, 2012, pp. 585–86. *Crossref*, pediatrics.aappublications.org/content/130/3/585.

[97] DiAngelo, Robin. *White Fragility: Why It's So Hard for White People to Talk About Racism*. Beacon Press, 2018, pp. 99-106.

DiAngelo, Robin. "White Fragility." *International Journal of Critical Pedagogy* 3(3), 2011: 54–70, p. 54.

[98] DiAngelo, Robin. *White Fragility: Why It's So Hard for White People to Talk About Racism*. Beacon Press, 2018, pp. 99-106.

[99] DiAngelo, Robin. *White Fragility: Why It's So Hard for White People to Talk About Racism*. Beacon Press, 2018, pp. 99-106.

[100] *American Circumcision*. Dir. Brendon Marotta. Gravitas Ventures, 2017. Film.

Doctors Opposing Circumcision. "Alleged Medical Benefits." *Doctors Opposing Circumcision*, 9 Jan. 2020, www.doctorsopposingcircumcision.org/for-professionals/alleged-medical-benefits. Accessed 6 Jan. 2021.

Intact America. "Falsehoods & Facts." Intact America, 30 Oct. 2019, www.intactamerica.org/falsehoods-and-facts. Accessed 6 Jan. 2021.

[101] Kendi, Ibram. *How to Be an Antiracist*. 1st ed., One World, 2019, pp. 20, 50-53.

[102] Kendi, Ibram. *How to Be an Antiracist*. 1st ed., One World, 2019, p. 20.

[103] Sensoy, Ozlem, and Robin DiAngelo. *Is Everyone Really Equal?: An Introduction to Key Concepts in Social Justice Education*, 1st ed., Teacher's College Press, 2012, pp. 2-12.

[104] Durkin, Keith F., and Clifton D. Bryant. "Propagandizing Pederasty: A Thematic Analysis of the on-Line Exculpatory Accounts of Unrepentant Pedophiles." *Deviant Behavior*, vol. 20, no. 2, 1999, pp. 103–27. *Crossref*, doi:10.1080/016396299266524.

Lanning, Kenneth. "Child Molesters: A Behavioral Analysis." *National Center for Missing & Exploited Children*. Dec 1992. https://www.ncjrs.gov/pdffiles1/Digitization/149252NCJRS.pdf. Accessed 4 Jan. 2021.

Pollock, Nathan L., and Judith M. Hashmall. "The Excuses of Child Molesters." *Behavioral Sciences & the Law*, vol. 9, no. 1, 1991, pp. 53–59. Crossref, doi:10.1002/bsl.2370090107.

[105] Wikipedia contributors. "North American Man/Boy Love Association." *Wikipedia*, 29 Nov. 2020, en.wikipedia.org/wiki/North_American_Man/Boy_Love_Association. Accessed 4 Jan. 2021.

[106] Wikipedia contributors. "Psychological Projection" *Wikipedia*, 3 Jan. 2021, https://en.wikipedia.org/wiki/Psychological_projection. Accessed 4 Jan. 2021.

[107] Kidd, Ian James, et al. *The Routledge Handbook of Epistemic Injustice* (Routledge Handbooks in Philosophy). 1st ed., Routledge, 2019, p. 1.

[108] Fricker, Miranda. *Epistemic Injustice: Power and the Ethics of Knowing.* 1st ed., Oxford University Press, 2010, pp. 1, 4.

[109] Fricker, Miranda. *Epistemic Injustice: Power and the Ethics of Knowing.* 1st ed., Oxford University Press, 2010, p. 9.

[110] Fricker, Miranda. *Epistemic Injustice: Power and the Ethics of Knowing.* 1st ed., Oxford University Press, 2010, pp. 4, 6, 27.

[111] *American Circumcision.* Dir. Brendon Marotta. Gravitas Ventures, 2017. Film.

[112] Farrell, Warren. *The Myth of Male Power.* Finch Publishing, 2001.

[113] "Types of Female Genital Mutilation." *World Health Organization*, 2021, www.who.int/teams/sexual-and-reproductive-health-and-research/areas-of-work/female-genital-mutilation/types-of-female-genital-mutilation. Accessed 31 March. 2021.

[114] Committee on Bioethics. "Ritual Genital Cutting of Female Minors." *Pediatrics*, vol. 125, no. 5, 2010, pp. 1088–93. *Crossref*, doi:10.1542/peds.2010-0187.

World Health Organization. "Types of Female Genital Mutilation." *World Health Organization*, 2021, www.who.int/teams/sexual-and-reproductive-health-and-research/areas-of-work/female-genital-mutilation/types-of-female-genital-mutilation. Accessed 31 March. 2021.

Archive: https://web.archive.org/web/20210205223602/www.who.int/teams/sexual-and-reproductive-health-and-research/areas-of-work/female-genital-mutilation/types-of-female-genital-mutilation.

[115] *American Circumcision.* Dir. Brendon Marotta. Gravitas Ventures, 2017. Film.

Sorrells, Morris L et al. "Fine-touch pressure thresholds in the adult penis." *BJU international* vol. 99,4 (2007): 864-9. doi:10.1111/j.1464-410X.2006.06685.x https://pubmed.ncbi.nlm.nih.gov/17378847/

[116] *American Circumcision.* Dir. Brendon Marotta. Gravitas Ventures, 2017. Film.

Sorrells, Morris L et al. "Fine-touch pressure thresholds in the adult penis." *BJU international* vol. 99,4 (2007): 864-9. doi:10.1111/j.1464-410X.2006.06685.x https://pubmed.ncbi.nlm.nih.gov/17378847/

Taylor, J. R., et al. "The Prepuce: Specialized Mucosa of the Penis and Its Loss to Circumcision." *British Journal of Urology*, vol. 77, no. 2, 1996, pp. 291–95. Crossref, doi:10.1046/j.1464-410x.1996.85023.x.

[117] Committee on Bioethics. "Ritual Genital Cutting of Female Minors." *Pediatrics*, vol. 125, no. 5, 2010, pp. 1088–93. *Crossref*, doi:10.1542/peds.2010-0187.

[118] Sales, Ben. "Dershowitz Advising Muslim Group Accused Of Promoting Female Genital Mutilation." *The Forward*, 12 June 2017, forward.com/fast-forward/374439/dershowitz-advising-muslim-group-accused-promoting-female-genital-mutilatio. Accessed 30 Oct. 2021.

[119] *American Circumcision Documentary Bonus Features*, "Fuambai Sia Ahmadu - Extended Interview." Dir. Brendon Marotta. Vimeo, 2019. https://vimeo.com/ondemand/circmoviebonus/296147378.

[120] Fricker, Miranda. *Epistemic Injustice: Power and the Ethics of Knowing*. 1st ed., Oxford University Press, 2010, pp. 1, 148-149, 151.

[121] Dotson, Kristie, 2014, "Conceptualizing Epistemic Oppression." *Social Epistemology*, 28(2), 2014: 115–138, p. 116.

[122] *American Circumcision*. Dir. Brendon Marotta. Gravitas Ventures, 2017. Film.

[123] Anand, K. and Scalzo, F., "Can Adverse Neonatal Experiences Alter Brain Development and Subsequent Behavior?" *Neonatology*, vol. 77, no. 2, 2000, pp. 69–82. Crossref, doi:10.1159/000014197.

Taddio, A. et al., "Effect of Neonatal Circumcision on Pain Response during Subsequent Routine Vaccination." *The Lancet* 349 (1997): 599–603.

[124] Loewen, James. "Circumcision and Sexual Function Difficulties." *YouTube*, uploaded by Bonobo3D, 6 Dec. 2012, https://youtu.be/yfGkZZ-KzpU. Accessed 5 Jan. 2020.

[125] Dotson, Kristie, 2014, "Conceptualizing Epistemic Oppression." *Social Epistemology,* 28(2), 2014: 115–138, p. 116.

[126] Fricker, Miranda. *Epistemic Injustice: Power and the Ethics of Knowing*. 1st ed., Oxford University Press, 2010, p. 158.

[127] Fricker, Miranda. *Epistemic Injustice: Power and the Ethics of Knowing*. 1st ed., Oxford University Press, 2010, p. 159.

[128] Schulman, Sarah. *Ties That Bind: Familial Homophobia and Its Consequences*. The New Press, 2012.

[129] Intact America. "Press Release: Having a Baby Boy? Get Ready for the Circumcision Sellers!" Intact America, 10 Dec. 2020, intactamerica.org/press-release-having-a-baby-boy-get-ready-for-the-circumcision-sellers. Accessed 31 March. 2021.

[130] Marotta, Brendon. "Peter Adler on Why Circumcision Is a Fraud and Landmark Legal Action." *Brendon Marotta Show*, 11 Apr. 2021, brendonmarotta.com/7994/peter-adler-on-why-circumcision-is-a-fraud-and-landmark-legal-action. Accessed 13 Oct. 2021.

Marotta, Brendon. "Anthony Losquadro on Lobbying to Change the Financial Incentives of the Foreskin Industry." *Brendon Marotta Show*, 11 Apr. 2021, brendonmarotta.com/8100/anthony-losquadro-lobbying. Accessed 13 Oct. 2021.

[131] Marotta, Brendon. "Georganne Chapin on How The Medical Machine Pushes Circumcision." *Brendon Marotta*, 12 Mar. 2021, brendonmarotta.com/8064/georganne-chapin-on-how-the-medical-machine-pushes-circumcision. Accessed 31 March. 2021.

[132] *American Circumcision*. Dir. Brendon Marotta. Gravitas Ventures, 2017. Film.

[133] "Circumcision Policy Statement." *PEDIATRICS*, vol. 130, no. 3, 2012, pp. 585–86. *Crossref*, pediatrics.aappublications.org/content/130/3/585.

[134] Intact America. "Press Release: Having a Baby Boy? Get Ready for the Circumcision Sellers!" Intact America, 10 Dec. 2020, intactamerica.org/press-release-having-a-baby-boy-get-ready-for-the-circumcision-sellers. Accessed 31 March. 2021.

Marotta, Brendon. "Peter Adler on Why Circumcision Is a Fraud and Landmark Legal Action." *Brendon Marotta Show*, 11 Apr. 2021, brendonmarotta.com/7994/peter-adler-on-why-circumcision-is-a-fraud-and-landmark-legal-action. Accessed 13 Oct. 2021.

Marotta, Brendon. "Georganne Chapin on How The Medical Machine Pushes Circumcision." *Brendon Marotta Show*, 11 Apr. 2021, brendonmarotta.com/8064/georganne-chapin-on-how-the-medical-machine-pushes-circumcision. Accessed 13 Oct. 2021.

[135] *Kalina v. General Hosp., Syracuse*, 31 Misc. 2d 18 (N.Y. Sup. Ct. 1961).

[136] Beverley, John. *Subalternity and Representation: Arguments in Cultural Theory*. Duke University Press, 1999, pp. 1-2.

[137] de Kock, Leon. "Interview With Gayatri Chakravorty Spivak: New Nation Writers Conference in South Africa." *ARIEL: A Review of International English Literature Archived 2011-07-06 at the Wayback Machine*. 23(3) 1992: 29-47. ARIEL.

[138] Beverley, John. *Subalternity and Representation: Arguments in Cultural Theory*. Duke University Press, 1999. p. 2.

[139] Beverley, John. *Subalternity and Representation: Arguments in Cultural Theory*. Duke University Press, 1999. p. 2.

[140] Dotson, Kristie, 2014, "Conceptualizing Epistemic Oppression." *Social Epistemology*, 28(2), 2014: 115–138, p. 116.

[141] Dotson, Kristie. "Tracking Epistemic Violence, Tracking Practices of Silencing." *Hypatia*, 26(2), 2011: 238–259, pp. 236–237.

[142] *American Circumcision*. Dir. Brendon Marotta. Gravitas Ventures, 2017. Film.

[143] Dotson, Kristie. "Tracking Epistemic Violence, Tracking Practices of Silencing." *Hypatia*, 26(2), 2011: 238–259, pp. 236–237.

[144] Sensoy, Ozlem, and Robin DiAngelo. *Is Everyone Really Equal?: An Introduction to Key Concepts in Social Justice Education*, 1st ed., Teacher's College Press, 2012, p. 49.

[145] Sensoy, Ozlem, and Robin DiAngelo. *Is Everyone Really Equal?: An Introduction to Key Concepts in Social Justice Education*, 1st ed., Teacher's College Press, 2012, p. 49.

[146] Wikipedia contributors. "Disability Justice." *Wikipedia*, 19 Mar. 2021, en.wikipedia.org/wiki/Disability_justice. Accessed 22 Nov. 2021.

[147] Goodley, Dan. *Dis/Ability Studies: Theorising Disablism and Ableism*. 1st ed., Routledge, 2014, pp. 4-6.

[148] Fricker, Miranda. *Epistemic Injustice: Power and the Ethics of Knowing*. 1st ed., Oxford University Press, 2010, p. 157.

[149] Fricker, Miranda. *Epistemic Injustice: Power and the Ethics of Knowing*. 1st ed., Oxford University Press, 2010, p. 157.

[150] Wikipedia contributors. "Ferber Method." *Wikipedia*, 30 Aug. 2021, en.wikipedia.org/wiki/Ferber_method. Accessed 13 Nov. 2021.

[151] Gottesman, Isaac. *The Critical Turn in Education: From Marxist Critique to Poststructuralist Feminism to Critical Theories of Race*. Routledge, 2016, p. 90.

[152] Braveman, Paula A. Braveman, Shiriki Kumanyika, Jonathan Fielding, et al. "Health Disparities and Health Equity: The Issue Is Justice." *American Journal of Public Health* 101(51): 2011.

[153] Wikipedia contributors. "White Feminism." *Wikipedia*, 30 Nov. 2021, en.wikipedia.org/wiki/White_feminism. Accessed 5 Dec. 2021.

[154] *American Circumcision*. Dir. Brendon Marotta. Gravitas Ventures, 2017. Film.

[155] Taddio, A. et al., "Effect of Neonatal Circumcision on Pain Response during Subsequent Routine Vaccination." *The Lancet* 349 (1997): 599–603.

[156] Taddio, A. et al., "Effect of Neonatal Circumcision on Pain Response during Subsequent Routine Vaccination." *The Lancet* 349 (1997): 599–603.

[157] Kolk, Van Bessel der, MD. *The Body Keeps the Score: Brain, Mind, and Body in the Healing of Trauma*. Reprint, Penguin Publishing Group, 2015, pp. 173-201.

[158] "Circumcision Policy Statement." *PEDIATRICS*, vol. 103, no. 3, 1999, pp. 686–93. *Crossref*, doi:10.1542/peds.103.3.686.

[159] Anda RF; Felitti VJ; Bremner JD; et al. "The Enduring Effects of Abuse and Related Adverse Experiences in Childhood. A Convergence of Evidence from Neurobiology and Epidemiology." *Child: Care, Health and Development*, vol. 32, no. 2, 2006, pp. 253–56. *Crossref*, doi:10.1111/j.1365-2214.2006.00614_2.x.

Downing, Nancy R., et al. "The Impact of Childhood Sexual Abuse and Adverse Childhood Experiences on Adult Health Related Quality of Life." *Child Abuse & Neglect*, vol. 120, 2021, p. 105181. Crossref, doi:10.1016/j.chiabu.2021.105181.

[160] Anda RF; Felitti VJ. "Origins and Essence of the Study." *ACE Reporter*, 2003. Retrieved 25 March 2014.

[161] World Health Organization; International Society for Prevention of Child Abuse and Neglect. *Preventing child maltreatment: a guide to taking action and generating evidence.* Geneva, Switzerland, 2006. p. 12. ISBN 978-9241594363.

[162] Bollinger, Dan, and Georganne Chapin. "Genital Cutting As An Adverse Childhood Experience." *Intact America*, Intact America, 19 Aug. 2019, adversechildhoodexperiences.net/CGC_as_an_ACE.pdf. Accessed 25 Oct. 2021.

Bollinger, Dan. "Adverse Childhood Experiences." *Adverse Childhood Experiences*, adversechildhoodexperiences.net. Accessed 25 Oct. 2021.

[163] If you want a longer exploration of circumcision trauma, the definitive book on this subject is: Goldman, Ronald. *Circumcision, The Hidden Trauma: How an American Cultural Practice Affects Infants and Ultimately Us All.* Vanguard Publications, 1997.

[164] Fisher, Janina. *Healing the Fragmented Selves of Trauma Survivors: Overcoming Internal Self-Alienation.* 1st ed., Routledge, 2017. pp. 19, 25.

[165] Fisher, Janina. *Healing the Fragmented Selves of Trauma Survivors: Overcoming Internal Self-Alienation.* 1st ed., Routledge, 2017. pp. 19-26.

[166] Fisher, Janina. *Healing the Fragmented Selves of Trauma Survivors: Overcoming Internal Self-Alienation.* 1st ed., Routledge, 2017. pp. 27-29.

[167] Fisher, Janina. *Healing the Fragmented Selves of Trauma Survivors: Overcoming Internal Self-Alienation.* 1st ed., Routledge, 2017. pp. 67-68.

[168] Fisher, Janina. *Healing the Fragmented Selves of Trauma Survivors: Overcoming Internal Self-Alienation.* 1st ed., Routledge, 2017.

[169] Fisher, Janina. *Healing the Fragmented Selves of Trauma Survivors: Overcoming Internal Self-Alienation.* 1st ed., Routledge, 2017. p. 28.

[170] Fisher, Janina. *Healing the Fragmented Selves of Trauma Survivors: Overcoming Internal Self-Alienation.* 1st ed., Routledge, 2017. p. 29.

[171] Fisher, Janina. *Healing the Fragmented Selves of Trauma Survivors: Overcoming Internal Self-Alienation.* 1st ed., Routledge, 2017. p. 28.

[172] deMause, Lloyd. *History of Childhood: The Untold Story of Child Abuse.* Peter Bedrick Books, 1988, p. 43.

[173] deMause, Lloyd. *History of Childhood: The Untold Story of Child Abuse.* Peter Bedrick Books, 1988, pp. 43-47.

[174] Ariès, Philippe. *Centuries of Childhood*, trans. by Robert Baldrick. Vintage Books, 1962, p. 103.

Postman, Neil. *The Disappearance of Childhood.* (Kindle Location 344-352). Kindle Edition, Vintage, 2011.

[175] deMause, Lloyd. *History of Childhood: The Untold Story of Child Abuse*. Peter Bedrick Books, 1988, pp. 48-49.

[176] deMause, Lloyd. *Foundations of Psychohistory*. Creative Roots Pub, 1982.

Note: Lloyd DeMause, the creator of psychohistory uses a psychotherapy analysis in much of his work. I use the term more broadly, to mean using childhood psychology to analyze history, and recognize other forms of psychology as more accurate.

[177] Sensoy, Ozlem, and Robin DiAngelo. *Is Everyone Really Equal?: An Introduction to Key Concepts in Social Justice Education*, 1st ed., Teacher's College Press, 2012, pp. 15–16.

[178] Bouie, Jamelle. "The Enlightenment's Dark Side: How the Enlightenment Created Modern Race Thinking, and Why We Should Confront It." *Slate Magazine*, 6 June 2018, slate.com/news-and-politics/2018/06/taking-the-enlightenment-seriously-requires-talking-about-race.html. Accessed 30 Oct. 2021.

Rattansi, Ali. *Racism: A Very Short Introduction (Very Short Introductions)*. 2nd ed., Oxford University Press, 2020, pp. 23, 25.

[179] Chamberlain, David. *Windows to the Womb: Revealing the Conscious Baby from Conception to Birth*. 1st ed., North Atlantic Books, 2013.

[180] Fildes, Valerie. "The English Wet-Nurse and Her Role in Infant Care 1538–1800." *Medical History*, vol. 32, no. 2, 1988, pp. 142–73. Crossref, doi:10.1017/s0025727300047979.

Fildes, Valerie. *Wet Nursing: A History from Antiquity to the Present (Family, Sexuality and Social Relations in Past Times)*. Illustrated edition, Blackwell Pub, 1988, pp. 74, 79.

"Wet Nursing", *Encyclopedia of Children and Childhood in History and Society*. http://www.faqs.org/childhood/Th-W/Wet-Nursing.html. Accessed 3 Jan. 2022.

[181] Fildes, Valerie. *Wet Nursing: A History from Antiquity to the Present (Family, Sexuality and Social Relations in Past Times)*. Illustrated edition, Blackwell Pub, 1988, pp. 79, 92-94.

[182] Fildes, Valerie. *Wet Nursing: A History from Antiquity to the Present (Family, Sexuality and Social Relations in Past Times)*. Illustrated edition, Blackwell Pub, 1988, pp. 79, 92-94, 97.

[183] Fildes, Valerie. *Wet Nursing: A History from Antiquity to the Present (Family, Sexuality and Social Relations in Past Times)*. Illustrated edition, Blackwell Pub, 1988, pp. 82-83

[184] Fildes, Valerie. *Wet Nursing: A History from Antiquity to the Present (Family, Sexuality and Social Relations in Past Times)*. Illustrated edition, Blackwell Pub, 1988, p. 82.

[185] Niceness has been cited by critical race theorists as one of the negative traits of whiteness. Source: DiAngelo, Robin. *Nice Racism: How Progressive White People Perpetuate Racial Harm.* Beacon Press, 2021.

[186] Marotta, Brendon. "Nick Duffell On The Wounded Leaders From Elite Boarding Schools That Shaped The World." *Brendon Marotta*, 13 June 2021, brendonmarotta.com/8182/nick-duffell-on-the-wounded-leaders-from-elite-boarding-schools-that-shaped-the-world. Accessed 30 Oct. 2021.

[187] Menakem, Resmaa. *My Grandmother's Hands: Racialized Trauma and the Pathway to Mending Our Hearts and Bodies.* Illustrated, Central Recovery Press, 2017, p. 9.

[188] Sensoy, Özlem, and Robin DiAngelo. *Is Everyone Really Equal? An Introduction to Key Concepts in Social Justice Education*, 1st ed., Teacher's College Press, 2012, p. 8.

[189] Fisher, Janina. *Healing the Fragmented Selves of Trauma Survivors: Overcoming Internal Self-Alienation.* 1st ed., Routledge, 2017. pp. 19-26.

[190] Sensoy, Özlem, and Robin DiAngelo. *Is Everyone Really Equal? An Introduction to Key Concepts in Social Justice Education*, 1st ed., Teacher's College Press, 2012, p. 48.

[191] Anand, K. and Scalzo, F., "Can Adverse Neonatal Experiences Alter Brain Development and Subsequent Behavior?" *Neonatology*, vol. 77, no. 2, 2000, pp. 69–82. *Crossref*, doi:10.1159/000014197.

[192] Loewen, James. "Circumcision Nightmares?" *YouTube*, uploaded by Bonobo3D, 21 May 2012, https://youtu.be/P-mngp8mrNg. Accessed 4 Jan. 2022.

[193] Edelstein, Ludwig. *The Hippocratic Oath, Text, Translation and Interpretation.* Amsterdam University Press, 1964.

[194] Crenshaw, Kimberle. "Mapping the Margins: Intersectionality, Identity Politics, and Violence against Women of Color." *Stanford Law Review*, vol. 43, no. 6, 1991, p. 1297. *Crossref*, doi:10.2307/1229039.

[195] Foucault, Michel. *Power/Knowledge: Selected Interviews and Other Writings*, 1972-1977. 1st ed., Vintage, 1980.

"Key Concepts." *Foucault News*, 1 Dec. 2019, michel-foucault.com/key-concepts. Accessed 19 Jan. 2021.

[196] Bohman, James. "Critical Theory (Stanford Encyclopedia of Philosophy)." *Stanford Encyclopedia of Philosophy*, Metaphysics Research Lab, Stanford University, 8 Mar. 2005, plato.stanford.edu/entries/critical-theory. Accessed 12 Oct. 2021.

[197] Shapiro, Ari. "'There Is No Neutral': 'Nice White People' Can Still Be Complicit In A Racist Society." *NPR*, 9 June 2020, www.npr.org/2020/06/09/873375416/there-is-no-neutral-nice-white-people-can-still-be-complicit-in-a-racist-society?t=1609613963293, Accessed 1 Jan. 2021.

198 Kendi, Ibram. *How to Be an Antiracist*. 1st ed., One World, 2019, pp. 22-23.

199 DiAngelo, Robin. "Antiracism Handout." *Robin DiAngelo*, https://robindiangelo.com/wp-content/uploads/2016/06/Anti-racism-handout-1-page-2016.pdf. Accessed 1 Jan. 2021.

Archive: https://archive.fo/O44Kv

200 Shapiro, Ari. "'There Is No Neutral': 'Nice White People' Can Still Be Complicit In A Racist Society." *NPR*, 9 June 2020, www.npr.org/2020/06/09/873375416/there-is-no-neutral-nice-white-people-can-still-be-complicit-in-a-racist-society?t=1609613963293, Accessed Jan 1, 2021.

201 Kendi, Ibram. *How to Be an Antiracist*. 1st ed., One World, 2019, p. 9.

202 Delgado, Richard, et al. *Critical Race Theory (Third Edition): An Introduction (Critical America, 20)*. 3rd ed., NYU Press, 2017, p. 174.

203 Adamson, Walter. *Hegemony and Revolution: Antonio Gramsci's Political and Cultural Theory*. Echo Point Books & Media, 2014.

204 "Why 'I'm Not Racist' Is Only Half the Story | Robin DiAngelo | Big Think" *YouTube*, uploaded by Big Think, 1 Oct. 2018, www.youtube.com/watch?v=kzLT54QjclA&feature=youtu.be. Accessed 2 Jan. 2021.

205 As far as I know, in Marxist theory there's no direct antonym of "false consciousness." The term "true consciousness" is my own creation to describe this opposite state.

206 Chamberlain, David. *Windows to the Womb: Revealing the Conscious Baby from Conception to Birth*. 1st ed., North Atlantic Books, 2013.

207 Chamberlain, David. *The Mind of Your Newborn Baby*. 3rd ed., North Atlantic Books, 1998.

208 Karlamangla, Soumya. "Male Doctors Are Disappearing from Gynecology. Not Everybody Is Thrilled about It." *Los Angeles Times*, 7 Mar. 2018, www.latimes.com/health/la-me-male-gynos-20180307-htmlstory.html. Accessed 6 Jan. 2021.

209 "Nursing Statistics in the US." *Minority Nurse*, 14 Apr. 2016, minoritynurse.com/nursing-statistics. Accessed 6 Jan. 2021.

210 McAllister, Ryan. "Child Circumcision: An Elephant in the Hospital by Professor R. McAllister." YouTube, uploaded by painfulquestioning, 8 July 2011, www.youtube.com/watch?v=Ceht-3xu84I&feature=youtu.be. Accessed 13 Oct. 2021.

211 *The Other Side of the Glass: A Birth Film for and about Fathers*. Dir. Janel Miranda. 2009. Film.

[212] "Breastfeeding: Why It Matters." *Centers for Disease Control and Prevention*, 29 Nov. 2020, www.cdc.gov/breastfeeding/about-breastfeeding/why-it-matters.html. Accessed 6 Jan. 2021

Wiessinger, Diane, et al. *The Womanly Art of Breastfeeding: Completely Revised and Updated 8th Edition*. 8th Revised, Updated ed., Ballantine Books, 2010.

[213] US Census Bureau. "Household Relationship and Living Arrangements of Children Under 18 Years, by Age and Sex: 2019." *The United States Census Bureau*, 16 Oct. 2019, www2.census.gov/programs-surveys/demo/tables/families/2019/cps-2019/tabc2-all.xls. Accessed 6 Jan. 2021.

[214] Farrell, Warren. *Why Men Are the Way They Are: The Male-Female Dynamic.* 1st ed., McGraw-Hill, 1986. p. 113

Susan Goldberg and Michael Lewis. "Play Behavior in the Year-Old Infant: Early Sex Differences," *Child Development*, vol. 40, no. I , March 1969, p. 29.

[215] Shpancer, Noam. "No Man's Land: Where Are the Male Daycare Caregivers?" *Psychology Today*, 5 July 2019, www.psychologytoday.com/us/blog/insight-therapy/201907/no-man-s-land-where-are-the-male-daycare-caregivers. 6 Jan. 2021.

[216] Ingersoll, Richard M.; Merrill, Elizabeth; Stuckey, Daniel; and Collins, Gregory. (2018). Seven Trends: The Transformation of the Teaching Force – Updated October 2018. *CPRE Research Reports*. https://repository.upenn.edu/cpre_researchreports/108. Accessed 6 Jan. 2021.

Wong, Alia. "The Growing Gender Divide Among U.S. Teachers." *The Atlantic*, 20 Feb. 2019, www.theatlantic.com/education/archive/2019/02/the-explosion-of-women-teachers/582622. Accessed 6 Jan. 2021.

[217] Wedge, Marilyn. "Are We Medicating the True Selves of Boys?" *Psychology Today*, 10 Apr. 2015, www.psychologytoday.com/us/blog/suffer-the-children/201504/are-we-medicating-the-true-selves-boys. 6 Jan. 2021.

Schwartz A. Thousands of Toddlers Are Medicated for A.D.H.D., Report Finds, Raising Worries. New York Times, May 14, 2014. http://www.nytimes.com/2014/05/17/us/among-experts-scrutiny-of-attention-disorder-diagnoses-in-2-and-3-year-olds.html. 6 Jan. 2021.

[218] Applebaum, Barbara. *Being White, Being Good: White Complicity, White Moral Responsibility, and Social Justice Pedagogy*. Lexington Books, 2010, pp. 123–124.

[219] DiAngelo, Robin. "White Fragility." *International Journal of Critical Pedagogy* 3(3), 2011: 54–70, p. 54.

[220] *American Circumcision*. Dir. Brendon Marotta. Gravitas Ventures, 2017. Film.

[221] Kendi, Ibram. *How to Be an Antiracist*. 1st ed., One World, 2019, p. 9.

[222] Abelove, Henry, et al. *The Lesbian and Gay Studies Reader*. 1st ed., Routledge, 1993, p. 10.

[223] Butler, Judith. *Bodies That Matter: On the Discursive Limits of Sex*. 1st ed., Routledge, 2011, p. xii.

[224] Boskey, Elizabeth. "What Does It Mean to Be Nonbinary or Enby?" *Verywell Mind*, 16 Nov. 2020, www.verywellmind.com/what-does-it-mean-to-be-non-binary-or-have-non-binary-gender-4172702. Accessed 24 Nov. 2021.

[225] Abelove, Henry, et al. *The Lesbian and Gay Studies Reader*. 1st ed., Routledge, 1993, pp. 9-10.

[226] Frellick, Marcia. "Remove Sex From Public Birth Certificates, AMA Says." *WebMD*, Web MD, 16 June 2021, www.webmd.com/a-to-z-guides/news/20210616/remove-sex-from-public-birth-certificates-ama-says. Accessed 24 Nov. 2021.

[227] Foucault, Michel. *Abnormal: Lectures at the Collège de France 1974-1975*. 1st ed., Picador, 2004, p. 42.

Foucault, Michel. *Security, Territory, Population: Lectures at the Collège de France 1977–1978*. 1st ed., Picador, 2009, p. 56.

[228] Foucault, Michel. *The History of Sexuality Volume 1: An Introduction*. Translated by Robert Hurley, Vintage Books, 1990.

[229] I also use the term man, because the way that circumcision is imposed as an identity on cisgender men is different from the way circumcision impacts transwomen who were assigned male at birth. Male circumcision intersects with a series of cultural norms, beliefs, and systems that are entirely different from the cultural norms, beliefs, and systems that impact transwomen. For example, there is no cultural norm that "transwomen don't cry," but there is a cultural norm that "men don't cry." If I say that systemic pedophilia impacts men in a certain way, I am not talking about "people with penises." I'm talking about men. The analysis of how circumcision impacts trans and non-binary people would be entirely different. This analysis is beyond the scope of this book and might require an entire book of its own. I hope an author with greater lived experience around trans issues writes it at some point.

[230] *American Circumcision Documentary Bonus Features*, "Deleted Scene - Symbolism." Dir. Brendon Marotta. Vimeo, 2019. https://vimeo.com/ondemand/circmoviebonus/650011219

American Circumcision Documentary Bonus Features, "Fuambai Sia Ahmadu - Extended Interview." Dir. Brendon Marotta. Vimeo, 2019. https://vimeo.com/ondemand/circmoviebonus/296147378

[231] Griaule, Marcel, and Germaine Dieterlen. *Conversations With Ogotemmeli: An Introduction to Dogon Religious Ideas*. International African Institute, 1975.

[232] Griaule, Marcel, and Germaine Dieterlen. *Conversations With Ogotemmeli: An Introduction to Dogon Religious Ideas*. International African Institute, 1975, p. 158.

[233] Farrell, Warren. *The Myth of Male Power*. Finch Publishing, 2001, pp. 67-101.

[234] "Maasai Culture | Ceremonies and Rituals." *Maasai Association*, www.maasai-association.org/ceremonies.html. Accessed 5 Jan. 2021.

[235] Fricker, Miranda. *Epistemic Injustice: Power and the Ethics of Knowing*. 1st ed., Oxford University Press, 2010, p. 157.

[236] *The Red Pill*. Dir. Cassie Jaye. 2016. Gravitas Ventures. Film.

[237] Wikipedia contributors. "White Feminism." *Wikipedia*, 22 Dec. 2021, en.wikipedia.org/wiki/White_feminism. Accessed 22 Dec. 2021.

[238] Foucault, Michel. *The Birth of the Clinic: An Archaeology of Medical Perception*. 1st ed., Vintage, 1994, pp. 111-122, 190-191.

[239] Foucault, Michel. *The Birth of the Clinic: An Archaeology of Medical Perception*. 1st ed., Vintage, 1994, pp. 190-191.

[240] *American Circumcision Documentary Bonus Features*, "Deleted Scene - Paul Fleiss." Dir. Brendon Marotta. Vimeo, 2019. https://vimeo.com/ondemand/circmoviebonus/296774901

[241] Auerbach, M. Richard, and John W. Scanlon. "Recurrence of Pneumothorax as a Possible Complication of Elective Circumcision." *American Journal of Obstetrics and Gynecology*, vol. 132, no. 5, 1978, p. 583. *Crossref*, www.ajog.org/article/0002-9378(78)90760-3/pdf.

[242] Palusci, Vincent J. "Adverse Childhood Experiences and Lifelong Health." *JAMA Pediatrics*, vol. 167, no. 1, 2013, p. 95. *Crossref*, doi:10.1001/jamapediatrics.2013.427.

[243] One entire book documents such a suicide: Roberts, Lesley. *A Is for Alex: A Bereaved Mother's Promise to Her Beloved Son*. Cherish Editions, 2021.

[244] *American Circumcision*. Dir. Brendon Marotta. Gravitas Ventures, 2017. Film.

[245] Earp, Brian. "Female Genital Mutilation and Male Circumcision: Toward an Autonomy-Based Ethical Framework." *Medicolegal and Bioethics*, 2015, p. 89. *Crossref*, doi:10.2147/mb.s63709.

[246] Mitchell, Harmeet Cnn Kaur And Skylar. "States Are Calling Racism a Public Health Crisis. Here's What That Means." *CNN*, 14 Aug. 2020, edition.cnn.com/2020/08/14/health/states-racism-public-health-crisis-trnd/index.html. Accessed 2 Jan. 20201.

Simon, Mallory Cnn. "Over 1,000 Health Professionals Sign a Letter Saying, Don't Shut down Protests Using Coronavirus Concerns as an Excuse." CNN, 5 June 2020, edition.cnn.com/2020/06/05/health/health-care-open-letter-protests-coronavirus-trnd/index.html. Accessed 1 Jan. 2021.

[247] Foucault, Michel. *The History of Sexuality Volume 1: An Introduction.* Translated by Robert Hurley, Vintage Books, 1990. p. 135-136.

[248] Foucault, Michel. *The History of Sexuality Volume 1: An Introduction.* Translated by Robert Hurley, Vintage Books, 1990. p. 140.

[249] Foucault, Michel. *The History of Sexuality Volume 1: An Introduction.* Translated by Robert Hurley, Vintage Books, 1990. p. 140.

[250] Foucault, Michel. *The History of Sexuality Volume 1: An Introduction.* Translated by Robert Hurley, Vintage Books, 1990. p. 135-136.

[251] Foucault, Michel. *The History of Sexuality Volume 1: An Introduction.* Translated by Robert Hurley, Vintage Books, 1990. p. 136.

[252] Foucault, Michel. *The History of Sexuality Volume 1: An Introduction.* Translated by Robert Hurley, Vintage Books, 1990. p. 138.

[253] In fact, this has already happened. In 2015, a mother named Heather Hironimus was arrested and forced to sign a consent form for her four-year-old son's circumcision. (There is obviously no such thing as forced consent.) For more on the Hironimus case:

The Associated Press. "'Intactivist' Mom Who Took Son into Hiding to Save His Foreskin Sobs in Court as She Signs Consent for Circumcision." Nationalpost, 25 May 2015, nationalpost.com/news/world/heather-hironimus-intactivist-mom-who-took-son-into-hiding-to-save-his-foreskin-sobs-in-court-as-she-signs-consent-for-circumcision. Accessed 13 Jan. 2021.

Freeman, Marc. "Handcuffed Mom Signs Consent for Son's Circumcision to Get out of Jail." *Sun Sentinel*, 22 May 2015, web.archive.org/web/20150522152728/http://www.sun-sentinel.com/local/palm-beach/fl-circumcision-mother-court-hearing-20150522-story.html. Accessed 13 Jan. 2021.

Sedensky, Matt. "Heather Hironimus: Mother Fighting to Stop Child's Circumcision Appears in Court in Florida." *The Independent*, 19 May 2015, www.independent.co.uk/news/world/americas/heather-hironimus-mother-fighting-stop-child-s-circumcision-appears-court-florida-10259445.html. Accessed Jan 13, 2021.

316 · Notes

[254] Merrefield, Clark. "'Defund the Police': What It Means and What the Research Says." *The Journalist's Resource*, 14 July 2021, journalistsresource.org/criminal-justice/defund-the-police. Accessed 30 Oct. 2021.

[255] Foucault, Michel. *The History of Sexuality Volume 1: An Introduction.* Translated by Robert Hurley, Vintage Books, 1990. p. 139.

[256] Foucault, Michel. *The History of Sexuality Volume 1: An Introduction.* Translated by Robert Hurley, Vintage Books, 1990. p. 139.

[257] Foucault, Michel. *The History of Sexuality Volume 1: An Introduction.* Translated by Robert Hurley, Vintage Books, 1990. p 139.

[258] Foucault, Michel. *The History of Sexuality Volume 1: An Introduction.* Translated by Robert Hurley, Vintage Books, 1990. p 140.

[259] Foucault, Michel. *Discipline & Punish: The Birth of the Prison.* 2nd ed., Vintage Books, 1995, p. 170-172.

[260] Foucault, Michel. *Abnormal: Lectures at the Collège de France 1974-1975.* 1st ed., Picador, 2004, p. 42.

[261] Foucault, Michel. *Abnormal: Lectures at the Collège de France 1974-1975.* 1st ed., Picador, 2004, p. 42.

[262] Foucault, Michel. *Abnormal: Lectures at the Collège de France 1974-1975.* 1st ed., Picador, 2004, p. 164.

[263] Foucault, Michel. *The History of Sexuality Volume 1: An Introduction.* Translated by Robert Hurley, Vintage Books, 1990. p. 104.

[264] Foucault, Michel. *Abnormal: Lectures at the Collège de France 1974-1975.* 1st ed., Picador, 2004, p. 233.

Glick, Leonard. *Marked in Your Flesh: Circumcision from Ancient Judea to Modern America.* 1st ed., Oxford University Press, 2005, p. 150-152.

[265] *American Circumcision.* Dir. Brendon Marotta. Gravitas Ventures, 2017. Film.

Foucault, Michel. *Abnormal: Lectures at the Collège de France 1974-1975.* 1st ed., Picador, 2004, p. 233, 236-237.

Glick, Leonard. *Marked in Your Flesh: Circumcision from Ancient Judea to Modern America.* 1st ed., Oxford University Press, 2005, p. 150-152.

[266] Foucault, Michel. *Abnormal: Lectures at the Collège de France 1974-1975.* 1st ed., Picador, 2004, p. 255.

[267] Foucault, Michel. *Abnormal: Lectures at the Collège de France 1974-1975.* 1st ed., Picador, 2004, p. 256.

[268] Foucault, Michel. *Abnormal: Lectures at the Collège de France 1974-1975.* 1st ed., Picador, 2004, p. 233, 239.

[269] Foucault, Michel. *Abnormal: Lectures at the Collège de France 1974-1975*. 1st ed., Picador, 2004, p. 240.

[270] Foucault, Michel. *Abnormal: Lectures at the Collège de France 1974-1975*. 1st ed., Picador, 2004, p. 241.

[271] Foucault, Michel. *Abnormal: Lectures at the Collège de France 1974-1975*. 1st ed., Picador, 2004, p. 241.

[272] Foucault, Michel. *Abnormal: Lectures at the Collège de France 1974-1975*. 1st ed., Picador, 2004, p. 242.

[273] Foucault, Michel. *Abnormal: Lectures at the Collège de France 1974-1975*. 1st ed., Picador, 2004, p. 245.

[274] Foucault, Michel. *Abnormal: Lectures at the Collège de France 1974-1975*. 1st ed., Picador, 2004, p. 242-243.

[275] Foucault, Michel. *Abnormal: Lectures at the Collège de France 1974-1975*. 1st ed., Picador, 2004, p. 245.

[276] Foucault, Michel. *Abnormal: Lectures at the Collège de France 1974-1975*. 1st ed., Picador, 2004, p. 247.

[277] Foucault, Michel. *Abnormal: Lectures at the Collège de France 1974-1975*. 1st ed., Picador, 2004, p. 247.

[278] Foucault, Michel. *Abnormal: Lectures at the Collège de France 1974-1975*. 1st ed., Picador, 2004, p. 252.

[279] "An Updated Definition of Rape." *The United States Department of Justice*, 7 Apr. 2017, www.justice.gov/archives/opa/blog/updated-definition-rape. Accessed 1 Jan. 2021.

"Rape." FBI, ucr.fbi.gov/crime-in-the-u.s/2019/crime-in-the-u.s.-2019/topic-pages/rape. Accessed 1 Jan. 2021.

[280] Foucault, Michel. *Abnormal: Lectures at the Collège de France 1974-1975*. 1st ed., Picador, 2004, p. 252.

[281] *American Circumcision*. Dir. Brendon Marotta. Gravitas Ventures, 2017. Film.

Glick, Leonard. *Marked in Your Flesh: Circumcision from Ancient Judea to Modern America*. 1st ed., Oxford University Press, 2005, p. 150-152, 172-173.

[282] Foucault, Michel. *Abnormal: Lectures at the Collège de France 1974-1975*. 1st ed., Picador, 2004, p. 252-253.

[283] Foucault, Michel. *Abnormal: Lectures at the Collège de France 1974-1975*. 1st ed., Picador, 2004, p. 252-253.

[284] Foucault, Michel. *Abnormal: Lectures at the Collège de France 1974-1975*. 1st ed., Picador, 2004, p. 256.

[285] Foucault, Michel. *The History of Sexuality, Vol. 1: An Introduction.* Translated by Robert Hurley, Vintage, 1990, p. 42.

[286] Foucault, Michel. *Abnormal: Lectures at the Collège de France 1974-1975.* 1st ed., Picador, 2004, p. 249.

[287] Foucault, Michel. *Abnormal: Lectures at the Collège de France 1974-1975.* 1st ed., Picador, 2004, p. 256.

[288] Foucault, Michel. *Abnormal: Lectures at the Collège de France 1974-1975.* 1st ed., Picador, 2004, p. 256.

[289] Foucault, Michel. *Abnormal: Lectures at the Collège de France 1974-1975.* 1st ed., Picador, 2004, p. 249.

[290] Feldhusen, Adrian. "The History of Midwifery and Childbirth in America: A Time Line." *Midwifery Today*, 2 Nov. 2019, midwiferytoday.com/web-article/history-midwifery-childbirth-america-time-line. Accessed 5 Jan. 2020.

The Business of Being Born. Dir. Abby Epstein. New Line, 2008. Film.

[291] Kortepeter, Mark. "Did Covid-19 Come From A Lab? Was It Deliberate Bioterrorism? A Biodefense Expert Explores The Clues." *Forbes*, 19 June 2020, www.forbes.com/sites/coronavirusfrontlines/2020/06/19/did-covid-19-come-from-a-lab-was-it-deliberate-bioterrorism-a-biodefense-expert-explores-the-clues. Accessed 5 Jan. 2020.

Lapin, Tamar. "Chinese Virologist Posts Report Claiming COVID-19 Was Made in Wuhan Lab." *New York Post*, 15 Sept. 2020, nypost.com/2020/09/14/chinese-virologist-posts-report-claiming-covid-19-was-made-in-wuhan-lab. Accessed 5 Jan. 2020.

[292] Ecarma, Caleb. "Joe Rogan and CNN Are Butting Heads Over 'Horse Dewormer' COVID Cure." *Vanity Fair*, 22 Oct. 2021, www.vanityfair.com/news/2021/10/joe-rogan-cnn-horse-dewormer-covid. Accessed 30 Oct. 2021.

[293] "Why You Should Not Use Ivermectin to Treat or Prevent COVID-19." *U.S. Food and Drug Administration*, 3 Sept. 2021, www.fda.gov/consumers/consumer-updates/why-you-should-not-use-ivermectin-treat-or-prevent-covid-19. Accessed 30 Oct. 2021.

[294] Rankovic, Didi. "Big Tech's Censorship of Ivermectin Stories Depend on Who's Sharing It." *Reclaim The Net*, 6 Sept. 2021, reclaimthenet.org/big-techs-censorship-of-ivermectin-stories-depend-on-whos-sharing-it. Accessed 30 Oct. 2021.

[295] Marotta, Brendon. "People Will Die If The Medical Establishment Censors COVID-19 Discussion." *Brendon Marotta*, 28 Mar. 2020, brendonmarotta.com/6420/covid-19-discussion. Accessed 5 Jan. 2021.

[296] Ross, Katherine. "Why Weren't We Wearing Masks From the Beginning? Dr. Fauci Explains." *TheStreet*, 18 June 2020, www.thestreet.com/video/dr-fauci-masks-changing-directive-coronavirus. Accessed 30 Oct. 2021.

[297] Niemiec, Emilia. "COVID-19 and misinformation: Is censorship of social media a remedy to the spread of medical misinformation?" EMBO Reports, vol. 21, no. 11, 2020. Crossref, doi:10.15252/embr.202051420.

Marotta, Brendon. "People Will Die If The Medical Establishment Censors COVID-19 Discussion." *Brendon Marotta*, 28 Mar. 2020, brendonmarotta.com/6420/covid-19-discussion. Accessed 5 Jan. 2021.

[298] *American Circumcision*. Dir. Brendon Marotta. Gravitas Ventures, 2017. Film.

[299] Doctors Opposing Circumcision. "HIV/AIDS." *Doctors Opposing Circumcision*, 14 Sept. 2020, www.doctorsopposingcircumcision.org/for-professionals/alleged-medical-benefits/hivaids. 5 Jan. 2021.

American Circumcision. Dir. Brendon Marotta. Gravitas Ventures, 2017. Film.

[300] Doctors Opposing Circumcision. "HIV/AIDS." *Doctors Opposing Circumcision*, 14 Sept. 2020, www.doctorsopposingcircumcision.org/for-professionals/alleged-medical-benefits/hivaids. 5 Jan. 2021.

American Circumcision. Dir. Brendon Marotta. Gravitas Ventures, 2017. Film.

[301] Riess, Thomas H., et al. "'When I Was Circumcised I Was Taught Certain Things': Risk Compensation and Protective Sexual Behavior among Circumcised Men in Kisumu, Kenya." *PLoS ONE*, edited by Landon Myer, vol. 5, no. 8, 2010, p. e12366. Crossref, doi:10.1371/journal.pone.0012366.

American Circumcision. Dir. Brendon Marotta. Gravitas Ventures, 2017. Film.

[302] CDC. "Male Circumcision | HIV Risk and Prevention | HIV/AIDS | CDC." *CDC*, www.cdc.gov/hiv/risk/male-circumcision.html. Accessed 5 Jan. 2021.

[303] U.S. Embassy & Consulates in South Africa. "U.S. Office of the Global AIDS Coordinator Provides Additional Funding of $11 Million to the PEPFAR South Africa Budget for Voluntary Medical Male Circumcision." *U.S. Embassy & Consulates in South Africa*, 22 Sept. 2015, za.usembassy.gov/u-s-office-of-the-global-aids-coordinator-provides-additional-funding-of-11-million-to-the-pepfar-south-africa-budget-for-voluntary-medical-male-circumcision. Accessed 5 Jan. 2021.

American Circumcision. Dir. Brendon Marotta. Gravitas Ventures, 2017. Film.

[304] Cairns, Gus. "PEPFAR Funded 15 Million Medical Male Circumcisions between 2007 and 2017." *Aidsmap.Com*, 26 Sept. 2018, www.aidsmap.com/news/sep-2018/pepfar-funded-15-million-medical-male-circumcisions-between-2007-and-2017. Accessed 5 Jan. 2021.

American Circumcision. Dir. Brendon Marotta. Gravitas Ventures, 2017. Film.

[305] Gathura, Gatonye. "35,000 Boys Get the Cut without Parental Consent." *Health*, 9 Aug. 2019, www.standardmedia.co.ke/health/article/2001337555/35000-boys-get-the-cut-without-parental-consent. Accessed 5 Jan. 2021.

[306] *American Circumcision*. Dir. Brendon Marotta. Gravitas Ventures, 2017. Film.

[307] PEPFAR. "PEPFAR 2020 Country Operational Plan Guidance for All PEPFAR Countries." *US Department of State*, 2019, www.state.gov/wp-content/uploads/2019/11/2019-11-25-COP20-Guidance-Full-Consolidated_Public-2-1.pdf. Accessed 5 Jan. 2021.

Marotta, Brendon. "PEPFAR To Experiment On African Children With The ShangRing." *Brendon Marotta*, 30 Nov. 2019, brendonmarotta.com/4475/pepfar-to-experiment-on-african-children-with-the-shangring. Accessed 5 Jan. 2021.

[308] Fish, M, Shahvisi, A, Gwaambuka, T, Tangwa, GB, Ncayiyana, D, Earp, BD. "A new Tuskegee? Unethical human experimentation and Western neocolonialism in the mass circumcision of African men." *Developing World Bioeth*. 2020; 00: 1– 16. https://doi.org/10.1111/dewb.12285

[309] Riess, Thomas H., et al. "'When I Was Circumcised I Was Taught Certain Things': Risk Compensation and Protective Sexual Behavior among Circumcised Men in Kisumu, Kenya." *PLoS ONE*, edited by Landon Myer, vol. 5, no. 8, 2010, p. e12366. Crossref, doi:10.1371/journal.pone.0012366.

[310] Sillars, Hannah. "White Paternalism Is Racism Too." *The Federalist*, 3 June 2020, thefederalist.com/2020/06/03/white-paternalism-is-racism-too. Accessed 23 Nov. 2021.

[311] Sillars, Hannah. "White Paternalism Is Racism Too." *The Federalist*, 3 June 2020, thefederalist.com/2020/06/03/white-paternalism-is-racism-too. Accessed 23 Nov. 2021.

[312] DiAngelo, Robin. *White Fragility: Why It's So Hard for White People to Talk About Racism*. Beacon Press, 2018, p. 9

[313] Intact America. "New Survey Finds That 4 Out of 10 Uncircumcised Boys Have Had Their Foreskins Forcibly Retracted by the Age of 7." *Intact America*, 20 July 2018, www.intactamerica.org/new-survey-finds-that-4-out-of-10-uncircumcised-boys-have-had-their-foreskins-forcibly-retracted-by-the-age-of-7. Accessed 5 Jan. 2021.

[314] "Forced Foreskin Retraction | What Does Forced Retraction Look Like? | After Forced Retraction What To Do Now." *Your Whole Baby*, www.yourwholebaby.org/forced-retraction. Accessed 26 Nov. 2021.

American Circumcision. Dir. Brendon Marotta. Gravitas Ventures, 2017. Film.

[315] "Implicit Bias (Stanford Encyclopedia of Philosophy)." *Stanford Encyclopedia of Philosophy*, 31 July 2019, plato.stanford.edu/entries/implicit-bias. Accessed 2 Dec. 2021.

[316] *American Circumcision Documentary Bonus Features*, "Deleted Scene - Dolores Sangiulano." Dir. Brendon Marotta. Vimeo, 2019. https://vimeo.com/ondemand/circmoviebonus/296785220.

[317] Sensoy, Ozlem, and Robin DiAngelo. *Is Everyone Really Equal?: An Introduction to Key Concepts in Social Justice Education*, 1st ed., Teacher's College Press, 2012, pp. 15–16.

[318] Sensoy, Ozlem, and Robin DiAngelo. *Is Everyone Really Equal?: An Introduction to Key Concepts in Social Justice Education*, 1st ed., Teacher's College Press, 2012, pp. 15–16.

[319] *American Circumcision*. Dir. Brendon Marotta. Gravitas Ventures, 2017. Film.

[320] *American Circumcision*. Dir. Brendon Marotta. Gravitas Ventures, 2017. Film.

[321] Milgram, Stanley (1963). "Behavioral Study of Obedience." *Journal of Abnormal and Social Psychology*. 67 (4): 371–8. CiteSeerX 10.1.1.599.92. doi:10.1037/h0040525.

[322] Perry, Gina. *Behind the Shock Machine: The Untold Story of the Notorious Milgram Psychology Experiments*. The New Press, 2013.

[323] Conscientious objection to circumcision is so rare, there is almost no data I can cite here other than the absence of data. While most hospitals have a conscientious objection policy to abortion, most do not even have one for circumcision, nor acknowledge it as something one can object to. When speaking with nurses who refused to do circumcisions for my documentary *American Circumcision*, many reported being reprimanded, harassed, abused, or wrongfully terminated for exercising their right to engage in conscientious objection to circumcision.

[324] Robinett, Patricia. *The Rape of Innocence: Female Genital Mutilation and Circumcision in the USA*. Nunzio Press, 2010, pp. 105-108.

[325] Data on the exact size of the circumcision industry is hard to find, and the medical system is deliberately opaque on many of their numbers. Circumcisions are billed to medical insurance between $300 and $5000. Just the sum total of all circumcisions per year in America at an average of this rate makes circumcision a multi-billion dollar industry. However, this doesn't even include the various secondary markets of circumcision tools, fixing botches, training, etc. The full industry is likely larger but the full information is not available to the public.

[326] Losquadro, Anthony. "Circumcision in America: Are Baby Boys' Foreskins for Sale?" *Medium*, 28 Feb. 2021, anthonylosquadro.medium.com/circumcision-in-america-are-baby-boys-foreskins-for-sale-e0b79fadc8cb. Accessed 23 Nov. 2021.

[327] Bell, Lauren. "What Is the Foreskin Facial, Why Does Kate Beckinsale like It and How Is the Serum Made?" *The Sun*, 27 Nov. 2018, www.thesun.co.uk/fabulous/7836602/foreskin-facial-kate-beckinsale-how-serum-made. Accessed 5 Jan. 2021.

Brucculieri, Julia. "What Is The 'Penis Facial' That Sandra Bullock Gets?" *Huffington Post*, 22 May 2018, www.huffpost.com/entry/penis-facial_n_5b02df5be4b0463cdba4a6fa. Accessed 5 Jan. 2021.

[328] Wikipedia Contributors. "Elizabeth Báthory." *Wikipedia*, 23 Nov. 2021, https://en.wikipedia.org/wiki/Elizabeth_Bathory. Accessed 23 Nov. 2021.

[329] "Fibronectin Human Foreskin Fibroblasts." *Millipore Sigma*, https://www.sigmaaldrich.com/catalog/product/sigma/f2518?lang=en&region=US. Accessed 5 Jan. 2021.

[330] "Erectile Dysfunction Drugs Market | 2021 - 26 | Industry Share, Size, Growth - Mordor Intelligence." *Mordor Intelligence*, mordorintelligence.com/industry-reports/erectile-dysfunction-drugs-market. Accessed 29 Nov. 2021.

[331] The Insight Partners. "Personal Lubricants Market Size ($2,933.62Mn by 2028) Lead by Water-Based Lubricant (10.9% CAGR) Impact of Coronavirus Outbreak and Global Analysis & Forecast by TheInsightPartners.Com." Yahoo, 29 Oct. 2021, finance.yahoo.com/news/personal-lubricants-market-size-2-164700245.html. Accessed 29 Nov. 2021.

[332] *American Circumcision*. Dir. Brendon Marotta. Gravitas Ventures, 2017. Film.

[333] *American Circumcision*. Dir. Brendon Marotta. Gravitas Ventures, 2017. Film.

[334] *American Circumcision*. Dir. Brendon Marotta. Gravitas Ventures, 2017. Film.

[335] *American Circumcision*. Dir. Brendon Marotta. Gravitas Ventures, 2017. Film.

336 Loewen, James. "Doctor Discusses Circumcision Controversy." *YouTube*, uploaded by Bonobo3D, 16 July 2011, https://youtu.be/XrcMYq0ASB8. Accessed 6 Dec. 2021.

337 *American Circumcision*. Dir. Brendon Marotta. Gravitas Ventures, 2017. Film.

338 Baudrillard, Jean. *Simulacra and Simulation (The Body, In Theory: Histories of Cultural Materialism)*. 1st ed., University of Michigan Press, 1994, p. 6.

339 Post Staff. "Here's a Breakdown of the $2T Coronavirus Bailout." *New York Post*, 28 Mar. 2020, nypost.com/2020/03/27/heres-a-breakdown-of-the-2t-coronavirus-bailout. Accessed Jan 1, 2020.

340 Marx, Karl. *The Economic and Philosophic Manuscripts of 1844 and the Communist Manifesto (Great Books in Philosophy)*. 1st ed., Prometheus, 1988.

341 DiAngelo, Robin. "White Fragility." *International Journal of Critical Pedagogy* 3(3), 2011: 54–70, p. 54.

342 DiAngelo, Robin. *White Fragility: Why It's So Hard for White People to Talk About Racism*. Beacon Press, 2018, p. 2.

343 Harsey, Sarah (June 1, 2017). "Perpetrator Responses to Victim Confrontation: DARVO and Victim Self-Blame". *Journal of Aggression, Maltreatment & Trauma*. **26** (6): 644–663. doi: 10.1080/10926771.2017.1320777.

344 Wang, Lucy, and Michael Xie. "Harvard 'Reviewing' Employee's Nude, Antisemitic Rant in Sanders Theatre." *Harvard Crimson*, 3 May 2018, www.thecrimson.com/article/2018/5/3/eric-clopper-production. Accessed 28 Nov. 2021.

345 Bailey, Alison. "Tracking Privilege-Preserving Epistemic Pushback in Feminist and Critical Race Philosophy Classes," *Hypatia* 32(4): 876–892, p. 879

346 Tuana, Nancy. "The Speculum of Ignorance: The Women's Health Movement and Epistemologies of Ignorance." *Hypatia*, 21(3), 2016: 1–19, p. 11.

347 The concept of pedophile stress is adapted from the critical social justice concept of racial stress. Racial stress describes the discomfort that many white people feel when forced to engage with racial issues. A source for that concept can be found here:

DiAngelo, Robin. *White Fragility: Why It's So Hard for White People to Talk About Racism*. Beacon Press, 2018, pp. 1–2.

348 DiAngelo, Robin. *White Fragility: Why It's So Hard for White People to Talk About Racism*. Beacon Press, 2018, pp. 1–2.

[349] Applebaum, Barbara. *Being White, Being Good: White Complicity, White Moral Responsibility, and Social Justice Pedagogy*. Lexington Books, 2011.

[350] DiAngelo, Robin. *White Fragility: Why It's So Hard for White People to Talk About Racism*. Beacon Press, 2018, pp. 4–5.

[351] Kendi, Ibram. *How to Be an Antiracist*. 1st ed., One World, 2019, pp. 9, 13.

[352] Delgado, Richard, et al. *Critical Race Theory (Third Edition): An Introduction (Critical America, 20)*. 3rd ed., NYU Press, 2017. p. 9.

Kendi, Ibram. *How to Be an Antiracist*. 1st ed., One World, 2019, pp. 44, 49.

[353] Kendi, Ibram. *How to Be an Antiracist*. 1st ed., One World, 2019, pp. 49-53.

[354] Delgado, Richard, et al. *Critical Race Theory (Third Edition): An Introduction (Critical America, 20)*. 3rd ed., NYU Press, 2017. pp. 9-10.

[355] DiAngelo, Robin. *White Fragility: Why It's So Hard for White People to Talk About Racism*. Beacon Press, 2018, p 150.

[356] Beltrán, Cristina. "To Understand Trump's Support, We Must Think in Terms of Multiracial Whiteness." *Washington Post*, 15 Jan. 2021, www.washingtonpost.com/opinions/2021/01/15/understand-trumps-support-we-must-think-terms-multiracial-whiteness. Accessed 21 Jan. 2021.

[357] DiAngelo, Robin. *White Fragility: Why It's So Hard for White People to Talk About Racism*. Beacon Press, 2018, p. 149.

[358] DiAngelo, Robin. *White Fragility: Why It's So Hard for White People to Talk About Racism*. Beacon Press, 2018, p. 150.

[359] DiAngelo, Robin. *White Fragility: Why It's So Hard for White People to Talk About Racism*. Beacon Press, 2018, p. 24.

[360] Fricker, Miranda. *Epistemic Injustice: Power and the Ethics of Knowing*. 1st ed., Oxford University Press, 2010, pp. 152-153

[361] Fricker, Miranda. *Epistemic Injustice: Power and the Ethics of Knowing*. 1st ed., Oxford University Press, 2010, pp. 152-153

[362] DiAngelo, Robin. *White Fragility: Why It's So Hard for White People to Talk About Racism*. Beacon Press, 2018, p 13.

Sensoy, Özlem, and Robin DiAngelo. *Is Everyone Really Equal? An Introduction to Key Concepts in Social Justice Education*, 1st ed., Teacher's College Press, 2012, p. 122.

[363] DiAngelo, Robin. *White Fragility: Why It's So Hard for White People to Talk About Racism*. Beacon Press, 2018, p 13.

Sensoy, Özlem, and Robin DiAngelo. *Is Everyone Really Equal? An Introduction to Key Concepts in Social Justice Education*, 1st ed., Teacher's College Press, 2012, p. 122.

[364] ADL. "ADL Urges Iceland Drop Bill Banning Male Circumcision." *Anti-Defamation League*, 23 Mar. 2008, www.adl.org/news/press-releases/adl-urges-iceland-drop-bill-banning-male-circumcision. Accessed Jan 1, 2021.

[365] Sokol, By Jta Sam. "Proposed Circumcision Ban a 'Sign of Antisemitism.'" *The Jerusalem Post*, 3 Oct. 2013, www.jpost.com/Jewish-World/Jewish-News/Proposed-circumcision-ban-a-sign-of-antisemitism-327821. Accessed 4, Jan 2021.

Baker, Andrew. "Banning Circumcision Is an Unnecessary Bar to Jewish Belonging in Europe." *Religion News Service*, 19 Nov. 2020, religionnews.com/2020/11/19/banning-circumcision-is-a-unnecessary-bar-to-jewish-belonging-in-europe. Accessed 4, Jan 2021.

Israel Ministry of Foreign Affairs. "Israel calls on Council of Europe to rescind anti-circumcision resolution." *Israel Ministry of Foreign Affairs*. 4 Oct, 2013. https://mfa.gov.il/MFA/PressRoom/2013/Pages/Israel-calls-on-Council-of-Europe-to-rescind-anti-circumcision-resolution-4-Oct-2013.aspx. Accessed 4, Jan 2021.

[366] NYC Health. "Metzitzah B'peh (Direct Oral Suctioning)." *NYC Health*, www1.nyc.gov/site/doh/health/health-topics/safe-bris.page. Accessed 6 Jan. 2021.

[367] James, Susan Donaldson. "Baby Dies of Herpes in Ritual Circumcision By Orthodox Jews." *ABC News*, 12 Mar. 2012, abcnews.go.com/Health/baby-dies-herpes-virus-ritual-circumcision-nyc-orthodox/story?id=15888618. Accessed 28 Nov. 2021.

[368] Hitchens, Christopher. "Cut It Off." *Slate Magazine*, 29 Aug. 2005, slate.com/news-and-politics/2005/08/another-disgusting-religious-practice.html. Accessed 4, Jan 2021.

[369] Zaklikowski, Dovid. "The One Who Holds the Baby – The 'Sandek.'" *Chabad*, www.chabad.org/library/article_cdo/aid/144125/jewish/The-One-Who-Holds-the-Baby-The-Sandek.htm. Accessed 6 Jan. 2021.

[370] van der Kolk, B A. "The compulsion to repeat the trauma. Re-enactment, revictimization, and masochism." The Psychiatric clinics of North America vol. 12,2 (1989): 389-411. https://pubmed.ncbi.nlm.nih.gov/2664732/.

[371] Menakem, Resmaa. *My Grandmother's Hands: Racialized Trauma and the Pathway to Mending Our Hearts and Bodies*. Illustrated, Central Recovery Press, 2017, p. 9.

[372] Menakem, Resmaa. *My Grandmother's Hands: Racialized Trauma and the Pathway to Mending Our Hearts and Bodies.* Illustrated, Central Recovery Press, 2017, p. 9.

[373] Kendi, Ibram. *How to Be an Antiracist.* 1st ed., One World, 2019, pp. 9, 13.

[374] DiAngelo, Robin. *White Fragility: Why It's So Hard for White People to Talk About Racism.* Beacon Press, 2018, pp. 40-44.

[375] Kendi, Ibram. *How to Be an Antiracist.* 1st ed., One World, 2019, pp. 9, 13.

[376] "Antisemitism." *Anti-Defamation League,* www.adl.org/antisemitism. Accessed 1 Nov. 2021.

[377] DiAngelo, Robin. *White Fragility: Why It's So Hard for White People to Talk About Racism.* Beacon Press, 2018, p. 12.

[378] DiAngelo, Robin. *White Fragility: Why It's So Hard for White People to Talk About Racism.* Beacon Press, 2018, p. 13.

[379] Sensoy, Ozlem, and Robin DiAngelo. *Is Everyone Really Equal?: An Introduction to Key Concepts in Social Justice Education*, 1st ed., Teacher's College Press, 2012, p. 119.

[380] DiAngelo, Robin. *White Fragility: Why It's So Hard for White People to Talk About Racism.* Beacon Press, 2018, pp. 5-13.

Sensoy, Ozlem, and Robin DiAngelo. *Is Everyone Really Equal?: An Introduction to Key Concepts in Social Justice Education*, 1st ed., Teacher's College Press, 2012, pp. 14-25.

[381] DiAngelo, Robin. *White Fragility: Why It's So Hard for White People to Talk About Racism.* Beacon Press, 2018, p. 10.

[382] DiAngelo, Robin. *White Fragility: Why It's So Hard for White People to Talk About Racism.* Beacon Press, 2018, p. 13.

Sensoy, Ozlem, and Robin DiAngelo. *Is Everyone Really Equal?: An Introduction to Key Concepts in Social Justice Education*, 1st ed., Teacher's College Press, 2012, p. 122.

[383] DiAngelo, Robin. *White Fragility: Why It's So Hard for White People to Talk About Racism.* Beacon Press, 2018, pp. 149-150.

[384] DiAngelo, Robin. *White Fragility: Why It's So Hard for White People to Talk About Racism.* Beacon Press, 2018, p. 150.

[385] DiAngelo, Robin. *White Fragility: Why It's So Hard for White People to Talk About Racism.* Beacon Press, 2018, p. 150.

[386] DiAngelo, Robin. *White Fragility: Why It's So Hard for White People to Talk About Racism.* Beacon Press, 2018, p. 150.

[387] DiAngelo, Robin. *White Fragility: Why It's So Hard for White People to Talk About Racism*. Beacon Press, 2018, p. 13.

Sensoy, Ozlem, and Robin DiAngelo. *Is Everyone Really Equal?: An Introduction to Key Concepts in Social Justice Education*, 1st ed., Teacher's College Press, 2012, p. 122.

[388] DiAngelo, Robin. *White Fragility: Why It's So Hard for White People to Talk About Racism*. Beacon Press, 2018, p. 149.

[389] Rattansi, Ali. *Racism: A Very Short Introduction (Very Short Introductions)*. 2nd ed., Oxford University Press, 2020, pp. 23, 25.

[390] Ignatiev, Noel. "Abolish the White Race." *Harvard Magazine*, 7 Aug. 2015, www.harvardmagazine.com/2002/09/abolish-the-white-race.html. Accessed 22 Nov. 2021.

DiAngelo, Robin. *White Fragility: Why It's So Hard for White People to Talk About Racism*. Beacon Press, 2018, pp. 149-150.

[391] Ignatiev, Noel. "Abolish the White Race." *Harvard Magazine*, 7 Aug. 2015, www.harvardmagazine.com/2002/09/abolish-the-white-race.html. Accessed 22 Nov. 2021.

[392] Ignatiev, Noel, et al. *Race Traitor*. 1st ed., Routledge, 1996, p. 10.

[393] Ignatiev, Noel. "Abolish the White Race." *Harvard Magazine*, 7 Aug. 2015, www.harvardmagazine.com/2002/09/abolish-the-white-race.html. Accessed 22 Nov. 2021.

[394] Ignatiev, Noel, et al. *Race Traitor*. 1st ed., Routledge, 1996, p. 11.

[395] Ignatiev, Noel, et al. *Race Traitor*. 1st ed., Routledge, 1996, p. 11.

[396] Ignatiev, Noel, et al. *Race Traitor*. 1st ed., Routledge, 1996, p. 10.

[397] Ignatiev, Noel, et al. *Race Traitor*. 1st ed., Routledge, 1996, p. 11.

[398] Ignatiev, Noel, et al. *Race Traitor*. 1st ed., Routledge, 1996, p. 10.

[399] Beltrán, Cristina. "To Understand Trump's Support, We Must Think in Terms of Multiracial Whiteness." *Washington Post*, 15 Jan. 2021, www.washingtonpost.com/opinions/2021/01/15/understand-trumps-support-we-must-think-terms-multiracial-whiteness. Accessed 21 Jan. 2021.

[400] DiAngelo, Robin. *White Fragilit: Why It's So Hard for White People to Talk About Racism*. Beacon Press, 2018, pp. 40-41.

[401] *American Circumcision*. Dir. Brendon Marotta. Gravitas Ventures, 2017. Film.

[402] O'Neill, Brendan. "The Latest Antisemitic Cry: Ban Circumcision | The Spectator." *Spectator*, 13 Oct. 2013, www.spectator.co.uk/article/the-latest-antisemitic-cry-ban-circumcision. Accessed 14 Oct. 2021.

[403] DiAngelo, Robin. *White Fragility: Why It's So Hard for White People to Talk About Racism*. Beacon Press, 2018.

DiAngelo, Robin. "White Fragility." *International Journal of Critical Pedagogy* 3(3), 2011: 54–70, p. 54.

[404] Beltrán, Cristina. "To Understand Trump's Support, We Must Think in Terms of Multiracial Whiteness." *Washington Post*, 15 Jan. 2021, www.washingtonpost.com/opinions/2021/01/15/understand-trumps-support-we-must-think-terms-multiracial-whiteness. Accessed 21 Jan. 2021.

[405] Kendi, Ibram. *How to Be an Antiracist*. 1st ed., One World, 2019, p. 9.

[406] DiAngelo, Robin. "White Fragility." *International Journal of Critical Pedagogy* 3(3), 2011: 54–70, pp. 1-2.

[407] DiAngelo, Robin. *White Fragility: Why It's So Hard for White People to Talk About Racism*. Beacon Press, 2018, p. 57.

[408] Sensoy, Ozlem, and Robin DiAngelo. *Is Everyone Really Equal?: An Introduction to Key Concepts in Social Justice Education*, 1st ed., Teacher's College Press, 2012, pp. 14-25.

DiAngelo, Robin. *White Fragility: Why It's So Hard for White People to Talk About Racism*. Beacon Press, 2018, pp. 5-13.

[409] Helms, J. E., Nicolas, G., & Green, C. E. *Racism and ethnoviolence as trauma: Enhancing professional training*. Traumatology, 2010. 16, 53-62. doi:10.1177/1534765610389595

Mental Health America. "Racial Trauma." *Mental Health America*, mhanational.org/racial-trauma. Accessed 13 Jan. 2021.

Ponds, Kenneth T. "The Trauma of Racism: America's Original Sin". *Reclaiming Children and Youth*, 2013. pp. 22-24.

[410] Narvaez, Darcia. *Neurobiology and the Development of Human Morality: Evolution, Culture, and Wisdom*. Illustrated, W. W. Norton & Company, 2014. pp. 14, 21-24, 134-135.

[411] Anand, K. and Scalzo, F., "Can Adverse Neonatal Experiences Alter Brain Development and Subsequent Behavior?" *Neonatology*, vol. 77, no. 2, 2000, pp. 69–82. *Crossref*, doi:10.1159/000014197.

Taddio, A. et al., "Effect of Neonatal Circumcision on Pain Response during Subsequent Routine Vaccination," *The Lancet* 349 (1997): 599–603.

[412] *American Circumcision*. Dir. Brendon Marotta. Gravitas Ventures, 2017. Film.

[413] ADL. "ADL Welcomes Establishment of Twitter Trust & Safety Council." *Anti-Defamation League*, 9 Feb. 2016, www.adl.org/news/press-releases/adl-welcomes-establishment-of-twitter-trust-safety-council. Accessed 30 Nov. 2021.

Webb, Whitney. "YouTube To Censor 'Controversial' Content, ADL On Board As Flagger." MintPress News, 21 June 2019, www.mintpressnews.com/youtube-censor-controversial-content-adl/230530. Accessed 30 Nov. 2021.

[414] Marcetic, Branko. "PayPal and the ADL: A Match Made in Censorship Hell." *Jacobin Magazine*, Aug. 2021, www.jacobinmag.com/2021/08/paypal-adl-anti-defamation-league-partnership-censorship-foxman-greenblatt-israel-zionism. Accessed 30 Nov. 2021.

[415] Kendi, Ibram. "The Mantra of White Supremacy." *The Atlantic*, 30 Nov. 2021, www.theatlantic.com/ideas/archive/2021/11/white-supremacy-mantra-anti-racism/620832. Accessed 30 Nov. 2021.

[416] LeVine, Mark. "Abolishing Whiteness Has Never Been More Urgent." *Racism | Al Jazeera*, 17 Nov. 2019, www.aljazeera.com/opinions/2019/11/17/abolishing-whiteness-has-never-been-more-urgent. Accessed 30 Nov. 2021.

[417] Cherry, Myisha. *The Case for Rage: Why Anger Is Essential to Anti-Racist Struggle*. Oxford University Press, 2021.

[418] Intact America. "New Survey Finds That 4 Out of 10 Uncircumcised Boys Have Had Their Foreskins Forcibly Retracted by the Age of 7." *Intact America*, 20 July 2018, www.intactamerica.org/new-survey-finds-that-4-out-of-10-uncircumcised-boys-have-had-their-foreskins-forcibly-retracted-by-the-age-of-7. Accessed 5 Jan. 2021.

[419] Sorrells, Morris L et al. "Fine-touch pressure thresholds in the adult penis." *BJU international* vol. 99,4 (2007): 864-9. doi:10.1111/j.1464-410X.2006.06685.x https://pubmed.ncbi.nlm.nih.gov/17378847/

[420] *American Circumcision*. Dir. Brendon Marotta. Gravitas Ventures, 2017. Film.

[421] *American Circumcision*. Dir. Brendon Marotta. Gravitas Ventures, 2017. Film.

Sorrells, Morris L et al. "Fine-touch pressure thresholds in the adult penis." *BJU international* vol. 99,4 (2007): 864-9. doi:10.1111/j.1464-410X.2006.06685.x https://pubmed.ncbi.nlm.nih.gov/17378847/

[422] *American Circumcision*. Dir. Brendon Marotta. Gravitas Ventures, 2017. Film.

Frisch, M., et al. "Male Circumcision and Sexual Function in Men and Women: A Survey-Based, Cross-Sectional Study in Denmark." *International Journal of Epidemiology*, vol. 40, no. 5, 2011, pp. 1367–81. Crossref, doi:10.1093/ije/dyr104.

[423] *American Circumcision Documentary Bonus Features*, "Deleted Scene - Patricia Robinett." Dir. Brendon Marotta. Vimeo, 2019. https://vimeo.com/ondemand/circmoviebonus/296104844.

Robinett, Patricia. The Rape of Innocence: Female Genital Mutilation and Circumcision in the USA. Nunzio Press, 2010.

[424] *American Circumcision*. Dir. Brendon Marotta. Gravitas Ventures, 2017. Film.

Hammond, T. "A Preliminary Poll of Men Circumcised in Infancy or Childhood." *BJU International*, vol. 83, no. S1, 2002, pp. 85–92. *Crossref*, doi:10.1046/j.1464-410x.1999.0830s1085.x.

Masters, William, and Virginia Johnson. *Human Sexual Response*. Illustrated, Ishi Press, 2010.

[425] Menakem, Resmaa. *My Grandmother's Hands: Racialized Trauma and the Pathway to Mending Our Hearts and Bodies*. Illustrated, Central Recovery Press, 2017, pp. 10, 37-56.

Narvaez, Darcia. *Neurobiology and the Development of Human Morality: Evolution, Culture, and Wisdom*. Illustrated, W. W. Norton & Company, 2014. pp. 14, 21-24, 134-135.

[426] Menakem, Resmaa. *My Grandmother's Hands: Racialized Trauma and the Pathway to Mending Our Hearts and Bodies*. Illustrated, Central Recovery Press, 2017, pp. 4-26.

[427] Menakem, Resmaa. *My Grandmother's Hands: Racialized Trauma and the Pathway to Mending Our Hearts and Bodies*. Illustrated, Central Recovery Press, 2017, p. 20.

[428] Menakem, Resmaa. *My Grandmother's Hands: Racialized Trauma and the Pathway to Mending Our Hearts and Bodies*. Illustrated, Central Recovery Press, 2017, pp. 19-30.

[429] Menakem, Resmaa. *My Grandmother's Hands: Racialized Trauma and the Pathway to Mending Our Hearts and Bodies*. Illustrated, Central Recovery Press, 2017, p. 37.

[430] Zehr, Howard. *The Little Book of Restorative Justice: Revised and Updated (Justice and Peacebuilding)*. 2nd ed., Good Books, 2015. pp. 20-21.

[431] Zehr, Howard. *The Little Book of Restorative Justice: Revised and Updated (Justice and Peacebuilding)*. 2nd ed., Good Books, 2015. pp. 21, 26-27.

[432] Zehr, Howard. *The Little Book of Restorative Justice: Revised and Updated (Justice and Peacebuilding)*. 2nd ed., Good Books, 2015. pp. 43-45.

[433] Zehr, Howard. *The Little Book of Restorative Justice: Revised and Updated (Justice and Peacebuilding)*. 2nd ed., Good Books, 2015. p. 57.

⁴³⁴ Davis, Fania. *The Little Book of Race and Restorative Justice: Black Lives, Healing, and US Social Transformation (Justice and Peacebuilding)*. Good Books, 2019.

⁴³⁵ Zehr, Howard. *The Little Book of Restorative Justice: Revised and Updated (Justice and Peacebuilding)*. 2nd ed., Good Books, 2015. p. 64.

⁴³⁶ *American Circumcision*. Dir. Brendon Marotta. Gravitas Ventures, 2017. Film.

American Circumcision Documentary. "Actor @NicoTortorella shows up at #NewYorkFashionWeek wearing a "Death To #Circumcision" t-shirt." *Twitter*, 7 July 2018, twitter.com/circmovie/status/1038106691848622080. Accessed 13 Oct. 2021.

⁴³⁷ *American Circumcision*. Dir. Brendon Marotta. Gravitas Ventures, 2017. Film.

American Circumcision Documentary Bonus Features, "Deleted Scene - Paul Fleiss." Dir. Brendon Marotta. Vimeo, 2019. https://vimeo.com/ondemand/circmoviebonus/296147378

Doctors Opposing Circumcision. "Doctors Opposing Circumcision | Facts About Circumcision." Doctors Opposing Circumcision | Why Not to Circumcise, 1 July 2021, www.doctorsopposingcircumcision.org. Accessed 13 Oct. 2021.

Fleiss, Paul, and Frederick Hodges. *What Your Doctor May Not Tell You About Circumcision*. 1st ed., Warner Books, 2021.

⁴³⁸ "Foregen." *Foregen*, www.foregen.org. Accessed 4 Jan. 2021.

⁴³⁹ Korioth, Trisha. "Featured Speaker Kendi to Pediatricians: Consider Racism 'a Diagnosis.'" *American Academy of Pediatrics*, 6 Oct. 2020, www.aappublications.org/news/2020/10/06/nce2020kendi100620. Accessed 13 Oct. 2021.

⁴⁴⁰ Kendi, Ibram. *How to Be an Antiracist*. 1st ed., One World, 2019, p. 18.

⁴⁴¹ Wikipedia contributors. "Eye for an Eye." *Wikipedia*, 16 Nov. 2021, en.wikipedia.org/wiki/Eye_for_an_eye. Accessed 1 Dec. 2021.

⁴⁴² Exodus 21, *Bible: New International Version (NIV)*, 2011. BibleHub, https://biblehub.com/niv/exodus/21.htm.

⁴⁴³ "ADL Joins In San Francisco Lawsuit Challenging Anti-Circumcision Ballot Initiative." *Anti-Defamation League*, 22 June 2011, www.adl.org/news/press-releases/adl-joins-in-san-francisco-lawsuit-challenging-anti-circumcision-ballot. Accessed 3 Dec. 2021.

ADL. "ADL Urges Iceland Drop Bill Banning Male Circumcision." *Anti-Defamation League*, 23 Mar. 2008, www.adl.org/news/press-releases/adl-urges-iceland-drop-bill-banning-male-circumcision. Accessed Jan 1, 2021.

⁴⁴⁴ ADL. "Remembering Leo Frank." *Anti-Defamation League*, www.adl.org/resources/backgrounders/remembering-leo-frank. Accessed 3 Dec. 2021.

⁴⁴⁵ This assertion might be controversial for those invested in pedophile-apologist narratives, but a full examination of the Leo Frank trial is beyond the scope of this book. For a deeper investigation of the Leo Frank trial, read the first chapter of:

Enless, Kaiter, and Tomislav Sunic. *Defamation Factory: The Sordid History of the ADL*. Reconquista Press, 2018.

⁴⁴⁶ In court transcripts, this racial slur is fully spelled out and was said aloud during the trial, but I have chosen to censor it in this book.

⁴⁴⁷ Atlanta Journal. "Prejudice and Perjury Constitute the State's Case." *Atlanta Journal*, Atlanta, Georgia, 22 Aug. 1913, p. 11.

⁴⁴⁸ Atlanta Constitution. "Arnold Ridicules Plot Alleged by Prosecution And Attacks the Methods Used by Detective," *Atlanta Constitution*, Aug. 22, 1913. p 2.

⁴⁴⁹ Moore, Deborah Dash (1981). *B'nai B'rith and the Challenge of Ethnic Leadership*. State University of New York Press. p. 108.

⁴⁵⁰ Kendi, Ibram. *How to Be an Antiracist*. 1st ed., One World, 2019, p. 226.

⁴⁵¹ DiAngelo, Robin. *White Fragility: Why It's So Hard for White People to Talk About Racism*. Beacon Press, 2018, pp. 40-43.

⁴⁵² Kendi, Ibram. *How to Be an Antiracist*. 1st ed., One World, 2019, pp. 6-8, 125-127,182.

DiAngelo, Robin. *White Fragility: Why It's So Hard for White People to Talk About Racism*. Beacon Press, 2018, pp. 139-140.

⁴⁵³ Kendi, Ibram. *How to Be an Antiracist*. 1st ed., One World, 2019, p. 226.

"Why 'I'm Not Racist' Is Only Half the Story | Robin DiAngelo | Big Think" *YouTube*, uploaded by Big Think, 1 Oct. 2018, www.youtube.com/watch?v=kzLT54QjclA&feature=youtu.be. Accessed 2 Jan. 2021.

⁴⁵⁴ Kendi, Ibram. *How to Be an Antiracist*. 1st ed., One World, 2019, pp. 9, 18.

⁴⁵⁵ Note that this reasoning only applies if the activist is effective. If the activists' outcome is greater systemic pedophilia, then this might not apply.

⁴⁵⁶ Dotson, Kristie, 2014, "Conceptualizing Epistemic Oppression." *Social Epistemology,* 28(2), 2014: 115–138, p. 116.

⁴⁵⁷ Dotson, Kristie. "Tracking Epistemic Violence, Tracking Practices of Silencing." *Hypatia*, 26(2), 2011: 238–259, pp. 236–237.

⁴⁵⁸ Weber, Peter. "'A Riot Is the Language of the Unheard,' Martin Luther King Jr. Explained 53 Years Ago." *The Week*, 29 May 2020, theweek.com/speedreads/917022/riot-language-unheard-martin-luther-king-jr-explained-53-years-ago. Accessed 3 Dec. 2021.

459 Freedman, A. L. "The Circumcision Debate: Beyond Benefits and Risks." *PEDIATRICS*, vol. 137, no. 5, 2016, p. e20160594. *Crossref*, doi: 10.1542/peds.2016-0594.

460 Intact America. "Circumcision Debate - User-Friendly Site for Circumcision Information." *Intact America*, 11 Feb. 2021, www.intactamerica.org/circumcision-debate-information. Accessed 13 Oct. 2021.

461 Davis, Susan. "New Studies Sharpen Circumcision Debate." *WebMD*, 25 Feb. 2008, www.webmd.com/baby/features/new-studies-sharpen-circumcision-debate#1. Accessed 13 Oct. 2021.

462 Anonymous. "The Risk Physicians Take When Going on Social Media." *KevinMD.Com*, 15 July 2019, www.kevinmd.com/blog/2019/07/the-risk-physicians-take-when-going-on-social-media.html. Accessed 13 Oct. 2021.

463 Sensoy, Özlem, and Robin DiAngelo. *Is Everyone Really Equal? An Introduction to Key Concepts in Social Justice Education*, 1st ed., Teacher's College Press, 2012, pp. 8, 14-27.

464 *American Circumcision*. Dir. Brendon Marotta. Gravitas Ventures, 2017. Film.

"San Francisco Circumcision Ban (November 2011)" *Ballotpedia*, 2011, ballotpedia.org/San_Francisco_Circumcision_Ban_(November_2011). Accessed 13 Oct. 2021.

465 Marotta, Brendon. "Why Would The American Academy Of Pediatrics Reject An Ad For A Film Featuring Their Leaders?" *Brendon Marotta*, 31 Oct. 2018, brendonmarotta.com/3236/aap-ads. Accessed 13 Oct. 2021.

466 Wikipedia contributors. "A Critique of Pure Tolerance." *Wikipedia*, 11 July 2021, en.wikipedia.org/wiki/A_Critique_of_Pure_Tolerance. Accessed 3 Dec. 2021.

467 Marcuse, Herbert, *The Essential Marcuse: Selected Writings of Philosopher and Social Critic Herbert Marcuse*. Beacon Press, 2007, p. 34.

468 Marcuse, Herbert, *The Essential Marcuse: Selected Writings of Philosopher and Social Critic Herbert Marcuse*. Beacon Press, 2007, p. 34.

469 Marcuse, Herbert, *The Essential Marcuse: Selected Writings of Philosopher and Social Critic Herbert Marcuse*. Beacon Press, 2007, p. 36.

470 Marcuse, Herbert, *The Essential Marcuse: Selected Writings of Philosopher and Social Critic Herbert Marcuse*. Beacon Press, 2007, p. 54.

471 Marcuse, Herbert, *The Essential Marcuse: Selected Writings of Philosopher and Social Critic Herbert Marcuse*. Beacon Press, 2007, p. 56.

472 Marcuse, Herbert, *The Essential Marcuse: Selected Writings of Philosopher and Social Critic Herbert Marcuse*. Beacon Press, 2007, p. 51.

473 Marcuse, Herbert, *The Essential Marcuse: Selected Writings of Philosopher and Social Critic Herbert Marcuse*. Beacon Press, 2007, p. 42.

474 Marcuse, Herbert, *The Essential Marcuse: Selected Writings of Philosopher and Social Critic Herbert Marcuse*. Beacon Press, 2007, p. 42.

475 Marcuse, Herbert, *The Essential Marcuse: Selected Writings of Philosopher and Social Critic Herbert Marcuse*. Beacon Press, 2007, p 51.

476 Marcuse, Herbert, *The Essential Marcuse: Selected Writings of Philosopher and Social Critic Herbert Marcuse*. Beacon Press, 2007, p. 50.

477 Lindsay, James. "How Not to Resolve the Paradox of Tolerance." *New Discourses*, 1 June 2021, newdiscourses.com/2021/01/how-not-to-resolve-the-paradox-of-tolerance. Accessed 14 Oct. 2021.

478 Marcuse, Herbert, *The Essential Marcuse: Selected Writings of Philosopher and Social Critic Herbert Marcuse*. Beacon Press, 2007, p. 46.

479 Marcuse, Herbert, *The Essential Marcuse: Selected Writings of Philosopher and Social Critic Herbert Marcuse*. Beacon Press, 2007, p. 46.

480 Marcuse, Herbert, *The Essential Marcuse: Selected Writings of Philosopher and Social Critic Herbert Marcuse*. Beacon Press, 2007, p. 46.

481 Marcuse, Herbert, *The Essential Marcuse: Selected Writings of Philosopher and Social Critic Herbert Marcuse*. Beacon Press, 2007, p. 46.

482 Marcuse, Herbert, *The Essential Marcuse: Selected Writings of Philosopher and Social Critic Herbert Marcuse*. Beacon Press, 2007, p. 51.

483 Marcuse, Herbert, *The Essential Marcuse: Selected Writings of Philosopher and Social Critic Herbert Marcuse*. Beacon Press, 2007, p. 46.

484 Marcuse, Herbert, *The Essential Marcuse: Selected Writings of Philosopher and Social Critic Herbert Marcuse*. Beacon Press, 2007, p. 51.

485 Marcuse, Herbert, *The Essential Marcuse: Selected Writings of Philosopher and Social Critic Herbert Marcuse*. Beacon Press, 2007, p. 43.

486 Hilton, Shani. "The BuzzFeed News Standards And Ethics Guide." *BuzzFeed News*, 13 Sept. 2019, www.buzzfeednews.com/article/shani/the-buzzfeed-editorial-standards-and-ethics-guide. Accessed 3 Dec. 2021.

487 Lenin, Vladimir Ilyich. *Essential Works of Lenin: "What Is to Be Done?" And Other Writings*. Dover Publications, 1987. p. 54.

488 Lenin, Vladimir Ilyich. *Essential Works of Lenin: "What Is to Be Done?" And Other Writings*. Dover Publications, 1987. p. 57.

489 Lenin, Vladimir Ilyich. *Essential Works of Lenin: "What Is to Be Done?" And Other Writings*. Dover Publications, 1987. p. 57.

490 Marotta, Brendon. *The Intactivist Guidebook: How to Win the Game of Intactivism and End Circumcision*. 2nd ed., Brendon Marotta, 2020, pp. 17-22.

491 Marotta, Brendon. *The Intactivist Guidebook: How to Win the Game of Intactivism and End Circumcision*. 2nd ed., Brendon Marotta, 2020, p. 26.

492 Marotta, Brendon. *The Intactivist Guidebook: How to Win the Game of Intactivism and End Circumcision*. 2nd ed., Brendon Marotta, 2020, pp. 17-22.

493 Foucault, Michel. *The Birth of the Clinic: An Archaeology of Medical Perception*. 1st ed., Vintage, 1994.

494 Applebaum, Barbara. *Being White, Being Good: White Complicity, White Moral Responsibility, and Social Justice Pedagogy*. Lexington Books, 2010, pp. 123–124.

495 Wikipedia contributors. "Epstein Didn't Kill Himself." *Wikipedia*, 29 Oct. 2021, en.wikipedia.org/wiki/Epstein_didn%27t_kill_himself. Accessed 30 Oct. 2021.

496 Gatto, John Taylor. *The Underground History of American Education*. Revised, Oxford, 2006.

497 Tyrone Hayes; Kelly Haston; Mable Tsui; Anhthu Hoang; Cathryn Haeffele; Aaron Vonk (2003). "Atrazine-Induced Hermaphroditism at 0.1 ppb in American Leopard Frogs" *Environmental Health Perspectives*. 111 (4): 568–75. doi:10.1289/ehp.5932.

Halpern, Daniel Noah. "Why Sperm Counts Are Dropping For Men Today." GQ, 17 Sept. 2018, www.gq.com/story/sperm-count-zero. Accessed 1 Jan. 2020.

498 Wikipedia contributors. "Kosher Certification Agency." *Wikipedia*, 3 Jan. 2021, en.wikipedia.org/wiki/Kosher_certification_agency#Fees. Accessed 5 Jan. 2021.

499 *An Open Secret*. Dir. Amy Berg. 2014. Film.

500 Iovino, Nicholas. "Judge Rules Twitter Can Be Sued for Failing to Take down Child Porn Videos." *Courthouse News Service*, 19 Aug. 2021, www.courthousenews.com/judge-rules-twitter-can-be-sued-for-failing-to-take-down-child-porn-videos. Accessed 4 Dec. 2021.

501 Hunt, Melissa G., et al. "No More FOMO: Limiting Social Media Decreases Loneliness and Depression." *Journal of Social and Clinical Psychology*, vol. 37, no. 10, 2018, pp. 751–68. *Crossref*, guilfordjournals.com/doi/10.1521/jscp.2018.37.10.751.

502 ADL. "Facebook, Google, Microsoft, Twitter, and ADL Announce Lab to Engineer New Solutions to Stop Cyberhate." *Anti-Defamation League*, 10 Aug. 2017, www.adl.org/news/press-releases/facebook-google-microsoft-twitter-and-adl-announce-lab-to-engineer-new. Accessed 4 Jan. 2021.

ADL. "ADL Welcomes Establishment of Twitter Trust & Safety Council." *Anti-Defamation League*, 9 Feb. 2016, www.adl.org/news/press-releases/adl-welcomes-establishment-of-twitter-trust-safety-council. Accessed Jan 2. 2021.

503 Ingham, Lucy. "YouTube CEO: We'll Ban Any Coronavirus Content against WHO Guidelines." *Verdict*, 24 Apr. 2020, www.verdict.co.uk/youtube-coronavirus-ban-who. Accessed Jan 4, 2021.

504 Sobey, Rick. "Boston's Aly Raisman Blasts FBI, USA Gymnastics over Handling of Larry Nassar Case: 'Like Serving Innocent Children up to a Pedophile on a Silver Platter.'" *Boston Herald*, 16 Sept. 2021, www.bostonherald.com/2021/09/15/bostons-aly-raisman-blasts-fbi-usa-gymnastics-over-handling-of-larry-nassar-case-like-serving-innocent-children-up-to-a-pedophile-on-a-silver-platter. Accessed 4 Dec. 20221.

505 Comey, James. "The FBI and the ADL: Working Toward a World Without Hate." *Federal Bureau of Investigation*, 26 July 2016, www.fbi.gov/news/speeches/the-fbi-and-the-adl-working-toward-a-world-without-hate. Accessed 2 Dec. 2021.

506 Leopold, Jason. "CIA Files Say Staffers Committed Sex Crimes Involving Children. They Weren't Prosecuted." *BuzzFeed News*, 4 Dec. 2021, www.buzzfeednews.com/article/jasonleopold/cia-employees-sex-crimes-children-secret-files-foia. Accessed 4 Dec. 2021.

507 Tom Newton Dunn, Political Editor. "UN Aid Workers Raped 60,000 People as It's Claimed Organisation Employs 3,300 Paedophiles..." *The Sun*, 13 Feb. 2018, www.thesun.co.uk/news/politics/5562215/un-aid-workers-raped-60000-people-as-its-claimed-organisation-employs-3300-paedophiles. Accessed 4 Dec 2021.

508 DiAngelo, Robin. *White Fragility: Why It's So Hard for White People to Talk About Racism*. Beacon Press, 2018, p. 9

509 Bellamy, Edward. *Looking Backward: 2000-1887*. Digibooks OOD / Demetra Publishing, 2019.

510 Wikipedia contributors. "Looking Backward." *Wikipedia*, 18 Dec. 2020, en.wikipedia.org/wiki/Looking_Backward. Accessed 6 Jan. 2021.

511 Bellamy, Edward. *Looking Backward: 2000-1887*. Digibooks OOD / Demetra Publishing, 2019, p. 28.

512 Bellamy, Edward. *Looking Backward: 2000-1887*. Digibooks OOD / Demetra Publishing, 2019, p. 28.

513 Gottesman, Isaac. *The Critical Turn in Education: From Marxist Critique to Poststructuralist Feminism to Critical Theories of Race*. Routledge, 2016, p. 90.

514 Pinker, Steven. *The Blank Slate: The Modern Denial of Human Nature*. Viking Penguin, 2002, pp. 287-305.

515 Wikipedia contributors. "Original Sin." *Wikipedia*, 29 Nov. 2021, en.wikipedia.org/wiki/Original_sin. Accessed 4 Dec. 2021.

516 Augustine, *Augustine: Confessions*. Trans. Albert C. Outler. Westminster Press, 1955. Book One, Chapter VI-VIII.

517 Augustine, *Augustine: Confessions*. Trans. Albert C. Outler. Westminster Press, 1955. Book One. Chapter VI, verse 8.

518 Augustine, *Augustine: Confessions*. Trans. Albert C. Outler. Westminster Press, 1955. Book One. Chapter VI, verse 8.

519 Augustine, *Augustine: Confessions*. Trans. Albert C. Outler. Westminster Press, 1955. Book One. Chapter IX, verse 14

520 Augustine, *Augustine: Confessions*. Trans. Albert C. Outler. Westminster Press, 1955. Book One, Chapter IX, verse 15.

521 Augustine, *Augustine: Confessions*. Trans. Albert C. Outler. Westminster Press, 1955. Book One, Chapter IX, verse15.

522 Augustine, *Augustine: Confessions*. Trans. Albert C. Outler. Westminster Press, 1955. Book One, Chapter X, verse16.

523 Augustine, *Augustine: Confessions*. Trans. Albert C. Outler. Westminster Press, 1955. Book One, Chapter XIII, verse 20.

524 Augustine, *Augustine: Confessions*. Trans. Albert C. Outler. Westminster Press, 1955. Book One, Chapter XI, verse 17.

525 Pinker, Steven. *The Blank Slate: The Modern Denial of Human Nature*. Viking Penguin, 2002, pp. 112-113.

526 Narvaez, Darcia. *Neurobiology and the Development of Human Morality: Evolution, Culture, and Wisdom*. Illustrated, W. W. Norton & Company, 2014. pp. 14, 21-24, 134-135.

527 Fahs, Breanne, and Michael Karger. "Women's Studies as Virus: Institutional Feminism, Affect, and the Projection of Danger." *Multidisciplinary Journal of Gender Studies*, vol. 5, no. 1, 2016, p. 929. *Crossref*, doi:10.17583/generos.2016.1683.

528 Dawkins, Richard. *The Selfish Gene: 40th Anniversary Edition (Oxford Landmark Science)*. 4th ed., Oxford University Press, 2016, pp. 245-260.

529 "Atheism Plus." *RationalWiki*, rationalwiki.org/wiki/Atheism_Plus. Accessed 14 Oct. 2021.

530 Alexander, Scott. "New Atheism: The Godlessness That Failed." *Slate Star Codex*, 22 July 2020, slatestarcodex.com/2019/10/30/new-atheism-the-godlessness-that-failed. Accessed 2 Jan. 2020.

531 Moldbug, Mencius. *How Dawkins Got Pwned*. Unqualified Reservations, 2016.

532 Wikipedia contributors. "COVID-19 Lab Leak Theory." *Wikipedia*, 30 Oct. 2021, en.wikipedia.org/wiki/COVID-19_lab_leak_theory. Accessed 30 Oct. 2021.

⁵³³ Racaniello, Vincent. "Gain of Function Research Explained." *Virology Blog*, 9 Sept. 2021, www.virology.ws/2021/09/09/gain-of-function-explained. Accessed 5 Dec. 2021.

Wikipedia contributors. "Gain-of-Function Research." *Wikipedia*, 17 Nov. 2021, en.wikipedia.org/wiki/Gain-of-function_research. Accessed 5 Dec. 2021.

⁵³⁴ Crane, Emily. "NIH Admits US Funded Gain-of-Function in Wuhan — despite Fauci's Denials." *New York Post*, 21 Oct. 2021, nypost.com/2021/10/21/nih-admits-us-funded-gain-of-function-in-wuhan-despite-faucis-repeated-denials. Accessed 5 Dec. 2021.

Wikipedia contributors. "COVID-19 Lab Leak Theory." *Wikipedia*, 30 Oct. 2021, en.wikipedia.org/wiki/COVID-19_lab_leak_theory. Accessed 30 Oct. 2021.

INDEX

AAFP, The American Academy of Family Physicians, 7, 11
AAP, American Academy of Pediatrics, 6-7, 11, 35, 43, 54, 64, 245-246, 251
abolish whiteness, 200-201, 214
ACE, Adverse Childhood Experiences, 64
ADL, Anti-Defamation League, 189, 198, 213, 237, 270
African circumcision campaigns, 143-147, 157, 159, 190, 236
Ahmadu, Fuambai Sia, 116
American Circumcision, 2, 10, 190, 246
anesthesia, 62-64, 232
antiracism, 5-6, 20, 34-35, 91, 124, 195, 198, 203, 231, 238-241
  definition, 5-6, 34-35
antipedophile,
  activism, 37, 241, 250-251, 265
  definition 33-34
  in relation to Jewishness, 197, 201, 207
  on becoming, 39, 107, 174, 182-183, 205, 221, 239, 262
antisemitism, 177, 191, 193, 195-198, 204-206, 212-215, 237, 241, 243
APPPAH, Association for Pre and Perinatal Psychology, 2
Apostle Paul, 15
Augustine, 275-276

Báthory, Elizabeth, 160
Baudrillard, Jean, 167
Being Good, Being White: White Complicity, White Moral Responsibility, and Social Justice Pedagogy, 181
Bellamy, Edward, 272-273
biopolitics, 133-134, 139
biopower, 132-136, 138, 140, 142-143
birth,
  birth system, 58-60, 100, 104-109, 111, 148, 158, 162, 183, 220, 262, 268-269
  of psychological defenses, 95-96
  gender assigned at, 113-114
  historical, 68, 104-109, 111
  hospital birth 27, 33, 48-50, 118, 142, 158, 171, 268-269, 286
  natural birth, 2, 170, 268-269
  race at birth, 201-203
  trauma around, 210-212, 222
Birth of the Clinic, 123
Black Lives Matter, 3
boarding schools, 68-69, 106
body-shaming, 42, 46, 71-72, 99
botched circumcision, 144, 159, 163-165

Butler, Judith, 113

Can the Subaltern Speak?, 68
capitalism, 9, 159-160, 171, 235
Catholicism, 15, 19, 282-283
CDC, Center for Disease Control, 8, 11
censorship, 142-143, 247-248, 250, 270
centering, 61, 139, 194
Christianity, 15, 18-19, 188, 275-276, 282
CIA, Central Intelligence Agency, 271
circumcision,
  and social justice, 9-11
  complications, 12, 133, 149, 163-164, 212
  definition, 10-11, 29-30
  discourses, 17-18, 27
  documentary on, 2, 10, 190, 246
  excuses, 32-33, 36-38, 54-55, 97, 101, 124-125, 144, 147, 151, 179, 182, 211, 228
  intersections, 27-31, 262
  Jewish, 50, 185, 189-190
  medical statements, 11-14, 43, 45-55, 64, 79, 82
  pain relief, 62-64, 232
  parental choice, 13, 29, 49-50, 83, 134, 136-140, 144, 150, 176, 179, 217, 219-221, 229, 245, 256
  symbolic meaning 116-119, 121
  trauma, 46, 62-64, 71, 75-77, 79, 110, 118, 127, 156, 208-224, 228, 231, 255
Circumcision, The Hidden Trauma: How an American Cultural Practice Affects Infants and Ultimately Us All, 10
coalition, social justice, 235-236, 238-239, 242-244, 258
coerced parents, 48
colonialism, 52, 67-70, 106, 170
color-blind racism, 5, 198, 203-204, 240
communism, 254-255, 273, 275
complicity principle
  definition, 33
  in relation to women 107-108
compulsory schooling, 56, 107, 118, 171, 268, 273
Confessions, 275
conservatives 92, 249, 258, 265-268
COVID-19, 8, 12, 129, 142, 146, 168, 172, 217, 261, 270, 281, 284
credentialism, 49, 261
Crenshaw, Kimberle, 84
critical race theory, 18, 92, 175, 185-186, 188, 195, 198-200, 203-205, 214, 233-234, 240, 264

critical theory,
  definition, 3-8, 17-26
  gender theory, 113-122, 264
  principles, 17-26
  queer theory, 19, 58, 113-114, 118, 122, 264
  race theory, 18, 92, 175, 185-186, 188, 195, 198-200, 203-205, 214, 233-234, 240, 264
  social justice theory, 17-26, 28, 33-38, 45, 52 55-58, 62, 67-70, 151, 162, 170, 175, 181-183, 186, 197-198, 229-230, 256-262, 280

DARVO, 177-179, 183, 227
Dawkins, Richard, 280-281
defund the police, 134
Dershowitz, Alan, 43
DiAngelo, Robin, 5, 55, 91-92, 175, 180-181, 199, 240
Dogon, 116, 118, 121
Duffell, Nick, 69

elites, 266-268
  education, 242-243, 281
  European boarding schools, 68-69, 106
endocrine disruptors, 269
epistemic injustice, 40-52, 61-63, 79, 82-84, 93, 109-110, 129, 155-156, 172, 178-180, 183-184, 187-188, 191, 195-197, 206, 209, 211, 223, 227, 230-232, 241, 243-244, 246, 260-261, 267
  hermeneutical injustice, 45-47, 49, 72, 93, 164, 187, 230, 266
  hermeneutical marginalization, 47, 60-61
  hermeneutical participation, 58, 199
  lived experience, 11, 13, 40-47, 50, 61, 69, 80-83, 155-156, 195, 243-244, 260-261, 282
  privilege-preserving epistemic pushback, 178-180, 183-184, 206, 211
  testimonial injustice, 40-42, 44-45, 50, 63, 93, 109, 223, 230, 237, 243
Epistemic Injustice: Power and The Ethics of Knowing, 40, 58, 187
epistemic violence, 54-55, 61, 172, 188, 195, 227, 232, 241, 243
Epstein, Jeffery, 267
equity,
  adult equity 109-111
  creating, 85
  definition, 5-6
  diversity, equity, inclusion, 146, 257-258
  applied to disability justice, 57
  health equity, 6-8
  in media, 251
  in restorative justice, 225-232
European boarding schools, 68-69, 106

false consciousness, 94-103, 120-121, 176, 181, 194, 246, 248, 286
fascism, 249, 254-255
father,
  absence, 106
  church fathers, 15, 276
  "look like his father" claim, 97-98, 145, 157
FBI, Federal Bureau of Investigations, 250, 271
Ferber Method, 60
FGM, Female Genital Cutting,
  double standards, 29, 43-45, 96, 114, 176, 179, 211, 217
  history 128
  Intactivist opposition, 14
  psychological impact, 156 218
  symbolic meaning 116-119, 121
feminism, 119-121, 253, 264, 280
fibroblasts, 160
forced retraction, 149-151, 217
forcible penetration, 30-31, 64
foreskin
  complications, 12, 133, 149, 163-164, 212
  forced retraction, 149-151, 217
  gender meaning, 115-117, 119-120
  in circumcision, 30, 80, 96, 123, 125-127, 133
  language, 72, 91-92
  myths, 28, 43, 98, 133, 142
  regeneration, 230-231
  selling foreskin, 159-161, 171
  sexual sensation, 43, 79, 115
Foucault, Michel, 23, 87, 89-90, 114-115, 123, 132-136, 138, 258, 260
  medical gaze, 123-131, 134-137, 157. 231, 232, 260, 269
  power/knowledge, 22, 87-93, 166, 168, 184, 204, 206, 244, 255, 258-259, 261
  definition, 87-88
fragility
  Jewish fragility, 191, 194-196, 202, 204, 206, 213, 232, 234
  parental fragility, 47, 180-182, 227-228
  pedophile fragility, 108, 175-180, 182-183, 215, 227, 241
  white fragility, 5, 175, 203-204, 206, 240
fragmentation, 65-66, 69-70, 75-77, 102, 145, 162, 230-231, 263, 275, 277-278, 282
  definition, 65-66, 75
  gender, 118-121
  healing, 227-228, 285-287
  medical, 124-125, 130-131, 157, 233, 269
  parental, 170
Frank, Leo, 237
Frankfurt School, 18, 247

Gatto, John Taylor, 268
Gramsci, Antonio, 97
gender,
  bias, 96

identity, 23, 24, 67, 72-73, 208
  intersection with circumcision, 28-30, 235, 262
  gender issues, 9, 13, 25, 58, 76, 102, 235
  gender movement, 3, 58, 235-236, 239
  social construction, 22, 67, 84, 172
  theory, 113-122, 264
  trauma, 208, 217-218
  violence, 105-122, 160, 208
Goldman, Ronald, 10
grooming, 100, 156-158, 231

hazing, 154, 202
hegemony,
  adult, 55, 60, 101, 169, 170
  changing, 265, 273, 283, 285
  cultural, 97-101, 270
  defintion, 97
  discourse, 53-55
  expanding, 146
  social justice as, 6, 15, 35, 256
  systemic pedophilia as, 9, 97-101, 103, 120, 151, 169, 170, 209-210, 216, 219-210, 245, 249-252, 270-271
hermeneutical hotspots, 58
hermeneutical injustice, 45-47, 49, 72, 93, 164, 187, 230, 266
hermeneutical marginalization, 47, 60-61
hermeneutical participation, unequal, 58, 199
Holocaust, 190, 202, 254
homeschooling, 100, 170
Horkheimer, Max 18
How To Be An Antiracist, 5, 7

Iceland genital cutting ban, 189
Ignatiev, Noel, 201-203
imperialism, 29, 44-45
imposed identity, 73-76, 115-116, 119, 233
Intact America, 64, 150
Intactivism, 2,14-15, 92, 254, 259
  activism, 64, 259-261
  definition, 14
  discourse and thinking, 17, 80, 82, 92-93, 204, 245-246, 253-255
  stories, 95, 190-191
The Intactivist Guidebook, 257-258
internalized dominance, 55-58, 102, 107, 145, 179, 206-207, 209, 237
intersectionality, 28, 72, 74, 84, 92, 234-235, 258
intersex, 14, 28, 155

Jesus, 15, 19
Jewish,
  antisemitism, 177, 191, 193, 195-198, 204-206, 212-215, 237, 241, 243
  circumcision, 50, 185, 189-190
  fragility, 191, 194-196, 202, 204, 206, 213, 232, 234
  Jewishness, 186-189, 191-208, 212-215, 223, 232, 237
  Judaism, 15
  kosher, 270
  Metzitzah B'Peh, 189
  privilege 187-188, 199-200, 206
  survivors, 177
  trauma, 190-194, 202-203, 206-207
Jones, Camara Phyllis, 7
Judaism, 15
  Jewish circumcision, 50, 185, 189-190

King, Martin Luther, 4-5, 243
Kendi, Ibram 3, 5, 7, 35, 92, 181, 205, 231, 240

labiaplasty, 29
Lenin, Vladimir, 252
lived experience, 11, 13, 40-47, 50, 61, 69, 80-83, 155-156, 195, 243-244, 260-261, 282
Looking Backward: 2000-1887, 272-273

Maasai, 118
Marcuse, Herbert, 247-252
Marx, Karl, 94, 172
Masturbation
  campaign against, 135-146
medical gaze, 123-131, 134-137, 157. 231, 232, 260, 269
Milos, Marilyn, 30
meme, 157, 265, 280-287
Menakem, Resmaa, 192, 221-222
Metzitzah B'Peh, 189
Mormonism, 282-283

Native, 69-70, 144, 229, 254
  European view of, 69-70
  Native Americans, 227, 229, 254
Nazi, 92, 176, 191, 249, 254
neutrality, 34-35, 91, 247-248
normalization, 10, 30, 35, 44, 49, 113-115, 134, 237
obstetrics, 105, 108, 182

Planned Parenthood, 236
parental choice, 13, 29, 49-50, 83, 134, 136-140, 144, 150, 176, 179, 217, 219-221, 229, 245, 256
parenting,
  attitudes, 11
  economics, 22, 169-170, 173
  choice, 13, 29, 49-50, 83, 134, 136-140, 144, 150, 176, 179, 217, 219-221, 229, 245, 256
  coerced parents, 48
  communication, 54
  complicity, 32-33, 43
  fragility, 47, 180-182, 227-228
  fragmentation, 170

historical, 68
norms, 59-60, 99-100, 106
paternalism, 145, 157
paternity, 98
peaceful parenting, 2, 60
power, 100, 133-134, 136-140, 144, 150, 157-158, 179
theory, 262, 276
trauma, 65, 95-96, 131, 181-182, 211-121, 217, 219-221
paternalism, 145, 157
paternity, 98
patriarchy, 104-112
PBTS, pedophilia-based traumatic stress, 209-223
peaceful parenting movement, 2, 60

pedophilia,
  definition, 31-32
  excuses for, 32-33, 36-38, 97, 101, 124-125, 144, 147, 151, 179, 182, 239
  grooming, 100, 156-158, 231
  hegemony of, 9, 97-101, 103, 120, 151, 169, 170, 209-210, 216, 219-210, 245, 249-252, 270-271
  pedophile fragility,108, 175-180, 182-183, 215, 227, 241
  PBTS, pedophilia-based traumatic stress, 209-223
  types, 32-33
privilege-preserving epistemic pushback, 178-180, 183-184, 206, 211
positionally, 74-75, 77
power/knowledge, 22, 87-93, 166, 168, 184, 204, 206, 244, 255, 258-259, 261
  definition, 87-88
psychohistory, 67-69
PTSD, Post-Traumatic Stress Disorder, 64

queer theory, 19, 58, 113-114, 118, 122, 264

race traitor, 202
racial justice, 3, 19, 34, 214, 221, 227, 231, 233, 236, 239, 264
racial narcissism, 191, 194-195
racial trauma, 208-210
  Jewish trauma, 190-194, 203, 207
racism,
  antiracism, 5-6, 34-35, 195, 196-198, 231, 238-241, 251
  antisemitism as, 196,198, 203-208, 237
  color-blind racism, 5, 198, 203-204, 240
  medical racism, 7-8, 129, 145-146
  movement against 4-7, 18, 256-258. 283
  origins, 67
  race-based traumatic stress, 208-212
  racial justice, 3, 19, 34, 214, 221, 227, 231, 233, 236, 239, 264

systemic, 6-8, 31-32, 90-93, 99, 119, 214-215, 238-241, 264
theory on, 10, 19-20, 31-32, 37, 46, 85, 90-93, 99, 102, 162, 170, 172, 201, 203-208, 214-215, 243, 254
white fragility, 5, 175, 203-204, 206, 240
RBTS, race-based traumatic stress, 208-212
The Rape of Innocence: Female Genital Mutilation and Circumcision in the USA, 156
reciprocal justice, 232
regret parents, 47-48
regeneration of foreskin, 230-231
reparations, 227, 229-230
restorative justice, 224-234
Robinett, Patricia, 156, 218

school, 56, 107, 118, 171, 268, 27
sexism, 29-30, 41, 45-46, 102, 119, 146, 160
simulacra, 167-168
Simulacra and Simulation, 167-168
simulacrum, 167-168
social justice,
  as current hegemony, 6, 9-16, 35, 256
  blindspots, 60-61, 73-77, 83-86, 105, 109-112, 128, 130, 146-148, 233-244
  coalition, 235-236, 238-239, 242-244, 258
  definition, 1, 3-8, 17-26
  discourse, 78, 83-92
  media, 251
  theory, 17-26, 28, 33-38, 45, 52 55-58, 62, 67-70, 151, 162, 170, 175, 181-183, 186, 197-198, 229-230, 256-262, 280
  utopian view, 272, 274-275, 277-278
socialization, 27, 67-70, 75, 98, 105, 109, 113, 151-158, 193, 205-206, 240, 246
sovereign power, 132-134, 140-141, 143
Spivak, Gayatri Chakravorty, 53
subaltern, 53-55, 61-62, 66
  Can the Subaltern Speak?, 68
  children as, 52-55, 61-62, 66, 85, 106, 110, 162, 166, 170-171, 231, 238, 242
  definition, 52-53
  internal, 68-71, 75-77, 101-103, 121, 145, 158, 162, 173, 179-181, 190, 230, 263, 274-276
  internalized dominance towards, 55-57
  needs, 179-181, 184, 219
  speech 53-55
  state of childhood, 85, 102-103, 121, 145, 170, 231, 238

systemic pedophilia,
  definition, 31-32
  excuses, 32-33, 36-38, 97, 101, 124-125, 144, 147, 151, 179, 182, 239
  grooming, 100, 156-158, 231

hegemony of, 9, 97-101, 103, 120, 151, 169, 170, 209-210, 216, 219-210, 245, 249-252, 270-271
narratives, 36-39, 82
pedophile fragility,108, 175-180, 182-183, 215, 227, 241
PBTS, pedophilia-based traumatic stress, 209-223
types, 32-33

testimonial injustice, 40-42, 44-45, 50, 63, 93, 109, 223, 230, 237, 243
tragic view, 274-278
transgender, 114, 155, 312

trauma,
ACE, Adverse Childhood Experiences, 64
as a virus, 285-287
birth, 210-212, 222
childhood, 2, 62-70, 75-79, 85, 104-111, 127, 148, 164, 170, 209, 218-219, 221-22, 231, 263, 265, 275-278, 286
ending, 285-287
European, 68-70, 106, 170, 275
fragmentation, 65-66, 69-70, 75-77, 102, 145, 162, 230-231, 263, 275, 277-278, 282
fragmentation explained, 65-66, 75
gender, 118-121
healing, 227-228, 285-287
Jewish, 190-194, 202-203, 206-207
medical, 124-125, 130-131, 157, 233, 269
parental, 65, 95-96, 131, 181-182, 211-121, 217, 219-221
racial trauma, 208-210
PBTS, pedophilia-based traumatic stress, 209-223
PTSD, Post-Traumatic Stress Disorder, 64

UN, United Nations, 236, 271
uncircumcised, 71, 73-74, 233
UNICEF, United Nations Children's Fund, 236
utopian view, 272, 274-275, 277-278

vaccination, 8, 63-64, 134, 142, 146

wet nurse, 68, 106, 275
white fragility, 5, 175, 203-204, 206, 240
White Fragility: Why It's So Hard for White People to Talk About Racism, 5, 175
white supremacy, 8, 13, 29, 203, 205-206, 221
whiteness, 67, 186, 188, 196, 198-206, 214-215
abolish whiteness, 200-201, 214
WHO, World Health Organization, 43, 236, 270
"Woke", 4, 265
Wuhan, 142, 281

For more, visit:
www.BrendonMarotta.com

www.ingramcontent.com/pod-product-compliance
Lightning Source LLC
Chambersburg PA
CBHW071658170426
43195CB00039B/2225